# A Practical Guide to Developing Computational Software

## Computational Software

– with emphasis on automated test, reusable code,
parallel programming, and Windows application

Yong-Ming Li

ISBN 978-1492973171

To My Family!

# Contents

# List of Figures

# Preface

In the past few years, I have been involved in the recruitment of both undergraduate and graduate students for the Intergraph Process, Power, & Marine (PP&M) division – the leading global provider of engineering software for the design, construction, and operation of plants, ships, and offshore facilities. In order to attract talented individuals from a diverse range of colleges, our job openings were posted not only in Alabama universities, but also in top ranked national universities such as Vanderbilt, Carnegie Mellon, Georgia Tech, Texas A&M, and Purdue. To identify the qualified candidates from amongst several hundred applicants, I sent the following seven pre-interview questions to the candidates and asked them to reply within two weeks with their answers to as many questions as possible. Many developers at Intergraph PP&M work with geometric creation and manipulation in one way or another. Therefore, the seven questions range from basic geometric analysis to numerical programming.

## 1. Area tolerance

No two components can be manufactured exactly the same. In practice, dimensional or geometric tolerances (e.g., distance and angular tolerances) are introduced in Computer Aided Design systems and manufacturing processes. The smaller the tolerance required, the more expensive the component will be to machine. Therefore, it is often desirable to specify the largest possible tolerance while maintaining proper functionality.

Denoting the distance tolerance by $\varepsilon$, then two circles are considered to be the same if

$$|R_1 - R_2| < \varepsilon,$$

where $R_1$ and $R_2$ are the radii of circles 1 and 2 respectively. Assume that we know the areas of the two circles (denoted by $A_1$ and $A_2$) and the radius of circle 1 (i.e., $R_1$). Please derive the "area tolerance" $\Delta$ in terms of the given distance tolerance $\varepsilon$ such that, when $|A_1 - A_2| < \Delta$, we know two circles are equal with respect to the distance tolerance. One should avoid computing radii via $R_i = \sqrt{A_i/\pi}, i = 2, 3, \cdots, n$, as the square root computation is an expensive arithmetic operation. Although a non-calculus based approach is acceptable, a calculus based approach is preferable since calculus is the study of change.

## 2. Angular tolerance

Again, we denote the distance tolerance by $\varepsilon$ and assume that the model space (the longest model we would create) is $10^4$ meters. Based on $\varepsilon$ and the limit of model space, I would like you to derive the angular tolerance $\Delta$ such that it can be used to determine whether two lines confined in the model space are collinear.

**Hint**: Two lines are considered to be collinear if the maximum deviation between these two lines is less than the distance tolerance $\varepsilon$. From this criterion, you may derive the angular tolerance such that you know two lines are collinear with respect to $\varepsilon$ if the angle between these two lines is less than the angular tolerance $\Delta$. Drawing two lines on a piece of paper may help you analyze the problem.

## 3. Improve performance of circle stroking

Most graphics programming tools provide only a line drawing capability. To display a circle on computer screen, we first need to break the circle into evenly spaced tiny pieces such that each piece can be well-approximated by a line. We then draw these lines on the screen. Because these lines are so small, a circle looks smooth on the screen.

Breaking a circle into many tiny pieces is equivalent to computing many evenly spaced points on the circle, a process known as *circle stroking*. If we want to stroke $n+1$ points on circle and start the first point at $\theta_0 = 0$, then the angle increment $\delta$ would be $2\pi/n$ as shown below.

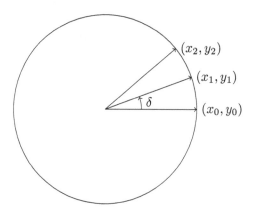

Accordingly, all other points may be computed as follows:

$$x_1 = r\cos(\theta_1) = r\cos(\theta_0 + \delta)$$
$$y_1 = r\sin(\theta_1) = r\sin(\theta_0 + \delta)$$

$$x_2 = r\cos(\theta_2) = r\cos(\theta_1 + \delta)$$
$$y_2 = r\sin(\theta_2) = r\sin(\theta_1 + \delta)$$

$$\cdots$$

$$x_n = r\cos(\theta_n) = r\cos(\theta_{n-1} + \delta)$$
$$y_n = r\sin(\theta_n) = r\sin(\theta_{n-1} + \delta)$$

The above formula indicates that we need to call trigonometric functions (i.e., sin and cos) for $2(n+1)$ times. Since trigonometric functions are relatively more expensive to compute than multiplication and division, the above approach is not optimized in terms of CPU usage. Please provide a suggestion on how you can speed up the computation.

## 4. Approximation by circular arc

A circle in quadratic form is

$$x^2 + y^2 + 2Ax + 2By + C = 0. \tag{0.0.1}$$

Its center and radius are given by $(-A, -B)$ and $\sqrt{A^2 + B^2 - C}$ respectively. Given $n$ points $(x_i, y_i)$ $(i = 1, 2, \cdots, n)$, we want to find a circle that interpolates $(x_1, y_1)$ and $(x_n, y_n)$ and approximates the remaining points in a least squares sense. Substituting $(x_1, y_1)$ and $(x_n, y_n)$ in the above equation gives

$$x_1^2 + y_1^2 + 2x_1 A + 2y_1 B + C = 0$$

$$x_n^2 + y_n^2 + 2x_n A + 2y_n B + C = 0$$

Subtracting the second equation from the first yields

$$2(x_1 - x_n)A + 2(y_1 - y_n)B + x_1^2 + y_1^2 - x_n^2 - y_n^2 = 0.$$

Assume that $|x_1 - x_n| \neq 0$ so we may express $A$ in terms of $B$, i.e.,

$$A = \frac{y_1 - y_n}{x_n - x_1} B + \frac{x_1^2 + y_1^2 - x_n^2 - y_n^2}{2(x_n - x_1)} = \alpha B + \beta \tag{0.0.2}$$

Replacing $A$ in equation (0.0.1) gives

$$2(x\alpha + y)B + C + x^2 + y^2 + 2x\beta = 0.$$

If an arbitrary point $\boldsymbol{p}_i = (x_i, y_i)$ is not on the circle, then

$$e_i = \left|2(x_i\alpha + y_i)B + C + x_i^2 + y_i^2 + 2x_i\right| > 0$$

is the approximation error. The sum of all squared errors is

$$\mathcal{E} = \sum_{i=2}^{n-1} \left(2(x_i\alpha + y_i)B + C + x_i^2 + y_i^2 + 2x_i\beta\right)^2$$

From calculus, $\mathcal{E}$ is minimized if

$$\frac{\partial \mathcal{E}}{\partial B} = 0 \quad \text{and} \quad \frac{\partial \mathcal{E}}{\partial C} = 0.$$

Optimized $B$ and $C$ are obtained by solving the above two linear equations and $A$ is computed via equation (0.0.2).

Implementing the above approach will not result in a circle that interpolates $(x_1, y_1)$ and $(x_n, y_n)$. Do you see a reasoning problem in this approach?

## 5. Evaluation of $e^x$

Exponential function $e^x$ and trigonometric functions such as $\sin x$ and $\cos x$ are often evaluated via the Maclaurin series (a special form of Taylor series). Expressing $e^x$ by the Maclaurin series gives

$$e^x = 1 + x + \frac{x^2}{2!} + \frac{x^3}{3!} + \cdots = \sum_{i=0}^{\infty} \frac{x^i}{i!}.$$

This Maclaurin series converges to $e^x$ absolutely and uniformly for $x \in (-\infty, +\infty)$. Please write a program to evaluate $e^x$ via Maclaurin series at $x = 1$ and $\pm 25$ and compare your results with the ones obtained by using either a pocket calculator or the C/C++ internal math function `exp(x)`. An explanation of your implementation and findings is expected.

**Hint:** Let $P_n = \sum_{i=0}^{n} \frac{x^i}{i!}$. Then, $P_n$ is said to be converged to $e^x$ with respect to the given tolerance $\varepsilon$ if $|P_n - P_{n-1}| = \left| \frac{x^n}{n!} \right| < \varepsilon$. Let's assume that $\varepsilon = 10^{-15}$.

## 6. Implementation of bisection method

Assume a continuous function $f$ is monotonic on the interval $[a, b]$ and $f(a) \times f(b) < 0$. Then, there exists a solution $x$ in $[a, b]$ such that $f(x) = 0$ as illustrated below.

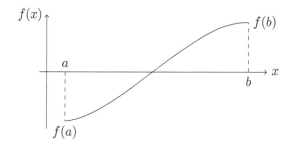

To find the solution numerically, we can use the bisecting method. As the name suggests, we start by selecting $x$ at the mid of the interval $[a, b]$ and compute $f(x)$. If $|f(x)| < \varepsilon$, $x$ is the root of function $f$. Otherwise, we reduce the interval by half using the following criterion:

```
if (f(a) * f(x) < 0.0)
{
    b = x;
}
else
{
    a = x;
}
```

Based on the reduced interval, we compute again $x = 0.5(a+b)$ and check if $|f(x)| < \varepsilon$. Repeating this process should find the root of $f = 0$.

If you are not familiar with object oriented programming, you may simply implement a workable recursive function to compute the root of $f(x) = x^3 + 2x - 2$ in $[0, 1]$. Otherwise, I would like you to demonstrate how you can implement, say, Bisection class to compute the root of the above function. Furthermore, you may want to show me how you can compute the root of another function $f(x) = \sin(x)$ in $[2, 4]$ based on Bisection class with minimum additional implementation.

# 7. Curve/Curve intersection

Simple curves such as lines and arcs are widely used in Computer Aided Design and Manufacturing (CAD/CAM) systems. In addition to a line and arc, a piecewise polynomial curve (either a composite Bézier curve or a B-spline curve) is also used to model complex geometric shapes.

Assume we already have an API to solve a line/line intersection problem. I would like you to derive a method to compute the intersection points of two generic curves as shown below by calling the line/line intersection API.

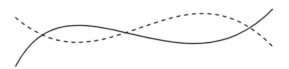

Two curves intersect each other at multiple places

I am not interested in C/C++ code implementation. Instead, I would like to see how you analyze the problem (math) and organize your data (computer science). If you want, you can write the pseudo code to clarify your approach.

Among those candidates who sent back their answers, very few could give satisfying analyses. I was quite surprised to find that candidates who were working toward their master's degrees in computer science were unable to demonstrate the desired programming skill, though they all indicated in their resumes that they are proficient in C/C++ and objected oriented programming.

It appears to me that there is a gap between academic training and real world computing. For example, mammals (or people) are often used in many text books to teach *inheritance* and *polymorphism* (the topics in *object oriented programming*). Engineering students are taught how mammals form a base class and how dogs and cats are derived from mammals and thus form the derived classes. The need for inheritance and polymorphism sounds very artificial and may fail to draw students' attention to the topic and may even cause their resistance to the idea. Therefore, when asked to use inheritance with polymorphism to design a bisection method that can be used to solve any function, candidates had no clue where to start. For this reason, I was motivated to write a numerical programming book to answer the above interview questions and, more importantly, to help serious science and engineering major students as well as entry level programmers learn the programming skills and become familiar with the software development process.

Readers may ask why I wanted to write another numerical programming book when there are already an abundance available. One simple reason is that those books emphasize more on numerical methods than on the software development process. Implementation of numerical methods is only one important part of developing computational software. Programming productivity, extensible and reusable code, quality control, and automated testing are also equally important parts of the software development process, which is the main theme of this book.

All examples in this book were carefully selected to demonstrate the strong need for mathematics and computer science in the software industry. To make this book accessible to wide spectrum of readers, the implementation of many algorithms emphasizes on understanding the underlying basics of techniques, not on the refinements that may, in practice, be needed to achieve optimal performance and reliability. Although most examples are mathematically oriented, they require no advanced mathematics beyond calculus and should be understood by engineering and computer science students and professional developers. Through these hands-on exercises, readers should be able to minimize the learning curve and become competent in designing and developing their own applications.

C/C++ and Microsoft Visual Studio are chosen in this book because they are both widely-used in software industry. If you do not have the professional version of Microsoft Visual Studio, you can download the Microsoft Visual Studio Express (a freeware) from the Microsoft web site or simply use whatever development platform you already have. It should be pointed out that all algorithms are implemented such that they are readily understood by beginners. Excessive use of C/C++ pointer operations, STL iterator operations, and C/C++ specific syntaxes are purposely avoided so that readers can convert them to other programming languages with minor efforts.

There is a Chinese saying,

$$抛砖引玉$$

which may be translated as *"By showing you how to make a brick, we hope that you will refine the technique and skill to figure out how to make a piece of jade jewelry."* Such is the intention of this book.

**Organization of this book:**

This book is written for those who want to pursue a career in developing computational software for engineering and scientific applications. Unlike traditional numerical programming books that focus on the analysis and implementation of numerical methods, this book emphasizes on the development of a reliable and reusable software package. Readers will not only learn implementation of numerical methods but also the software development process that includes creating and using a dynamic-link library, designing flexible test drivers, writing scripting tools for productivity, performing and validating an automated test suite. Based on the computational library developed in this book, readers will also learn how to develop a windows-based application for data visualization and manipulation. Multi-core processors bring parallel computing to mainstream customers. The shift to parallel computing leads to fundamental changes in the design of software. As a result, computer science students and programmers now need to learn parallel computing techniques that allow software to take advantage of the shift toward parallelism. For this reason, this book discusses also how classical numerical programs can be parallelized via Open Multi-Processing (OpenMP). In particular, readers will learn how to create multi-threaded applications with minimal and manageable changes in their serial code.

Numerical methods discussed in this book include evaluation of polynomial and series, root-finding, linear and nonlinear systems, inverse of a matrix, eigenvalues and eigenvector, integration, and least squares approximation. These methods are grouped and taught based on their implementation styles rather than their relevance. By completing these hands-on programming exercises, readers will gain an assured confidence and the sound programming skills needed to design and implement their own computational software that include creation of sharable library, test drivers, test suites, automation scripts, data comparison and validation tools.

Chapter 1 is a fast-paced brief introduction to C/C++ programming under Microsoft Visual Studio to familiarize readers with basic C/C++ syntax and commonly used debugging tools.

Chapter 2 discusses floating-point notation, comparison, and arithmetic. One important thing about computing over a set of floating-point numbers is that it is not arithmetically closed. If we take two floating-point numbers x, y and choose an arithmetic operator $(+, -, \times, \div)$ then, in general, the result will not be exactly representable in the floating-point system no matter how high precision is used. Failure to understand such limitation is often the source of problems in numerical programming. Therefore, rudimentary understanding of floating-point is a pre-requisite for programmers.

Chapter 3 continues the study of advanced C/C++ programming such as default arguments, data structure and class, double pointers, dynamic memory allocations, and STL containers. Algorithm efficiency analysis and big O notation will also be discussed. This chapter is designed to help readers to gain the required C/C++ proficiency in implementing numerical methods as well as to understand the importance of good analysis and design of numerical methods. Examples in this chapter are specially selected to illustrate how well-designed numerical methods can improve not only performance but also numerical stability.

Chapter 4 is devoted to give readers an insight on how a computational software library may actually be developed in a software house. Readers will learn how to create and use a dynamic-link library, how to design flexible test drivers, and how to write scripts to improve productivity, to execute test suites automatically, and to compare the test results with the predicted outcomes.

Chapter 5 deals with recursive algorithm. Because of its problem-solving power and simplicity in implementation, the recursive algorithm is a preferred powerful problem-solving tool. Recursion in numerical methods will be discussed in this chapter with emphasizes on performance and memory usage.

Chapter 6 discusses linear systems. Topics include solution to system of linear equations, matrix manipulation, inverse of a matrix, eigenvalue and eigenvector.

Chapter 7 and 8 cover an important topic in software engineering: design extensible and reusable code. Many numerical programming books focus more on understanding the underlying basics of techniques than on how to design a reusable code. These two chapters explore how to use function pointers, "generic" data pointer, and inheritance with polymorphism to design extensible and reusable code.

Chapter 9 discusses the least square approximation method whose applications can be found in many fields such as computer aided design, metrology, image processing, and so on. Starting with the best fit line, circle, arc, and plane, we expand the discussion to the generic normal equations of least squares approximation. Examples are specially selected to draw readers' attention to how math plays a vital role in software development.

Chapter 10 aims to develop a simple windows-based application for data visualization and manipulation. CAD/CAM systems have revolutionized much of the engineering design and manufacturing processes. A CAD system is essentially a collection of sophisticated tools that are exposed to users via graphical user interface (GUI) for creating, visualizing, and manipulating data. Through this miniature application, readers will get a glimpse of how sophisticated CAD/CAM systems are developed.

Chapter 11 discusses how classical numerical methods can be parallelized to take the advantage of multi-thread programming. As multi-core processors bring parallel computing to mainstream customers, the key challenge in computing today is to transition the software industry to parallel programming. Programmers at all levels will soon find that they will have to deal with parallel programming whether they are ready or not. Common problems associated with parallel computing such as data race conditions, workload balance, synchronization, and parallel slowdown are discussed in detail.

Appendix A is a brief introduction to Perl programming.

Appendix B contains answers to all seven pre-interview questions presented in the preface.

**Reference resources**:

Wikipedia, Microsoft Developer Network (MSDN), and Intel web sites have been the primary resources of reference for terminologies and historical events such as advancements of parallel programming and Microsoft products.

**Acknowledgement**:

I would like to take this opportunity to thank my colleagues at the Intergraph Math department. It is my honor and privilege to work with and learn from those talented individuals. In particular, I want to thank Dr. Lujun Wang who, as a new developer, used the manuscript of this book as training material and provided me with valuable feedback. My special thank also goes to my friend and former colleague Dr. Jean-Jacques Malosse, who was my mentor and set a high bar for me when I joined Intergraph nineteen years ago.

**About the author**:

Dr. Yong-Ming Li is a senior technical manager at Intergraph Corporation with 19 years of professional software development experience. Dr. Li specializes in curve, surface and solid modeling. He has developed numerous geometric modeling algorithms to support SolidEdge®, SmartPlant®, and SmartMarine®. He received his bachelor's degree in mechanical engineering from Chengdu University of Science and Technology in China. While studying for his master's degree at Northwestern Polytechnical University in Xi'an, China, Yong-Ming Li received the *Sino-British Friendship Scholarship* and went to England in 1988 to continue his postgraduate study. At the University of Birmingham, he earned an M.Sc. in production engineering and Ph.D. in mechanical engineering with an emphasis on geometric modeling and computer-aided design.

# Chapter 1

# Introduction to C/C++ Programming

This book is about learning numerical programming skill and the software development process. Therefore, it requires a lot of hands-on programming exercises. In consideration that not every reader has programmed in C/C++ under Microsoft Visual Studio, we start this book with the basics of C/C++ programming. After overcoming the initial hurdles of C/C++ language syntax, readers will find that numerical programming is simply translating mathematic logic and evaluation into C/C++ programming statements.

In scientific and engineering calculations, exact symbolic results are usually very desirable when they can be found via, for example, Macsyma (originally developed at MIT) and Maple (originated at the University of Waterloo). However, it is not always possible to get symbolic results. In such cases, we must resort to numerical methods. Since most engineering and scientific computations involve evaluation of mathematical functions, they do not necessarily require *graphical user interface (GUI)* and hence can be implemented and maintained efficiently as *console applications*. A console application is a computer program designed to be used via a text-only computer interface. It accepts input and sends output to the console, which is also known as the *command prompt*. In much older operating systems, the command prompt was widely known as DOS (*Disk Operating System*) or MS-DOS prompt. Most programs in this book will be implemented as console applications. Therefore, we start this section with the creation of few simple console applications to help readers get familiar with basic C/C++ syntax and Microsoft Visual Studio development environment.

In the early days of programming, most programmers used *Emacs* (the text editor developed initially at MIT AI lab in 1970's) to implement FORTRAN, PASCAL, and C programs. When the implementation is completed, the source file is compiled at the command line to generate an executable program whose suffix is usually `.exe`. To see how this works, we will use a text editor (either `Notepad` or `Emacs`) to implement a program to compute the factorial

$$n! = n(n-1)(n-2)\cdots 1.$$

Translating the above formula into C or C++ code would be something like:

```
Result = n;
for (i=n-1; i>1; i--)
{
    Result = Result * i;
}
```

Here, we use a `for` loop to perform repeated execution. Loop index i is initialized to $n - 1$. The statement

```
Result = Result * i;
```

is repeatedly executed if i is larger than 1. After each execution, the index is reduced by 1 with *post-decrement* arithmetic operator. In C and C++, there are four commonly-used *unary increment* or *decrement* operators:

| Expression | Called | Explanation |
|---|---|---|
| ++i | pre-increment | Increment i by 1, then use the new value of i in the expression in which i resides |
| i++ | post-increment | Use the current value of i in the expression in which i resides, then increment i by 1 |
| --i | pre-decrement | Decrement i by 1, then use the new value of i in the expression in which i resides |
| i-- | post-decrement | Use the current value of i in the expression in which i resides, then decrement i by 1 |

If you do not want to use a unary decrement operator, it is fine to write the above code as

```
Result = n;
for (i=n-1; i>1; i -= 1)
{
    Result *= i;
}
```

It is noted that *compound assignment operator* `*=` and `-=` are used in the above code. In C/C++ programming, addition (`+=`) and division (`/=`) are also widely-used compound assignment operators.

Based on the preference, we may also replace the `for` loop by a `while` loop as

```
Result = 1;
while (n > 1)
{
    Result *= n;
    n--;
}
```

We can also combine two statements inside the `while` loop into one as

```
    Result = 1;
    while (n > 1)
    {
        Result *= n--;
    }
```

However, I personally do not recommend it since the code becomes more difficult to understand for beginners. To be able to test the implementation of factorial computation, we need a driver `main` to initialize $n$, call the method `Factorial`, and print out the result. The full implementation is listed below:

```
1    #include <stdio.h>
2
3    int Factorial(int n)
4    {
5        int Result = 1;
6        while (n > 1)
7        {
8            Result *= n;
9            n--;
10       }
11       return Result;
12   }
13
14   int main (void)
15   {
16       int result, n = 6;
17       result = Factorial(n);
18       printf("result = %d\n", result);
19       return 0;
20   }
```

Since this is our first console application implemented in C/C++, we shall explain the above code in detail. The C and C++ programming languages are closely related. C++ grew out of C and was designed to support *object oriented programming*. The incompatibilities between C and C++ were reduced as much as possible in order to maximize interoperability between the two languages. Examples in this book are mostly numerical algorithms that are usually implemented as functions rather than as object oriented *classes*. Therefore, it is possible to implement such algorithms so that they are compatible with both C and C++. If any code is specific to C++, it will be mentioned. Otherwise, we simply say in this book that *"the implementation in C/C++ is ..."*

Referring to the above code list, the statement `#include <stdio.h>` in line 1 is to include a standard C/C++ library header file that contains the prototypes or signatures of input/output (I/O) functions such as `printf`. Without it, we would get a compiling error about `printf` since the compiler does not know the prototype of `printf`.

Lines 3 through 12 illustrate the implementation of the computation of factorial $n!$. In particular, line 3 is a function *declaration* (also known as *prototype* or *signature*). It precedes the function definition and specifies the name, return type, storage class, and other attributes of a function. To be a prototype, the function declaration must also establish types and identifiers for the function's arguments. In our case, the return type of this function is `int`, indicating that an integer will be returned by this function. It is also noted that this function has one argument `int n` that is sent to this function from `main` via *passing-by-value* mechanism. When an argument is passed by value, a copy of the argument is passed to the function. Modification of this argument in the callee function has no effect on the variable in the caller function. Accordingly, $n = 6$ in `main` will not be changed when the copy of `n` gets modified inside the `while` loop in the callee function.

Implementation of `main` starts from line 14 and ends at line 20. For a console application, the only absolute requirement is a function called `main`. It is the starting point of execution for all C and C++ console programs. The operating system calls `main` when we run the program, and from that point on, we implement our algorithm and can use any programming structure we want. The argument in `main` declaration is `void`, indicating that no specific input arguments are declared. In chapter 4 we shall see how we can add input arguments to `main` to access the command-line arguments. From line 16 to 18 inside the `main` function, we initialize `n`, call the function `Factorial` to compute $n!$, and print out the result at the command prompt. The `printf` function at line 18 formats and prints a series of characters and values to the standard output stream. If arguments follow the format string, the format string must contain specifications (beginning with %) that determine the output format for the arguments. At line 18, `%d` indicates its corresponding argument is a signed decimal integer. Additional frequently-used format specifiers in this book are `%lf` (long float) and `%e` (scientific notation). For example, the following code fragment

```
double pi = 3.14159265358979323846;
printf("pi = %lf or %.10lf or %.15e\n", pi, pi, pi);
```

will print $\pi$ in three different formats:

```
pi = 3.141593 or 3.1415926536 or 3.141592653589793e+000
```

It is noted that the first, second, and third printout has 6, 10, and 15 decimal places. Besides `printf`, we also frequently use `fprintf` in this book. It formats and prints a series of characters and values to a user-defined stream as oppose to the standard output stream. We will cover it in subsequent chapters.

We now discuss how to compile and run the `Factorial` program. Let us create a new folder in D: drive and name it `ArtProgram`. It is all right if you prefer to create this folder in another drive. In this case, however, you have to make necessary changes whenever the directory path is presented. We create also a subfolder `test` and save the above code as `ComputeFactorial.cpp` in this subfolder. We then invoke Microsoft's Visual C++ compiler `cl.exe` at the command prompt as

```
D:\ArtProgram\test>cl ComputeFactorial.cpp
```

The following information will be displayed at the command line

```
Microsoft (R) 32-bit C/C++ Optimizing Compiler
    Version 16.00.40219.01 for 80x86
Copyright (C) Microsoft Corporation.  All rights reserved.

ComputeFactorial.cpp
Microsoft (R) Incremental Linker Version 10.00.40219.01
Copyright (C) Microsoft Corporation.  All rights reserved.

/out:ComputeFactorial.exe
ComputeFactorial.obj
```

We may suppress the display of the above copyright information by using /nologo options as follows:

```
D:\ArtProgram\test>cl /nologo ComputeFactorial.cpp
```

Upon the completion of compilation, we should see ComputeFactorial.exe in the test folder and may invoke this executable to generate the desired output at the command line as

```
D:\ArtProgram\test>ComputeFactorial
result = 720
```

The above development process is fine if we just do some simple and casual programming. Even so, we may still have a problem in debugging the code when a program does not generate the expected results. In this case, we may have to detect bugs by putting print instructions inside our programs to print out intermediate results. By doing so, we may be able to isolate the problematic code and eventually track down the bugs or problems.

In software companies nowadays, professional software developers usually reply on an *integrated development environments (IDEs)* to develop their programs. IDEs normally consist of a source code editor, source code management, build automation tools, and a debugger. They are designed to maximize programmers' productivity by providing tight-knit components with similar user interfaces.

In developing *windows-based applications* (programs written to run under the Microsoft Windows operating system), Microsoft Visual Studio is unarguably the primary choice of IDEs. For this reason, Microsoft Visual studio is the chosen integrated development environment for this book. At the write of this book, Microsoft Visual Studio 2012 was just released. In consideration that many readers may not have upgraded their versions, we use Microsoft Visual Studio 2010 exclusively in this book. If you do not have Microsoft Visual Studio installed in your computer, you may download Microsoft Visual Studio Express from the Microsoft web site. The Express version is a lightweight freeware that has almost everything we need except for the support of parallel programming via OpenMP.

We now look how to use Visual Studio IDE to develop a console application. Start Visual Studio 2010 and click File->New->Project from Visual Studio *menu bar* to bring up New Project wizard. The Visual Studio menu bar is also known as IDE menu bar. It contains menu categories such as `File`, `Edit`, `View`, $\cdots$, `Window`, and `Help` as shown below. This IDE menu bar will be referred to frequently in subsequent chapters.

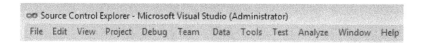

Figure 1.1: IDE menu bar

In the Visual C++ project types pane, click `Win32 Console Application` and type or browse the location of the project. In our case, the location is the folder in which `ComputeFactorial.cpp` resides. We then type the project name `ComputeFactorial` as shown below and click the `OK` button.

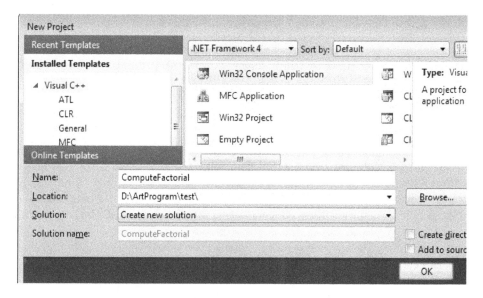

Figure 1.2: Create a Visual C++ project

When the Win32 Application Wizard pops up, we click `Next`, then select the `Empty Project` check box and click the `Finish` button. The wizard will create several empty folders under `ComputeFactorial` project in *Solution Explorer* as seen in figure 1.3. If Solution Explorer is not visible, click Solution Explorer on the View menu.

Let's move the mouse cursor to `Source Files` folder and click the right mouse button to select `Add->Existing Item` as shown in figure 1.3. Browse to find the existing source file `ComputeFactorial.cpp` and click the `Add` button. We should now find that the source file has been added to the `Source Files` folder as illustrated in figure 1.4. If a `.cpp` source file is created from scratch by using Microsoft Visual Studio IDE text editor, we need to select `Add->New Item`. In this case, the Wizard will ask whether it is a `.cpp`, or `.h`, or any other type of file. By selecting a correct file type and entering the name of file, the Wizard will add the specified file to the `Source Files` folder in Solution Explorer and a tabbed window will appear where we type in the code.

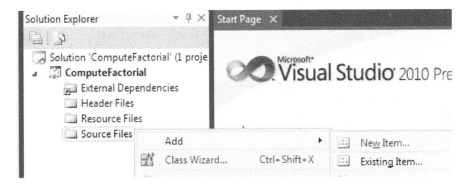

Figure 1.3: Add existing files to source folder

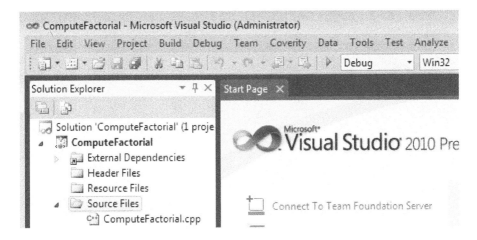

Figure 1.4: Appearance of Visual C++ project (build mode is `Debug`)

We are ready to compile and run the program under Visual Studio IDE. From the menu bar, click `Build->Build Solution` from the menu bar or press the `F7` key to build the project. By default it is set to `Debug` mode as shown in the Solution Configurations list box in figure 1.4. Compiling the program with `Debug` setting generates a debug version of executable with full symbolic debug information so that we can set a *breakpoint* at any statement to watch the execution. The use of breakpoints is best illustrated with an example. Let us move the mouse cursor to this statement:

```
result = Factorial(n);
```

and press `F9` to set a breakpoint that is indicated by the red solid spherical glyph as shown in figure 1.5. Next, press the `F5` key to run the program. The execution halts and breaks into the debugger when it hits the breakpoint. We can now use a `Watch` window to watch or evaluate variables and expressions. To open the `Watch` window, the debugger must be running or in break mode. From the `Debug` menu, select `Windows`, then `Watch` and click either `Watch 1`, `Watch 2`, `Watch 3`, or `Watch 4`. For this simple case, we just need one `Watch` window. Let's add `n` and `result` in `Watch 1` and press

F10 to execute the program. As we do so, the values of variables in Watch 1 window change as shown in figure 1.5.

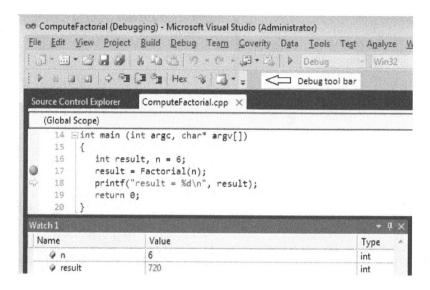

Figure 1.5: Watch variables in debug mode

As opposed to pressing F10 to step over the subfunction Factorial(n) when the execution halts at the breakpoint, we may also press the F11 key to step into Factorial to watch how the value of Result changes at each iteration.

It is noted that the Debug Toolbar is shown in figure 1.5. We can access the debugger's most commonly-used commands and windows through the Debug Toolbar. To display the Debug Toolbar, on the View menu click Toolbars and then select Debug. It is also noted that the line numbers are displayed in code for reference. If they are not shown in your Microsoft Visual Studio IDE, you can turn on the display of line numbers by choosing Tool->Option from menu bar, then expanding the Text Editor node and selecting either All Languages or the specific language (e.g., C/C++), and marking the Line numbers checkbox.

A breakpoint can be set and deselected by pressing F9 key. We can also press Ctrl+F9 to disable and enable a breakpoint instead of deselecting it. In this case, the disabled breakpoint is marked by a hollow glyph. It is also possible to set a *conditional breakpoint*. Conditional breakpoints can be very useful when we are trying to find bugs in our code. They cause a break to occur only if a specific condition is satisfied. A conditional breakpoint is created by combining a breakpoint command with a valid expression and is best illustrated with an example. Let us set a breakpoint at line 11. In a source, right-click a line containing a breakpoint glyph and choose Condition from Breakpoints in the shortcut menu as shown below.

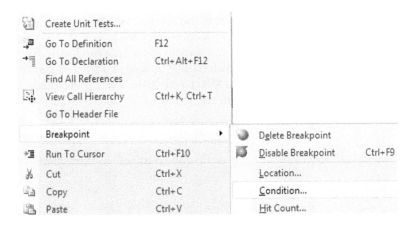

Figure 1.6: Conditional breakpoint

In the `Breakpoint Condition` dialog box, enter `n < 5` in the `Condition` box as illustrated below. A conditional breakpoint is indicated by a solid glyph with + sign in the middle. When n is reduced to 4 or less in the `while` loop, the execution halts at the conditional breakpoint.

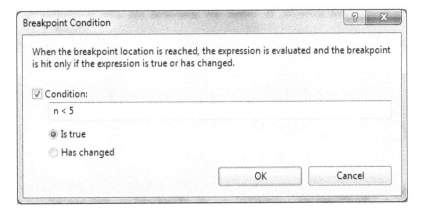

Figure 1.7: Specify a valid break condition

So far we have been running the program in debug mode. On the Standard toolbar, we can also choose `Release` from the `Solution Configurations` list box so that the compiler will generate an optimized executable that runs much faster. This is usually the final version delivered to customers. It should be pointed that you can debug the code in release mode to investigate a problem specific to the release code (e.g., local variables not explicitly initialized by the program are initialized differently in debug and release modes). However, you may find some strange behaviors such as the data in `Watch` windows not making any sense at all. It is possible to turn off optimization and enable debugging of a release build. However, the behavior under such configuration may be different from the fully optimized version.

Our next example demonstrates how to find the smallest and largest integer number in a one-dimensional array. It is designed to help readers without C/C++ programming experience become familiar with additional argument passing mechanisms and C/C++ pointers. Start Visual Studio to create an empty project named **FindMinMax** in **test** folder (referring to figure 1.2). We then select **Add->New Item** (referring to figure 1.3) to create a **apiFindMinMax.cpp** file with the following implementation

```
1    #include <stdio.h>
2
3    void apiFindMinMax(int n, int *myArray, int nMin, int nMax)
4    {
5        int   i;
6        nMin = nMax = myArray[0];
7        for (i=1; i<n; i++)
8        {
9            if (nMin > myArray[i])
10                nMin = myArray[i];
11            else if (nMax < myArray[i])
12                nMax = myArray[i];
13        }
14        return;
15    }
16
17    int main(void)
18    {
19        int   nMin = 0, nMax = 0, n = 10;
20        int   myArray[10] = {6,7,3,10,22,7,11,18,20,19};
21
22        apiFindMinMax(n, myArray, nMin, nMax);
23        return 0;
24    }
```

Referring to line 3, the return type of function **apiFindMinMax** is **void**. If a function was declared with return type **void**, the **return** statement at the end of this function should be either omitted or left there without any return value. There are four arguments in this function: n specifies the size of the array, **myArray** is sent to this function via *passing-by-pointer mechanism* (more discussion later), **nMin** and **nMax** are intended to be the output arguments that store respectively the smallest and largest integer value. Save and compile this project. Set a breakpoint at line 14 and press **F5** to run the program. The execution will halt at the breakpoint. By adding **nMin** and **nMax** to a **Watch** window we will see that they have correct results: 3 and 22. Press the **F10** key to step over and return to the calling function. At this moment we shall see that both **nMin** and **nMax** at the **Watch** window are back to zero – the computed results are gone! This is because both **nMin** and **nMax** were passed to **apiFindMinMax** via passing-by-value, which means copies of **nMin** and **nMax** were created for **apiFindMinMax**. Changes to these local copies have no effect on **nMin** and **nMax** in **main** and these copies were destroyed when **apiFindMinMax** ends.

One solution to this problem is to use the passing-by-pointer mechanism. *Pointers* are a very powerful feature of the C/C++ languages that has many uses in advanced programming. However, they are among C/C++'s most difficult capabilities to master. A very intimate relationship exists between arrays and pointers, which is why an array was used in the above program for discussion of pointers. Referring to line 20 of the above program, a static integer array of size ten was declared and initialized. When this program is compiled and executed, a block of memory is reserved and initialized to the specified values. Memory addresses and corresponding values can be viewed when the execution breaks into the debugger. Let's set a breakpoint at line 22 and run the program by pressing F5. When the execution halts at the breakpoint, we add myArray in the Watch window and click Debug->Windows->Memory->Memory 1 from the main menu bar. When Memory 1 window pops up, type the address of myArray in the address field as shown in figure 1.8. As is seen, each integer value is stored in a uniquely addressed memory "cell" that is intended for integer. Since an integer in 32bit machine has 4 bytes, the memory address from one cell to the next one is increased by 4, which can be verified by using hexadecimal number arithmetic. It should be pointed out that figure 1.8 is for illustration only. The actual memory addresses vary at each execution.

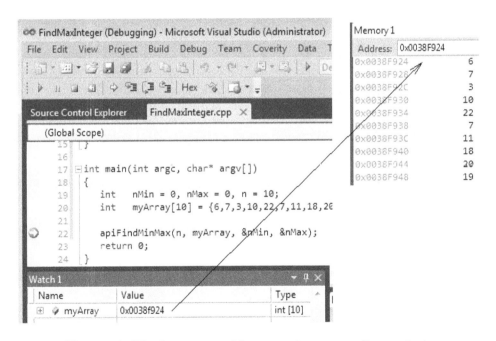

Figure 1.8: Watch memory addresses and corresponding contents

C and C++ are the programming languages that include features of both high-level and low-level programming languages. For example, they allow direct access to memory address locations via pointers. A pointer is a special variable whose value is the *address* of a memory location where a specific data type is stored. When a pointer variable is declared, the data type it can point to is also specified. The notations

```
int     *pA;
double  *pD;
```

declare **pA** as an integer-pointer variable and **pD** as a double-pointer variable. A pointer declaration merely creates the pointer variables; it neither initializes the pointer nor allocates memory space for the pointer. Therefore, before it is used, a pointer variable must be assigned the address of a variable, of an array, or of dynamically allocated memory space. Two unary operators are important in dealing with pointers:

& – the address-of operator,

* – the value-of operator.

Having already declared *pA, the statement

```
pA = &myArray[2];
```

assigns to **pA** the address of **myArray[2]**. Since the array index starts from 0 in C/C++, **pA** holds the address of the third memory cell, i.e., 0x0038F92C (referring to figure 1.8). To access the content of the pointer, we use the value-of operator as *pA. It was said that **pA** points at the third cell (or holds the address of third cell), the content of **pA** is thus 3. If we print *pA via

```
printf("%d\n", *pA);
```

we should see the value 3 at the command prompt. With the use of a pointer, we may pass to the callee function the address of a variable defined inside the **main**. By modifying the content of this variable through the pointer, the callee function is permitted to modify the actual argument declared in caller function. Let us modify our code to pass the addresses of **nMin** and **nMax** to the callee so that **apiFindMinMax** can indirectly modify the contents of **nMin** and **nMax** that are declared in **main**:

```
1    #include <stdio.h>
2
3    void apiFindMinMax(int n, int *myArray, int *nMin, int *nMax)
4    {
5        int    i;
6        *nMin = *nMax = myArray[0];
7        for (i=1; i<n; i++)
8        {
9            if (*nMin > myArray[i])
10               *nMin = myArray[i];
11           else if (*nMax < myArray[i])
12               *nMax = myArray[i];
13       }
14       return;
15   }
16
17   int main(void)
18   {
19       int    nMin = 0, nMax = 0, n = 10;
```

```
20      int   myArray[10] = {6,7,3,10,22,7,11,18,20,19};
21
22      apiFindMinMax(n, myArray, &nMin, &nMax);
23      return 0;
24   }
```

Pointers are powerful and efficient in that C/C++ allows pointer arithmetic. Arithmetic on pointers takes into account the size of the type. For example, adding an integer number to a pointer produces another pointer that points to an address that is higher by that number times the size of the type. Therefore, pA += 2 is equivalent to assigning (referring to figure 1.8)

```
0x0038F934 (= 0x0038F92C + 2 * sizeof(int) = 0x0038F92C + 8)
```

to pA. Accordingly, pA += 2 changed the address of pA from the current &myArray[2] to &myArray[4]. With basic knowledge about pointer arithmetic, we may potentially improve the efficiency of code by avoiding array indexing as follows:

```
1    void apiFindMinMax(int n, int *myArray, int *nMin, int *nMax)
2    {
3        int   i, *ptr;
4        *nMin = *nMax = myArray[0];
5        ptr = myArray + 1;
6        for (i=1; i<n; i++)
7        {
8            if (*nMin > *ptr)
9                *nMin = *ptr;
10           else if (*nMax < *ptr)
11               *nMax = *ptr;
12           ptr++;
13       }
14   }
```

However, I personally do not encourage this for beginners. In addition, modern compilers are likely to generate the same code for pointer accesses and array accesses. Therefore, we should probably not be worrying about that level of performance.

In C++ (not in C), it is also possible to pass the address of a variable to the callee via *passing-by-reference*. This is done by placing & in front of an argument in the decoration of function. Passing an argument by reference means that the function or method is permitted to modify the actual argument. For illustration we modify our implementation of **apiFindMinMax** as follows:

```
1    #include <stdio.h>
2
3    void apiFindMinMax(int n, int *myArray, int &nMin, int &nMax)
4    {
5        int   i;
6        nMin = nMax = myArray[0];
7        for (i=1; i<n; i++)
```

```
8       {
9           if (nMin > myArray[i])
10              nMin = myArray[i];
11          else if (nMax < myArray[i])
12              nMax = myArray[i];
13      }
14      return;
15  }
16
17  int main(void)
18  {
19      int    nMin = 0, nMax = 0, n = 10;
20      int    myArray[10] = {6,7,3,10,22,7,11,18,20,19};
21
22      apiFindMinMax(n, myArray, nMin, nMax);
23      return 0;
24  }
```

For now, this is adequate information to allow us to move on and be comfortable with implementing algorithms that will be discussed in the next two chapters. When encountering new terminologies and new Microsoft IDE environments, I shall continue to provide necessary explanations.

# Chapter 2

# Floating-point Computing

*"Floating-point numbers are like piles of sand; every time you move them around, you lose a little sand and pick up a little dirt."* – Dr. Brian Kernighan (Princeton professor and contributor of UNIX) and Dr. P. J. Plauger (entrepreneur and author of many programming books).

Computers use a fixed number of bits to represent a piece of data, which could be a number, a character, etc. A $n$-bit storage location can represent up to $2^n$ distinct entities. For example, a 32-bit computer can hold unsigned integers ranging from 0 to 4,294,967,295 ($= 2^{32} - 1$). Integers provide an exact representation for numeric values. However, they suffer from two major drawbacks: the inability to represent fractional values and a limited dynamic range. Floating-point arithmetic solves these two problems at the expense of accuracy and speed. Some of the greatest achievements of the 20th century would not have been possible without the floating-point capabilities of digital computers. Nevertheless, this subject is not well understood by software developers and is a regular source of confusion. In a February, 1998 keynote address entitled *Extensions to Java for Numerical Computing*, Dr. James Gosling, the creator of Java programming language, asserted *"95% of folks out there are completely clueless about floating-point."* His assertion may sound far-fetched to many but has good ground in consideration of the following examples:

- In 1982 the Vancouver Stock Exchange instituted a new index much like the Dow-Jones Index. It began with a nominal value of 1,000.000 and was recalculated based on the selling price of all listed stocks after each recorded transaction. This computation was done using four decimal places and truncating (not rounding) the result to three. Stock transactions happen 2,800 times a day. After 22 months of accumulated roundoff error, the Vancouver Stock Exchange index was undervalued by almost 50% even though the exchange was setting records for volume and value. When this computation problem was found and corrected by rounding off (not truncating) the fourth decimal place, the index sat at 1098.892.

- On February 25, 1991 an American Patriot missile failed to track and destroy an Iraqi Scud missile. Instead it hit an Army barrack, killing 26 people. The cause was later determined to be an inaccurate calculation caused by measuring time in a tenth of a second that cannot be represented exactly since a 24-bit floating-point was used.

- Ariane 5's first test flight on 4 June 1996 failed, with the rocket self-destructing 37 seconds after launch because of a malfunction in the control software. The malfunction was traced to unanticipated overflow in converting 64-bit floating-point number to a 16-bit signed integer.

- A few years ago, the company where I work started to use the commercialized static code analysis tool Coverity® to automatically test source code for software defects that could lead to product crashes, unexpected behavior, security breaches, or catastrophic failures. One of the top five defect criterions was the direct comparison of floating-point values for equality, which, as a rule of thumb, should rarely be used in floating-point computing.

- Geometric models created at different computer-aided design (CAD) systems may use different units for measurement. Commonly-used units are the millimeter, meter, inch, foot, etc. When a model generated in one system is imported to another system, it is important to use a correct scaling factor to scale the model geometry to obtain consistent measurements. For example, to convert a drawing created in millimeters to meters, the scaling factor of $1/1,000$ needs to be used. AutoCAD® (developed by Autodesk) is probably the only popular CAD system that allows users to create the so-called *unitless* drawings and models. It is, however, emphasized in a 2007 *Autodesk University*'s article that "this (unitless) selection can only make sense if you never ever switch between metric and imperial, or never exchange files with other companies." If a unitless model has to be imported to a different system, it is important to derive a scaling factor based on the allowed workspace and properly scale the model to maintain model integrity. Unfortunately, this is not always the case. As a manager and developer at Math and Geometric Modeling group, I have seen numerous cases in which unitless models were imported without scaling. Therefore, a model may sit so far away that the distance between the model and the origin of coordinate system is equivalent to the distance from the Moon to the Earth (roughly $4 \times 10^8$ meters). When geometric operations fail to create consistent results with respect to the tolerance of $10^{-6}$ meter, people blame the "unstable" math and geometric algorithms. Apparently, those developers who imported the foreign models are unaware of floating-point representation in a digital computer and hence fail to understand that a `double` data type in a 32-bit machine has at most 16 significant digits. Eight or more significant digits are required to represent a model sitting on the Moon. Additional six digits are required to describe the measurement with accuracy in micrometer (i.e., $10^{-6}$ meter). Therefore, 14 or more significant digits will be consumed, leaving no room for round-off error that occurs in numerical computation and approximation.

Floating-point arithmetic is a very important subject, and a rudimentary understanding of it is a pre-requisite for programmers, operating system designers, programming language and compiler writers. For this reason, floating-point representation, arithmetic, and limitations will be reviewed in this chapter prior to any discussion of numerical method.

Digital computers cannot represent all real numbers exactly, so we are constantly facing challenges when designing computer algorithms for real number computations. Such challenges are further exacerbated since many important scientific algorithms make additional approximations when exact solutions are not practical. It is not uncommon that a targeted computation result can be achieved in several ways, all of which may be equivalent in theory, but in practice when performed on digital computers yield different results. Some calculations might dampen out approximation errors (also known as *numerical noises*); others might magnify such errors. Calculations that can be proven not to magnify approximation errors are referred to as *numerically stable*. In this chapter, we will also discuss general rules in reducing numerical errors and how to determine if an algorithms is robust based on some examples.

## 2.1 Floating-point representation

A modern digital computer represents data using the binary numeral system. Text, numbers, pictures, audio, and nearly any other form of information can be converted into a string of *bits*, or *binary digits*, each of which has a value of 1 or 0. The most common unit of storage is the *byte*, which is equal to 8 bits.

Computers use a fixed number of bits to represent a piece of data, which could be a character, an integer, a double, etc. An $n$-bit storage location can represent up to $2^n$ distinct entities. For example, a 2-bit memory location can hold one of these four binary patterns:

$$00, \quad 01, \quad 10, \quad 11.$$

Hence, it can represent at most 4 distinct entities (e.g., integer numbers 0 to 3). Modern personal computers have either 32 bit or 64-bit architectures that can hold unsigned integers ranging

| 32-bit | 0 to 4,294,967,295 ($= 2^{32} - 1$). |
|---|---|
| 64-bit | 0 to 18,446,744,073,709,551,615 ($= 2^{64} - 1$). |

These ranges are "huge" for counting but very limited for real world computing. For example, the factorial of 21 is

$$21! = 51,090,942,171,709,440,000$$

which means that a 64-bit computer would not be able to compute factorials of 21 or higher if it has only integer representation. Lack of dynamic range is not the only limitation of integer representation. Another significant drawback of integer presentation is the inability to represent fractional values.

The term floating-point refers to the fact that its decimal point can "*float*" anywhere relative to the significant digits of the number with the help of exponents. For example, we can let the decimal "float" by writing 3141.59 in *scientific notation* as

$$314.159 \times 10, \quad 31.4159 \times 10^2, \quad 3.14159 \times 10^3$$

with the last one being also called the *normalized scientific notation.* In scientific notation all real numbers are written in the form of

$$m \times 10^n$$

where the exponent $n$ is an integer, and the coefficient $m$ is any real number called the *mantissa* or *significand.* When $1 \leq |m| < 10$, the notation is then the normalized scientific notation.

The significand (or mantissa) is part of a number in scientific notation, consisting of its *significant digits.* The significant digits of a number are those digits that carry meaning contributing to its accuracy. Every science and engineering student knows that no measurement of a physical quantity can be entirely accurate. It is important to know, therefore, just how much the measured value is likely to deviate from the unknown, true value of the quantity. For example, if I say I weigh 135 lbs, what I am really saying is:

$$134.5 \, \text{lbs} < \text{my weight} < 135.5 \, \text{lbs}$$

This is because I have confidence that my scale is accurate to within a half pound, and that I read the number correctly off the dial. But I don't say that I weigh 135.000 lbs, since that would imply extraordinary precision of my scale:

$$134.9995 \, \text{lbs} < \text{my weight} < 135.0005 \, \text{lbs}$$

By saying I weigh 135 lbs, I imply that three digits in the number are known to be correct. Accordingly, these three digits are significant.

Non-zero digits are always significant. With zeroes, the situation is more complicated:

1. Zeroes placed between other digits are always significant; 5004 has four significant digits and 601 has three.

2. Zeroes placed before other digits are not significant. They are simply placeholders. For example, the diameter of my watch without crown is 28 millimeters. This measurement has two significant digits. If the diameter is written in meter, it is then 0.028 meter. Zeros are simply placeholders. Therefore, 0.028 has only two significant numbers.

3. Zeroes placed after other digits but behind a *decimal point* are significant. If there is no decimal point, they are usually considered as placeholders and hence are not counted. For example, when you are told that the population in Huntsville, Alabama is approximately 181000, it often means that the figure is rounded to the nearest thousand. Therefore, 181000 has only three significant digits. However, 3.700 has four significant digits since zeroes are placed after a decimal point to indicate a measurement precise to three decimal places.

To avoid confusion and make counting easy, always write the number in the normalized scientific notation. In this case, all digits are significant.

Floating-point notation in computers is analogous to scientific notation for decimal numbers. Suppose

$$x = \pm m \times 2^E$$

where $1 \leq m = (b_0 b_1 b_2 \cdots)_2 < 2$ and $b_0, b_1, \cdots$ are bits. To store a number in floating-point representation, a computer word is divided into 3 fields, representing the sign (0 for positive and 1 for negative), the exponent $E$, and the significand (or mantissa) $m$ respectively. A 32-bit word is used for the *single-precision* floating-point format (known as float in C/C++) and is divided into fields as follows: 1 bit for the sign, 8 bits for the exponent and 23 bits for the significand (23 bits is equivalent to $\log_{10} 2^{23} \approx 7$ significant decimal digits). Since the exponent field is 8 bits, it can be used to represent signed exponents between $-126$ and $127$ (approximately between -38 and 38 in base 10 since $2^{-126} \approx 1.1755 \times 10^{-38}$ and $2^{127} \approx 1.7014 \times 10^{+38}$). The significand field can store the first 23 bits of the binary representation of $m$, namely

$$b_0 b_1 b_2 \cdots b_{22}.$$

To store a base-10 number in computer, we first convert the integer part to its binary equivalent. This may be done by repeatedly dividing the integer by two until the quotient becomes zero. Depending on the dividend is odd or even, we write respectively the remainder 1 or 0 on the right of each division process. The binary equivalent is then obtained by reading the sequence of remainders upwards to the top. For example, the processes to convert $(71)_{10}$ are

$$
\begin{array}{r|l}
2|71 & 1 \\
2|35 & 1 \\
2|17 & 1 \\
2|8 & 0 \\
2|4 & 0 \\
2|2 & 0 \\
2|1 & 1 \\
\end{array}
$$

We thus have $(71)_{10} = (1000111)_2$ or, in the normalized form, $(1.000111)_2 \times 2^6$. Accordingly, it is stored in 32-bit computer as

| 0 | $E = 6$ | 1.00011100000000000000000 |
|---|---------|---------------------------|

Reversely, we can convert $(1000111)_2$ to the its decimal equivalent as follows:

$$1 \times 2^6 + 0 \times 2^5 + 0 \times 2^4 + 0 \times 2^3 + 1 \times 2^2 + 1 \times 2^1 + 1 \times 2^0 = (71)_{10}.$$

Note that the exponent $E = 6$ should actually be stored in binary numbers as well. For now, we use decimal number 6 for simplicity.

Converting a decimal fraction to binary number is done by repeatedly multiplying the decimal fraction by 2. The whole number (either 1 or 0) is the binary number repeatedly appended to the right of the point. For example, the steps to convert 0.625 to the binary representation are

- $0.625 \times 2 = 1.25$, the first binary digit to the right of the point is a 1.

- Discard the whole number part of the previous result and multiply the fraction by 2: $0.25 \times 2 = 0.5$. So, the second binary digit to the right of the point is a 0.

- Multiply the fraction by 2 again: $0.5 \times 2 = 1.0$. So, the thrid binary digit to the right of the point is a 1.

- Terminate the process since the fraction part is now zero.

Therefore, we have $(0.625)_{10} = (.101)_2$ or, in the normalized form, $(.101)_2 = (1.01)_2 \times 2^{-1}$. Reversely, we can convert the binary number to the decimal fraction as follows:

$$0.625 = 1 \times 2^{-1} + 0 \times 2^{-2} + 1 \times 2^{-3}.$$

Since computers have only a finite number of bits for storing a real number, any number that has an infinite number of digits such as $1/3$, $\sqrt{2}$ and $\pi$ cannot be represented completely in computer. It may surprise some people that even a number with finite decimal digits cannot be represented precisely because of the way of encoding real numbers. For example, when 0.1 in base 10 is represented in a binary system, it is

$$(1.100110011 \cdots)_2 \times 2^{-4},$$

which is stored in a 32-bit machine with truncation as:

| 0 | $E = -4$ | 1.10011001100110011001100110 |
|---|----------|------------------------------|

Thus, there is loss of precision. In general, a fraction with finite decimal expansions can be represented as a rational number $a/b$. This rational number has finite binary expansions if and only if the denominator has 2 as the only prime factor, i.e., $b = 2^n$. It should be pointed out that a fraction number that has finite binary expansions may still have to be stored as an approximation because it may have more binary expansions than the available bits can hold.

We now discuss representation of exponents in computers. In IEEE 754 floating-point numbers, the exponent is *biased* in the engineering sense of the word – the value stored is offset from the actual value by the exponent bias. Biasing is done because exponents have to be signed values in order to be able to represent both tiny and huge values, but two's complement, the usual representation for signed values, would make comparison harder. To solve this problem, the exponent is biased before being stored, by adjusting its value to put it within an unsigned range suitable for comparison. For example, if the real exponent of a number is $X$, then it is represented as $(X + \text{bias})$. When interpreting the floating-point number, the bias is subtracted to retrieve the actual exponent. IEEE single-precision uses a bias of 127. Therefore, an exponent of

$-4$ is represented as $-4 + 127 = 123 = (01111011)_2$

$\;\;0$ is represented as $0 + 127 = 127 = (01111111)_2$

$+1$ is represented as $+1 + 127 = 128 = (10000000)_2$

$+6$ is represented as $+6 + 127 = 133 = (10000101)_2$

After understanding the representation of an exponent, we can convert 71 in base 10 to binary system to store in computers as

| 0 | 10000101 | 1.00011100000000000000000 |
|---|----------|----------------------------|

Similarly, 0.1 would be

| 0 | 01111011 | 1.10011001100110011001100110 |
|---|----------|------------------------------|

For most programmers, it may not be so important to know the exact representation of floating-point numbers. It is, however, very important to remember that a computer has only a finite number of bits for storing the exponent and significand. Therefore,

- When the result of a calculation is too large to represent in a floating-point number system, we say that *overflow* has occurred. This happens when a number's exponent is larger than allowed.

- Just as overflow occurs when an exponent is too big, *underflow* occurs when an exponent is too small.

- Finite number of bits for storing the significand requires an infinite number of digits to be truncated. Such roundoff errors may be further exacerbated by floating-point arithmetic in the numerical process, which will be discussed in subsequent sections.

It should be pointed out that a *double-precision* floating-point format (known as `double` in C/C++) is more widely used than single-precision in numerical computations in order to retain maximum significant digits in spite of its performance and bandwidth cost. Computers with 32-bit storage locations use two memory locations to store a 64-bit double-precision number. The 64-bit is divided into three fields as follows: 1 bit for the sign, 11 bits for the exponent and 52 bits for the significand (52 bits is equivalent to $\log_{10} 2^{52} \approx 15 \sim 16$ significant decimal digits). Since the exponent bias for a double-precision floating-point format is 1023 and the exponent is stored as $X + \text{bias}$, the true exponent range is:

$$X_{\min} + \text{bias} = 1 \qquad \Rightarrow \qquad X_{\min} = 1 - \text{bias} = -1022$$
$$X_{\max} + \text{bias} = 2046 \qquad \Rightarrow \qquad X_{\max} = 2046 - \text{bias} = 1023$$

Note that $2046 = 2^{11} - 2$ (one bit for the sign and one bit for zero). Converting the exponent range between $-1022$ and $1023$ to the exponent for base 10 is approximately between $-308$ and $308$ ($2^{-1022} \approx 2.225074 \times 10^{-308}$ and $2^{1023} \approx 1.0 \times 10^{+308}$).

## 2.2 Floating-point comparison

As a rule of thumb in programming, we should avoid direct comparison of two floating-point values for equality because computers have limited precision. It is widely regarded that direct comparisons of floating-point values are the sources of instability that can be triggered by arithmetic computations, change of compilers, or even change of compiling options. For this reason, any direct comparison of floating-point values is considered a defect by Coverity® and must be scrutinized carefully to determine if a defect truly exists or if the comparison is being performed in an appropriate context. Some people may think that a solution to such anomalies is simply not to compare floating-point numbers for equality, but instead to consider them equal if they are within some error bound $\varepsilon$. This is hardly a cure-all, because it raises as many questions as it answers. What should the value of $\varepsilon$ be? If the absolute values of $x < 0$ and $y > 0$ are within $\varepsilon$, should they really be considered equal, even though they have different signs? We will try to answer these questions in this section.

## 2.2.1   Machine precision

Because of the approximate representation of real numbers in computers, a direct comparison of equality as illustrated below is instable as it may perform `operation 1` now and `operation 2` in the future when an environment such as a compiler and operating system changes.

```
if (a == b)
{
    // operation 1
}
else
{
    // operation 2
}
```

A tolerance should be used while comparing two floating-point values. In floating-point arithmetic, the *machine epsilon* $\varepsilon$ (also called *machine precision* or *machine tolerance*) is a very useful quantity in numerical error analysis. For any given format (e.g., `float`, `double`, or `long double`), the machine epsilon is the difference between 1 and the next larger number that can be stored in that format. For a single-precision floating format, there are 23 bits for the significand. Accordingly, the next larger binary number is

$$1.00000000000000000000001$$

which is $1 \times 2^0 + 1 \times 2^{-23} \approx 1 + 1.19 \times 10^{-7}$ in the decimal number system. Due to the restriction of the 23-bit significand, it is clear that $1 + 2^{-24}$ cannot be stored exactly. Therefore, the machine epsilon for a `float` is approximately $1.19 \times 10^{-7}$. Similarly, 52 bits are used for the significand of a double-precision floating-point format. Consequently, the machine epsilon for a `double` is $2^{-52} \approx 2.22 \times 10^{-16}$.

The machine epsilon can also be determined via a C program. For example, we can use the following C program to determine the machine precision for `double` data type:

```
double epsilon = 1.0;

while ((1.0 + epsilon) != 1.0)
{
    epsilon /= 2.0;
}
printf( "\nCalculated Machine epsilon: %.15e\n\n", 2 * epsilon );
```

The while loop breaks when adding epsilon to 1 no longer makes difference (i.e., the condition 1.0 + epsilon == 1.0 is true). Since $\varepsilon$ should be the smallest positive floating-point number such that $1 + \varepsilon > 1$, we thus need to restore the previous value by printing the machine epsilon with 2 * epsilon. Running the above program under Microsoft Visual C++ 2010 compiler, we would get

$$\varepsilon = 2.2204460492503131 \times 10^{-16},$$

which is $2^{-52}$. Machine epsilons for float and double are available in C/C++ header file float.h as FLT_EPSILON and DBL_EPSILON.

## 2.2.2   Comparison with absolute error bound

The absolute difference $|a - b|$ is computed and compared to a fixed error bound $\varepsilon$. If the following condition is true,

$$|a - b| < \varepsilon$$

then $a$ is considered equal to $b$. We must exercise with care when choosing the value for the error bound. It should be a value greater than the minimum representable difference for the range and type of float we are dealing with. For example, $\varepsilon$ is recommended to be larger or equal to the machine epsilon when comparing two values whose types are double.

The absolute difference comparison might be used to identify numbers that are approximately the same. The advantages of comparisons with absolute are speed, simplicity and portability. A severe disadvantage is lack of consideration of the size of a number. For example, a 1 millimeter error in the length of a one-meter long household pipe is certainly more serious than a 1 millimeter error in a 1000-meter long oil transportation pipe. With absolute error bound, however, both cases will be treated equally. Furthermore, it pays no attention to differences in significant digits. Assume $a = 2.2204460 \times 10^{-16}$ and $b = 1.110223024625157 \times 10^{-16}$. By using the absolute error bound, we would consider them to be equal even though their *relative error*

$$\frac{|a - b|}{|a|}$$

is 0.5 (more in the next section).

## 2.2.3   Comparison with relative error bound

In many applications, we are interested in knowing the differences of significant digits rather than the absolute difference of two floating-point numbers. In this case, the following comparison makes more sense than the absolute error bound:

$$|a - b| < \frac{max(|a|, |b|)}{10^{15}}$$

If such condition is true, we say $a$ and $b$ are equal within 15 digits. In some publications, the following formula is used:

$$|a - b| < max(|a|, |b|) \times \varepsilon.$$

If neither $|a|$ nor $|b|$ is zero, we can write the above relation as:

$$\frac{|a - b|}{max(|a|, |b|)} < \varepsilon.$$

As is seen above, this is a relative error bound. In other words, the error is measured as the percentage of the size of the larger number. In general, the relative error makes more sense than the absolute error since it takes into consideration the size of the number. However, users need to pay special attentions to the following aspects:

1. When both $a$ and $b$ are very small, it may result in underflow without a safeguard in division by $10^{15}$ or multiplication by $\varepsilon$. The term floating-point underflow is a condition in a computer program where the result of a calculation is a number smaller than the computer can actually store in memory.

2. From a practical point of view, we would treat $a = 1.0 \times 10^{-30}$ as zero. However, it would not be considered equal to zero using the relative error bound since they do not have equal significant digits.

## 2.2.4   Geometric comparison

At Intergraph Corporation, we develop CAD/CAM software systems and work with geometric entities created by using parametric curves and surfaces all the time. In order to maintain model integrity, we must impose a set of tolerances to ensure proper interpretation of positions, such as determining whether two curves intersect, a position lies on a curve, or a position is inside or outside a volume. The following three tolerances are widely used to control modeling operations in CAD/CAM systems:

**Distance tolerance** If the Euclidean distance of two positions is less than this tolerance, we consider the two points coincident. By default, distance tolerance is set to $10^{-6}$ unit (e.g., meter).

**Angular tolerance** For 32-bit computer, a double-precision floating-point format uses 52-bit for the significand, which is equivalent to 15 or 16 significant decimal digits ($\log_{10} 2^{52} \approx 15.654$). We consider five of the least significant digits to represent numeric round-off errors that occur during calculations. Thus, there are roughly 10 digits that represent the dynamic range of numbers (smallest and largest numbers) within object space. Accordingly, the angular tolerance, which is the smallest of all three tolerances, is set to $10^{-10}$.

**Fit tolerance** This tolerance is used when approximation is involved (e.g., fitting point cloud by spline curve via the least squares approximation method). By default, it is set to $10^{-3}$ unit.

When the distance and angular tolerances are defined, the longest line we can model would be

$$\frac{10^{-6}}{10^{-10}} = 10,000 \, \text{units}$$

Reversely, the angular tolerance can be derived from the distance tolerance and the limit of model space. Since the longest line in the confined model space is $10^4$ units, the deviation incurred by rotating this line by a small angle (say, the angular tolerance $\Delta$) is $10^4 \times \Delta$. If the rotated line is still considered to be the same as the original one with respect to the distance tolerance, the deviation has to be less than the distance tolerance, i.e.,

$$10^4 \times \Delta < \varepsilon.$$

Therefore, the angular tolerance is

$$\Delta < \frac{\varepsilon}{10^4} = 10^{-10},$$

which answers the second pre-interview question in the preface.

Sometime we need to derive a tolerance from the above three. The first pre-interview question in the preface asked for a derivation of a tolerance to measure the area of circle. It was assumed that the radius $(R_1)$ and area $(A_1)$ of circle 1 is known. We further assumed that the radius of the $i$th circle is $R_i = R_1 \pm \varepsilon$. Then, the area tolerance is given by

$$\Delta = |A_i - A_1| = \pi |(R_1 \pm \varepsilon)^2 - R_1^2| = \pi |\pm 2R_1\varepsilon + \varepsilon^2| = \pi |2R_1\varepsilon \pm \varepsilon^2|.$$

Since $\varepsilon^2$ is negligible, we have $\Delta = 2\pi R_1 \varepsilon$. Calculus is the mathematical study of change. We may derive the area tolerance based on calculus. Since $A = \pi R^2$. By the rule of differentials,

$$dA = 2\pi R\, dR.$$

It is known that $dA$ measures the change of area with respect to the small change of radius (i.e., $dR$). Since $dR$ needs to be smaller than $\varepsilon$, we have $\Delta = 2\pi R\varepsilon$. Replacing $R$ by the known $R_1$, we obtain $\Delta = 2\pi R_1 \varepsilon$.

## 2.2.5 Round number to given decimal place

It is often desirable to round a number to a specified decimal place. Assuming we want to round 0.084849999 to the third decimal place to obtain 0.085, we would

- Multiply the number by 1000 to get 84.849999.

- Add 0.5 to round to the nearest integer. The result would be 85.349999.

- Truncate all decimals. The result is 85.0.

- Finally, divide the truncated number by 1000.

By generalizing the above steps, we have the following implementation:

```
double apiRoundValue(
    double   dValue,      // Input: the number to be rounded
    int      nDecimals)   // Input: the decimal digits to keep
{
    double   temp, dScale;

    // Scale the number and add 0.5 so the first decimal of
```

```
// enlarged number is rounded to the nearest integer if
// it's equal or larger than 0.5.
dScale = pow(10.0, nDecimals);
temp = dScale * dValue + 0.5;

// Truncate the decimal numbers and scale it back
temp = floor(temp);
return temp / dScale;
}
```

As previously discussed, computers have only limited precision. Therefore, most numbers just cannot be presented exactly. We take the same number (0.084849999) as an example. Assume we want to round it to the fifth decimal place. The expected result is 0.08485. Instead, we will get

$$0.084849999999999995$$

when running Microsoft Visual C++ 2010.

## 2.3   Design numerically stable algorithms

Numerical stability is an important notion in numerical analysis. An algorithm is called numerically stable if an error, whatever its cause, does not grow to be much larger during the calculation. This happens if the problem is *well-conditioned* , meaning that the solution changes by only a small amount if the problem data are changed by a small amount. On the other hand, if a problem is *ill-conditioned* , then any small error in the data will grow to be a large error. The *condition number* is measured as

$$C_p = \frac{\text{relative change in solution}}{\text{relative change in input data}}$$

The condition number determines how sensitive a problem is to small perturbations of input values. If $C_p$ is not much larger than 1 we call the problem well-conditioned; in the case of $C_p \gg 1$ we call the problem ill-conditioned. For a function $f(x)$, the condition number at $x_0$ is

$$C_p = \left| \frac{(f(x) - f(x_0))/f(x_0)}{(x - x_0)/x_0} \right| \approx \left| \frac{x_0 f'(x_0)}{f(x_0)} \right|$$

It is beyond the scope of this section to study well-conditioned and ill-conditioned systems in detail. For most developers, it is important to realize that floating-point mathematics (as implemented in all modern computer systems) is usually not exact but an approximation to the real number system. In practice we can improve numerical stability by paying special attention to the following floating-point arithmetic:

- Avoid dividing a large number by a very small one, as it is equivalent to multiplying a very large number to the numerical noise. If possible, try to divide numbers that have the same relative magnitudes.

- Avoid subtraction between two similar numbers. Subtracting two numbers that are almost equal results in great loss of significant digits. The numerical instability may be understood by looking at the relative error of subtraction. Let $\bar{a} = a(1 + \Delta a)$ and $\bar{b} = b(1 + \Delta b)$ be two approximation numbers to $a$ and $b$. The relative error caused by small perturbations $\Delta a$ and $\Delta b$ is

$$\frac{|\bar{x} - x|}{|x|} = \frac{|a\Delta a - b\Delta b|}{|a - b|},$$

where $\bar{x} = \bar{a} - \bar{b}$ and $x = a - b$. If $a \approx b$, small $\Delta a$ and $\Delta b$ can lead to very large relative error in $x$ (known as the *cancellation error*).

- Avoid adding a very small number to a large number. Floating-point computation has limited precision. If a large float is added to a small float, the small float may be too negligible to change the value of the larger float. In performing a sequence of additions, the numbers should be added in the order of smallest in magnitude to largest in magnitude. This ensures that the cumulative sum of many small arguments is not negligible.

- Reduce arithmetic computations to minimize cumulative error. Each arithmetic operation adds numerical noise at least linearly if not exponentially (Please note some numerical noises may cancel each other out due to different sign). Therefore, reduction of arithmetic operations generally improves numerical stability.

- Select the most stable algorithm when several approaches are available.

- Transform geometric models to the origin before doing complex geometric computations. It is not uncommon for CAD system users to create their models far away from the origin of global coordinate system. In this case, any geometry will have large $(x, y, z)$ components and hence leave fewer decimal digits for computations. Transforming them close to the origin will greatly improve the stability of numerical computation.

A few examples are given below to illustrate how numerical stability can be improved.

**Example 1**: In high school, we were all taught that solutions to a quadratic equation $ax^2 + bx + c = 0$ is

$$x_1 = \frac{-b + \sqrt{b^2 - 4ac}}{2a}, \quad x_2 = \frac{-b - \sqrt{b^2 - 4ac}}{2a}.$$

The above solutions can be numerically unstable if $b^2 \gg 4|ac|$ because of subtraction between two similar numbers. In this case, it is better to utilize the identity $x_1 x_2 = c/a$ to calculate one root from another.

- If $b < 0$, calculate $x_1 = \dfrac{-b + \sqrt{b^2 - 4ac}}{2a}, \quad x_2 = \dfrac{c}{ax_1}.$

- If $b > 0$, calculate $x_2 = \dfrac{-b - \sqrt{b^2 - 4ac}}{2a}, \quad x_1 = \dfrac{c}{ax_2}.$

If you are not convinced, try the following code fragment

```
float x2, x1_bad, x1_good, delta;
delta = (float)sqrt(b * b - 4.0 * a * c);
x2 = (-b - delta)/(2.0 * a);
x1_bad = (-b + delta)/(2.0 * a);
x1_good = c / (a * x2);
```

with

$$a = 1.0,$$
$$b = 200.0,$$
$$c = -1.5 \times 10^{-3}, -1.5 \times 10^{-4}, -1.5 \times 10^{-5}.$$

You will get three sets of solutions:

```
c = 1.0e-3:
    x2                  -200.00000
    x1_bad              -7.6293945e-006
    x1_good             -7.5000003e-006

c = 1.0e-4:
    x2                  -200.00000
    x1_bad               0.00000000
    x1_good             -7.5000003e-007

c = 1.0e-5:
    x2                  -200.00000
    x1_bad               0.00000000
    x1_good             -7.4999996e-008
```

One can verify that x1_good should be the correct results. Since float holds only 7 decimal digits after the decimal point, subtraction of two similar numbers (i.e., $-b + \Delta$) results in the loss of significance.

**Example 2**: We want to compute

$$\frac{1 - \cos^2(x)}{x^2}$$

at $x = 10^{-3}$. Since $x$ is small, $\cos(x) \approx 1.0$. To avoid the loss of significance caused by subtraction of two similar numbers, it is recommended to use

$$\frac{\sin^2(x)}{x^2}.$$

If we run the following code fragment, we will see that $f_1 = 0.95367402$ and $f_2 = 0.99999976$, with $f_2$ being the better solution.

```
float x = 1.0e-3, cos_x, sin_x, f1, f2;
cos_x = cos(x);
sin_x = sin(x);
f1 = (1.0 - cos_x * cos_x)/(x * x);
f2 = sin_x * sin_x / (x * x);
```

Readers may not be convinced by the above examples, as they may argue that a higher accuracy is achievable when `double` instead of `float` is used. Then, the following example will clear any doubt.

**Example 3**: Evaluation of many functions such as $\sin x$, $\cos x$, $e^x$ and so on is often performed via evaluation of a truncated *Taylor series* – provided that these functions have converging series. For example,

$$e^x = 1 + x + \frac{x^2}{2!} + \frac{x^3}{3!} + \cdots + \frac{x^n}{n!} + \cdots$$

This Taylor (or Maclaurin) series converges uniformly and absolutely for all values of $x$. Without thoughtful analysis of numerical stability (a necessary step for a good design), one may implement the evaluation as follows:

```
inline long long Factorial(long long n)
{
    long long Result = 1;
    while (n > 1)
    {
        Result *= n;
        n--;
    }
    return Result;
}

void EvaluateExpX(int n, double x, double &f)
{
    int i;

    f = 1.0;
    for (i=1; i<=n; i += 1)
    {
        f += pow(x, i) / Factorial(i);
    }
}
```

It is noted that `Factorial` is declared as an *inline function*. The `inline` specifier instructs the compiler to insert a copy of the function body into each place the function is called. Using inline functions can make our program faster because they eliminate the overhead associated with function calls, but at the cost of larger code size. In computing the factorial $n!$, a `long long` data type is used to avoid overflow. In programming, an overflow occurs when an arithmetic operation attempts to create a numeric value that is too large to be represented within the available storage range. For a 32bit machine, `long long` is equivalent to _int64 and has the data range of

$$-9,223,372,036,854,775,808 \quad \text{to} \quad 9,223,372,036,854,775,807.$$

This means $n$ should be less than or equal to 20. When $n$ is larger than 20, we will have an integer overflow. We may use `double` to store the factorial and improve the performance with the following implementation:

```
void EvaluateExpX(int n, double x, double &f)
{
    int      i;
    double   factorial;

    f = factorial = 1.0;
    for (i=1; i<=n; i += 1)
    {
        factorial *= i;
        f += pow(x, i) / factorial;
    }
}
```

This is a big improvement in terms of eliminating integer overflow and boosting performance. However, it is still numerically unstable. If you are not convinced, try to evaluate $x = -25$ and compare your result with the one obtained from a pocket calculator or the C internal function $exp(x)$. I will explain why the above implementation is numerically unstable when $x$ is negative in the next chapter. Further improvement in performance and numerical stability of the above implementation will also be discussed.

**Example 4**: The angle between two unit vectors $v_1$ and $v_2$ may be computed via a *dot-product* of two vectors as follows:

$$v_1 \cdot v_2 = \|v_1\| \times \|v_2\| \cos\theta = \cos\theta \quad \Longrightarrow \quad \theta = acos(v_1 \cdot v_2)$$

noting that $\|v_1\| = 1$ and $\|v_2\| = 1$. In Cartesian coordinates , $v_1 = (x_1, y_1, z_1)$ and $v_2 = (x_2, y_2, z_2)$. Hence,

$$v_1 \cdot v_2 = x_1 x_2 + y_1 y_2 + z_1 z_2.$$

If we use the above formula to compute $\theta$, we will get noticeable numerical noise when two vectors are almost parallel (i.e., $\theta$ is very small). To illustrate this instability issue, let's try the following code fragment:

```
double alpha = 1.7453292519943297e-007;
double theta;
double cos_alpha = cos(alpha);
theta = acos(cos_alpha);
```

We expect to obtain $\theta = \alpha$ with respect to a small tolerance $\varepsilon$. However, $\theta = 1.7441362009524762e{-}007$. A numerically stable way to compute $\theta$ is to also compute the *cross product* of two vectors:

$$\|v_1 \times v_2\| = \|v_1\| \|v_2\| \sin\theta = \sin\theta,$$

where

$$v_1 \times v_2 = \begin{bmatrix} i & j & k \\ x_1 & y_1 & z_1 \\ x_2 & y_2 & z_2 \end{bmatrix}$$

with $i, j$, and $k$ being the standard basis vectors that represent, in our case, the $x$-, $y$-, and $z$- axes respectively. Then, the angle is obtained by

$$\theta = \arctan\left(\frac{\sin\theta}{\cos\theta}\right) \quad \text{or} \quad \theta = atan2(\sin\theta, \cos\theta).$$

We now analyze why it is numerically stable to compute $\theta$ via arctan or atan2. Floating-point computation has limited precision. The loss of some precision can be reflected by introducing small change of angle $\delta$. Accordingly, we have

$$\frac{\sin(\theta \pm \delta)}{\cos(\theta \pm \delta)}.$$

From trigonometry it is known that

$$\cos(\theta \pm \delta) = \cos(\theta)\cos(\delta) \mp \sin(\theta)\sin(\delta)$$

$$\sin(\theta \pm \delta) = \sin(\theta)\cos(\delta) \pm \cos(\theta)\sin(\delta)$$

When $\delta$ is small (caused by numerical noise), we have $\sin(\delta) \approx 0$ and hence:

$$\cos(\theta + \delta) \approx \cos(\theta)\cos(\delta)$$

$$\sin(\theta + \delta) \approx \sin(\theta)\cos(\delta)$$

Consequently,

$$\frac{\sin(\theta)\cos(\delta)}{\cos(\theta)\cos(\delta)} = \frac{\sin(\theta)}{\cos(\theta)} = \tan\theta.$$

This indicates that we should have a "clean" operand for arctan by introducing both sin and cos in computation since numerical noise has been canceled.

We now show that the function arctan is numerically stable when $\theta$ approaches zero. Denoting $\tan\theta$ by $x$, the condition number of $\arctan(x)$ is

$$C_p \approx \left|\frac{xf'(x)}{f(x)}\right| = \frac{1}{1+x^2}\left|\frac{x}{\arctan(x)}\right|$$

When two vectors are almost parallel, $\theta$ is small and $x = \tan\theta \to 0$. Accordingly,

$$\lim_{x \to 0}\frac{x}{\arctan(x)} = \lim_{\theta \to 0}\frac{\tan\theta}{\theta} = \lim_{\theta \to 0}\frac{\sin\theta}{\theta}\cos\theta = \lim_{\theta \to 0}\frac{\sin\theta}{\theta} = 1.$$

Therefore, $C_p = 1$ when $x$ approaches zero, indicating that $\arctan(x)$ is stable when $x$ is very small. The proof of

$$\lim_{\theta \to 0}\frac{\sin\theta}{\theta} = 1$$

is often carried out via the Squeeze Theorem but can also be done via L'Hôpital's Rule as:

$$\lim_{\theta \to 0}\frac{\sin\theta}{\theta} = \lim_{\theta \to 0}\frac{\sin'\theta}{\theta'} = \lim_{\theta \to 0}\frac{\cos\theta}{1} = 1.$$

We now look at why arccos is numerically unstable. Denoting $\cos\theta$ by $x$, the condition number of $\arccos(x)$ is

$$C_p \approx \left|\frac{xf'(x)}{f(x)}\right| = \left|\frac{-1}{\sqrt{1-x^2}}\right|\left|\frac{x}{\arccos(x)}\right|$$

When $\theta$ approaches zero, $x = \cos\theta \to 1$. So

$$\lim_{x \to 1}\frac{x}{\arccos(x)} = \lim_{\theta \to 0}\frac{\cos\theta}{\theta} = \infty.$$

Accordingly $C_p \to \infty$, indicating arccos is ill-conditioned near zero.

## 2.4  Summary

Although integers provide an exact representation of numeric values, they suffer from two major drawbacks: the inability to represent fractional values and a limited dynamic range. Floating-point arithmetic solves these two problems at the expense of accuracy and speed. For many applications, the benefits of floating-point outweigh the disadvantages. Some of the greatest achievements of the 20th century would not have been possible without the floating-point capabilities of digital computers. The fact that floating-point numbers cannot precisely represent all real numbers, as well as the fact that floating-point operations cannot precisely represent true arithmetic operations, is not fully understood by all software developers. Direct comparison of two floating-point values is a bad operation that leads to many surprising situations. In this chapter, we discussed in general how we should compare two floating-point values. There are many research papers that cover more details about floating-point computation. Readers are encouraged to read these papers.

Many engineering and scientific computations are complex and have to be done via computers. A big problem with floating-point arithmetic is that it does not follow the standard rules of algebra. Normal algebraic rules apply only to infinite precision arithmetic. Complex formulae can suffer from larger errors due to round-off. The loss of accuracy can be substantial if a problem or its data are ill-conditioned, meaning that the correct result is hypersensitive to tiny perturbations in its data. One approach to remove the risk of such loss of accuracy is the designing and analysis of numerically stable algorithms, which is a goal of the branch of mathematics known as numerical analysis. Another approach that can protect against the risk of numerical instabilities is the computation of intermediate values in an algorithm at a higher precision than the final result requires, which can remove or reduce such risk by orders of magnitude. For example, we should always use `double` rather than `float` for our intermediate variable in order to retain the highest possible precision even if the final result does not need that much decimal precision.

Numerical analysis is a rigorous mathematical discipline in which such problems and algorithms for their solution are analyzed in order to establish the condition of a problem or the stability of an algorithm and to gain insight into the design of better and more widely applicable algorithms. Numerical analysis is often taught in engineering schools as a graduate-level course. This book is written for a wide range of engineering students and does not assume a very high level of mathematics. Without going into much detail, we discussed how we can minimize the effect of accuracy problems and presented a few practical examples to draw readers' attention. In the subsequent chapters, we will come across more topics related to floating-point computation and numerical analysis.

# Chapter 3

# Performance by Design

In this chapter we continue to learn advanced topics in C/C++ programming such as default arguments, data structure and class, double pointers, dynamic memory allocations, and STL containers. The hands-on exercises in this chapter are specially selected from real world applications in order to draw readers' attentions to the importance of good analysis and design of numerical algorithms.

Every developer who creates real-time applications is concerned about performance optimization. By looking at the code developed by experienced C/C++ programmers, you will likely find an extensive use of C/C++ pointers because they allow programmers to efficiently manipulate memory addresses and corresponding contents. You will also find the use of register to store frequently used local variables to boost performance. Such practice improves program performance. However, it will not make a poorly-designed algorithm run faster than a well-designed one. It has been proven in every software company that the most efficient program always starts with good analysis and design.

To have a good design of computational algorithm, you do not have to have a Ph.D. in mathematics or computer science. With calculus and other preceding high school math, you can achieve most of the goals. In this chapter we will use some examples to illustrate the importance of design in terms of obtaining optimized performance and numerical stability. Algorithm efficiency analysis and big O notation are also discussed.

## 3.1 Horner's method

Polynomials are widely used in many domains including computer graphics, compute-aided design, approximation theory, and numerical computations. For example, many transcendental and trigonometric functions have a uniformly-converged Taylor series. With respect to some given tolerance, we may truncate the series to obtain a polynomial of degree $n$. Evaluation of this polynomial at $x$ gives the approximate result to the original function. In this section, we discuss how to evaluate a polynomial efficiently.

Given the following cubic polynomial (i.e., a polynomial of degree 3)

$$f(x) = 2x^3 - 6x^2 + 2x - 1,$$

we want to evaluate $f$ for $x = 3$. If one does not give the performance much thought, he or she may implement the code as follows

```
f = 2.0 * x * x * x - 6.0 * x * x + 2.0 * x - 1.0;
```

It is readily seen that the above evaluation involves 6 multiplications and 3 additions (subtraction is considered as addition with a negative sign). In general, it requires

$$\frac{n(n+1)}{2}$$

multiplications and $n$ additions for a polynomial of degree $n$. Therefore, it is an n-square or quadratic algorithm. Whenever $n$ doubles, the running time of the algorithm increases by a factor of 4.

If we write a generic cubic polynomial as follows

$$f(x) = x[x(a_3x + a_2) + a_1] + a_0,$$

then Horner's method to evaluate the cubic polynomial value is

- Let $f = a_3$.

- Compute $f \times x + a_2$ and assign the value to $f$.

- Compute $f \times x + a_1$ and assign the value to $f$.

- Compute $f \times x + a_0$ and output the result $f$.

As is seen above, the evaluation of $f$ involves only three multiplications and three additions, which is well optimized.

For a polynomial of degree $n$

$$f = a_0 + a_1x + a_2x^2 + \cdots + a_nx^n = \sum_{i=0}^{n} a_ix^i,$$

Horner's method is implemented as follows:

```
// Evaluate canonical polynomial of degree n at x
void apiHornerEval(int ndeg, double *pA, double x, double &f)
{
    int      i;
    f = pA[ndeg];
    for (i=ndeg; i>= 1; i--)
    {
        f = f * x + pA[i-1];
    }
}
```

It involves in total $n$ multiplications and $n$ additions to evaluate a polynomial of degree $n$, which is a significant reduction of computation in comparison to $\dfrac{n(n+1)}{2}$ multiplications and $n$ additions required by the sloppy implementation. Fewer arithmetic computations means less cumulative round off errors. Therefore, Horner's method is not only fast but also numerically stable.

Putting an & sign in front of $f$ indicates that $f$ is passed to the callee via the passing-by-reference mechanism. If there is no & sign in front of a function variable, it is known as passing-by-value. In this case, a local copy of the variable is created for the callee. When the function call ends, the local variables are out of scope and hence destroyed. To bring the local copy back to the caller, a variable should be passed either by reference (available only in C++) or by pointer (available in both C and C++). For the latter case, the memory address of a variable is passed to the callee. It is regarded that passing-by-reference is safer but less flexible than passing-by-pointer.

It is often desirable to evaluate not only a polynomial value but also its derivatives at $x$. Let's see how a thoughtful design can efficiently utilize the evaluations in a single loop. Let $t$ be any fixed value and consider the division of polynomials in variable $x$

$$q(x) = \frac{f(x) - f(t)}{x - t} \iff f(x) = q(x)(x - t) + f(t)$$

where the quotient polynomial $q(x)$ is of degree $n - 1$

$$q(x) = \sum_{i=0}^{n-1} b_i x^i.$$

Differentiating $f$ at $x$ gives

$$f'(x) = q'(x)(x - t) + q(x).$$

Thus, $f'(t) = q(t)$. To derive $b_i$ for the quotient polynomial $q(x)$, we expand

$$f(x) = q(x)(x - t) + f(t)$$

as follows:

$$f(x) = (f(t) - tb_0) + (b_0 - tb_1)x + \cdots + (b_{n-2} - tb_{n-1})x^{n-1} + (b_{n-1})x^n.$$

By comparing the coefficient of the same term between the above expansion and $f(x) = \sum a_i x^i$, we have

$$b_{n-1} = a_n$$
$$b_{n-2} = tb_{n-1} + a_{n-1}$$
$$b_{n-3} = tb_{n-2} + a_{n-2}$$
$$\vdots$$
$$b_0 = tb_1 + a_1$$
$$b_{-1} = f(t) = tb_0 + a_0$$

Therefore, $f(x)$ and $f'(x) = q(x)$ can be evaluated via Horner's method as follows:

| | |
|---|---|
| $f_n = a_n$ | $q_{n-1} = b_{n-1} = a_n$ |
| $f_{n-1} = xf_n + a_{n-1}$ | $q_{n-2} = xq_{n-1} + b_{n-2} = xq_{n-1} + (xa_n + a_{n-1}) = xq_{n-1} + f_{n-1}$ |
| $f_{n-2} = xf_{n-1} + a_{n-2}$ | $q_{n-3} = xq_{n-2} + b_{n-3} = xq_{n-2} + (xb_{n-2} + a_{n-2}) = xq_{n-2} + f_{n-2}$ |
| $\vdots$ | $\vdots$ |
| $f_2 = xf_3 + a_2$ | $q_1 = xq_2 + b_1 = xq_2 + f_2$ |
| $f_1 = xf_2 + a_1$ | $q_0 = xq_1 + b_0 = xq_1 + f_1$ |
| $f_0 = xf_1 + a_0$ | |

Upon completion of iterations, we have $f(x) = f_0$ and $f'(x) = q_0$. We now modify
apiHornerEval to evaluate polynomial value $f$ and, optionally, its first derivative $q$. In
C/C++ *optional arguments* are also known as *default arguments*. A default argument is
a function parameter that has a default value provided to it. If the caller does not supply
a value for this parameter, the default value will be used. If the user does supply a
value for the default parameter, the user-supplied value is then used. Default arguments
are used only in function calls in which trailing arguments may or may not be omitted.
In other words, default argument(s) must be the last argument(s) with default values
when declaring a function. We thus modify the prototype of apiHornerEval as follows:

```
void apiHornerEval(int ndeg, double *pA, double x,
                   double &f, double *q = NULL);
```

It is noted that q is passed to the callee by pointer. By default, it is a NULL pointer,
indicating no first derivative should be computed inside apiHornerEval if users call
apiHornerEval without specifying q, as indicated below:

```
    apiHornerEval(ndeg, pA, x, f);
```

If the first derivative is desired, users call apiHornerEval with q as follows:

```
    double q;
    apiHornerEval(ndeg, pA, x, f, &q);
```

The new implementation of apiHornerEval is listed below:

```
/*-------------------------------------------------------------
API Name
    apiHornerEval

Description
    It evaluates polynomial and optionally its first derivative.

Signature
    void apiHornerEval(int ndeg, double *pA,
            double x, double &f, double *q)
```

```
INPUT:
   ndeg      degree of polynomial
   pA        coefficients of polynomial
   x         variable at which polynomial is evaluated
OUTPUT:
   f         polynomial value
   q         (optional) first derivative of polynomial


History

   Y.M. Li     10/15/2012 : Creation date
-----------------------------------------------------------------*/
#include "MyHeader.h"

void apiHornerEval(int ndeg, double *pA, double x,
                   double &f, double *q)
{
   int   i;
   f = pA[ndeg];
   if (q)
   {
      *q = 0.0;
      for (i=ndeg; i>= 1; i--)
      {
         *q = *q * x + f;
         f = f * x + pA[i-1];
      }
   }
   else
   {
      for (i=ndeg; i>= 1; i--)
      {
         f = f * x + pA[i-1];
      }
   }
}
```

It is noted that comments and history about **apiHornerEval** have been added at the top of the function. This is a good practice and usually imposed by software companies. It helps users understand the functionality and required input/output arguments. When modifications have been made to the function, a brief description should be added under "History" for tracking. We also added

```
#include "MyHeader.h"
```

in our implementation. **MyHeader.h** is a C/C++ *header* file that usually contains the standard library headers and user-defined function prototypes (also known as declarations or signatures), definitions of data structure or class, and constants to allow functions and variables in one file to be used by functions in other files. At

this moment, MyHeader.h contains simply the C library headers and the prototype of
apiHornerEval:

```
#include <stdio.h>
#include <stdlib.h>
#include <time.h>
#include <math.h>
#include <string>
```

```
void apiHornerEval(int ndeg, double *pA, double x,
                   double &f, double *q = NULL);
```

We now discuss how to test the above program via a main function. As was discussed
in chapter 1, the main function is where a program starts execution. It is responsible
for the high-level organization of the program's functionality (e.g., preparing data to
call a function) and typically has access to the *command-line arguments* given to the
program when it was executed. Thus, it is essential to have a main function to run
our code. Up to now, the main functions we have implemented were simple and saved
in the same source file as the function to be tested. From now on we will implement
the main function in a separate source file since it merely serves as a test driver and is
not usually delivered to customers. Our implementation of main is a little bit complex
because we want it to be flexible enough to execute a polynomial of any degree. For
this reason, main opens a data file to read required information (i.e., ndeg, coefficients
$a_i$, and the variable $x$) and then to call apiHornerEavl to compute the function value.
It also prints out the result at the command prompt. Here is the code list:

```
1    #include "MyHeader.h"

2

3    void main(void)

4    {

5        int          i, ndeg = 0;

6        double       x, f, f1;

7        double       *pA = NULL;

8        FILE         *infile = NULL;

9

10       // Open a txt data file named HornerEval.d1

11       fopen_s(&infile, "HornerEval.d1", "r");

12       if (NULL == infile)

13       {

14           exit(1);

15       }

16

17       // Read the degree of polynomial from HornerEval.d1

18       fscanf_s(infile, "%d", &ndeg);

19

20       // Allocate memory and read the coefficients of polynomial

21       pA = (double *)malloc((ndeg+1) * sizeof(double));

22       if (NULL == pA)

23       {
```

```
24          exit(1);
25      }
26      for (i=0; i<=ndeg; i++)
27      {
28          fscanf_s(infile, "%lf", &pA[i]);
29      }
30
31      // Read the variable value
32      fscanf_s( infile, "%lf", &x);
33
34      // Invoke the function
35      apiHornerEval(ndeg, pA, x, f, &f1);
36
37      printf("f = %.10e,   f1 = %.10e\n", f, f1);
38
39      if (infile)
40      {
41          fclose(infile);
42      }
43      if (pA)
44      {
45          free(pA);
46      }
47  }
```

At line 11, `fopen_s` is equivalent to the conventional C `fopen` that opens the file whose name is specified in the filename parameter `HornerEval.d1` and associates it with a stream that can be identified in future operations by the returned FILE pointer `infile`. The C string character `"r"` indicates this file stream is opened for *read only*. If this file does not exist, the file pointer `infile` is set to NULL. Besides `"r"`, the commonly-used C string that determines a file access mode includes `"w"` for writable file and `"a"` for appending file. Upon completion of reading data from the opened stream, the associated file needs to be closed by calling `fclose` as seen above (lines 39 through 42). At line 18, `fscanf_s` is equivalent to the conventional C `fscanf` that reads formatted data from the named stream.

The above `main` driver does not have any hard-coded data. All required information is read from a data file. When users want to use it to evaluate different polynomials, they simply modify the information in the text file `HornerEval.d1`. There is no need to change the implementation of `main`. In the next chapter, we will discuss how to make `main` drivers truly flexible to run any specific test case.

It is worth mentioning that `malloc` and `free` are used to dynamically allocate and delete *heap memory*. Both `malloc` and `free` are supported by C and C++. However, `new` and `delete` are recommended for C++, especially when working with C++ classes with *constructors* and *destructors*. The C++ `new` and `delete` will trigger calls to a constructor and destructor respectively; while `malloc` and `free` will not. A member function with the same name as its class is a constructor function. It is implemented to initialize an object of that class type prior to use in a program. Destructor functions are the inverse of constructor functions. They are often implemented to properly release resources (e.g., internal memory) and, if necessary, reset member variables. Destructors are called when objects are destroyed (deallocated).

## 3.2   Variation of Horner's method

It is common that a polynomial is not directly represented as

$$\sum_{i=0}^{n} a_i x^i.$$

For example, the truncated Maclaurin series (a special case of Taylor series ) for $e^x$ is

$$e^x \approx 1 + x + \frac{x^2}{2!} + \frac{x^3}{3!} + \cdots + \frac{x^i}{i!} + \cdots + \frac{x^n}{n!}.$$

In this case, $a_i = \frac{1}{i!}$. It is unwise to compute factorials to obtain all $a_i$ as it is inefficient and can cause an overflow when $i$ is large. By examining the above series, it is noted that the $i$th term is equal to multiplying the $(i-1)$th term by $\frac{x}{i}$. Accordingly, we can efficiently evaluate the above polynomial at $x$ via a variation of Horner's method as:

```
void apiEvalExp(double x, int n, double &f)
{
    int          i;
    double       term;

    f = 0.0;
    term = 1.0;
    for (i=1; i<=n; i += 1)
    {
        f += term;
        term = term * x / i;
    }
}
```

The above implementation requires the user to specify $n$, which is impractical since he or she may not know at what $n$ the evaluation yields a converging result. A feasible approach is to specify the convergence tolerance rather than $n$. Denoting

$$P_n(x) = \sum_{i=0}^{n} \frac{x^i}{i!},$$

then $P_n(x)$ is said to be converged to $e^x$ with respect to the given tolerance $\varepsilon$ if

$$|P_n(x) - P_{n-1}(x)| < \varepsilon.$$

It is noted that $|P_n(x) - P_{n-1}(x)|$ gives the last term of $P_n(x)$. Therefore, the convergence criterion is to check whether the $i$th **term** is less than the given accuracy. So the complete implementation is:

```
void apiEvalExp(double x, double epsilon, double &f)
{
    int         i;
    double      term;

    f = 0.0;
    term = 1.0;
    i = 1;
    while (true)
    {
        f += term;
        if (fabs(term) < epsilon)
            break;
        term = term * x / i;
        i++;
    }
}
```

Since the Maclaurin series converges to $e^x$ uniformly and absolutely for all $x$, one may assume that the above implementation will always give a correct result for any $x$. This is true only if $x \geq 0$. When $x$ is negative, the above implementation may not produce a good result. For example, if $x = -25$ is used to test the above code, the result is

$$-7.1297804036720779e - 007,$$

but the correct answer is

$$1.3887943864964021e - 011,$$

which is obtained via the C internal function exp(x). The two results are not only significantly different but also have different signs. How could a converging series lead to diverging results? As discussed in the previous chapter, many standard computation rules apply only to infinite precision arithmetic. In floating-point computation, it is very important to design an algorithm that minimizes the loss of significant digits. Referring to the above Maclaurin series, the even terms are positive and odd terms are negative, so the numerical instability is caused by subtraction of similar numbers. To avoid such a catastrophic problem, we should always treat $x$ as a positive value and compute $f$. If $x < 0$, we have $e^{-x} = 1/e^x$. Accordingly, $1/f$ is the result for $e^{-x}$. Therefore, a numerically stable implementation should be

```
void apiEvalExp(double u, double epsilon, double &f)
{
    int         i;
    double      x, term;

    x = abs(u);
    f = 0.0;
    term = 1.0;
    i = 1;
```

```
while (true)
{
    f += term;
    if (fabs(term) < epsilon)
        break;
    term = term * x / i;
    i++;
}
if (u < 0)
    f = 1.0 / f;
}
```

If we try the above implementation again with $u = -25$, we should be able to get a result that matches the one from a pocket calculator or from the C internal function exp(x).

Similar variations of Horner's method may also be derived to evaluate a truncated series of many familiar trigonometry and logarithm functions. When discussing parallel programming in chapter 11, we will have another chance to see how $\sin x$ is evaluated via a variation of Horner's method.


## 3.3   Circle stroking

Have you ever wondered how a curve is drawn on a computer screen? It usually involves two steps. First, the curve is approximated by line segments called a *polyline* in computer graphics. The process to break a curve into many tiny pieces that can be approximated by lines is often referred to as *curve stroking*. Next, the polyline is rendered via an API (*Application Programming Interface*) in a graphics library such as *OpenGL* or Microsoft's *Graphics Device Interface (GDI)*. In general, the more line segments generated, the smoother the curve looks on the computer screen. However, too many line segments will degrade the performance.

Similarly, display of a curved surface also involves two steps. It is first approximated by triangular planes (three non-collinear points define a unique plane) – a process known as *tessellation* in computer graphics. Then, the triangulated polyhedra are rendered via an API in a graphics library.

For simplicity, we consider how to approximate a circle by line segments. Assume that we want to approximate a circle with a radius $r$ by line segments such that a distance from any line to the circle is less than the given tolerance. Referring to the following figure, it is readily derived that the chord-height $h$ of the arc corresponding to the small angle $\delta$ is

$$h = r - r\cos(\frac{\delta}{2}).$$

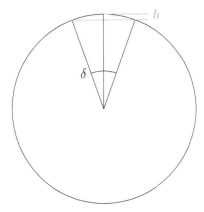

Figure 3.1: Chord and chord-height $h$

We want $h \leq \varepsilon$. Hence

$$\delta \leq 2\arccos(1 - \frac{\varepsilon}{r}).$$

Recall that I said in the previous chapter that arccos is ill-conditioned when the angle is very small. Here, it is all right to call arccos since $\delta$ will not be too small in practice. This is because we usually choose $\varepsilon$ to be the fit tolerance that is 1,000 times larger than the distance tolerance in order to avoid getting too many stroking points. Therefore, it is fine to compute $\delta$ via arccos. Otherwise, it is numerically more stable to compute very small $\delta$ via arctan as

$$\delta = 2\arctan\left(\frac{\sqrt{(2r-h)h}}{r-h}\right).$$

Each chord is a line that approximates the corresponding arc with respect to the given tolerance $\varepsilon$. The number of lines required to approximate the full circle can be determined by the following formula:

$$n = \frac{2\pi}{\delta}.$$

Therefore, we will need to evaluate $n+1$ evenly-spaced points on the circle to form $n$ line segments, which is known as the circle stroking process. Assume the first stroking point starts at $\theta_0 = 0$ as shown below.

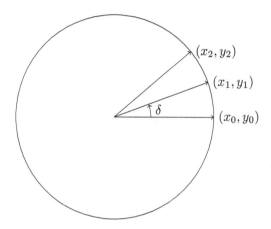

Figure 3.2: Stroking a circle centered at (0, 0)

Then, the second, third, and the $i$th points would be computed as follows:

$$x_1 = r\cos(\theta_1) = r\cos(\theta_0 + \delta)$$
$$y_1 = r\sin(\theta_1) = r\sin(\theta_0 + \delta)$$
$$x_2 = r\cos(\theta_2) = r\cos(\theta_1 + \delta)$$
$$y_2 = r\sin(\theta_2) = r\sin(\theta_1 + \delta)$$
$$\cdots$$
$$x_i = r\cos(\theta_i) = r\cos(\theta_{i-1} + \delta)$$
$$y_i = r\sin(\theta_i) = r\sin(\theta_{i-1} + \delta)$$

The above formula indicates that we need to call trigonometric functions (i.e., sin and cos) for $2(n+1)$ times. Since trigonometric functions are relatively more expensive to compute than multiplications and divisions, the above approach is not optimized in terms of CPU usage.

From high school math it is known that

$$\cos(\theta_i + \delta) = \cos(\theta_i)\cos(\delta) - \sin(\theta_i)\sin(\delta)$$
$$\sin(\theta_i + \delta) = \sin(\theta_i)\cos(\delta) + \cos(\theta_i)\sin(\delta)$$

With the above formulas we can compute the $(i+1)$th point as follows:

$$x_{i+1} = r\cos(\theta_i + \delta) = r\cos(\theta_i)\cos(\delta) - r\sin(\theta_i)\sin(\delta) = x_i\cos(\delta) - y_i\sin(\delta)$$
$$y_{i+1} = r\sin(\theta_i + \delta) = r\sin(\theta_i)\cos(\delta) + r\cos(\theta_i)\sin(\delta) = y_i\cos(\delta) + x_i\sin(\delta)$$

Therefore, we compute $\sin(\delta)$ and $\cos(\delta)$ once and use them to derive all stroking points via the recursive relation. The code fragment is given below:

```
sin_delta = sin(delta);
cos_delta = cos(delta);
x[0] = r;
```

```
y[0] = 0.0;
for (i=1; i<=n; i++)
{
    x[i] = x[i-1] * cos_delta - y[i-1] * sin_delta;
    y[i] = y[i-1] * cos_delta + x[i-1] * sin_delta;
}
```

Alternatively, we create a rotation transformation with the rotating angle being $\delta$ and then compute $(x_{i+1}, y_{i+1})$ as follows:

$$\begin{pmatrix} x_{i+1} \\ y_{i+1} \end{pmatrix} = \begin{pmatrix} \cos \delta & -\sin \delta \\ \sin \delta & \cos \delta \end{pmatrix} \begin{pmatrix} x_i \\ y_i \end{pmatrix}$$

This example demonstrates again how our training in high school and college can help us design and implement an optimized algorithm.

Let's introduce two new data types before implementing a circle stroking algorithm. Numerical methods can fail for many reasons such as invalid or ill-conditional data sets, limitation of algorithm or its implementation, division by zero, memory allocation failure, etc. When such incidents occur, the caller needs to know exactly what has caused the failures. For this reason, many of our implementations will return an error code whose type is apiError. It is fine to simply use the integer type for the return error code. For example, 0 for "success without incident," 1 for "generic failure," and so on. By doing so, however, the error code looks arbitrary and meaningless. In practice, it is recommended to use an *enumerated type* consisting of a set of named values called *elements* or *enumerators* of the type. We thus define our apiError as

```
typedef enum{
    api_OK            = 0,
    api_FAIL          = 1,
    api_NOTSUPPORTED  = 2,
    api_INVALIDARG    = 3,
    api_INCONSISTENT  = 4,
    api_DEGENERATE    = 5,
    api_DIVIDEBYZERO  = 6,
    api_NOMEMORY      = 7} apiError;
```

Here, we explicitly specified a value for each enumerator (the value can be randomly chosen). If we do not specify the value for each enumerator, the first enumerator has a value of 0 by default, and each successive enumerator is one larger than the value of the previous one. Enumerated types make the code more self-documenting. For example, programmers can check the error code based on a meaningful constant (or enumerator) instead of some arbitrary, meaningless number.

Our second data type is GPosition2d that will be used throughout this book to store a position vector $(x, y)$ in the Cartesian plane. In C/C++, different pieces of relevant data can be combined in a logical way to form an information unit called *data structure*. There are several ways to define an information unit. In C++ (not in C), the information unit GPosition2d can be defined as *class* by using the class keyword:

```
class GPosition2d{
public:
    double  x;
    double  y;
};
```

Variables in a class are by default *private* , meaning those members are accessible only from member functions and friends of the class. We may explicitly define the member variables as *protected* (accessible from member functions and friends of the class and derived classes) or *public* (accessible from any function). In our case, we explicitly define the member variables as public to grant other functions direct access to member variables. After it is defined, we can use this new data type in a similar way as we do for an `int` or `double` data type. For example, we can initialize its member variables and assign values to member variables as follows:

```
GPosition2d point = {0}; // initialization

// Assignment
point.x = 2.0;
point.y = 1.0;
```

In both C and C++, we can also use the `struct` keyword to define `GPosition2d` as a structure type:

```
typedef struct{
    double  x;
    double  y;
} GPosition2d;
```

In C++, a structure is the same as a class except that its members are public by default.

We are now ready to implement the circle stroking algorithm. In our analysis, all stroking points were computed from a circle centered at the origin. If it is not, we need to move the obtained stroking points by a constant distance defined by the center (the process known as the *translation*). A generic circle stroking method is hence implemented as follows:

```
/*-----------------------------------------------------------------
API Name
    apiStrokeCircleV1

Description
    It strokes a circle with respect to the chord-height tolerance.

Signature
    void apiStrokeCircleV1(
            GPosition2d &center, double radius, double tol,
            int &nStrkPts, GPosition2d *&pStrkPts, apiError &rc)

    INPUT:
```

```
      center     center of circle
      radius     radius of circle
      tol        chord-height tolerance
   OUTPUT:
      nStrkPts   number of returned stroking points
      pStrkPts   pointer to the array that stores stroking points
      apiError   error code: api_OK if no error

History

   Y.M. Li     10/15/2012 : Creation date
------------------------------------------------------------------*/
#include "MyHeader.h"

void apiStrokeCircleV1(
        GPosition2d &center, double radius, double tol,
        int &nStrkPts, GPosition2d *&pStrkPts, apiError &rc)
{
   int        i;
   double     delta, sin_delta, cos_delta;

   // Initialize data and determine the number of stroking points
   rc = api_OK;
   pStrkPts = NULL;
   delta = 2.0 * acos(1.0 - tol / radius);
   nStrkPts = 2 + (int)(2.0 * GPI / delta);
   delta = 2.0 * GPI / (nStrkPts - 1);

   // Allocate memory for storing stroking points
   pStrkPts = new GPosition2d[nStrkPts];
   if (!pStrkPts)
   {
      rc = api_NOMEMORY;
      goto wrapup;
   }

   // Loop to compute stroking points on circle centered at (0,0)
   sin_delta = sin(delta);
   cos_delta = cos(delta);
   pStrkPts[0].x = radius;
   pStrkPts[0].y = 0.0;
   for (i=1; i<nStrkPts; i++)
   {
      pStrkPts[i].x = pStrkPts[i-1].x * cos_delta -
                      pStrkPts[i-1].y * sin_delta;
      pStrkPts[i].y = pStrkPts[i-1].y * cos_delta +
                      pStrkPts[i-1].x * sin_delta;
```

```
    }

    // Translate the points based on the given center
    for (i=0; i<nStrkPts; i++)
    {
        pStrkPts[i].x += center.x;
        pStrkPts[i].y += center.y;
    }

wrapup:

    if (rc != api_OK && pStrkPts)
    {
        delete [] pStrkPts;
        pStrkPts = NULL;
        nStrkPts = 0;
    }
}
```

From the declaration of `apiStrokeCircleV1`, it should be noted that two new data types, `GPosition2d` and `apiError`, have been used. These data types are defined in `MyHeader.h` as

```
#include <stdio.h>
#include <stdlib.h>
#include <time.h>
#include <math.h>
#include <string>

#define GPI 3.14159265358979323846264338332795

typedef enum{
    api_OK              = 0,
    api_FAIL            = 1,
    api_NOTSUPPORTED    = 2,
    api_INVALIDARG      = 3,
    api_INCONSISTENT    = 4,
    api_DEGENERATE      = 5,
    api_DIVIDEBYZERO    = 6,
    api_NOMEMORY        = 7} apiError;


class GPosition2d{
public:
    double  x;
    double  y;
};
```

```
void apiHornerEval(int ndeg, double *pA, double x,
                   double &f, double *q = NULL);

void apiStrokeCircleV1(GPosition2d &center, double radius,
                       double tol, int &nStrkPts,
                       GPosition2d *&pStrkPts, apiError &rc);
```

In subsequent chapters, we shall no longer list the full content of `MyHeader.h` unless it is absolutely necessary. Every time we create a new function or define a new data type, we should always assume that the prototype of new function or new data type will be added to `MyHeader.h`.

It should be pointed out that the pointer `pStrkPts` is passed into the callee function `apiStrokeCircleV1` via *passing-by-reference*. This is because we want to assign the pointer the address of allocated heap memory inside `apiStrokeCircleV1` and be able to preserve the address when `apiStrokeCircleV1` ends. In other words, passing a pointer by reference means that the callee function or method is permitted to modify the actual pointer value defined in the calling function. Otherwise, a local copy of pointer will be created when `apiStrokeCircleV1` is called. Modification to the local pointer will be lost when exiting the callee function.

The purpose of this section is to demonstrate that high school math can help us improve the design and, hence, the performance. However, it should be pointed out that trigonometric functions are widely available across programming languages and platforms. Most CPU architectures have built-in instructions for trigonometric functions. Therefore, it will not be terribly slow if our circle stroking method is simply implemented as follows:

```
for(i=0; i<nStrkPts; i++)
{
    pStrkPts[i].x = center.x + radius * cos(i * delta);
    pStrkPts[i].y = center.y + radius * sin(i * delta);
}
```

Based on our timing, it is roughly 3 to 4 times slower when repeatedly calling the standard sin and cos math functions.

## 3.4 STL vector

The *Standard Template Library (STL)* is a programmer's dream. It offers efficient ways to store, access, manipulate, and view data and is designed for maximum extensibility. Once getting over the initial syntax hurdles, we will quickly learn to appreciate the STL's sheer power and flexibility.

The STL is logically divided into four pieces:

**Containers** At the heart of the STL is a collection of container classes, allowing us to specify what objects are allowed in the containers. Containers in STL can be divided into three categories: sequence containers (e.g., `vector`, `deque`, `list`), associative containers (e.g., `set`, `map`), and container adapters (e.g., `queue`, `priority_queue`, and `stack`).

**Iterators** Each STL container exports iterators – objects that view and modify ranges of stored data. Iterators have a common interface, allowing us to write code that operates on data stored in arbitrary containers.

**Algorithms** STL algorithms are functions that operate over ranges of data specified by iterators. The scope of the STL algorithms is staggering – there are algorithms for searching, sorting, reordering, permuting, creating, and destroying sets of data.

**Functors** The STL includes classes that overload the function call operator. Instances of such classes are called functors or function objects. Because so much of the STL relies on user-defined callback functions (e.g., callback functor in `std::sort` algorithm), the STL provides facilities for creating and modifying functions at runtime.

STL `vector` is the most commonly-used container in engineering and scientific computations. It is usually used as an array to store data because of its simplicity and extensibility. We thus confine our discussion to STL `vector`. There are already many excellent online tutorials about STL `vector`. However, not many tutorials explicitly discuss the performance of STL `vector`. By reviewing STL `vector` in this section, we want to emphasize how STL `vector` may affect the performance. It should be noted that elements in STL `vector` are accessed via indices rather than iterators to make the code more readable for beginners.

Referring to `apiStrokeCircleV1`, the number of stroking points generated is determined based on the input tolerance and the radius of circle. After knowing the number of stroking points, we dynamically allocate a block of heap memory to store the stroking points. Upon completion of the computation, the memory address is returned to the caller. It is then the caller's responsibility to free the heap memory. Failure to do so will cause a memory leak – one of the most common mistakes in software development. Furthermore, the number of stroking points may not be readily derived when stroking a complex curve as opposed to a circle. In this case, we have to guess the possible number to allocate memory. When the limit is reached during the stroking process, we either return an error or add more code to reallocate a larger memory block and copy the stored data to new memory.

With the use of STL `vector`, both issues can be addressed easily. Let's rewrite the code to store stroking points via STL `vector` and name it `apiStrokeCircle`:

```
/*------------------------------------------------------------------
API Name
    apiStrokeCircle


Description
    It strokes a circle with respect to the chord-height tolerance.
```

Signature
```
    void apiStrokeCircle(GPosition2d &center, double radius, double tol,
                     std::vector<GPosition2d>& pStrkPts, apiError &rc)
```

    INPUT:
       center      center of circle
       radius      radius of circle
       tol         chord-height tolerance
    OUTPUT:
       pStrkPts    STL vector that stores stroking points
       apiError    error code: api_OK if no error

History

    Y.M. Li      10/15/2012 : Creation date
---------------------------------------------------------------------*/
```c
#include "MyHeader.h"
#include <vector>
using namespace std;

void apiStrokeCircle(GPosition2d &center, double radius, double tol,
                 std::vector<GPosition2d>& pStrkPts, apiError &rc)
{
    int         i, nStrkPts;
    double      delta, sin_delta, cos_delta;
    GPosition2d pt;

    // Initialize data and determine the number of stroking points
    rc = api_OK;
    pStrkPts.clear();
    delta = 2.0 * acos(1.0 - tol / radius);
    nStrkPts = 2 + (int)(2.0 * GPI / delta);
    delta = 2.0 * GPI / (nStrkPts - 1);

    // Loop to compute stroking points on the circle centered at (0,0)
    sin_delta = sin(delta);
    cos_delta = cos(delta);
    pt.x = radius;
    pt.y = 0.0;
    pStrkPts.push_back(pt);
    for (i=1; i<nStrkPts; i++)
    {
        pt.x = pStrkPts[i-1].x * cos_delta - pStrkPts[i-1].y * sin_delta;
        pt.y = pStrkPts[i-1].y * cos_delta + pStrkPts[i-1].x * sin_delta;
        pStrkPts.push_back(pt);
    }
```

```
// Translate the points based on the given center
for (i=0; i<nStrkPts; i++)
{
    pStrkPts[i].x += center.x;
    pStrkPts[i].y += center.y;
}
}
```

The statement `using namespace std` is used to resolve any name clash. Without it, we would have to use the prefix `std::` when calling any STL function in case the same name has been used by other programs or libraries. For example, we may have implemented our own `sort` somewhere in the library. When calling STL `sort` without the `using namespace std` statement, we will have to type `std::sort` to avoid name clash with the one we implemented. By adding the statement `using namespace std`, we can simply type `sort` and the compiler will know that the method `sort` in this implementation actually means the STL function `std::sort`.

It is noted that no heap memory allocation is presented in the code. Memory space allocation and deletion are managed by STL `vector`. We simply use it as a "magic" array. Let us compile it in release mode and run the executable at the command line with `StrokeCircle.d1` for 1 million times. It takes 2.14 seconds in release mode on a Sony VAIO VCPF1 laptop computer with a Core i7 processor, which is roughly 31 percent slower (2.14 vs 1.63 seconds) than `apiStrokeCircleV1` that dynamically allocates heap memory.

To investigate why it is slow to use a STL `vector`, we add a statement in the loop to print the memory address of STL `vector`

```
for (i=1; i<nStrkPts; i++)
{
    pt.x = pStrkPts[i-1].x * cos_delta - pStrkPts[i-1].y * sin_delta;
    pt.y = pStrkPts[i-1].y * cos_delta + pStrkPts[i-1].x * sin_delta;
    pStrkPts.push_back(pt);
    printf("%p  ", (void*)&pStrkPts[0]);
    if ((i % 4) == 0)
        printf("\n");
}
```

As is seen below, the memory addresses change in a certain pattern. At beginning it changes every time when a point is added, which means memory allocation and data copy happen when a point is added. It then changes less frequently and hence has less memory allocation and copy activities. Obviously, `vector` implementations intelligently adjust and maintain a buffer of memory to minimize the memory allocation and data copy. This is likely achieved by allocating larger and larger blocks of memory when such activities increase.

```
002221E8  00229F20  00229F48  00229F80
002214D0  002214D0  00229F20  00229F20
00229F20  002214D0  002214D0  002214D0
```

```
002214D0   00448408   00448408   00448408
00448408   00448408   00448408   00448540
00448540   00448540   00448540   00448540
00448540   00448540   00448540   00448540
00448708   00448708   00448708   00448708
00448708   00448708   00448708   00448708
00448708   00448708   00448708   00448708
00448708   00448708   004489B0   004489B0
004489B0   004489B0   004489B0   004489B0
004489B0   004489B0   004489B0
```

After understanding the behavior of STL vector and where the performance overhead
comes from, we can design the code to optimize the performance. Since the number of
stroking points is known, the reserve() operation may be used to prevent unnecessary
reallocations. After a call to reserve(n), the vector's capacity is guaranteed to be
at least $n$. In other words, adding stroking points to vector will not trigger memory
reallocation as long as the number of points added is less than or equal to the reserved
space.

```cpp
void apiStrokeCircle(GPosition2d &center, double radius, double tol,
                std::vector<GPosition2d>& pStrkPts, apiError &rc)
{
    int         i, nStrkPts;
    double      delta, sin_delta, cos_delta;

    // Initialize data and determine the number of stroking points
    rc = api_OK;
    delta = 2.0 * acos(1.0 - tol / radius);
    nStrkPts = 2 + (int)(2.0 * GPI / delta);
    delta = 2.0 * GPI / (nStrkPts - 1);
    pStrkPts.reserve(nStrkPts);

    // Loop to compute stroking points on the circle centered at (0,0)
    sin_delta = sin(delta);
    cos_delta = cos(delta);
    pt.x = radius;
    pt.y = 0.0;
    pStrkPts.push_back(pt);
    for (i=1; i<nStrkPts; i++)
    {
        pt.x = pStrkPts[i-1].x * cos_delta -
                pStrkPts[i-1].y * sin_delta;
        pt.y = pStrkPts[i-1].y * cos_delta +
                pStrkPts[i-1].x * sin_delta;
        pStrkPts.push_back(pt);
    }
}
```

```
// Translate the points based on the given center
for (i=0; i<nStrkPts; i++)
{
    pStrkPts[i].x += center.x;
    pStrkPts[i].y += center.y;
}
}
```

It should be pointed out that we still have to call **push_back** to add elements to `vector`. If an element was added by accessing the `vector` via index as follows

```
{
    pStrkPts[0].x = radius;
    pStrkPts[0].y = 0.0;
    for (i=1; i<nStrkPts; i++)
    {
        pStrkPts[i].x = pStrkPts[i-1].x * cos_delta -
                        pStrkPts[i-1].y * sin_delta;
        pStrkPts[i].y = pStrkPts[i-1].y * cos_delta +
                        pStrkPts[i-1].x * sin_delta;
    }
}
```

we would see the following assertion in debug mode.

Figure 3.3: Visual C++ assertion dialog box

This is because a call to **reserve** does not allocate but *reserve* the memory block. It is worth mentioning that, when the debugger halts because of a C runtime library assertion, it navigates to the point in the source file where the assertion occurred (if the source is available). The assertion message appears in the Output window as well as the *Assertion Failed dialog box*. If we click **Retry**, it brings us to the source code where the assertion was thrown out. This is very useful in investigating an assertion problem.

The above improved `apiStrokeCircle` program avoids repeatedly reallocating memory when elements are added to `vector` and hence improves the performance. In our case, the improvement is not so significant because STL `vector` stores `GPosition2d` that is simply a C++ class without a constructor and destructor. If it stores a C++ class with a complex constructor and destructor, the overhead is then significant since memory allocation and data copy inside `vector` will trigger calls to the constructor and destructor. Accordingly, the performance improvement will be significant by preventing unnecessary reallocations.

Alternatively, we can call `resize` to allocate and initialize memory for STL `vector`. After a call to `resize`, elements are added to STL `vector` via an index operation as shown below. It should be pointed out that, if we call `push_back` to add elements, these elements would be appended to the end of allocated memory, which is not what we want.

```
void apiStrokeCircle(GPosition2d &center, double radius, double tol,
                std::vector<GPosition2d>& pStrkPts, apiError &rc)
{
    int         i, nStrkPts;
    double      delta, sin_delta, cos_delta;

    // Initialize data and determine the number of stroking points
    rc = api_OK;
    delta = 2.0 * acos(1.0 - tol / radius);
    nStrkPts = 2 + (int)(2.0 * GPI / delta);
    delta = 2.0 * GPI / (nStrkPts - 1);
    pStrkPts.resize(nStrkPts);

    // Loop to compute stroking points on the circle centered at (0,0)
    sin_delta = sin(delta);
    cos_delta = cos(delta);
    pStrkPts[0].x = radius;
    pStrkPts[0].y = 0.0;
    for (i=1; i<nStrkPts; i++)
    {
        pStrkPts[i].x = pStrkPts[i-1].x * cos_delta -
                        pStrkPts[i-1].y * sin_delta;
        pStrkPts[i].y = pStrkPts[i-1].y * cos_delta +
                        pStrkPts[i-1].x * sin_delta;
    }

    // Translate the points based on the given center
    for (i=0; i<nStrkPts; i++)
    {
        pStrkPts[i].x += center.x;
        pStrkPts[i].y += center.y;
    }
```

```
}
```

Running this version 1 million times takes 1.85 seconds, which is almost as fast as running `apiStrokeCircleV1` that dynamically allocates heap memory. Therefore, it is recommended to call `resize` to let STL allocate and initialize memory for `vector` when the size is known in advance.

It is worth mentioning that STL `vector` stores elements in a single *contiguous* memory block. Therefore, we can pass the pointer of STL `vector` directly to a callee function that takes a pointer of array as an input parameter. Assume that we have an API that draws a polyline from given 2D points:

```
void apiDraw(int n, GPosition2d *p2DPoints)
{
    int i;
    // Move cursor to start point
    MoveTo((int)p2DPoints[0].x, (int)p2DPoints[0].y);
    for (i=1; i<n; i++)
    {
        // draw a line to current point
        LineTo(p2DPoints[i].x, p2DPoints[i].y);
    }
}
```

After obtaining the stroking points stored in STL `vector`, we can call the above API as follows:

```
    apiDraw((int)pStrkPts.size(), &pStrkPts[0]);
```

Here, we simply pass the address of the memory block allocated by STL `vector` to the callee.

## 3.5    double-pointer and two-dimensional STL vector

So far the use of STL `vector` has been limited to one-dimensional. A typical two-dimensional array is a grid containing rows and columns in which each element is uniquely specified by means of row and column coordinates. As an example, we will see how memory is allocated to perform the following matrix multiplication:

$$B = A^T A$$

where $A$ is an $n \times m$ matrix, $A^T$ the transpose matrix of $A$, and $B$ the square and symmetric matrix of $m \times m$. The need to compute $A^T A$ arises in linear least squares approximation that will be discussed in chapter 9. The following code illustrates how $A^T A$ is computed:

```
void apiAtTimesA(int n, int m, double **pA, double **pAtA)
{
    int     i, j, k;
```

```
for (i=0; i<m; i++)
{
    for (j=0; j<m; j++)
    {
        pAtA[i][j] = 0.0;
        for (k=0; k<n; k++)
        {
            pAtA[i][j] += pA[k][i] * pA[k][j];
        }
    }
}
}
```

There are several ways to allocate heap memory for a two-dimensional array in C/C++. One solution is to declare a double-pointer and allocate an array of $n$ pointers as follows:

```
double **pA = NULL;
pA = (double **)malloc(n * sizeof(double *));
```

A *double-pointer* is a *pointer-to-pointer-to-data type*. In our case, the double-pointer is a pointer-to-pointer-to-double. The above code fragment allocated $n$ double-pointers that will be used to hold the *entry* addresses of $n$ memory blocks of type double. At this moment, none of the double-pointers has been assigned a valid address since memory blocks of type double have not yet been allocated. Therefore, we need to loop through the array of $n$ pointers to allocate a memory block that holds $m$ doubles for each pointer:

```
double **pA = NULL;
pA = (double **)malloc(n * sizeof(double *));
if (!pA)
{
    rc = api_NOMEMORY;
    goto wrapup;
}
for (i=0; i<n; i++)
{
    pA[i] = (double *)malloc(m * sizeof(double));
    if (!pA[i])
    {
        rc = api_NOMEMORY;
        goto wrapup;
    }
}
```

A double-pointer is a difficult concept for beginners. In plain English, the above code fragment allocates a block of memory to store $n$ pointers and assign the entry address of allocated memory to a double-pointer pA via the statement

```
pA = (double **)malloc(n * sizeof(double *));
```

Each pointer can be accessed via index as pA[i]. At this moment, pA[i] is simply an uninitialized pointer whose type is double. The loop

```
for (i=0; i<n; i++)
{
    pA[i] = (double *)malloc(m * sizeof(double));
}
```

allocates a memory block to store m double and assign the entry address of allocated memory to each pointer pA[i] as illustrated below.

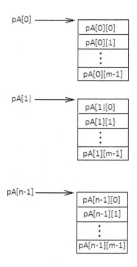

Figure 3.4: Illustration of double-pointer

In total, n blocks of memory have been allocated in the above loop to store $n \times m$ elements. Each block of memory may or may not be contiguously connected to any other memory block. How elements are stored in these blocks of memory is illustrated in figure 3.4, noting that pA[0], pA[1],$\cdots$, pA[n-1] store the *entry* address of the first, second, ..., and nth memory block.

Knowing the concept of a double-pointer, we can implement a main driver to illustrate the allocation of a two-dimensional array to read $n \times m$ matrix from an input data file. The output matrix $A^T A$ is a two-dimensional array of size $m \times m$ and is also allocated in the main driver. The main driver is designed to

- open the input (AtTimesA.d1) and output file (AtTimesA.n1),

- read elements of matrix $A$,

- call apiAtTimesA to compute $A^T A$,

- print the output results, and

- free all allocated heap memory.

The full implementation is listed below:

```c
int main(void)
{
   // Open input and output files
   FILE *infile = NULL, *outfile = NULL;
   fopen_s(&infile, "AtTimesA.d1", "r");
   if (!infile)
   {
      printf(" *** Cannot open %s\n", "AtTimesA.d1");
      exit(1);
   }

   fopen_s(&outfile, "AtTimesA.n1", "w");
   if (!outfile)
   {
      printf(" *** Cannot open %s\n", "AtTimesA.n1");
      exit (1);
   }

   // Local variables to call the testing function:
   apiError    rc = api_OK;
   int         i, j, n, m;
   double      **pA = NULL, **pAtA = NULL;

   // Allocate memory for matrix A and read in data
   fscanf_s(infile, "%d %d", &n, &m);
   pA = (double **)malloc(n * sizeof(double *));
   for (i=0; i<n; i++)
      pA[i] = (double *)malloc(m * sizeof(double));
   for (i=0; i<n; i++)
   {
      for (j=0; j<m; j++)
         fscanf_s(infile, "%lf",  &pA[i][j]);
   }

   // Allocate memory for output matrix AtA
   pAtA = (double **)malloc(m * sizeof(double *));
   for (i=0; i<m; i++)
   {
      pAtA[i] = (double *)malloc(m * sizeof(double));
   }

   // Invoke the function
   apiAtTimesA(n, m, pA, pAtA);

   // Print the output
   for (i=0; i<m; i++)
```

```
{
    for (j=0; j<m; j++)
        fprintf(outfile, "%lf ", pAtA[i][j]);
    fprintf(outfile, "\n");
}

// Free allocated heap memory
if (pA)
{
    for (i=0; i<n; i++)
    {
        if (pA[i])
            free(pA[i]);
    }
    free(pA);
}

if (pAtA)
{
    for (i=0; i<m; i++)
    {
        if (pAtA[i])
            free(pAtA[i]);
    }
    free(pAtA);
}

// Close opened input/output files
if (infile)
    fclose(infile);
if (outfile)
    fclose(outfile);
return rc;
}
```

Upon completion, all allocated memory must be properly freed. The above implementation involves many memory allocations and deletions, which is inefficient and may cause *memory fragmentation*. When a computer program requests blocks of memory from the computer system, the blocks are allocated in chunks. When the computer program is finished with a chunk, it frees the chunk back to the computer. The size and the amount of time a chunk is held by a program varies. During its lifespan, a computer program can request and free many chunks of memory. When a program is started, the free memory areas are long and contiguous. Over time and with use, the long contiguous regions become fragmented into smaller and smaller contiguous areas. Eventually, it will take significant longer time to find large chunks of memory. In the worst case scenario, memory allocation can fail even when the total available memory in the heap is enough to satisfy a request, because no single block of memory is large enough.

The following code fragment reduces the total number of memory allocations/deletions by allocating a large block of memory, dividing it into smaller chunks, and assigning the addresses to an array of pointers. By doing so, it improves the performance slightly (roughly ten percent).

```
fscanf_s(infile, "%d %d", &n, &m);
// Allocate n pointers for n rows
pA = (double **)malloc(n * sizeof(double *));
// Alocate n * m doubles
pA[0] = (double *)malloc(n * m * sizeof(double));
// Assign addresses to row pointers via pointer arithmetic
for (i=1; i<n; i++)
    pA[i] = pA[i-1] + m;
// Read in data
for (i=0; i<n; i++)
{
    for (j=0; j<m; j++)
        fscanf_s(infile, "%lf",  &pA[i][j]);
}

// Allocate memory for output matrix AtA
pAtA = (double **)malloc(m * sizeof(double *));
pAtA[0] = (double *)malloc(m * m * sizeof(double));
for (i=1; i<m; i++)
{
    pAtA[i] = pAtA[i-1] + m;
}
    :
wrapup:

if (pA)
{
    if (pA[0])
        free(pA[0]);
    free(pA);
}

if (pAtA)
{
    if (pAtA[0])
        free(pAtA[0]);
    free(pAtA);
}
```

Some experienced programmers may simply allocate one-dimensional array to store a two-dimensional data such that rows are stored one after another. This is known as *row-major* storage. Accordingly, matrix elements are accessed via indices operations as illustrated below.

```c
void apiAtAMatrixV2(int n, int m, double *pA, double *pAtA)
{
    int      i, j, k, im, km;
    for (i=0; i<m; i++)
    {
        im = i * m;
        for (j=0; j<m; j++)
        {
            pAtA[im+j] = 0.0;
            for (k=0; k<n; k++)
            {
                km = k * m;
                pAtA[im+j] += pA[km+i] * pA[km+j];
            }
        }
    }
}
```

The above implementation does not improve performance but minimizes memory allocation and deletion, because only one allocation is required for each one dimensional pointer as shown below

```c
    fscanf_s(infile, "%d %d", &n, &m);
    // Allocate n * m doubles and read in data
    pA = (double *)malloc(n * m * sizeof(double));
    if (!pA)
    {
        rc = api_NOMEMORY;
        goto wrapup;
    }
    for (i=0; i<n; i++)
    {
        for (j=0; j<m; j++)
            fscanf_s(infile, "%lf",  &pA[i*m+j]);
    }

    // Allocate memory for output matrix AtA
    pAtA = (double *)malloc(m * m * sizeof(double));
    if (!pAtA)
    {
        rc = api_NOMEMORY;
        goto wrapup;
    }
    :
wrapup:
```

```
if (pA)
{
    free(pA);
}

if (pAtA)
{
    free(pAtA);
}
```

Using two-dimensional arrays makes code easier to read and faster to run. However, memory allocation and deletion can be painful and may degrade the overall performance due to memory fragmentation in a large software system. We now look at how STL vector can help us address such issues. Analogous to the way heap memory was allocated for a double-pointer (pA and pAtA) in mnAtAMatrixV1.cpp, a tow-dimensional STL vector has to be properly initialized before use. The following code fragment in mnAtAMatrix.cpp shows how this is done:

```
// Local variables to call the testing function:
apiError    rc = api_OK;
int         i, j, n, m;
vector<std::vector<double>> pA, pAtA;

fscanf_s(infile, "%d %d", &n, &m);

// Let STL allocate n rows
pA.resize(n);
// Let STL allocate m elements for each row
for (i=0; i<n; i++)
    pA[i].resize(m);

for (i=0; i<n; i++)
{
    for (j=0; j<m; j++)
        fscanf_s(infile, "%lf", &pA[i][j]);
}

// Let STL allocate m rows
pAtA.resize(m);
// Let STL allocate m elements for each row
for (i=0; i<m; i++)
    pAtA[i].resize(m);
```

Since both pA and pAtA are STL vectors, memory deletion is managed by STL. The implementation of matrices multiplication via STL vector is listed below. Although it runs roughly fifteen percent slower than apiAtAMatrixV1, two-dimensional STL vector is still preferred since it minimizes memory fragmentation and eliminates the need to properly free memory – a common resource-leaking bug in software development.

```
/*-------------------------------------------------------------------
API Name
    apiAtAMatrix

Description
    It computes matrix multiplication in the form of A^t x A,
    where A^t is the transpose matrix of A.

Signature
    void apiAtAMatrix(std::vector<std::vector<double>> &pA,
                    std::vector<std::vector<double>> &pAtA)

    INPUT:
        pA        matrix of n x m
    OUTPUT:
        pAtA      the resulting matrix of A^t x A

History

    Y.M. Li      03/10/2013 : Creation date
-----------------------------------------------------------------*/
#include "MyHeader.h"

void apiAtAMatrix(std::vector<std::vector<double>> &pA,
                std::vector<std::vector<double>> &pAtA)
{
    int      i, j, k, n, m;

    n = (int)pA.size();
    m = (int)pA[0].size();
    for (i=0; i<m; i++)
    {
        for (j=0; j<m; j++)
        {
            pAtA[i][j] = 0.0;
            for (k=0; k<n; k++)
            {
                pAtA[i][j] += pA[k][i] * pA[k][j];
            }
        }
    }
}
```

## 3.6   Know how to count beads

Mathematicians and computer scientists traditionally use certain criteria to measure the amount of computation involved in executing an algorithm. The criteria often include the number of comparison tests, the number of assignment statements, and the number of arithmetic operations used by an algorithm. These types of measures are independent of any particular computer system and depend solely on the design and implementation of the algorithm. These criteria describe the *computational complexity* of an algorithm. As far as this book is concerned, computational complexity measures the computational efficiency of the algorithm relative to $n$, the number of data items. The computational complexity of an algorithm indicates how fast it performs, so the *running time* will be clocked in every main driver to measure the efficiency of an algorithm.

In mathematics and computer algorithm analysis, "big $O$ notation" is used to characterize functions according to their growth rates: different functions with the same growth rate may be represented using the same $O$ notation. For example, $O(n)$ describes an algorithm whose performance will grow linearly and in direct proportion to the size of the input data set. $O(n^2)$ represents an algorithm whose performance is directly proportional to the square of the size of the input data set. This is common with algorithms that involve nested iterations over the data set. An algorithm could have different running times for the best, average, and worst cases, so we may compute a specific big $O$ estimation for each case. The best case for an algorithm is often not important because the circumferences are exceptional and hence not a useful criterion when choosing an algorithm. The worst case can be important, despite its exceptionality. Its efficiency could be so poor that an application could not tolerate the performance. For this reason, a designer may prefer an algorithm with better worst-scenario behavior even though the average performance is not as good.

One of my favorite questions when interviewing candidates is

> Assume that we have $n$ sorted integers saved in an array. If we want to find a particular number (i.e., the key) in this array, the simplest way is to perform *linear search* (the $O(n)$ algorithm). Please tell us the best and worst scenario for this linear search.

> In general, a *binary search* is preferred. We start by comparing the element in the middle of the sorted array. If this key is larger than the middle number, we discard the first half of elements and repeat the same search to the remaining elements. Please show us what algorithm the binary search is.

> **Hint**: The worst scenario for binary search is that you find the key only when all other elements have been eliminated. So, find out how many search operations you would need.

Every candidate could tell me that the best and worst scenario for linear search is that the key is respectively the first and last element. Most of them could also answer that a binary search is a logarithmic algorithm. However, they were unable to prove it. The ability to analyze a piece of code or an algorithm and understand its efficiency is vital for software development.

The binary search algorithm is a typical example of an $O(\log n)$ algorithm. Let us see how it is proved:

After the first search, there are $\dfrac{n}{2}$ elements remaining.

After the second search, there are $\dfrac{n}{2^2}$ elements remaining.

$$\vdots$$

The worst scenario is that, after $m$ searches, we find the key, and it is the only remaining element. So, the equation is

$$\frac{n}{2^m} = 1,$$

Solving this equation for $m$ gives $m = \log_2 n$. Therefore, the binary search is an $O(\log n)$ algorithm. For $n = 100$, $m = \log_2 100 \approx 6.644$, indicating that we need, at most, 7 searches to find the key. The implementation of a binary search algorithm is given below:

```
/*--------------------------------------------------------------
API Name
    apiBinarySearch

Description
    It finds the key in a sorted array and returns the index of array

Signature
    int apiBinarySearch(int key, int *pIntArray,
            int i_beg, int i_end, apiError &rc)

        INPUT:
            key             the specific integer to be found in integer array
            pIntArray       pointer to the integer array
            i_beg           starting index of the array
            i_end           ending index of the array
        OUTPUT:
            rc              error code: api_OK if no error

History

    Y.M. Li       03/10/2013 : Creation date
-----------------------------------------------------------------*/
#include "MyHeader.h"

int apiBinarySearch(int key, int *pIntArray,
        int i_beg, int i_end, apiError &rc)
{
    int  i0, i1, i_mid;
```

```
// Validate the key
rc = api_OK;
if (i_end < i_beg || key < pIntArray[i_beg] ||
                     key > pIntArray[i_end])
{
    rc = api_INVALIDARG;
    return -1;
}

i0 = i_beg;
i1 = i_end;
while (i1 - i0 >= 0)
{
    i_mid = (i0 + i1) / 2;
    if (key == pIntArray[i_mid])
    {
        return i_mid;
    }

    if (key < pIntArray[i_mid])
    {
        i1 = i_mid - 1; // key is in the left half
    }
    else
    {
        i0= i_mid + 1; // key is in the right half
    }
}

    return -1;
}
```

Computational complexity is usually studied in data structure and algorithm analysis. Readers may think that algorithms can exhibit hundreds of these big-$O$ measures of running time. In reality, a small set of measures defines the running time of most algorithms. The following are categories for the different measures, along with short descriptions.

**Constant time** An algorithm has an efficiency $O(1)$ when its running time is independent of the number of data items. The algorithm runs in constant time. For example, the algorithm for finding the smallest or the largest key in a pre-sorted array has efficiency $O(1)$ regardless of the size of the array.

**Linear** An algorithm has efficiency $O(n)$ when its running time is proportional to the size of the data items. Such an algorithm is said to be linear. When the number of elements doubles, so does the number of operations. For example, finding the minimum value in an $n$-element unsorted array is $O(n)$.

**Quadratic and Cubic** Algorithms whose running time is $O(n^2)$ are quadratic. Most simple sorting algorithms such as the selection sort are $O(n^2)$. Quadratic algorithms are practical only for relatively small $n$. Whenever $n$ doubles, the running time of the algorithm increases by a factor of 4. An algorithm is cubic if its running time is $O(n^3)$. The efficiency of such an algorithm is generally poor, because doubling the size of $n$ increases the running time of the algorithm by an eightfold. Solving a linear system with $n$ unknowns usually involves computing $n^3$ products and thus is an $O(n^3)$ algorithm.

**Logarithmic** As discussed, finding a key in a sorted array is logarithmic since it involves $O(\log n)$ comparisons in the worst case. Besides $O(\log n)$, many good sorting algorithms (e.g., *QuickSort*, *Merge Sort*, etc.) require average $O(n \log n)$ comparisons and are also termed logarithmic. These running times occur when the algorithm repeatedly subdivides the data into sublists whose size are $1/2, 1/4, 1/8, \cdots$ of the original size. This type of algorithm running time is good and desirable!

**Exponential** Some algorithms deal with problems that involve searching through a large number of potential solutions before finding an answer. Such algorithms often have running time $O(a^n)$ with $a > 1$ and hence are termed exponential running time. Recursive solution to the problem of generating Fibonacci numbers has an exponential running time. The Tower of Hanoi puzzle to be discussed in chapter 5 is also an exponential algorithm, as it requires $2^n - 1$ disk movements. Exponential algorithms are used only when $n$ is small. Modern computers are fast and can perform roughly $2^{30}$ operations per second. One may ask what the big deal is to have a large $n$. The following table answers their concern:

| Operations: | $2^{30}$ | $2^{36}$ | $2^{42}$ | $2^{48}$ | $2^{54}$ |
|---|---|---|---|---|---|
| Time: | 1 sec | 1 min | 1 hour | 3 days | 6 months |

## 3.7   CPU cache

In the previous section, it was emphasized that an analysis of computational complexity is an essential and important starting point for an optimal performance. But, having an algorithm with minimum computational complexity may not necessarily lead to an optimal performance. For example, it is known that inserting an element in a linked list is $O(1)$ algorithm, while inserting an element in an array is $O(n)$. In reality, however, it is usually slow to work with a linked list. It is also known that accessing an arbitrary element in an array is an $O(1)$ algorithm. However, the real performance in accessing an array varies vastly due to CPU caching mechanism. For this reason, I want to end this chapter by discussing how the performance of a program can be further improved by understanding the basics of CPU caching.

CPU caches are small pools of high speed static random-access memory (SRAM) that store information the CPU most likely needs for the next operation. Almost all modern CPUs have multiple levels of CPU caches named L1, L2, etc. with L1 being the fastest CPU cache. Which information is cached depends on sophisticated algorithms and certain assumptions about programming code. The goal of the cache system is to increase likelihood that the next bit of data CPU will need has already been loaded into cache to reduce the average cost to access data from the main memory. If the CPU finds the needed data in caches, it is called a *cache hit*. A *cache miss*, on the other hand, means the CPU has to go scampering off to find the data elsewhere in L2, L3, or main memory (DRAM).

In general, L1 cache is extremely fast (1 cycle to access) but relatively small; L2 cache is a secondary cache and is 10 times slower to access data; DRAM is 80 times slower than L1 to access. Therefore, well-optimized code depends not only on minimal computational complexity, but also on reducing cache misses.

Modern computers deploy sophisticated algorithms to determine what information needs to be loaded into cache. For example, it may assume that:

- Temporal: memory accessed recently will likely be required again soon.

- Spatial: adjacent memory is likely to be required soon.

- Striding: memory access is likely to follow a predictable pattern.

Because of these assumption, it comes no surprise that accessing an array sequentially is much faster than accessing it randomly. To illustrate it, let us take a look at the performance of matrix multiplication. Given two $n \times n$ matrices $A$ and $B$, the product of two matrices is

$$A \times B = \begin{pmatrix} a_{1,1} & a_{1,2} & \cdots & a_{1,n} \\ a_{2,1} & a_{2,2} & \cdots & a_{2,n} \\ \vdots & \vdots & \ddots & \vdots \\ a_{n,1} & a_{n,2} & \cdots & a_{n,n} \end{pmatrix} \begin{pmatrix} b_{1,1} & b_{1,2} & \cdots & b_{1,n} \\ b_{2,1} & b_{2,2} & \cdots & b_{2,n} \\ \vdots & \vdots & \ddots & \vdots \\ b_{n,1} & b_{n,2} & \cdots & b_{n,n} \end{pmatrix}$$

$$= \begin{pmatrix} \sum_{k=1}^{n} a_{1,k} b_{k,1} & \sum_{k=1}^{n} a_{1,k} b_{k,2} & \cdots & \sum_{k=1}^{n} a_{1,k} b_{k,n} \\ \sum_{k=1}^{n} a_{2,k} b_{k,1} & \sum_{k=1}^{n} a_{2,k} b_{k,2} & \cdots & \sum_{k=1}^{n} a_{2,k} b_{k,n} \\ \vdots & \vdots & \ddots & \vdots \\ \sum_{k=1}^{n} a_{n,k} b_{k,1} & \sum_{k=1}^{n} a_{n,k} b_{k,2} & \cdots & \sum_{k=1}^{n} a_{n,k} b_{k,n} \end{pmatrix}$$

As seen above, the product of matrices requires repeatedly accessing elements in $A$ *sequentially* along each row, but accessing elements in $B$ along each column. If all elements in both matrices are stored in a one-dimensional array in a row-major order, the above product has no performance problem in accessing elements in $A$ sequentially (a *predictable* pattern), but it has a "cache-miss" issue in accessing elements in $B$ (*unpredictable*) and thus results in a significant performance hit.

To improve the performance, we can create a temporary matrix that stores the elements of $B$ in a column-major order (Note that it is equivalent to store the transpose matrix of $B$ in a row-major order). Accordingly, accessing elements in $B$ along column becomes accessing elements sequentially along one-dimensional array. With this approach, the accumulative time in generating transpose matrix and computing the product of two square matrices is about three times faster than the direct product of unarranged matrices.

## 3.8   Summary

In this chapter we learned advanced topics in C/C++ programming such as default arguments, data structure and class, double-pointer, dynamic memory allocation, and STL containers. By now we should have gained the required level of proficiency in implementing numerical methods.

A better design not only boosts performance but also reduces cumulative numerical noises. Each arithmetic operation adds numerical noise linearly, if not exponentially (Please note some numerical noises may cancel each other out due to different signs). Rushing to implementation without a sound analysis and design will only result in a buggy and unstable code. In real world computation, we often have to take into consideration these aspects: number of arithmetic computations, code clarity, straightforwardness, modularity, layering, design, efficiency, best coding practices, etc.

Horner's method and its variations are good examples in evaluating polynomials as they use the least number of arithmetic computations. The circle stroking method presented in this chapter is another good example of how thoughtful design can greatly improve the performance. In the chapter on parallel programming, we shall have an opportunity to see that repeatedly computing sin and cos cannot compete with the circle stroking method implemented in this chapter even with the help of multi-thread programming on a quad-core computer.

STL `vector` discussed in this chapter plays an important role in software development. It is true that we often find that STL `vector` performs slightly slower than a dynamically allocated array. But it is still preferred by professional developers because of its sheer power and flexibility. Furthermore, memory allocation and deletion of STL containers are managed automatically, so developers do not need to worry about dynamic growth of storage and memory deletion. For these reasons, we shall exclusively use STL `vector` in this book whenever storage is required.

Optional or default arguments were discussed in implementing `apiHornerEval`. They are widely used in software development for two reasons:

**Flexibility** In many cases, functions have control arguments (e.g., distance tolerance, angular tolerance, etc.) in which a default value would suffice. Such control arguments can be implemented as optional arguments with pre-assigned default values. When users call these functions without optional arguments, the default values are passed to the callee. If users are not happy about the default control values, they can call these functions with their desired values, which makes these functions flexible to use.

**Minimizing massive code change** Some functions were created to meet specific tasks at the time of implementation. Assume that we have an API to compute an intersection between two curves. At the time of implementation, the system default tolerance was used to compute the intersection. It has worked well for many years until one day, when we found it does not work for imported data since different CAD systems may use different default distance tolerances. In this case, we would like to allow users to specify the tolerance. Adding an additional input argument would require a code change in the calling functions, which can be massive. If the tolerance variable is implemented as an optional argument with the default system tolerance value, then only the translator team needs to modify their code to use different tolerances when importing a CAD file into our system.

# Chapter 4

# Software Development Process

In software companies, developers do not just sit down, turn on their computers, and start writing code. Instead, they follow an organized plan or methodology that breaks the process into a series of tasks. Even a very specialized software system such as the software library for numerical computations has a high inherent complexity so engineering principles have to be used in software development. The application of a systematic, disciplined, quantifiable approach to the design, development, operation, and maintenance of software makes up the discipline of software engineering. There are several development models of software engineering. The so-called *Waterfall Model* has traditionally been adopted by many software development companies. In this model, developers follow these phases in order:

1. Requirements specification (Requirements analysis)

2. Software design

3. Implementation and Integration

4. Testing (or Validation)

5. Maintenance

Most recently, the *Agile* software development has become increasingly popular. It uses iterative development as a basis but advocates a lighter and more people-centric viewpoint than traditional approaches. Agile processes use feedback, rather than planning, as their primary control mechanism. The feedback is driven by regular tests and releases of the evolving software.

It is beyond the scope of this chapter to give a broad perspective of software development processes and techniques. Instead, it focuses on how computational software may be developed in software houses. The presentation is biased, to some extent, towards my own experience in developing numerical computing and geometric modeling systems in two software companies.

No matter what software development model is used, the ultimate goal is to find repeatable, predictable processes that improve productivity, reusability, and quality of software systems. For a practical illustration of how this goal is met, we confine our discussion to the development of a reliable computational library. It includes writing script tools to improve the productivity of software development, designing flexible main drivers to perform functional and regression tests, automatically running and validating a unit and suite test overnights. Techniques and tools discussed in this chapter will be the protocol and standard in developing numerical methods in this book.

## 4.1    Create dynamic-link library

In the previous chapter, each functional program was saved in a different source file. When we need them, we may copy and add the source files in our project to build an executable program. This is okay for casual programming but can be a hurdle for professional development. In a software development company, there are tens of thousands of source files. In general, functions that are related (e.g., transformation functions, 2D geometry creation and manipulation functions, etc.) are grouped together and stored in the same place. Each of these sections is then compiled and linked to form a function library. When developers want to call functions in certain libraries, they simply link these libraries in their projects. A library usually contains both program code and data that provide services to independent programs. The use of library files encourages the sharing and changing of code and data in a modular fashion and eases the distribution of the code and data. Library files are not executable programs. They are either *static libraries* that are merged with an executable when the executable is being compiled and linked, making them "statically linked," or they are *dynamic libraries* that are loaded by a dynamic linker while the executable is running, making them "dynamically linked."

In a statically-linked case, linking (to other functions) is performed during the creation of an executable, known as *early binding* or *static linking*. This process usually produces a stand-alone executable program. In other words, you can copy the executable program to any compatible machine (e.g., machines with the same Windows operating system) and run it there regardless of the configuration of the computer. This is one of the significant advantages of using statically linking libraries. Another advantage is that static linking will result in a performance improvement. However, a statically-linking library is inflexible. When a function in the library is modified, all applications that depend on this library have to be recompiled and linked even though those applications have not had a code change. Another disadvantage is that the executable file size is usually large, as the library code is stored within the executable rather than in separate files.

Dynamic linking or *late binding* refers to the linking performed while a program is being loaded (load time) or executed (run time), rather than when the executable file is created. A dynamically linked library (commonly known as DLL) is a library intended for dynamic linking. Only a minimum amount of work is done by the linker when the executable file is created; it only records what library routines the program needs and the index names or numbers of the routines in the library. The majority of linking is done at the time the application is loaded (load time) or during execution (run time). The necessary linking program, called a dynamic linker or linking loader, is actually part of the underlying operating system. Since the library code is not stored within the executable but linked at the run time, the executable file size is much less than the statically-linked one. As far as the signature (i.e., the interface or prototype) of each function in the library remains the same, modification to the code does not trigger re-compiling and re-linking the application programs that depend on this library. Therefore, when bug fixes are made to one or more functions in the library, we simply recompile this library and deliver only this library DLL, instead of a full platform, to the customers. These advantages make the dynamic linking libraries very attractive in the software development process. For this reason, we limit our discussion to the creation of a dynamic-link library. It is a tedious process but is done only once.

We first create a few folders under `ArtProgram` as shown below. Folder `src` is for program source files, `mn` for main drivers, `data` for input data files, `outp` for the output/result files, and `include` for header files. Folders `bin` and `lib` are for DLL and Lib files respectively. Besides DLL files, the `bin` folder also stores executable scripts such as the `.bat` and `.cmd` files.

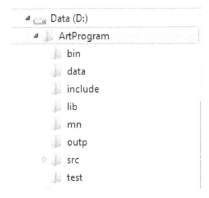

Figure 4.1: Folder structure

So far we have implemented the following algorithms:

```
apiAtAMatrix
apiAtAMatrixV1
apiAtAMatrixV2
apiBinarySearch
apiHornerEval
apiStrokeCircle
apiStrokeCircleV1
```

Let's move source, main driver, input data, and output data files respectively to their destination folders. Although Microsoft Visual Studio 2010 is selected to be the development platform for this book, the process to create DLL can similarly be applied to other versions of Microsoft Visual Studio. In this chapter, numerous screenshots are used to help you complete each step. Since the appearance and behavior of the Visual

Studio integrated development environment (IDE) are customizable in many ways, you may find some screenshots to be different from the screen of your environment. For example, the `Solution Explorer` appears on the left pane by default. You may have configured your settings to make it appear on the right pane. It is possible to reset the integrated development environment to the default settings so that your environment will closely match my descriptions and screenshots. To do so, click

`Tools->Import and Export Settings ...`

In the popup wizard window, select the `Reset all settings` radio button and follow the instructions to complete resetting. It is highly recommended to change the default `Tab` key setting to `Insert spaces` as shown below. This guarantees that any `.cpp` source file will have a consistent look when it is opened by a different editor (e.g., `Emacs` or `notepad`). This is done by clicking from the menu bar

`Tools->Options->Text Editor->C/C++->Tabs`

as indicated below:

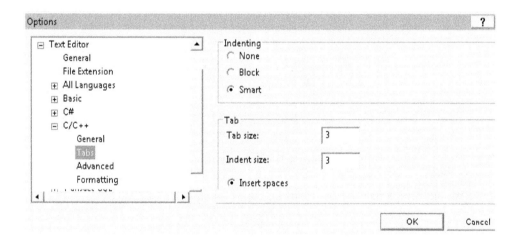

Figure 4.2: Configuration of Tab key

It should be pointed out that your current settings can be exported to a file for use on other computers or to revert your settings when your settings get messed up.

Let's start Visual Studio 2010 and click `File->New->Project` to invoke a New Project wizard. We select Visual C++ on the left pane and `Win32 Console Application` on the right pane; then either type or browse `D:\ArtProgram\src` as the location of the project and name the project `FunctDLL` as shown below.

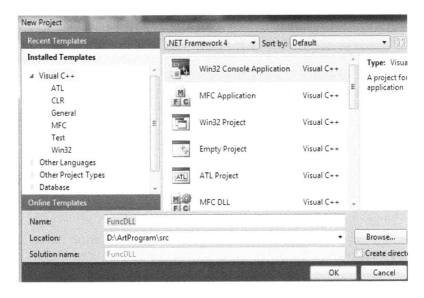

Figure 4.3: Create a DLL project

Click `Ok` to go to the next stage. In the new popup window, select `Empty project` and check `DLL` and then click `Finish` as shown below.

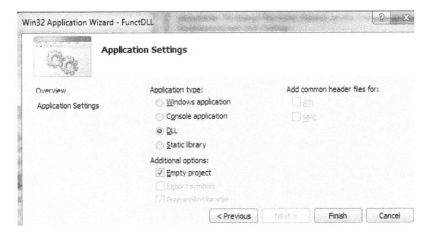

Figure 4.4: DLL project settings

The `Win32 Application Wizard` usually creates a subfolder named `FunctDLL` under `D:\ArtProgram\src`. In this subfolder, we will find that the following files have been created to manage the project in the solution:

.sln

> The *solution* file. It organizes all elements of a project or multiple projects into one solution.

.suo

The *solution options* file. It stores your customizations for the solution so that every time you open a project or file in the solution, it has the appearance and behavior you want.

.std

The *browsing database* file. It supports browsing and navigation features such as Goto Definition, Find All References, and Class View. It is generated by parsing the header files.

.vcxproj

The *project* file. It stores information specific to each project.

.vcxproj.filters

The *filters* file. It specifies where to put a file that is added to the solution. For example, a .h file is put in the Header Files folder.

.vcxproj.user

The *migration user* file. After a project is migrated from Visual Studio 2008, this file contains information that was converted from any .vsprops file.

We need neither the FunctDLL subfolder nor most of the project files in this folder. Let us close the opened Visual Studio project so that both FunctDLL.vcxproj and FuncDLL.vcxproj.filters can be moved to D:\ArtProgram\src. The subfolder FunctDLL and the remaining files in this folder will not be used and can safely be deleted. By expanding D:\ArtProgram\src, we should see the following files:

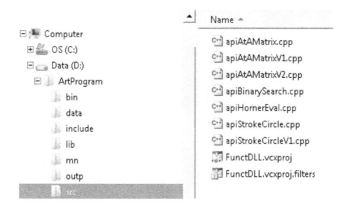

Figure 4.5: Source file folder

It is worth mentioning that, prior to Visual Studio 2010, only FunctDLL.vcproj was needed for our applications. Starting with 2010, FuncDLL.vcxproj.filters is also required as it contains information about folders of a project. Double-click FunctDLL.vcxproj to open the project. We will see several folders in the Solution Explorer pane. Move the mouse cursor to Source Files and click the right mouse button to select Add->Existing Items to add all source files as shown below.

Figure 4.6: Adding source files to project

The `FunctDLL.def` is a *module-definition* (.def) text file that we need to create via either Visual Studio's editor or any other text editor. It provides the `linker` with information about exports to allow our application projects to link with the DLL and call the exported functions. There are three ways to export functions in C/C++ files:

- Place the *decorated names* in the `.def` file. C++ allows specification of more than one function of the same name, provided that their parameter types and/or number is different. These are called *overloaded functions*. How does a compiler pick the appropriate version of overloaded functions? Microsoft resolved this problem by using the so-called decorated names or *mangled names*. A decorated name contains at least the function name and types of the function's parameters in decorated forms that have internal meaning only for the compiler and the linker. For example, the following function

      int func1(char myChar)

  is encoded in the decorated name as `?func1@@YAHD@Z`. The decorated names can be obtained by using the `DUMPBIN` tool or by using the `linker` /MAP option. Conversely, a decorated name can be converted to an undecorated form by invoking the `undname.exe` at the command line as

      D:\ArtProgram>undname ?func1@@YAHD@Z
      Microsoft (R) C++ Name Undecorator
      Copyright (C) Microsoft Corporation. All rights reserved.

      Undecoration of :- "?func1@@YAHD@Z"
      is :- "int __cdecl func1(char)"

- Use *standard C linkage* by placing `extern "C"` in front of each function definition. In C language, overloaded functions are not allowed. Therefore, there is no need to mangle the name. Placing `extern "C"` in front of function tells the compiler to use C linkage without mangling.

- Use the `__declspec(dllexport)` keyword to export the DLL's functions without the need of the `.def` file.

Both the second and third option will be used in this book. For now, we will start with the standard C linkage for simplicity. Since there are seven functions to export, the `FunctDLL.def` looks like

```
EXPORTS
apiAtAMatrix @1
apiAtAMatrixV1 @2
apiAtAMatrixV2 @3
apiBinarySearch @4
apiHornerEval @5
apiStrokeCircle @6
apiStrokeCircleV1 @7
```

It should be noted that `@ordinal` lets us specify that a *number*, not the function name, will go into the DLL's export table. This helps minimize the size of our DLL. The `.LIB` file (to be discussed later) will contain the mapping between the ordinal and the function, which allows us to use the function name as we normally would in projects that use the DLL. So far, seven function names have been added. As the book progresses, many more new functions will be developed and added to the library. Readers should always assume that new function names and ordinal numbers will similarly be added to `FunctDLL.def` whenever they are included in the `FunctDLL` library even if not explicitly stated.

Since the standard C linkage is chosen to export functions, we need to modify the header file to add `extern "C"` in front of each function definition. So, declarations of APIs in `MyHeader.h` look like

```
extern "C" void apiAtAMatrix(std::vector<std::vector<double>> &pA,
                             std::vector<std::vector<double>> &pAtA);

extern "C" void apiAtAMatrixV1(int n, int m, double **pA,
                                             double **pAtA);

extern "C" void apiAtAMatrixV2(int n,int m, double *pA, double *pAtA);

extern "C" int apiBinarySearch(int key, int pIntArray[],
                     int i_beg, int i_end, apiError &rc);
```

$\vdots$

Before compiling the project, we need to make some configuration changes for our convenience. Move the mouse cursor to `FunctDLL` in the `Solution Explorer` pane

and click the right mouse button to select Properties. At the FunctDLL Property
Pages, click General under Configuration Properties and type FunctDLL_d and
D:\ArtProgram\bin\ as shown below. This tells the compiler to create the debug
FunctDLL_d.dll in the folder D:\ArtProgram\bin\.

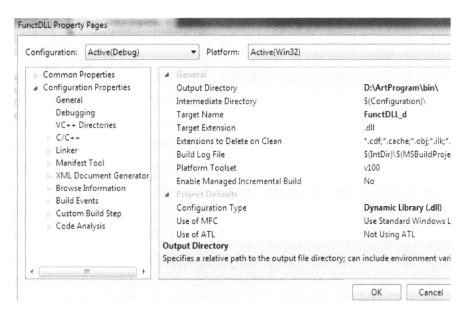

Figure 4.7: Specify DLL name and path

We need to do the same thing for release. At the top left corner of the above figure,
Active(Debug) indicates that the current (active) setting is for debugging. Change
it to Release and specify the path and release DLL name FunctDLL_r as we did for
debugging (note: FunctDLL_d.dll for the debug version and FunctDLL_r.dll for the
release version). When prompted to save changes, click OK to save the changes.

Under C/C++, click General and type D:\ArtProgram\include in the Additional
Include Directories field as shown below (this needs to be done for both debug and
release modes), which tells the compiler where to look for a header file.

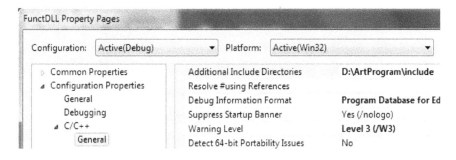

Figure 4.8: Specify header file directory

We also need to let the `linker` know where to look for the module-definition file
`FunctDLL.def`. Click `Input` under `Linker` and type

`.\FunctDLL.def`

in the `Module Definition File` field. Again, the module-definition file provides the
linker with information about exports, attributes, and other details about the program
to be linked.

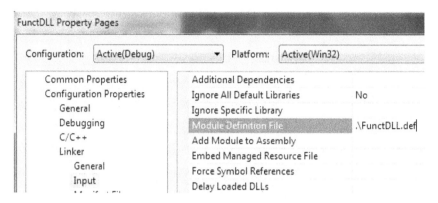

Figure 4.9: Specify module definition file

Next, we need to tell the `linker` to create an import library that contains the mapping
between the ordinal and the exported function. This import library will be included in
an application project if this application needs to call any exported function in DLL.
Click `Advanced` under `Linker` and type

`D:\ArtProgram\lib\FunctDLL_d.lib`

in the field of `Import Library` and click `Apply` as shown below (Note: we need to do
this for `Release` by typing `D:\ArtProgram\lib\FunctDLL_r.lib` in release mode).

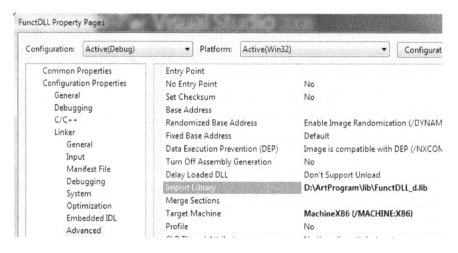

Figure 4.10: Specify `Linker` option

Finally, let's add a *versioning* mechanism to the DLL. A software company usually maintains and supports several versions of products. Therefore, it is important to assign a visioning number to a DLL so that users can tell which version of DLL they are using when reporting problems. At the `Solution Explorer` pane (referring to Figure 4.6), highlight `Resource Files` and click the right mouse button to select `Add->New Item`. At the popup window, select `Resource File (.rc)` and type the name `FunctDLL.rc` as shown in figure 4.11. Click the `Add` button to add `FunctDLL.rc` in the `Resource Files` folder.

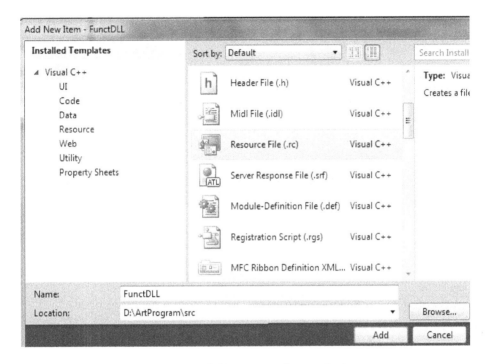

Figure 4.11: Add resource for versioning

Expand the `Resource Files` folder and then highlight `FunctDLL.rc` and click the right mouse button to select `Add Resource`. At the popup window, double-click `Version` as indicated in figure 4.12. In the new popup window, we can specify version information that consists of company and product identification, a product release number, and copyright and trademark notification.

It is time to compile the project in both debug and release mode. When it is done, we should see `FunctDLL_d.dll`, `FunctDLL_d.pdb`, `FunctDLL_r.dll`, and `FunctDLL_r.pdb` files in the `bin` folder. The *program database* (`.pdb`) files are big in size, as they hold debugging information. They are used by developers for debugging and usually not delivered to customers. By highlighting a DLL and clicking the right mouse button to select `Properties` and then the `Details` tab, we should see the DLL versioning information we previously typed in (see figure 4.13).

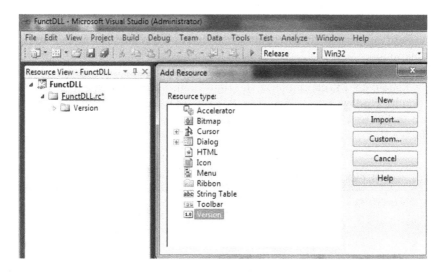

Figure 4.12: DLL versioning

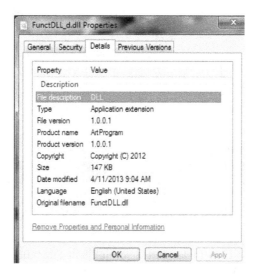

Figure 4.13: View versioning information

In the lib folder, we have FunctDLL_d.lib, FunctDLL_d.exp, FunctDLL_r.lib, and FunctDLL_r.exp. These files are small in size. They contain information about exported functions. The .lib files contain the mapping between the ordinal and the exported function and will be used for importing respective DLL when we write application programs. Export(.exp) files also contain information about exported functions and data items. When the Microsoft Library Manager LIB.exe creates an import library, it also creates an .exp file. The .exp files are used for exporting when multiple DLLs with cross-dependency are involved. In our case, we will not create multiple DLLs that both export to and import from another program. Therefore, .exp files will not be used in this book.

## 4.2 Use dynamic-link library

Using DLLs is a great way to reuse code. Rather than re-implementing these routines in every new program, we write them once and reference them from applications that need the functionality. In this walk-through section, we shall create an application that references the dynamic-link library FunctDLL_d.dll for debug or FunctDLL_r.dll for release. Before doing so, we need to add D:\ArtProgram\bin in User Path so that Windows can find the DLLs in the directories listed in the PATH environment variable.

To test the DLL, copy mnHornerEval.cpp and HornerEval.d1 created in the previous chapter to the folder test. Start Visual Studio 2010 and create a Win32 Console Application with the name mnHornerEval. Next, add mnHornerEval.cpp to Source Files. Since we will not use the Header Files and Resource Files folders created by Wizard, we can delete Resource Files and rename Header Files to Lib Files. Move the mouse cursor to Lib Files and click the right mouse button to select Add->Existing Items. Browse D:\ArtProgram\lib to add both FunctDLL_d.lib and FunctDLL_r.lib. We now need to exclude the release .Lib file from building a debug application. This is done by highlighting FunctDLL_r.lib and clicking right mouse button to set the value in the Exclude From Build field to Yes as shown below.

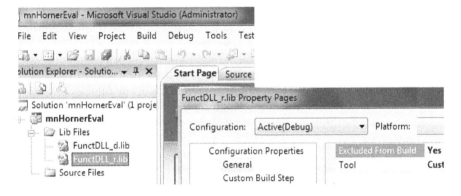

Figure 4.14: Exclude release library from debug build

Similarly, we exclude the debug .Lib file from building a release application. Next, we add D:\ArtProgram\include in the Additional Include Directories field (referring to Figure 4.8) so that the compiler knows where to find MyHeader.h. Finally, we tell the Linker where to output the executable. By default, it saves the debug and release executable in the subfolders Debug and Release respectively. In our case, project, source, and data files are all copied to the test folder. If we do not change the default setting, the debug or release executable will be saved in test\Debug or test\Release. Since our main driver is designed to open an input file from the same directory where the executable resides, we have to move either the executable to the test folder or move the input file to the Debug or Release folder. It is simpler to change the IDE setting to output the executable to the folder where the project (and hence the input data files) resides. This is done by selecting `Project` from menu bar, clicking `Properties`, expanding the `Configuration Properties` tab, clicking `Linker->General`, and typing

`.\$(ProjectName).exe`

in the `Output Files` field.

We are done with the settings. Compiling the project in either debug or release mode generates the executable in the `test` folder. We run the executable by either pressing the `F5` key under Visual Studio or invoking it at the command prompt as follows:

`D:\ArtProgram\test>mnHornerEval`

Open the test driver `mnHornerEval.cpp` in IDE windows and set a breakpoint at the statement where `apiHornerEval` is called. Press `F5` to run the program. When it halts at the breakpoint, press `F11` to step into the function. We will find that the debugger steps into the source file `apiHornerEval.cpp` in `D:\ArtProgram\src`. When we created this project, our intention was to call the function built into the DLL. Therefore, we did not copy `apiHornerEval.cpp` to the `test` folder to include it in the project. When we pressed `F11` to step into the callee function, the debugger knew exactly where to find the program database (`.pdb`) file that contains the original location of the source files when the DLL was built. The debugger used this information to determine two key pieces of information: the source file and line number that are displayed in the Visual Studio IDE. Based on the timestamp of the source file and information in `.pdb` file, the debugger also knew whether the source file had been modified since the last build of DLL. A warning would be issued if the debugger found timestamp differences between the source file and saved symbols in the `.pdb` file.

From time to time, we may want to modify a particular function to fix a bug or to improve performance. Accordingly, we copy the source file of the function to the current working directory and include it in the working project. In this case, the same API in DLL will be excluded automatically so that we work with the local copy of the source file.

It is a lengthy and tedious process to create a correct Visual Studio C/C++ project (i.e., `.vcxproj file`) for each application. In the next section, we will write scripts to simplify the process.

## 4.3  Write scripts for productivity

Microsoft Visual Studio's integrated development environment provides a user-friendly environment to write C/C++ programs, design graphical user interface, compile, run, and debug a program. However, as seen in the previous section, it is a tedious process to create a new Visual Studio project. If any required step is missing, we would not be able to compile and run the program. In this section, we discuss how to simplify this process to improve productivity.

In the previous section, we created the project `mnHornerEval` that references to the DLL to call `apiHornerEval`. This project and its configurations are managed by two files: `mnHornerEval.vcxproj` and `mnHornerEval.vcxproj.filters`. Opening these two files with any text editor (e.g., `Notepad`), we will see that both files are *Extensible Markup Language (XML)* files that contain information needed to build a C/C++ project. XML is a markup language that defines a set of rules for encoding documents in a format that is both human-readable and machine-readable. Since XML is a textual data format with strong support via Unicode for the languages of the world, the XML files can safely be tailored to create a specific new project by using a scripting language. Among several scripting languages, Perl is an ideal text manipulation language. It was originally developed for text manipulation but is now also used for a wide range of tasks including system administration, web development, network programming, and GUI development. Furthermore, Perl has a similar syntax to C. For these reasons, we choose Perl to write scripts. It is free to download and install Perl. If you are new to Perl, you may refer to the appendix or online Perl tutorials for information regarding installation and basic Perl programming.

Let's create the `template` folder under `D:\ArtProgram` and copy

```
mnHornerEval.vcxproj
mnHornerEval.vcxproj.filters
```

to the `template` folder. These two files will be used constantly as our template project files to create a new project. Since the new project files will have the same configurations as the template project files, we can write a Perl script to open `mnHornerEval.vcxproj` as `INFILE` and the destination file with the new function name as `OUTFILE`. We then loop through `INFILE` line-by-line to search for `HornerEval` and replace it by the new function name. In the meantime, we write line-by-line to `OUTFILE`. When it is done, we should have a new `.vcxproj` file in the destination folder that is ready to use. The same procedures apply to the `vcxproj.filters` file. Let us name the Perl script as `getvcproj` and implement it as follows:

```perl
@rem = '
@goto endofperl
';
#Y.M. Li 11/10/2012
# Modify the template vcproj file to be used for specified program


if ($ARGV[0] eq "")
{
    print "Error: cmmond line argument is empty.\n";
    print "Usage: getvcproj <function name>\n";
    die;
}

# Copy and modify vcxproj template
$template = "D:\\ArtProgram\\template\\mnHornerEval.vcxproj";
open(INFILE, "$template") || die "Cannot open $$template\n";

open(OUTFILE, ">mn$ARGV[0].vcxproj") || die "Cannot open mn$ARGV[0]\n";
```

```perl
foreach $line (<INFILE>) # For each line in INFILE
{
  # Check if $line contains "HornerEval".
  # If so, replace it by new function name
  if ($line =~ /HornerEval/)
  {
    $line =~ s/HornerEval/$ARGV[0]/g;
  }
  print OUTFILE "$line";
}
close(INFILE);
close(OUTFILE);

# Copy and modify vcxproj.filters template
$template = "D:\\ArtProgram\\template\\mnHornerEval.vcxproj.filters";
open(INFILE, "$template") || die "Cannot open $$template\n";

open(OUTFILE,">mn$ARGV[0].vcxproj.filters") || die "Can't open file\n";

foreach $line (<INFILE>)
{
  if ($line =~ /HornerEval/)
  {
    # When found, replace HornerEval by new function name
    $line =~ s/HornerEval/$ARGV[0]/g;
  }
  print OUTFILE "$line";
}
close(INFILE);
close(OUTFILE);

__END__
:endofperl
@perl -S %0.cmd %1
```

The above scripts are self-explanatory with a few exceptions. The new function name is brought in via the first command-line argument $ARGV[0], which is similar to C/C++ main (more detail in next section). The statements goto endofperl and perl -S %0.cmd %1 may not be found in most Perl script books and online examples. Here, the goal is to save Perl scripts in D:\ArtProgram\bin and be able to invoke them from any directory. As is known, the Windows command prompt will search through the Environment Variable "PATH" for executables, DLLs, and Windows scripts such as .bat and .cmd files. If a Perl script is saved in D:\ArtProgram\bin with the default suffix .pl and the current working folder is not bin, the command prompt will not be able to find it. Hence, we have to invoke it with the full path such as

```
D:\ArtProgram\test>perl D:\ArtProgram\bin\filename.pl
```

To avoid typing the full path, we write the above Perl script that is compatible with both Windows script and Perl. Save it in `D:\ArtProgram\bin` as `getvcproj.cmd` and type the following at the command line:

`D:\ArtProgram\test>getvcproj BinarySearch`

We will see that the following ready-to-use project files have been created in the current destination folder `test`:

`mnBinarySearch.vcxproj`
`mnBinarySearch.vcxproj.filters`

In the software industry, our work is not only to create new functions but also to fix bugs and/or to improve the existing functionality. In this case, we would like to create XML-based project files and copy existing source, driver, input and output data files to the current working directory with dedicated scripts. For this reason, we will write a few more scripting tools.

The following batch file (`getsrcfl.bat`) copies a named source file to the current directory:

```
@echo off
rem  getsrcfl.bat copies a source file to current directory.
rem  Y.M. Li  11/10/2012

if "%1" == "" goto help

if exist D:\ArtProgram\src\api%1.cpp goto copy
echo *** No api%1.cpp found.
goto end

:copy
echo Copy api%1.cpp from D:\ArtProgram\src ...
copy D:\ArtProgram\src\api%1.cpp .
goto end

:help
echo "Usage: getsrcfl <filename>"

:end
```

We can similarly create `getmnfl.bat` and `getdofl.bat` to copy a specific main driver, input, and output files to the current directory. Finally, we write the `getafl.bat` batch file to call each script to copy the named source, main driver, input, and output files to the current directory and also to create the ready-to-use XML project files:

```
@echo off
rem  getafl.bat copies source, driver, data, output, and vcxproj files
rem  Y.M. Li   11/10/2012
```

```
if "%1" == "" goto help

call getsrcfl %1
call getmnfl %1
call getdofl %1
call getvcproj %1
goto end

:help
echo "Usage: getafl <filename>"

:end
```

To see how these scripts work together to improve productivity, let us delete everything in D:\ArtProgram\test and type the following at the command line:

D:\ArtProgram\test>getafl StrokeCircle

Consequently, we should see the following files in the test folder:

```
apiStrokeCircle.cpp
mnStrokeCircle.cpp
mnStrokeCircle.vcxproj
mnStrokeCircle.vcxproj.filters
StrokeCircle.d1
```

Let's start Visual Studio and click File->Open->Project/Solution and then browse and open mnStrokeCircle.vcxproj. Alternatively, we can browse the folder via Windows Explorer to locate and double-click mnStrokeCircle.vcxproj to start Visual Studio. We will see that

```
apiStrokeCircle.cpp
mnStrokeCircle.cpp
```

have been added to the Source Files folder of the Visual C++ project. Furthermore, FunctDLL_d.lib and FunctDLL_r.lib files have been added to the Lib Files folder and all required configuration settings have also been done automatically. We can simply compile the project and run the program.

The scripts we wrote in this section eliminate the tedious work of creating a desired project and hence greatly improves productivity. Imagine if you have to create and maintain several thousands functional programs like I do at work; you would certainly appreciate those productivity tools.

## 4.4   Design flexible drivers

The main driver mnHornerEval.cpp created in the previous chapter opens an input file to read required information. The purpose is to avoid hard-coded data and make the driver flexible to test different cases without modifying the driver. However, this main driver is not flexible enough, as it opens only `HornerEval.d1`. If we want to keep this test case and create a new one, say `HornerEval.d2`, we have to modify the driver to open `HornerEval.d2`. In real world computing, several test cases will usually be created to test different workflows of a new function during the development cycle. This is known as an acceptance or certification test in the software development life cycle. When this new function is released and used by other applications, it is likely that a bug, function limitation, and/or performance issue of this new function will be found. Accordingly, failure incidents will be filed against this new function. When developers investigate these incidents, they will convert the failures into new test cases. Year after year, tens of thousands of test cases will be collected to form a test suite for a specific library (e.g., numerical computing library). It is obvious that a flexible test driver is required to test multiple cases.

Furthermore, it is desirable to be able to clock the execution time of a functional program. To minimize fluctuation of timing, we often need to run the same program multiple times to obtain the accumulative CPU time and then average it. Therefore, there is also a need to design a driver to call the function for specified times. The purpose of this section is to discuss how to make a main driver truly flexible to achieve these two goals without need of repeatedly modifying the main driver.

In many programming languages, the `main` function is where a program starts execution. It is responsible for the high-level organization of the program's functionality (e.g., preparing data to call a function) and typically has access to the command-line arguments when it was executed. The `main` function receives command-line arguments via a *command-line interface* (CLI). It is a means of interacting with a computer program where the user issues commands to the program in the form of successive lines of text at the command line. These successive lines of text are known as the command-line arguments. Although the command-line arguments are usually issued at the command line, they can also be specified and accessed in Microsoft Visual Studio IDE when the program is run under the debugger.

How command-line arguments may help us design a flexible main driver is best understood by an example. Let us copy all files required to build the `mnHornerEval` project to the `test` folder by invoking the script `getalf` at the command line as

`D:\ArtProgram\test>getafl HornerEval`

Open the project and double-click `mnHornerEval.cpp` in the `Source files` folder under `Solution Explorer` to open the main driver source file. We then add two input arguments in the declaration of `main` as shown below:

`int main(int argc, char* argv[])`

The first argument `argc` tells us how many command-line arguments are sending to `main`. This count includes the name of the program itself, so it will always have a value of at least one. The second argument `argv[]` is a pointer array that stores the string name of each command-line argument delimited by white spaces. For example, `argv[0]` contains the name of the program since the program name is always included.

Microsoft Visual Studio IDE allows the user to specify command-line arguments before launching the application for debugging. Let's see how it works: highlight mnHornerEval project at the Solution Explore pane and click the right mouse button to bring up the Configuration Properties window. Next, click Debugging and type command-line arguments "1 1" in the Command Arguments field as shown below:

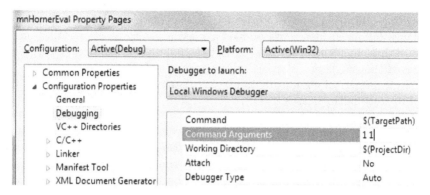

Figure 4.15: Specify command-line arguments

The first "1" is indented to specify that the suffix of test data is 1 and the second "1" is intended to tell the main drive to call apiHornerEval once. To view these command-line arguments in debug, we set a breakpoint at the first statement and press the F5 key to run the program. When the execution stops at the breakpoint, we add argc, argv[0], etc. in the Watch window as shown below:

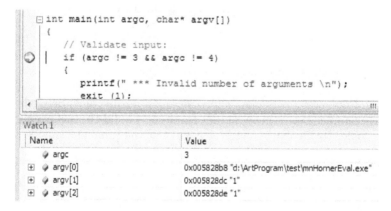

Figure 4.16: View command-line arguments

As seen above, there are three command-line arguments:

argv[0] = D:\ArtProgram\test\mnHornerEval.exe
argv[1] = 1
argv[2] = 1

The above information indicates that we can use command-line arguments to compose the correct file name to open HornerEval.d1, HornerEval.d2, etc. For example, we

extract HornerEval from argv[0] and concatenate it with .d and argv[1] to form
the name of an input data file: HornerEval.d1. We can similarly compose the output
file name HornerEval.n1. The third command-line argument argv[2] tells the main
driver to call testing API repeatedly for a specific number of times, which is useful in
evaluating the performance of this API.

It should be noted that argv[0] stores the name of program (i.e., mnHornerEval)
without path when the executable is invoked from the command line as:

D:\ArtProgram\test>mnHornerEval 1 1

Accordingly, we need two different ways to extract HornerEval from argv[0]. The
improved main driver is listed as follows:

```
#include "MyHeader.h"

int main(int argc, char* argv[])
{
    // Validate input:
    if (argc != 3)
    {
        printf(" *** Invalid number of arguments \n");
        exit (1);
    }

    std::string driverName;

    // Extract the name of program from argv[0]. When running from IGE,
    // argv[0] contains D:\ArtProgram\test\mnHornerEval.exe In this
    // case, we need to remove the full path and the suffix ".exe"
    // Lets set a string pointer to the last backlash
    char *pStr = strrchr(argv[0], '\\');
    if (pStr)
    {
        // Run from Visual Studio. Shift pointer by 3 to delete "\mn"
        pStr += 3;

        // Remove ".exe" that has 4 characters
        std::string tmpStr = pStr;
        driverName = tmpStr.substr(0, tmpStr.length()-4);
    }
    else // if (pStr == NULL)
    {
        // pStr is NULL pointer since argv[0] doesn't have full path
        // when running from DOS. We only need to shit pointer by 2
        // to delete "mn" (note argv[0] doesn't have ".exe")
        pStr = argv[0] + 2;
        driverName = pStr;
    }
```

```cpp
// Compose input and output file names:
std::string inputFileName = driverName + ".d" + argv[1];
std::string outpFileName = driverName + ".n" + argv[1];

// Open input and output files
FILE *infile = NULL, *outfile = NULL;
fopen_s(&infile, inputFileName.c_str(), "r");
if (!infile)
{
   printf(" *** Cannot open %s\n", inputFileName.c_str());
   exit(1);
}

fopen_s(&outfile, outpFileName.c_str(), "w");
if (!outfile)
{
   printf(" *** Cannot open %s\n", outpFileName.c_str());
   exit (1);
}

// Local variables to call the testing function:
int         nIter, nLoops = atoi(argv[2]);
int         i, rc = 0, ndeg = 0;
double      f, x;
double      *pA = NULL;

clock_t     tStart, tFinish;
double      duration;

// Read data from input file
fscanf_s(infile, "%d", &ndeg);
pA = new double[ndeg+1];
if (NULL == pA)
{
   rc = 1;
   goto wrapup;
}

for (i=0; i<=ndeg; i++)
{
   fscanf_s(infile, "%lf", &pA[i]);
}

// Read the variable value
fscanf_s( infile, "%lf", &x);
```

```
    // Invoke the function
    tStart = clock();

    for (nIter=0; nIter < nLoops; nIter++)
    {
        f = apiHornerEval(ndeg, pA, x);

        if (rc)
        {
            printf("*** rc = %d at nIter = %d\n", rc, nIter);
            goto wrapup;
        }
        else if (nIter != nLoops - 1)
        {
            //   If it is not the last iteration, delete memory
            //   that was allocated by the function being called.
            ;
        }
    }

    tFinish = clock();
    duration = (double)(tFinish - tStart) / CLOCKS_PER_SEC;
    printf("\n CPU time = %lf seconds for %d iteration.\n",
                                        duration, nLoops);

    if (rc == 0)
    {
        fprintf(outfile, "f = %.10e\n", f);
    }

wrapup:

    if (pA)
    {
        delete [] pA;
    }
    if (infile)
        fclose(infile);
    if (outfile)
        fclose(outfile);
    return rc;
}
```

With these improvements, this main driver is able to test any data file without modifying the code. For example,

`D:\ArtProgram\test>mnHornerEval 2 1`

indicates running the executable with `HornerEval.d2` once, and

`D:\ArtProgram\test>mnHornerEval 2 1000`

means running the executable with `HornerEval.d2` repeatedly 1,000 times.

When writing a new driver to test a program, we can use this one (or any other similar one) as a template and tailor it to meet a specific requirement. Since it is trivial to implement a new driver based on the template, we shall not discuss it explicitly in subsequent chapters unless it is necessary. However, all main drivers will be available for readers who purchased this book.

## 4.5   Automated regression testing

There are at least three reasons for software developers to modify or rewrite existing functions:

1. Fix defects or bugs reported by customers.

2. Improve the performance.

3. Eliminate the limitation of functionality.

Experience has shown that as software is fixed, emergence of new and/or reemergence of old faults is quite common. Sometimes reemergence occurs because a fix gets lost through poor revision control practices (or simple human error in revision control). Often, a fix for a problem will be "fragile" in that it fixes the problem in the narrow case where it was first observed but not in more general cases which may arise over the lifetime of the software. Frequently, a fix for a problem in one area inadvertently causes a software bug in another area. Reemergence of old faults and/or change of program behavior are known as software *regression*. To prevent regression from happening, it is considered good software development practice, when a bug is located and fixed, to record a test that exposes the bug and to rerun that unit test and a full test suite regularly after subsequent changes to the program. Software regression testing is an important and critical part of the software development process, on which the quality and reliability of the delivered product strictly depend. Testing is not limited to the detection of bugs in the software but also increases confidence in its proper functioning and assists with the evaluation of functional and nonfunctional properties.

Although regression testing may be done through manual testing procedures, it is often done using automated testing tools in software houses. There are many commercially-available testing software packages such as Rational Visual Test, QuickTest Professional, and Testing Anywhere. These packages are automated testing software designed for testing various software applications and environments. They perform functional and regression testing through a user interface such as a native GUI or web interface. For testing numerical methods, we do not have to rely on a third party testing software. In this section, we will explore how to design and implement very effective testing tools for engineering and scientific computations.

In the previous section, we learned how to design a flexible driver that reads input data from a named file and calls the corresponding API to generate an output. For the purpose of regression testing, we need to save the output as the "baseline" (or predicted outcome) and use it to compare the new output in the next run. If all results match our saved baseline results, we have confidence in believing that our changes have not caused a regression.

When calling, for example, `apiHornerEval` with the test case `HornerEval.d1`, the main driver saves the output result in `HornerEval.n1`, where .n denotes a new result. If it is the first time running the test, we rename it as `HornerEval.o1` with .o standing for an old result. All .o files will be saved in `D:\ArtProgram\outp` as the baseline results. When running `apiHornerEval` again in the future, we compare `HornerEval.n1` with the saved `HornerEval.o1`. If there is no difference or if the differences are less than the specified tolerance, `HornerEval.n1` will be discarded. Otherwise, it will be kept for investigation.

So, how do we compare the results? In this book, we are primarily concerned with engineering and scientific computations. The output results are usually numerical numbers. However, texts are often printed out with numbers to make numerical numbers meaningful. For example, we print

```
f = 8.4800000000e+002
```

in `HornerEval.n1` and

```
key index = 18
```

in `BinarySearch.n1`. Accordingly, it is the so-called *alphanumeric* string when reading line-by-line from a text file. It is not trivial to extract numerical numbers properly from an alphanumeric string. A big part of this section is dedicated to describing how to design and implement a program to extract numerical numbers and compare them with a specified tolerance. Let's name this program `mydiff`. The first thing `mydiff` needs to do is to open two text files (e.g., `testdata.o1` and `testdata.n1`) specified by command-line arguments. It then reads line-by-line from both files and checks whether the two alphanumeric strings match exactly. If the two strings do not match, they will be split into two collections of sub-strings based on the specified *separators* for further comparison. The separators used in this program are the equality sign, parentheses (or round brackets), colon, and empty space. Given an alphanumeric string, the desired splitting function will search from the first character to the last to find separators and split the string there. For example, the following alphanumeric string

```
key index = 18
```

has an empty space and the equality sign as separators and thus will be split into three sub-strings: "key," "index," and "18." The program `mydiff` then checks whether a sub-string from one collection matches the corresponding sub-string from another collection. It should be noted that the sub-string consisting of numerical numbers is first converted to `double` and then compared with respect to the given tolerance. If any pair of sub-strings do not match, the program prints either a warning at the command

prompt or the detailed differences to a named file for reviewing, depending on the
option passed into `mydiff`.

The program `mydiff` will be implemented in C/C++ rather than Perl for performance,
since we may have output files that contain tens of thousands of lines. The program
`mydiff` takes five command-line arguments to meet the desired requirements and is
called with the following syntax:

```
mydiff <filename> <file-number> <detail> <precision-digit>
```

The usages of the last four arguments are explained below:

- `filename` specifies the name of two files to be compared.

- `file-number` is combined with `filename` to form a full name.  Assume that
  `filename` is HornerEval and `file-number` is 2.  Then the combined full names
  would be `HornerEval.o2` and `HornerEval.n2`.  In other words, these two files
  will be opened by `mydiff` for comparison.

- `detail` is a boolean flag to indicate whether line-by-line differences need to be
  documented for later investigation.

- `precision-digit` is used to derive the tolerance to compare two **doubles**.  If
  `precision-digit` is 10, for example, then the tolerance is $10^{-10}$.

With the described requirements in mind, it is easier to understand the following
implementation of `mydiff`:

```
/*------------------------------------------------------------------
Name
    mydiff

Abstract
    It is called by mntest.cmd and showdiff.cmd to check/display
    differences between old and new results.

Usage
    mydiff <filename> <file-number> <detail> <precision-digit>
    (e.g., mydiff HornerEval 1 TRUE 12)

    - filename:    name of o & n files to be compared (e.g. HornerEval)
    - file-number: 1 - compare HornerEval.n1 with HornerEval.o1
                   2 - compare HornerEval.n2 with HornerEval.o2
                     ...
    - detail:      TRUE if we want to print differences to named file
    - precision-digit: the number of digits to be matched.

History
    Y.M. Li     02/15/2013 : Creation date.
------------------------------------------------------------------*/
```

```cpp
#include <direct.h>
#include <sstream>
#include <vector>
using namespace std;

// This function splits alphanumeric string into sub-strings.
// Standard STL string methods are used to achieve the goal.
static void myStrSplit(string& str, string& separators,
                                    vector<string>& subStrs)
{
    // Find the start position of non-separator string
    string::size_type i_beg = str.find_first_not_of(separators,0);

    // Find end position of non-separator string
    string::size_type i_end = str.find_first_of(separators, i_beg);

    while (string::npos != i_end || string::npos != i_beg)
    {
        // Extract non-separator string and store in subStrs
        subStrs.push_back(str.substr(i_beg, i_end - i_beg));

        // Continue to find start position of non-separator string
        i_beg = str.find_first_not_of(separators, i_end);

        // Continue to find end position of non-separator string
        i_end = str.find_first_of(separators, i_beg);
    }
} // End of myStrSplit


// This function compares two alphanumeric strings by splitting
// them into sub-string, then comparing sub-string pair-by-pair
static bool isTwoAlphanumericSame(char *str1, char *str2, double tol)
{
    int      i, n;
    double   a, b;
    string   separators = "=,(,),:, ";
    string   myStr1(str1), myStr2(str2);
    vector<string> subStrs1, subStrs2;

    // Split two strings with given separators
    myStrSplit(myStr1, separators, subStrs1);
    myStrSplit(myStr2, separators, subStrs2);
    if (subStrs1.size() != subStrs2.size())
        return false;

    // We have the same number of sub-strings.
```

```cpp
    // Loop through each to check equality
    n = (int)subStrs1.size();
    for (i=0; i<n; i++)
    {
        // Save sub-string in an istringstream object so
        // that we can parse the string to decimal number
        istringstream iStr1(subStrs1[i]);
        istringstream iStr2(subStrs2[i]);
        if (iStr1 >> a)
        {
            // This sub-string is decimal number
            if (iStr2 >> b)
            {
                if (fabs(a - b) > tol)
                    return false;
            }
            else
            {
                return false;
            }
        }
        else if (subStrs1[i] != subStrs2[i])
        {
            return false;
        }
    }

    return true;
} // End of isTwoAlphanumericSame


int main(int argc, char* argv[])
{
    int     nline, result_match;
    double  tol;
    char    str_i[_MAX_PATH], str_j[_MAX_PATH];
    FILE    *ofile=NULL, *nfile=NULL, *detail_file=NULL;

    string  dirname, dtFileName, nFileName, oFileName;

    // Five command line arguments are expected. They are:
    // mydiff <filename> <numerical-sufix> <detail> <precision-digits>
    if (argc != 5)
    {
        printf("\t *** Invalid input arguments.\n\n");
        exit(1);
    }
```

```cpp
// Setup tolerance to compare two doubles
if (isdigit(argv[4][0]))
{
   std::string tmpStr = "1.0e-";
   tmpStr += argv[4];
   tol = atof(tmpStr.c_str());
}
else
{
   tol = 1.0e-10;
}

// Get the path and name of current working directory
if (_getcwd(str_i, _MAX_PATH) == NULL)
   exit(1);
dirname = str_i;
dirname += "\\";

// Compose the file name and open the named n file:
nFileName = dirname + argv[1] + ".n" +  argv[2];
fopen_s(&nfile, nFileName.c_str(), "r");
if (!nfile)
{
   printf("\t *** Cannot open %s.\n\n", nFileName.c_str());
   exit(1);
}

// Compose the file name and open the named baseline file:
oFileName = dirname + argv[1] + ".o" + argv[2];
fopen_s(&ofile, oFileName.c_str(), "r");
if (!ofile)
{
   // If no o file, move the n file to o file
   _fcloseall();
   rename(nFileName.c_str(), oFileName.c_str());
   printf("\n");
   return 0;
}

// Check if we need to open a file to which
// the detailed differences will be printed
if (strcmp(argv[3], "TRUE") == 0)
{
   dtFileName = dirname + argv[1] + "_d.txt";
   fopen_s(&detail_file, dtFileName.c_str(), "w");
   if (!detail_file)
```

```
        exit(1);
}


// Let's check line-by-line whether two files are same
nline = 0;
result_match = 1;
fgets(str_i, _MAX_PATH, nfile);
fgets(str_j, _MAX_PATH, ofile);
while(!feof(nfile) && !feof(ofile))
{
    nline++;
    if (0 != strcmp(str_i, str_j))
    {
        // Two strings do not match. Do complex comparison:
        if (!isTwoAlphanumericSame(str_i, str_j, tol))
        {
            result_match = 0;
            if (detail_file)
            {
                fprintf(detail_file, "\nLine %d:\n", nline);
                fprintf(detail_file, "new: %s", str_i);
                fprintf(detail_file, "old: %s", str_j);
            }
            else
            {
                printf("\t *** Results differ from previous ones.\n\n");
                break;
            }
        }
    }

    fgets(str_i, _MAX_PATH, nfile);
    fgets(str_j, _MAX_PATH, ofile);
}

// We need to check if we have reached the end of both files
if (feof(nfile) != feof(ofile))
{
    if (detail_file)
        fprintf(detail_file, "\n *** File sizes are different.\n");
    else
        printf("\t *** File sizes are different.\n");
    _fcloseall();
}
else
{
    _fcloseall();
```

```
    if (result_match)
    {
        // Since results match, discard these files:
        if (dtFileName.c_str())
            remove(dtFileName.c_str());
        remove(nFileName.c_str());
        printf("\t Results match previous ones.\n");
    }
}

return 0;
}
```

Compile the above program in release mode for optimized performance and copy `mydiff.exe` to `D:\ArtProgram\bin` so that it can be accessed from any directory. Necessary comments were added to the above implementation to help readers understand the code. Even so, it is still a challenge for unexperienced C/C++ programmers. It is recommended to run the above program in debug mode with pre-saved `.o` and `.n` files in the `D:\ArtProgram\mydiff` folder. Set a breakpoint at the entry of **main** and execute the program step-by-step by pressing **F10** repeatedly. It helps you understand the code by watching the variables when moving the execution from one statement to another.

It is fine to run **mydiff.exe** at the command line to compare the named `.o` and `.n` files as

`D:\ArtProgram\mydiff>mydiff testdata 1 TRUE 10`

However, it is more convenient to call **mydiff** implicitly by scripts when executing an application API or when examining the differences between existing `.o` and `.n` files. We will first look at how to write a script to run an executable and compare the output result with the saved baseline result. With our flexible main driver design, we can run an executable at the command line with a specific data file. For example,

`D:\ArtProgram\test>mnHornerEval 1 1`

indicates running **mnHornerEval.exe** with `HornerEval.d1` once. Assume that we have collected 100 data files to test **mnHornerEval.exe**. It would be painful to repeatedly type the following at the command line to run all 100 test cases.

`D:\ArtProgram\test>mnHornerEval 1 1`
`D:\ArtProgram\test>mnHornerEval 2 1`
$\vdots$
`D:\ArtProgram\test>mnHornerEval 100 1`

This kind of tedious manual work is more productively handled by a Perl script that runs the application API and calls **mydiff** to check whether `.o` and `.n` files match with the default tolerance. Recall that `.o` files are our baseline results and `.n` files are new results generated when running an executable. Assume that this Perl script is named **mntest.cmd**. We wish to invoke it at the command prompt with the following syntax:

```
mntest <filename> <file-range> <iteration number>
```

The usages of the last three arguments are explained below:

- `filename` specifies the name of the testing file.

- `file-range` may be a number, number range, or character 'a'. If it is a number, it is combined with `filename` to form the unique test file name. For example, 1 is combined with `HornerEval` to indicate that the executable is run with `HornerEval.d1`. If it is a number range, e.g., 1-2, then the executable is run with `HornerEval.d1` and `HornerEval.d2`. If it is the character 'a,' then the executable is run with all available test cases.

- `iteration number` indicates how many times the executable needs to be called. This is useful in evaluating the performance of the program.

With these tasks in mind, the implementation of `mntest.cmd` is readily understood:

```
@rem = '
@goto endofperl
';

if ($ARGV[0] eq "" || $ARGV[1] eq "" || $ARGV[2] eq "")
{
    print "\nUsage: mntest <name of routine><which data file> <loop>\n";
    print "Example 1: mntest HornerEval 1 1 - run 1st data file once\n";
    print "Example 2: mntest HornerEval 1-2 1 - run data file 1 & 2\n";
    print "Example 3: mntest HornerEval a 10 - run all data 10 times\n";
    die "\n";
}

$i0 = $i1 = 0;
$name = $ARGV[0];
$name =~ tr/A-Z/a-z/;   # make it lower case
$range = $ARGV[1];
$loop = $ARGV[2];
if ($range =~ /-/)
{
    # It comes here only if a range (e.g., 1-20) is specified.
    # Extract the number on the left of "-"
    $rg = $range;
    $temp = chop $rg;
    while ($temp ne "-")
    {
        $temp = chop $rg;
    }
    $i0 = $rg;

    # Extract the number on the right of "-"
    $rg = reverse $range;
```

```perl
    $temp = chop $rg;
    while ($temp ne "-")
    {
        $temp = chop $rg;
    }
    $i1 = reverse $rg;
}
elsif ($range eq "a")
{
    # It comes here only if "a" is given as range.
    # Count how many *.d files to determine the range
    system "dir/b $name.d* > num_test_file.txt";
    open(INFILE, "num_test_file.txt") || die "Can't open file.\n";
    $i0 = 1;
    $i1 = 0;
    foreach $file (<INFILE>)
    {
        # Check if filename matches $name.d by ignoring the case
        if ($file =~ /$name.d/i)
        {
            $i1 += 1;
        }
    }
    close(INFILE);
    unlink("num_test_file.txt");
}
else
{
    $i0 = $i1 = $range;
}

for ($i=$i0; $i <= $i1; $i++)
{
    #make sure this data file exists
    if ( -e "$ARGV[0].d$i")
    {
        print "\n Processing data file $ARGV[0].d$i ...\n";
        system "call mn$ARGV[0] $i $loop";
        system "mydiff $ARGV[0] $i FALSE 10";
    }
}

__END__
:endofperl
@perl -S %0.cmd %1 %2 %3
```

Save this Perl script as `mntest.cmd` in `D:\ArtProgram\bin`. Invoking this script at the command line gives:

```
D:\ArtProgram\test>mntest HornerEval a 1

 Processing data file HornerEval.d1 ...

CPU time = 0.000000 seconds for 1 iteration.
        Results match previous ones.

 Processing data file HornerEval.d2 ...

CPU time = 0.000000 seconds for 1 iteration.
        Results match previous ones.
```

To see how it catches regression, let's modify apiHornerEval.cpp to declare $f$ as float and compile it. Invoking mntest script at the command line gives

```
D:\ArtProgram\test>mntest HornerEval a 1

 Processing data file HornerEval.d1 ...

CPU time = 0.000000 seconds for 1 iteration.
        *** Results differ from previous ones.


 Processing data file HornerEval.d2 ...

CPU time = 0.000000 seconds for 1 iteration.
        *** Results differ from previous ones.
```

Whenever there is a difference, the corresponding .n file is kept for investigation. It is possible to use windiff (a graphical file-comparison program published by Microsoft) or other programs to examine the differences. However, these third party programs may not be flexible enough to perform the desired comparison tasks. For example, the differences were caught with respect to the tolerance $10^{-10}$. When investigating the differences, we would like to know if these differences can go away with respect to a coarser tolerance (e.g., $10^{-6}$). The program mydiff is an ideal comparison tool, as it was designed to compare a pair of data files with a specified tolerance. To compare multiple pairs of data files, we will need a script program to loop though each pair. Let us name this script program showdiff.cmd. It takes two command-line arguments – filename and precision-digit – that, in turn, are passed to mydiff.exe. The main tasks of showdiff.cmd include:

- Create temp_n.txt that constrains all undeleted .n* files in the current working folder. This is done via the DOS redirection operator ">" as

  dir /b filename.n* > temp_n.txt

- For each recorded .n filename in temp_n.txt, extract the file number to call

  mydiff <filename> <file-number> TRUE <precision-digit>

  Recall that the TRUE flag indicates that the differences will be printed to a file named filename_d.txt.

- If differences exist with respect to the specified precision, the subfunction inside
  showdiff will display the differences written to filename_d.txt by mydiff and
  ask the user whether he or she wants to fix the differences.

Again, keeping these tasks in mind helps understand the following implementation of
showdiff.cmd:

```
@rem = '
@goto endofperl
';

#  Syntax:  showdiff <filename> <precision-digit>
if ($ARGV[0] eq "" || $ARGV[1] eq "")
{
    print "\nInvalid. Syntax: showdiff <filename> <precision-digit>\n";
    die "\n";
}

# Create a temporary file that contains all named n files
$filename = @ARGV[0];
system "dir/b $filename.n* > temp_n.txt";
open(INFILE, "temp_n.txt") || die "Cannot open temp_n.txt\n";

# Compare each n file with corresponding o file
foreach $Line (<INFILE>)
{
    if ($Line =~ /$filename/)
    {
        # Remove newline symbol
        chop $Line;

        # Extract the file number (e.g., extract 2 from HornerEval.n2)
        $num = chop $Line;
        $temp = chop $Line;
        while ($temp ne "n")
        {
            $num = "$temp$num";
            $temp = chop $Line;
        }

        print "\nComparing $filename.n$num with $filename.o$num ...\n";
        system "mydiff $ARGV[0] $num TRUE @ARGV[1]";
        $nfile = "$filename.n$num";
        if (-e $nfile)
        {
            HandleDiff(@_=($filename, $num));
        }
        else
```

```perl
        {
            print "\t Moving $nfile to $filename.o$num\n";
        }

        # Removed file created by mydiff containing difference details
        $dfile = "$filename\_d.txt";
        if (-e $dfile)
        {
            unlink($dfile);
        }
    }
}
close(INFILE);
unlink("temp_n.txt");


# This subroutine display differences line-by-line on screen
# and prompt users with option to fix differences.
sub HandleDiff
{
    local($filename, $num) = @_;
    $nfile = "$filename.n$num";
    $ofile = "$filename.o$num";
    $dfile = "$filename\_d.txt";

    open(DETAIL, "$dfile") || die "No difference files found.\n";
    $ncount = 0;
    foreach $Line (<DETAIL>)
    {
        print $Line;
        $ncount += 1;
        if ($ncount == 60)
        {
            print "Continue? (y/n)-> ";
            $answer = <STDIN>;
            if ($answer =~ "y" || $answer =~ "Y")
            {
                $ncount = 0;
            }
            else
            {
                last;
            }
        }
    }

    print "fix n-file? (y/n)-> ";
```

```
    $answer = <STDIN>;
    if ($answer =~ "y" || $answer =~ "Y")
    {
        print "moving $nfile -> $ofile\n";
        unlink $ofile;
        @command = 'rename $nfile $ofile';
    }

    close(DETAIL);
}


__END__
:endofperl
@perl -S %0.cmd %1 %2
```

The implementation is lengthy but mostly self-explanatory. Recall that we modified the declaration of $f$ in apiHornerEval.cpp from double to float, which resulted in differences. These differences can be viewed by running the Perl script we just wrote at the command prompt:

```
D:\ArtProgram\test>showdiff HornerEval 10

Comparing HornerEval.n1 with HornerEval.o1 ...

Line 1:
new: f = 1.047829589843750e+003
old: f = 1.047829559470038e+003
fix n-file? (y/n)-> n

Comparing HornerEval.n2 with HornerEval.o2 ...

Line 1:
new: f = 5.187295675277710e-001
old: f = 5.187294043770239e-001
fix n-file? (y/n)-> n
```

The command-line argument "10" indicates that the precision tolerance is $10^{-10}$. If we use "5," the new and old results match with respect to the coarser tolerance $10^{-5}$. Therefore, all .n files will be discarded as shown below:

```
D:\ArtProgram\test>showdiff HornerEval 5

Comparing HornerEval.n1 with HornerEval.o1 ...
        Results match previous ones.
        Discarding HornerEval.n1.

Comparing HornerEval.n2 with HornerEval.o2 ...
        Results match previous ones.
        Discarding HornerEval.n2.
```

In this section, we discussed the importance of regression testing and implemented several tools to perform regression testing automatically. These tools are practical and cost-effective for catching regressions. The implementations of `mydiff.cpp`, `mntest.cmd`, and `showdiff.cmd` are lengthy and may not be readily understood by beginners. A good way to understand the implementation of these tools is to play with these tools on a few cases by altering the code as we did in this section.

## 4.6　Automated suite testing

The Perl script `mntest.cmd`, in conjunction with `mydiff.exe` and `showdiff`, provides a convenient way to run a named executable for functional and regression testing. However, `mntest.cmd` is of little help if we want to run a *test suite*, or a collection of test cases of all numerical methods. It is often the case that one numerical method is called by many other methods to complete complex computations. For example, `apiHornerEval` will be repeatedly called by the Netwon iteration method for root-finding of a polynomial equation (see chapter 8 for detail). Testing `apiHornerEval` alone may not guarantee that the Netwon iteration method still works correctly. Therefore, it is important to run the test suite whenever there is a change in any function.

In the previous section, we wrote `mntest.cmd` to perform a unit test. It works only if the executable for that unit test (e.g., `mnHornerEval.exe`) has been created prior to the test. If all executables have been created and saved somewhere, it is possible to write a script program to call `mntest.cmd` repeatedly with different function names to perform an automated suite test. Obviously, this approach requires all executables to be saved in advance and is thus less flexible. A better approach is to compile a main driver on the fly to create an `.obj` file of the driver and then link it with the DLL library to form an executable by the dedicate script before calling `mntest`. The executable is discarded after it completes the test. Our task in this section is to write two more scripting programs to run the test suite automatically.

Up until now, we have depended on Microsoft Visual Studio IDE to compile a project and create an executable. This is, of course, not the only way. Any C/C++ source file can actually be compiled at the command line via Microsoft's C/C++ compiler `cl.exe` as follows:

```
D:\ArtProgram\test>cl simple.cpp
```

If `simple.cpp` is a stand-alone application, the `cl.exe` compiler generates an executable program `simple.exe`. In our case, all main drivers depend on the DLL library to run. We thus need to compile each main driver without a link to obtain an object file (i.e., `.obj` file), then link the object file with the DLL library to create an executable. Furthermore, we want the compiling options to closely match the settings imposed in Visual Studio IDE. For these reasons, we write the following batch file `lnkrunmn.bat` to perform the compiling, linking, and invoking the executable:

```
@echo off

cd D:\ArtProgram\mnexe
```

```
copy D:\ArtProgram\mn\mn%1.cpp .
copy D:\ArtProgram\data\%1.d* .
copy D:\ArtProgram\outp\%1.o* .

cl  /nologo /c /MD /EHsc /O2 /I D:\ArtProgram\include mn%1.cpp

link /nologo /OUT:mn%1.exe mn%1.obj D:\ArtProgram\lib\FunctDLL_r.lib

if errorlevel 1 goto end

if exist D:\ArtProgram\outp\%1.n* del /q D:\ArtProgram\outp\%1.n*

call mntest %1 a 1

if exist %1.n* copy %1.n* D:\ArtProgram\outp\
del /q *%1*

:end
```

This script takes one command-line argument (denoted by %1) that contains the name of main driver without the prefix mn. As is seen, it copies the main driver and all input and baseline output files to the directory D:\ArtProgram\mnexe. The statement

```
cl  /nologo /c /MD /EHsc /O2 /I D:\ArtProgram\include mn%1.cpp
```

invokes the cl.exe compiler to compile the named main driver with options that match our settings in Visual Studio IDE. These options are:

- /nologo Suppresses display of copyright and sign-on banner.

- /c Compiles without linking.

- /MD Creates a multithreaded DLL.

- /EHsc Instructs the compiler to enable C++ exception handling.

- /O2 Creates fast and optimized code.

- /I Searches a directory for include files.

The statement

```
link /nologo /OUT:mn%1.exe mn%1.obj D:\ArtProgram\lib\FunctDLL_r.lib
```

calls the linker (i.e., link.exe) to link the object file with the release DLL and output an executable with the specified name. When this statement is done, we should have an executable in the folder. Therefore, the next statement

```
call mntest %1 a 1
```

runs the executable with all testing cases for the named function. If there are .n files left in the directory, differences must have occurred. The next-to-last statement is to copy all named .n files to outp folders for investigation. Finally, the last statement cleans out all copied files in the current directory.

Running the script at the command line performs a series of tasks as shown below:

```
D:\ArtProgram\mnexe>lnkrunmn HornerEval
        1 file(s) copied.
D:\ArtProgram\data\HornerEval.d1
D:\ArtProgram\data\HornerEval.d2
        2 file(s) copied.
D:\ArtProgram\outp\HornerEval.o1
D:\ArtProgram\outp\HornerEval.o2
        2 file(s) copied.
mnHornerEval.cpp

 Processing data file HornerEval.d1 ...

CPU time = 0.000000 seconds for 1 iteration.
        Results match previous ones.

 Processing data file HornerEval.d2 ...

CPU time = 0.000000 seconds for 1 iteration.
        Results match previous ones.
```

With this newly created batch file, it is then trivial to write a Perl script to loop through each source file in either src or mn folders and call lnkrunmn.bat to run all the tests automatically. We name this Perl script program lnkrunall.cmd and implement it as follows:

```
@rem = '
@goto endofperl
';

$dirname = "D:\\ArtProgram\\src";
opendir(DIR, $dirname) || die "Cannot find $dirname\n";
@files = readdir(DIR);

foreach $file (@files)
{
    if ($file =~ /\.cpp/)
    {
        $file =~ s/\.cpp//;  # Remove .cpp
        $file = reverse $file;  # To remove prefix "api"
        chop $file;
        chop $file;
        chop $file;
```

```
        $file = reverse $file;
        system ("lnkrunmn $file");
    }
}

close(DIR);

__END__
:endofperl
@perl -S %0.cmd %1 %2 %3 %4 %5 %6 %7 %8 %9
```

Recall that `lnkrunmn.bat` cleans all files in current directory upon completion. It is thus recommended to create the empty testing folder D:\ArtProgram\mnexe and invoke `lnkrunall.cmd` from there. All exiting APIs will be executed in alphabetical order as follows:

```
D:\ArtProgram\mnexe\lnkrunall

Processing data file BinarySearch.d1 ...

CPU time = 0.000000 seconds for 1 iteration.
        Results match previous ones.

 Processing data file BinarySearch.d2 ...

CPU time = 0.000000 seconds for 1 iteration.
        Results match previous ones.
        1 file(s) copied.

Processing data file HornerEval.d1 ...

CPU time = 0.000000 seconds for 1 iteration.
        Results match previous ones.

 Processing data file HornerEval.d2 ...

CPU time = 0.000000 seconds for 1 iteration.
        Results match previous ones.

Processing data file StrokeCircle.d1 ...

CPU time = 0.000000 seconds for 1 iteration.
        Results match previous ones.

    ⋮
```

As seen above, a full test suite is executed by running a single script at the command line. Therefore, it is possible to arrange the Windows scheduler to run the test suite overnight so that any regression will be caught daily. To do so, you must be logged on as an administrator to perform the following steps:

1. Open Task Scheduler by clicking the `Start` button, clicking `Control Panel`, clicking `System and Security`, clicking `Administrative Tools`, and then double-clicking `Task Scheduler`. If you're prompted for an administrator password or confirmation, type the password or provide confirmation.

2. Click the `Action` menu, and then click `Create Basic Task`.

3. Type a name for the task (e.g., TestSuite) and an optional description (e.g., Test Suite for Numerical Methods), and then click Next.

4. Setup a schedule by clicking `Daily` and then click `Next`.

5. Specify the time for the program to start (e.g., 9:00PM), check the `Start a program` radio button, and then click `Next`.

6. Click `Browse` to find the script program `lnkrunall.cmd`, and then click `Next`.

7. Click `Finish`.

It is also possible to start Test Scheduler by typing `Taskschd.msc` at the command prompt or `Run` command via the `Start` button. It should be noted that the `Run` command is not available by default in Windows 7 but can be restored.

## 4.7   Summary

Software engineering is concerned with developing and maintaining software systems that are reliable and reusable. Instead of giving a broad perspective about software engineering and the software development process, this chapter focused on essential elements and techniques that are required to develop a numerical computing software system. In particular, creation and use of a dynamic-link library, script tools to improve productivity, and automated regression testing were discussed in detail in this chapter.

A dynamic-link library is a module that contains functions and data that can be used by another module (application or DLL). DLLs provide a way to modularize applications so that their functionality can be updated and reused more easily. Dynamic linking has the following advantages over static linking:

- Multiple processes that load the same DLL at the same base address share a single copy of the DLL in physical memory. Doing this saves system memory and reduces swapping.

- When the functions in a DLL change, the applications that use them do not need to be recompiled or relinked as long as the function arguments, calling conventions, and return values do not change. In contrast, statically linked object code requires that the application be relinked when the functions change.

- A DLL can provide after-market support. For example, a display driver DLL can be modified to support a display that was not available when the application was initially shipped.

- Programs written in different programming languages can call the same DLL function as long as the programs follow the same calling convention that the function uses. The calling convention (such as C, Pascal, or standard call) controls the order in which the calling function must push the arguments onto the stack, whether the function or the calling function is responsible for cleaning up the stack, and whether any arguments are passed in registers.

Working in software companies, developers deal with DLLs, *load-time dynamic linking*, and *run-time dynamic link* daily. Unfortunately, information about DLLs is often missing in introductory C/C++ programming text books. No wonder so many computer science graduates I interviewed had little knowledge about dynamic-link libraries. This chapter started with the creation of a dynamic-link library. Examples were given to show how main drivers were compiled and linked with a DLL to create executables. Readers will have a chance to see how the DLL developed in this book is used to create a windows-based application for data visualization and manipulation. In this book, both the debug and release DLLs are copied to `D:\ArtProgram\bin`. In practice, DLLs may be copied to any directory as far as this directory is listed in the `PATH` environment variable.

Back to the early 1980s, it was common for developers to use text editors such as `Emacs` (developed at the MIT AI Lab during 1970s) to implement programs. Nowadays, professional developers rely on software development kits such as Microsoft Visual Studio's integrated development environment to write programs. These development kits usually have a rich collection of tools, templates, and documents that allow programmers to develop applications with ease and productivity. Under Visual Studio IDE, for example, we can move the mouse cursor to a particular function and click the right mouse button to invoke the following context menu.

Figure 4.17: Context menu that exposes functionality

By selecting a different entry, we can find where this function was declared and where it was called. In order to take this and many other advantages, we have to develop our application under Microsoft Visual Studio IDE with proper configuration settings. As was demonstrated in this chapter, this could be a tedious process. Therefore, we discussed

how to write Perl scripts to modify XML based `.vsxproj` and `.vcxproj.filters`
template files to make our life much easier in developing a new function.

Software testing is very important. A primary purpose of testing is to detect software
failures so that defects may be discovered and corrected. When new functions are
developed, either developers or certification personnel will create collections of data
to test these new functions. Depending on availability, they may deploy professional
testing packages to analyze whether their data sets have covered all work flows – a
process known as dynamic software coverage profiling. Testing can never completely
identify all the defects within software. Therefore, we will receive bug or problem
reports from either internal or external customers. These problems are then converted
to our test cases. Year after year, we eventually build a large collection of data that
is used for regression testing. There are many commercially-available testing software
packages such as Rational Visual Test, QuickTest Professional, and Testing Anywhere.
These packages are automated testing software designed for testing various software
applications and environments. They perform functional and regression testing through
a user interface such as a native GUI or web interface. For engineering and scientific
computation, our end results are often numerical numbers. In this case, our low cost,
and yet very effective, tools developed in this chapter are ideal to perform functional
and regression testing automatically.

The software development process and associated techniques discussed in this chapter
not only reflect what I do at work but also serve as the protocol and standard in this
book for developing numerical methods in subsequent chapters.

# Chapter 5

# Recursive Algorithm

A recursive algorithm is an algorithm that calls *itself*. Many problems are solvable by a type of algorithm that reduces the original problem into several smaller problems of exactly the same nature. These subproblems can be further reduced by applying the same algorithm *recursively* until they become simple enough to solve. A recursive algorithm can be implemented most naturally by a recursive function that usually consists of

1. **Termination condition**: Always begin a recursive function with a termination condition to prevent it from performing infinite recursions. The termination condition usually checks if a problem is already simple enough to solve. If so, solve it and exit.

2. **Reduction of problem to subproblems**: In this part, the problem is broken down into smaller problems of the same nature. Each is solved by a recursive call to the function itself with reduced size or complexity.

3. **Recombination of solutions**: In some cases, the results from each recursion will need to be combined to form the final result.

Recursive functions are concise and easy to implement once we recognize the recursive nature of problems. Though concise, elegant, and powerful, a recursive function saves neither storage nor execution time. In fact, it usually consumes more memory and degrades the performance due to the overhead of maintaining the stack for many levels of nested function calls. But the logic behind the recursion algorithm provides a problem-solving mechanism unparalleled by other methods. Many seemingly complicated problems can be solved easily with a recursive approach. Because of the advantages of problem-solving power and simplicity in implementation, the recursive algorithm is a preferred, powerful problem-solving tool in developing numerical methods.

## 5.1 Beauty of recursive algorithm

A binary search algorithm was studied in chapter 3 and was implemented via the `while` loop. Given an array of sorted data, we started by comparing the element in the middle

117

of the sorted array. If this key is larger than the middle number, the left half of the
elements is discarded. Otherwise, the right half of the elements is discarded. This
process is repeated until the key is found. By nature this is a recursion and can be
implemented by the recursive function as shown below:

```
/*-----------------------------------------------------------------
API Name
    apiBinarySearch

Description
    It finds the key in a sorted array and returns the index of array

Signature
    int apiBinarySearch(int key, int *pIntArray,
            int i_beg, int i_end, apiError &rc)

    INPUT:
      key           the specific integer to be found in integer array
      pIntArray     pointer to the integer array
      i_beg         starting index of the array
      i_end         ending index of the array
    OUTPUT:
      rc            error code: api_OK if no error

History

    Y.M. Li     03/10/2013 : Creation date
-----------------------------------------------------------------*/
#include "MyHeader.h"

int apiBinarySearch(int key, int *pIntArray,
        int i_beg, int i_end, apiError &rc)
{
    int i_mid = (i_beg + i_end) / 2;

    // Terminate condition
    if (pIntArray[i_mid] == key)
        return i_mid;
    if (i_beg >= i_end)
    {
        rc = api_INVALIDARG; // key is not in the array
        return -1;
    }

    // Reduce the complexity of problem via recursion
    if (pIntArray[i_mid] > key)
        return apiBinarySearch(key, pIntArray, i_beg, i_mid - 1, rc);
    else
```

```
        return apiBinarySearch(key, pIntArray, i_mid + 1, i_end, rc);
}
```

In comparison with the non-recursive implementation, the above recursive function is very concise and reflects our design analysis very well. However, it is not as efficient as the non-recursive counterpart we implemented previously. In the next section, we shall discuss why a recursive function usually takes more storage and time to complete the work than its non-recursive counterpart.

If you are not convinced of how powerful the recursive method is, consider the well-known *Tower of Hanoi* puzzle. It is said that monks in Hanoi spent their time moving disks to and from three poles marked by A, B, and C as shown below. These disks are different in size. In the beginning, all of the disks are stacked on pole A, with the smallest on top. The goal of the puzzle is to move all of the disks to pole C whilst obeying the following rules:

- Only one disk may be moved at a time, and this disk has to be the top disk on the given pole.

- A disk must be moved from one pole to another pole directly. It cannot be placed somewhere else.

- No disk may be placed on top of a smaller disk.

With three disks, the puzzle can be solved in seven moves:

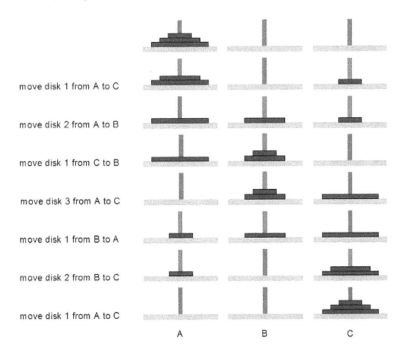

move disk 1 from A to C

move disk 2 from A to B

move disk 1 from C to B

move disk 3 from A to C

move disk 1 from B to A

move disk 2 from B to C

move disk 1 from A to C

A      B      C

Figure 5.1: Tower of Hanoi

For $n$ disks it requires $2^n - 1$ moves to solve the puzzle. When $n$ increases, we soon find that the problem becomes increasingly harder with no discernable pattern or rule to follow. Fortunately, the puzzle becomes very easy if we think about it recursively. A key to solving this puzzle is to recognize that it can be solved by breaking the problem down into a collection of smaller problems and further breaking those problems down into even smaller problems until a solution is reached. Referring to the above illustration, it is noted that all seven movements can be divided into three steps:

1. Move two discs from A to B through C in $2^2 - 1 = 3$ steps. When completed, only disc 3 (the largest one) remains on pole A.

2. Move disc 3 (the largest one) from A to C. This requires just 1 step.

3. Move two discs from B to C through A in again $2^2 - 1 = 3$ steps.

In total, $2(2^2 - 1) + 1 = 2^3 - 1 = 7$ movements are required. We can generalize it to $n$ disks. Let us number the discs from 1 (the smallest and topmost) to $n$ (the largest and bottommost). To move n discs from pole A to pole C:

1. Recursively move $n - 1$ discs from A to B through C. This can be done in $2^{n-1} - 1$ steps. When completed, only disc $n$ (the largest one) remains on pole A.

2. Move disc $n$ (the largest one) from A to C. This requires just 1 step.

3. Recursively move $n - 1$ discs from B to C through A so they sit on disc $n$. Again, $2^{n-1} - 1$ steps are required.

The total required movements are $2(2^{n-1} - 1) + 1 = 2^n - 1$, and the implementation is given below.

```
#include "MyHeader.h"

static void HanoiTower(int n, char *pA, char *pB, char *pC)
{
    if (n == 1)
    {
        // Terminate condition
        printf("Move disk 1 from %s to %s\n", pA, pC);
        return;
    }

    // Step 1
    HanoiTower(n-1, pA, pC, pB);

    // Step 2
    printf("Move disk %d from %s to %s\n", n, pA, pC);

    // Step 3
    HanoiTower(n-1, pB, pA, pC);
}
```

```
void main(void)
{
    int   n = 0;

    while (n <= 0)
    {
        printf("\nHow many disks to move --> ");
        scanf_s("%d", &n);
        if (n <= 0)
            printf("\nError: The number has to be larger than zero.\n");
    }

    HanoiTower(n, "A", "B", "C");
}
```

Compiling and running the above program at the command line gives

```
D:\ArtProgram\test>mnHanoiTower

How many disks to move --> 4
Move disk 1 from A to B
Move disk 2 from A to C
Move disk 1 from B to C
Move disk 3 from A to B
Move disk 1 from C to A
Move disk 2 from C to B
Move disk 1 from A to B
Move disk 4 from A to C
Move disk 1 from B to C
Move disk 2 from B to A
Move disk 1 from C to A
Move disk 3 from B to C
Move disk 1 from A to B
Move disk 2 from A to C
Move disk 1 from B to C
```

One can verify the correctness of the results by following the above instructions to move four disks.

Moving disks from one pole to another through an intermediate pole is an exponential algorithm. When the number of disks increases, it can become a computational bottleneck even for a modern computer, not to mention the poor monks in Hanoi. Assume that our computer can perform $2^{30}$ operations per second. The time required to move $n$ disks increases exponentially as shown:

| Operations: | $2^{30}$ | $2^{36}$ | $2^{42}$ | $2^{48}$ | $2^{54}$ |
|---|---|---|---|---|---|
| Time: | 1 sec | 1 min | 1 hour | 3 days | 6 months |

## 5.2   Bisection method

The bisection method in mathematics is a root-finding method that repeatedly bisects an interval and then selects a subinterval in which a root must lie for further processing. Assume that $f$ is a continuous function on an interval $[a, b]$ and that $f(a) \times f(b) < 0$. By the *intermediate value theorem*, there must exist at least one solution $x$ in $[a, b]$ such that $f(x) = 0$ as illustrated below.

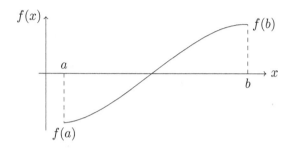

Figure 5.2: Illustration of the intermediate value theorem

To find the solution numerically, we start by selecting $c = (a + b)/2$ at the middle of the interval $[a, b]$ and compute $f(c)$. If $|f(c)| < \varepsilon$, $c$ is the root of function $f$. Otherwise, we reduce the interval in half using the following criterion:

```
if (f(a) * f(c) < 0.0)
{
    b = c;
}
else
{
    a = c;
}
```

We repeat this process based on the reduced interval until $|f(c)| < \varepsilon$. This is very similar to the binary search algorithm we just covered and can be implemented by a recursive function. As an example, we consider finding a root of the polynomial

$$f(x) = \sum_{i=0}^{n} a_i x^i$$

at the interval $[a, b]$. The recursive implementation is

```
/*-----------------------------------------------------------
API Name
    apiBisection

Description
    It finds the root of polynomial function in the interval [a, b].
```

Signature
```
   double apiBisection(int ndeg, double *pA,
             double a, double b, double tol)
```

```
   INPUT:
      ndeg          degree of polynomial
      pA            pointer to the array of polynomial coefficients
      a, b          defines the interval where the root is
      tol           convergency tolerance
   OUTPUT:
      return the root of polynomial
```

History

   Y.M. Li     03/10/2013 : Creation date
------------------------------------------------------------------*/
```c
#include "MyHeader.h"

double apiBisection(int ndeg, double *pA,
          double a, double b, double tol)
{
   double f_a, f_b, f_mid, x_mid;

   // Terminate condition
   x_mid = 0.5 * (a + b);
   apiHornerEval(ndeg, pA, x_mid, f_mid);
   if (fabs(f_mid) < tol)
      return x_mid;

   // Recuce the complexity via recursion
   apiHornerEval(ndeg, pA, a, f_a);
   apiHornerEval(ndeg, pA, b, f_b);
   if (f_a * f_mid < 0.0)
      return apiBisection(ndeg, pA, a, x_mid, tol);
   else if (f_a * f_mid > 0.0)
      return apiBisection(ndeg, pA, x_mid, b, tol);
   else
      return api_INCONSISTENT;
}
```

The following cubic polynomial is used to test the above program:

$$f(x) = x^3 - 5x^2 - 2x + 10.$$

Given $a = 1.0$, $b = 3.0$, and tol $= 10^{-10}$, it takes 37 recursions to reach the required accuracy as indicated below.

```
x = 1.414213562369696e+000 and f(x) = 3.447553353908006e-011
```

The bisection method is very simple and robust, but it is relatively slow (linear convergency). Because of this, it is often used to obtain a rough approximation to a solution which is then used as a starting point for more rapidly converging methods such as Newton's method.

As was said at beginning of this chapter, a recursive function usually consumes more stack memory and takes more CPU time to complete than its non-recursive counterpart due to the overhead of maintaining many levels of call stacks. In computer science, a *call stack* is a stack data structure that keeps track of the point to which each active function should return control when it finishes executing. An *active function* is one that has been called but has yet to complete execution. Since a function may be called from different places (e.g., recursive calls), the call stack needs to include at least the following information:

- Function's return address.

- Function parameters.

- Local variables inside the function at each level of recursion.

For observation, let's set a break point at the termination **return x_mid** and run the test case via the Visual C++ debugger. As is seen, the input parameters for each level of recursion is recorded in call stacks (To display the **Call Stack** window, click **Debug** from the menu bar, then select **Windows->Call Stack**).

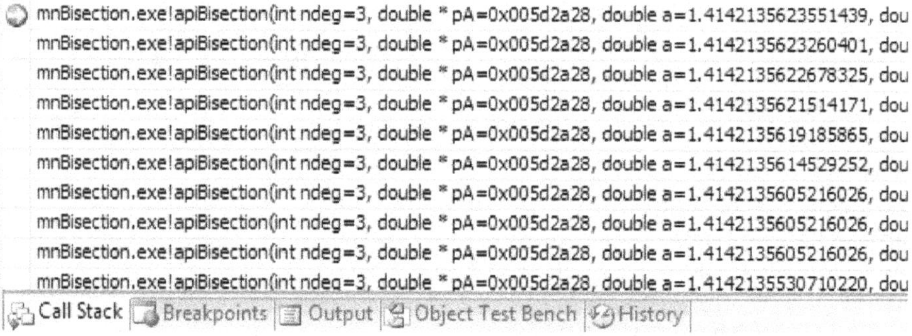

```
  mnBisection.exe!apiBisection(int ndeg=3, double * pA=0x005d2a28, double a=1.4142135623551439, dou
  mnBisection.exe!apiBisection(int ndeg=3, double * pA=0x005d2a28, double a=1.4142135623260401, dou
  mnBisection.exe!apiBisection(int ndeg=3, double * pA=0x005d2a28, double a=1.4142135622678325, dou
  mnBisection.exe!apiBisection(int ndeg=3, double * pA=0x005d2a28, double a=1.4142135621514171, dou
  mnBisection.exe!apiBisection(int ndeg=3, double * pA=0x005d2a28, double a=1.4142135619185865, dou
  mnBisection.exe!apiBisection(int ndeg=3, double * pA=0x005d2a28, double a=1.4142135614529252, dou
  mnBisection.exe!apiBisection(int ndeg=3, double * pA=0x005d2a28, double a=1.4142135605216026, dou
  mnBisection.exe!apiBisection(int ndeg=3, double * pA=0x005d2a28, double a=1.4142135605216026, dou
  mnBisection.exe!apiBisection(int ndeg=3, double * pA=0x005d2a28, double a=1.4142135605216026, dou
  mnBisection.exe!apiBisection(int ndeg=3, double * pA=0x005d2a28, double a=1.4142135530710220, dou
 Call Stack   Breakpoints   Output   Object Test Bench   History
```

Figure 5.3: Recursion call stack

Clicking each recursion level, we will see that all values of local variables are available, indicating they have been stored for retrieval. For performance, all needed information is stored in *stack memory* instead of *heap memory* . In most programming languages, the stack space available to a thread is much less than the space available in the heap, and recursive algorithms tend to require more stack space than iterative algorithms. For this reason, we have to be very careful in using local array variables, as they grow in recursions and may consume the available stack memory. When a program attempts to use more space than is available on the call stack, the stack is said to be *overflow* , which typically resulting in a program crash. To see how this may happen, let's open **Bisection.dl** and change the tolerance to **1.0e-15** and run the program under Visual Studio IDE. Roughly at the $3356^{th}$ recursion, we will see the following exception dialog:

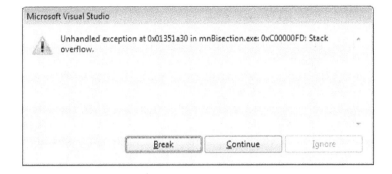

Figure 5.4: Deep recursion causes stack overflow

The size of available stack depends on many factors, including the programming language, machine architecture, multi-threading, and amount of available memory. In the Visual Studio development environment, it is possible to change the default stack size by specifying *reserve* and/or *commit* values. The reserve value specifies the total stack allocation in virtual memory. For x86 and x64 machines, the default stack size is 1 MB. On the Itanium chipset, the default size is 4 MB. The commit value is subject to interpretation by the operating system. In Windows NT and Windows 2000, it specifies the amount of physical memory to allocate at a time. Committed virtual memory causes space to be reserved in the paging file. A higher commit value saves time when the application needs more stack space but increases the memory requirements and possibly the startup time. For x86 and x64 machines, the default commit value is 4 KB. On the Itanium chipset, the default value is 16 KB. To change the default size, let us bring up the project's **Property Pages** by selecting **Linker->System** under **Configuration Properties**. We then type the desired size in bytes in either the **Stack Commit Size** or **Stack Reserve Size** field as shown below, which will change respectively the total stack allocation size in physical or virtual memory

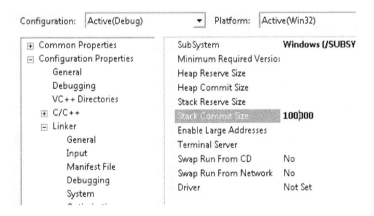

Figure 5.5: Modification of default stack memory size

It is also possible to change the stack size of an executable at command prompt as

```
>editbin/STACK:100000 filename.exe
```

which changes the stack memory size to 10 MB. The bisection method discussed here has only linear convergency speed. By increasing the reserved stack memory size to, for example, 500 MB, the recursion will go deeper to 16,334 before stack overflow. It should be noted that stack overflow is preventable in this case if we also check the subdivided interval $[a, b]$ and terminate the recursion when the subinterval is less than a certain tolerance (e.g., the machine epsilon). We purposely left the algorithm unprotected so that readers can experiment with committed/reserved stack size. In practice, the bisection method is rarely used to find the accurate result, as it has only linear convergency speed. It is often used to find a reasonably good approximation of the true solution, then a faster converging algorithm is used to refine the solution. This will be discussed in chapter 8. It should also be pointed out that a higher committed/reserved value increases the memory requirements and possibly startup time.

## 5.3   Numerical integration

In this section, we discuss how a recursive algorithm can be used for creating and traversing a binary tree implicitly and dynamically. The example here is to compute a definite integral numerically. In particular, we will see how to apply the numerical integration technique to compute the arc length of a curve.

Let $f$ be a smooth function on $[a, b]$ (i.e., $f$ has a continuous first derivative everywhere on $[a, b]$). We wish to compute a definite integral

$$\int_a^b f(t)\, dt.$$

If there exists a function $F(t)$ such that $F'(t) = f(t)$, then the definite integral is given by the relation

$$\int_a^b f(t)\, dt = F(b) - F(a).$$

In practice, it is often the case that we cannot find $F$, so that we have to use a numerical method to compute an approximate solution to the definite integral. For completeness, we will briefly review a *quadrature formula* used for numerical integration. It has the following form:

$$\int_a^b f(t)\, dt \simeq \sum_{i=0}^n A_i f(t_i) \qquad (5.3.1)$$

where $A_0, A_1, \cdots, A_n$ are known as the *weights*. In plain English, the quadrature formula is a weighted sum of function values at specified points within the domain of integration. The summation approximates the definite integral of a function.

The formal study of the quadrature method usually begins with an approximation of $f$ by an interpolation polynomial since integration of a polynomial is easy. If we choose

$t_0, t_1, \cdots, t_n$ from the interval $[a, b]$, the Lagrange interpolating polynomial of degree at most $n$ is given by

$$P_n(t) = \sum_{i=0}^{n} f(t_i)L_i(t),$$

where $L_i(t)$ is the $i$th Lagrange interpolating polynomial

$$L_i(t) = \prod_{k=0, k\neq i}^{n} \frac{(t - t_k)}{(t_i - t_k)} = \frac{(t - t_0)\cdots(t - t_{i-1})(t - t_{i+1})\cdots(t - t_n)}{(t_i - t_0)\cdots(t_i - t_{i-1})(t_i - t_{i+1})\cdots(t_i - t_n)}.$$

Since $L_i(t_i) = 1$, it is readily seen that $P_n(t_i) = f(t_i)$ for $i = 0, 1\cdots, n$. Consequently, $P_n(t)$ interpolates $f(t)$ at $t_i$. If $f$ is approximated by $P_n(t)$, the truncation error is

$$\frac{f^{(n+1)}(\xi(t))}{(n+1)!}(t - t_0)(t - t_1)\cdots(t - t_n) = \frac{f^{(n+1)}(\xi(t))}{(n+1)!}\prod_{k=0}^{n}(t - t_k).$$

Accordingly, the integration of $f$ may be obtained by

$$\int_a^b f(t)dt = \int_a^b \sum_{i=0}^{n} f(t_i)L_i(t)dt + \int_a^b \prod_{k=0}^{n}(t - t_k)\frac{f^{(n+1)}(\xi(t))}{(n+1)!}dt$$

$$= \sum_{i=0}^{n} A_i f(t_i) + \int_a^b \prod_{k=0}^{n}(t - t_k)\frac{f^{(n+1)}(\xi(t))}{(n+1)!}dt$$

where $A_i = \int_a^b L_i(t)dt$. By ignoring the truncation error, we obtain the quadrature formula (5.3.1). It is noted that integration (5.3.1) is exact if $f(t)$ is a polynomial of degree equal to or less than $n$ since $f^{(n+1)}(\xi(t)) = 0$. From this fact, we have an alternative and simpler way to determine the coefficients $A_i$ by taking $f(t)$ to be monomials $1, t, t^2, \cdots, t^n$ so as to obtain $n+1$ linear equations with $n+1$ unknowns $A_i$:

$$\sum_{i=0}^{n} A_i t_i^n = \int_a^b t^k dt = \frac{1}{k+1}(b^{k+1} - a^{k+1}), \qquad (k = 0, 1, \cdots, n).$$

Accordingly, $A_0, A_1, \cdots, A_n$ are obtained by solving a system of linear equations. It is noted that computation of $A_i$ is independent of $f(t)$. Therefore, $A_i$ can be computed in advance and saved in the coefficient table. As an example, let $n = 2$ and take $t_0 = a, t_1 = (a + b)/2, t_2 = b$. We thus have

$$b - a = A_0 + A_1 + A_2$$

$$\frac{1}{2}(b^2 - a^2) = A_0 a + A_1 \left(\frac{a + b}{2}\right) + A_2 b$$

$$\frac{1}{3}(b^3 - a^3) = A_0 a^2 + A_1 \left(\frac{a + b}{2}\right)^2 + A_2 b^2$$

Solving the above system of linear equations gives

$$A_0 = \frac{1}{6}(b - a),$$

$$A_1 = \frac{2}{3}(b - a),$$

$$A_2 = \frac{1}{6}(b - a).$$

The integration formula

$$\int_a^b f(t)dt \simeq \frac{b - a}{6}\left( f(a) + 4f\left(\frac{b+a}{2}\right) + f(b)\right)$$

is known as the *Simpsion's three-point rule* .

For simplicity, $t_i$ is chosen to be evenly spaced. The corresponding quadrature rule is known as the *Newton-Cotes formula*. If $t_i$ is not equally spaced, is it possible for the integration rule given in (5.3.1) to have the greatest degree of precision? From the theorem of *Gaussian quadrature*, the answer is yes! It states that the quadrature formula (5.3.1) is exact for any polynomial $f(x)$ with degree up to $2n - 1$ if and only if $t_i \in [a, b]$ is chosen to be the roots of an orthogonal polynomial of degree $n$. The proof of Gaussian Theorem can be found in many numerical analysis text books.

Among the family of classical and well-studied orthogonal polynomials (e.g., Chebyshev and Legendre polynomials ), it is the simplest to choose $t_i$ as the roots of the Legendre polynomial and the corresponding quadrature method is usually known as *Gauss-Legendre quadrature.*

A *Legendre polynomial* of degree $n$ is given by

$$P_n(t) = \frac{1}{2^n n!}\frac{d^n}{dt^n}\left[(t^2 - 1)^n\right].$$

An important property of the Legendre polynomials is that they are *orthogonal* with respect to the inner product on the interval $[-1, 1]$., i.e.,

$$\int_{-1}^{+1} P_m(t)P_n(t)dt = 0 \quad \text{if} \quad m \neq n.$$

Legendre polynomials can also be defined by the following recursive rule:

$$P_0(t) = 1,$$
$$P_1(t) = t,$$
$$nP_n(t) = (2n - 1)tP_{n-1}(t) - (n - 1)P_{n-2}(t).$$

The roots of these polynomials are in general not analytically solvable, so they have to be computed numerically. In the case of classical orthogonal polynomials, the roots are practically known and readily available online. However, the published roots may not have enough decimal precision. If required, we can refine them by, for example, Newton-Raphson iteration.

Legendre polynomials are orthogonal on the interval $[-1, 1]$. If the integrand $f(t)$ is defined over an arbitrary interval $[a, b]$ rather than $[-1, 1]$, we may reparametrize $f$ by

$$t(u) = \frac{b-a}{2}u + \frac{a+b}{2}$$

such that $u \in [-1, 1]$. It is readily checked that $t = a$ and $b$ if $u = -1$ and $1$ respectively. This permits the Gaussian-Legendre quadrature to be applied to any interval $[a, b]$ since

$$\int_a^b f(t)dt = \frac{b-a}{2} \int_{-1}^1 f(t(u))du = \frac{b-a}{2} \sum_{i=1}^n A_i f(t(u_i)).$$

It should be noted that summation starts with $i = 1$, which is different from (5.3.1). This is because we have chosen $t_i$ to be the the $n$ roots of the Legendre polynomial of degree $n$ as opposed to $n + 1$ evenly spaced points for (5.3.1).

We now consider the determination of $A_i$ for the Gauss-Legendre quadrature. Since the roots of the Legendre polynomial of degree $n$ are known, we can similarly take $f(t)$ to be monomials $1, t, t^2, \cdots$ and form $n$ linear equations. Solving this system of linear equations gives all $A_i$ $(i = 1, 2, \cdots, n)$. Again, we do not have to compute $A_i$ since they are also readily available online.

Assume that we have the roots of a Legendre polynomial of degree $n$ and the associated weights $A_i$. The procedure to compute a definite integral

$$\int_a^b f(t)\, dt$$

by Gauss-Legendre quadrature is outlined below:

1. Obtain the roots of Legendre polynomial of degree $n$ and store them in an array, say, roots.

2. For each Legendre root,

   (a) Reparametrize it by $t = \dfrac{b-a}{2} \times \text{roots}[i] + \dfrac{a+b}{2}$, noting that Legendre roots are defined in $[-1, 1]$.

   (b) Evaluate $f(t)$ and store it in an array, say, functs.

3. Get $A_i$ $(i = 1, \cdots, n)$ and compute dValue$= \displaystyle\sum_{i=1}^n A_i \times \text{functs}[i]$.

4. Compute dValue $= \dfrac{b-a}{2} \times$ dValue.

Readers may ask how to choose $n$ to obtain a result that converges to the true integral. It is possible to estimate $n$ based on the given tolerance when the upper bound of $f^{(2n)}(t)$ (i.e., order $2n$ derivative) is known. It is, however, impractical for two reasons: difficult to estimate the upper bound and the actual error may be much less than a bound established by the derivative. In practice, we take one of the following two approaches:

- Choose $n = 4, 6, \cdots$ to compute the integration $\int_a^b f(t)\, dt$ until the absolute difference of two subsequent results is less than the tolerance (some books use a relative difference to compare). Obviously, this approach requires a large table to store the roots of Legendre polynomials of degree $4, 6, \cdots$ and the corresponding weights $A_i$. There is an additional reason why we do not want to choose a very large $n$. It is known that Gauss-Legendre quadrature has twice the order of accuracy as the Newton-Cotes formula when $f(t)$ is a polynomial. If $f$ is not a polynomial, "high order" is not the same as high accuracy. High order translates to high accuracy only when the integrand is very smooth, in the sense of being well-approximated by a polynomial.

- Choose two fixed $n$ (e.g., $n = 8$ and $n = 10$) to compute $\int_a^b f(t)\, dt$. If the absolute difference of the two results is less than the tolerance, our work is done. Otherwise, we bisect the interval and compute the definite integrals on the left and right intervals. This subdivision process may need to be repeated several times until the convergence criterion is reached. Every time we bisect the interval, the graph of the subdivided function becomes flatter and hence can be better approximated by polynomials. In an extreme case, $f$ is approximated by a collection of line segments when the recursions go deep enough (recall the discussion associated with circle stroking algorithm). It is obvious that subdivided intervals form a binary tree. Tree traversal here will be naturally described by recursion in which case the deferred nodes are stored implicitly in the call stack.

The second approach is preferred since it does not require a large collection of the roots of Legendre polynomials of different degrees. Furthermore, it is at least as efficient as the first approach. In our implementation, we save the roots of Legendre polynomials of degree 8 and 10 in dLdgRoots and corresponding weights in dGaussLdgWts. It should be pointed out that the Gauss-Legendre weights are symmetric and positive. Accordingly, we save only half of them in dGaussLdgWts. Both static arrays dLdgRoots and dGaussLdgWts are declared and initialized in MyHeader.h as follows

```
static double dLgdRoots[18] = {
-0.9602898564975362316835609,
-0.796666477413626739591553 9,
-0.525532409916328985817739 0,
-0.183434642495649804939476 1,
0.183434642495649804939476 1,
0.525532409916328985817739 0,
0.796666477413626739591553 9,
0.960289856497536231683560 9,
```

```
-0.97390652851717172007799640,
-0.86506336668898451073209967,
-0.67940956829990244062343274,
-0.43339539412924719079926599,
-0.14887433898816312108848260,
 0.14887433898816312108848260,
 0.43339539412924719079926599,
 0.67940956829990244062343274,
 0.86506336668898451073209967,
 0.97390652851717172007799640
};

static double dGaussLdgWts[9] = {
0.10122853629037625915255314,
0.22238103445337447054435560,
0.31370664587788728723793622,
0.36268378337836198296515504,

0.06667134430868818137593568,
0.14945134915058059314577633,
0.21908636251598204399553493,
0.26926671930999635509122699,
0.29552422471475287017389300
};
```

*Static variables* are variables that have been allocated statically and whose lifetime extends across the entire run of the program. Both static arrays contain two sets of roots and weights. To access each set of information correctly, we need to provide an API to return the correct entry address of static memory, depending on whether callers want 8 or 10 Legendre roots and corresponding weights. API `apiGetGaussLdgRtWts` is implemented for this purpose:

```
/*--------------------------------------------------------------
API Name
    apiGetGaussLdgRtWts

Description
    It returns the proper addresses of Legendre roots and the
    Gauss-Legendre quadrature weights, depending on n=8 or 10.
    It is noted that pointers are passed in and out via the
    passing-by-reference mechanism.

Signature
    void apiGetGaussLdgRtWts(int n, double *&pRoots,
                        double *&pA, apiError &rc)

    INPUT:
```

```
     n            number of required Legendre roots
OUTPUT:
     pRoots       pointer to the roots of Legendre polynomial
     rc           error code: api_OK if no error
     pA           pointer to the Gauss-Legendre weights
```

```
History

     Y.M. Li      03/10/2013 : Creation date
-------------------------------------------------------------------*/
#include "MyHeader.h"

void apiGetGaussLdgRtWts(int n, double *&pRoots,
                         double *&pA, apiError &rc)
{
    rc = api_OK;
    if (n == 8)
    {
        pRoots = dLgdRoots;
        pA = dGaussLdgWts;
    }
    else if (n == 10)
    {
        pRoots = dLgdRoots + 8;
        pA = dGaussLdgWts + 4;
    }
    else
    {
        rc = api_INVALIDARG;
    }
}
```

As an example, we implement a program to compute the length of the following planar curve on the interval $[\frac{1}{2}, 2]$:

$$f(x) = \frac{x^3}{6} + \frac{1}{2x}.$$

In calculus, it is taught that the arc length of $f(x)$ is

$$s = \int_a^b \sqrt{1 + f'^2(x)}\, dx.$$

Since

$$f'(x) = \frac{1}{2}\left(x^2 - \frac{1}{x^2}\right),$$

the exact solution of the arc length is:

$$s = \int_{1/2}^2 \sqrt{1 + \left[\frac{1}{2}\left(x^2 - \frac{1}{x^2}\right)\right]^2}\, dx = \frac{1}{2}\left(\frac{x^3}{3} - \frac{1}{x}\right)\Big|_{\frac{1}{2}}^2 = \frac{33}{16} = 2.0625.$$

If it is solved by Gauss-Legendre quadrature, the implementation is

```
/*------------------------------------------------------------
API Name
   apiCurveLength

Description
   It computes the curve (or girth) length of a particular
   function via Gauss-Legendre quadrature.

Signature
   void apiCurveLength(double a, double b, double tol,
                   double &dValue, apiError &rc)

   INPUT:
     a, b      integral interval [a, b]
     tol       convergency tolerance
   OUTPUT:
     dValue    the integral value
     rc        error code: api_OK if no error

History

   Y.M. Li     03/10/2013 : Creation date
-----------------------------------------------------------*/
#include "MyHeader.h"


static double myEval(double x)
{
   double xx, dy;
   xx = x * x;
   dy = 0.5 * (xx - 1.0/xx);
   return sqrt(1.0 + dy * dy);
}

void apiCurveLength(double a, double b, double tol,
                double &dValue, apiError &rc)
{
   int      i, k, n, num_roots[2] = {8, 10};
   double   *pRoots = NULL, *pA = NULL;
   double   alpha, beta, x, d[2], f_i[10];
   double   dLeft, dRight;

   // Compute approximate value at n=8 and 10
   rc = api_OK;
   alpha = (b - a) / 2.0;
   beta =  (a + b) / 2.0;
```

```
    for (k=0; k<2; k++)
    {
        n = num_roots[k];
        apiGetGaussLdgRtWts(n, pRoots, pA, rc);
        if (rc != api_OK)
            goto wrapup;

        d[k] = 0.0;
        for (i=0; i<n; i++)
        {
            x = alpha * pRoots[i] + beta;
            f_i[i] = myEval(x);
        }

        for (i=0; i<n/2; i++)
        {
            d[k] += f_i[i] * pA[i];
            d[k] += f_i[n-1-i] * pA[i];
        }

        d[k] *= alpha;
    }

    // Terminate condition
    if (fabs(d[1] - d[0]) < tol)
    {
        dValue = d[1];
        goto wrapup;
    }

    // Reduce the complexity by halving the interval
    x = 0.5 * (a + b);
    apiCurveLength(a, x, tol, dLeft, rc);
    if (rc != api_OK)
        goto wrapup;
    apiCurveLength(x, b, tol, dRight, rc);
    if (rc != api_OK)
        goto wrapup;

    // Combine the results
    dValue = dLeft + dRight;

wrapup:

    return;
}
```

It is noted that `myEval` is implemented to evaluate the integrand

$$\sqrt{1 + \left[\frac{1}{2}\left(x^2 - \frac{1}{x^2}\right)\right]^2}$$

at the roots of a Legendre polynomial. Except for `myEval`, the above implementation is independent of a particular integrand function. In chapter 7, we shall discuss how to design a reusable code such that the above implementation can be used to solve a generic definite integral.

Let's compile the above program and run it with the tolerance being $10^{-10}$. At the first node whose interval is $[\frac{1}{2}, 2]$, we obtain

```
d[0] = 2.0624996018215116 for n=8
d[1] = 2.0624999938823447 for n=10
fabs(d[1] - d[0]): 3.9206083313203521e-007
```

Since the two results did not converge, we have to subdivide the interval into two sub-intervals, $[\frac{1}{2}, \frac{5}{4}]$ and $[\frac{5}{4}, 2]$, as shown below.

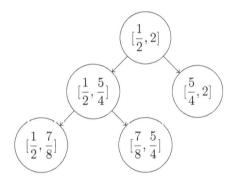

Figure 5.6: Binary tree for bisection

At the node whose interval is $[\frac{1}{2}, \frac{5}{4}]$, we have

```
d[0] = 0.90468749935834947 for n=8
d[1] 0.90468749999795017 for n=10
fabs(d[1] - d[0]): 6.3960070573187977e-010
```

The two results still did not converge. Therefore, the interval is recursively subdivided until converging results are obtained. The final result is obtained by combining results from recursions at the end of program via the statement: `dLength = dLeft + dRight`.

## 5.4  Summary

A common computer programming technique is to divide a problem into subproblems of the same type, solve those problems, and combine the results. This is often referred to as the *divide-and-conquer* method and is the key to the design of many important algorithms. Divide-and-conquer algorithms can be implemented by a non-recursive program that stores the partial sub-problems in some explicit data structure, such as a stack, queue, or priority queue. However, they are more naturally implemented by recursive algorithms. By working on four cases (binary search, Tower of Hanoi, bisection, and computation of definite integral), we have seen how simple to implement and yet very powerful a recursive algorithm is.

Since function parameters and local variables are all stored in call stacks, we need to be very careful about stack overflow. As a rule of thumb, we need to have a proper termination criterion to prevent recursions from going too deep. Local variables are automatic variables stored on the call stack directly. This means that when a recursive function calls itself, local variables in each instance of the function are given distinct addresses. For this reason, we should avoid using arrays as local variables in recursive functions since they may quickly consume all available stack memory and lead to unexpected crashes.

It is true that a recursive implementation is slower than its non-recursive counterpart due to overhead in managing the function call stacks. However, we should not rule it out because of some performance consideration, especially when it greatly reduces the complexity of code and data structure. For example, the implementation of Gauss-Legendre quadrature would need a *last-in-first-out* stack to manage the binary tree nodes that store the sub-intervals if the algorithm is implemented non-recursively.

Gauss-Legendre quadrature is a powerful tool to solve a definite integral problem. It usually converges very quickly if the integrand is a smooth and well-behaved function. The method is not, for example, suitable for functions with singularities. In mathematics, *singularities* are either discontinuities of a function or discontinuities of the derivative. For the purpose of computing the arc length of a curve, a common singularity is a cusp on the curve at which the first derivative is discontinuous. In this case, we can subdivide the curve at the singular point and apply the Gauss-Legendre quadrature to each subdivided curve.

# Chapter 6

# System of Linear Equations

No doubt we have all encountered linear equations many times in high schools and colleges, as well as during our careers as engineers and scientists. The study of a system of linear equations is a fundamental part of linear algebra, a subject which is used in most parts of modern mathematics. Computational algorithms for finding the solutions are an important part of numerical linear algebra and play prominent roles in engineering, physics, chemistry, computer science, and economics.

MATLAB (Matrix Laboratory) is a leading numerical computing environment developed by MathWorks. It started as an interactive program for doing matrix calculations and has now grown to a high-level technical computing language and interactive environment for algorithm development, data visualization, data analysis, and numerical computation. MATLAB has a rich collection of sophisticated functions for solving linear equations. Behind the scenes, they were rewritten to use a newer set of libraries for matrix manipulation, LAPACK (*Linear Algebra Package*). Since MATLAB is taught and widely used in universities worldwide, readers may ask why there is a need to devote a chapter to a system of linear equations. First, without some basic APIs to solve linear equations and eigenvalues and eigenvectors, we would have to eliminate several examples from this book that have practical importance. Secondly, it is often the case that many commercial software companies do not license MATLAB and hence have to develop their own solvers. Even if solutions of linear equations written in C/C++ and other languages are widely available in the *public domain*, software companies usually do not use them to avoid license complication.

While a system of three or four linear equations can be readily solved by hand, numerical methods are often used for larger systems. There are essentially two types of numerical methods:

**Direct method** for solving a system of linear equations is based on Gaussian elimination with some modifications. The Gaussian elimination is widely regarded as a fundamental method for solving a dense, unstructured linear system of equations on a serial computer. It is essential to avoid division by small numbers, which may lead to inaccurate results. This can be done by reordering the equations if necessary – a process known as *pivoting*. With some modifications, the Gaussian elimination method is also used for matrix decomposition.

**Iterative method** starts with an initial estimation to the solution and generates a sequence of new solutions until two adjacent solutions converge. An iterative method is seldom used for solving linear systems of small dimension since the time required for sufficient accuracy exceeds that required for the direct method. For large systems with a high percentage of 0 elements, however, this technique is efficient in terms of both computer storage and computation.

It is beyond the scope of this book to discuss all possible solutions to linear systems. Instead, we will discuss Gaussian elimination without and with pivoting. Gauss-Jordan elimination with full pivoting is also covered since it can be used not only to solve a linear system of equations but also to compute an *inverse matrix*.

The determination of the eigenvalues and eigenvectors of a system is extremely important in physics and engineering. In classical mechanics, for example, moment of inertia is a property of a distribution of mass in space that measures its resistance to rotational acceleration about an axis. The greater its value, the greater the moment required to provide a given acceleration about a fixed axis. For a given coordinate system, moments of inertia form a symmetric matrix called the *inertia matrix* (note that $I_{xy} = I_{yx}$, etc.):

$$\begin{bmatrix} I_{xx} & -I_{xy} & -I_{xz} \\ -I_{yx} & I_{yy} & -I_{yz} \\ -I_{zx} & -I_{zy} & I_{zz} \end{bmatrix}$$

When the coordinate system changes, so do the moments of inertia. It is always possible to find a particular orientation for which products of inertia (i.e., $I_{xy}$, $I_{xz}$, $I_{yz}$, etc.) are all zeros. In other words, the inertia matrix is diagonal. In this case, the three mutually orthogonal coordinate axes are known as *principal axes* and the corresponding moments of inertia are the *principal moments of inertia*. The three planes formed by the principal axes are called *principal planes*. Determination of the principal axes is equivalent to solving an eigenvalue and eigenvector problem.

Computation of eigenvalue and eigenvector (known as the *eigenpair*) is studied in linear algebra and numerical analysis text books. In this chapter, we will briefly review the properties of the eigenpair and present a numerical method to compute the dominant eigenpair. This algorithm will frequently be called by the least squares approximation methods to be discussed in chapter 9.

It should be pointed out that the numerical methods presented in this chapter emphasize on understanding the underlying basics of techniques, not on the refinements that may, in practice, be needed to achieve optimal performance and reliability.

## 6.1   Gaussian elimination without pivoting

Gaussian elimination is considered the workhorse of computational science for the solution of a system of linear equations. It is a systematic application of elementary row operations to a system of linear equations in order to convert the system to the upper *triangular* (or *reduced*) form. Once the coefficient matrix is in the upper triangular form, the unknowns can be solved by a *backward-substitution* process.

Gaussian elimination is best understood by an example. Let's consider a system of three equations

$$
\begin{aligned}
E_1: & \quad x_1 + x_2 + x_3 = 6, \\
E_2: & \quad 4x_2 - x_3 = 5, \\
E_3: & \quad 2x_1 - 2x_2 + x_3 = 1.
\end{aligned}
$$

It is known that elementary row and column operations do not change the final solutions. We first multiply $E_1$ by $-2$ and add $-2E_1$ to $E_3$ to eliminate $x_1$ in $E_3$:

$$
\begin{aligned}
E_1: & \quad x_1 + x_2 + x_3 = 6, \\
E_2: & \quad 4x_2 - x_3 = 5, \\
E_3: & \quad -4x_2 - x_3 = -11.
\end{aligned}
$$

We then add $E_2$ to $E_3$ to further eliminate $x_2$:

$$
\begin{aligned}
E_1: & \quad x_1 + x_2 + x_3 = 6, \\
E_2: & \quad 4x_2 - x_3 = 5, \\
E_3: & \quad -2x_3 = -6.
\end{aligned}
$$

Solutions are thus obtained by the backward-substitution process:

$$
\begin{aligned}
x_3 &= 6/2 = 3, \\
x_2 &= (5 + x_3)/4 = 8/2 = 2, \\
x_1 &= 6 - x_2 - x_3 = 6 - 2 - 3 = 1.
\end{aligned}
$$

The above processes are readily solvable by computer program via elementary row operations on the augmented matrix. An *augmented matrix* is a matrix obtained by appending the columns of two given matrices, usually for the purpose of performing the same elementary row operations on each of the given matrices. Writing the original three equations in the augmented matrix and performing the Gaussian elimination gives

$$
\left[\begin{array}{ccc|c}
1 & 1 & 1 & 6 \\
0 & 4 & -1 & 5 \\
2 & -2 & 1 & 1
\end{array}\right]
\xrightarrow{-2E_1 + E_3}
\left[\begin{array}{ccc|c}
1 & 1 & 1 & 6 \\
0 & 4 & -1 & 5 \\
0 & -4 & -1 & -11
\end{array}\right]
\xrightarrow{E_2 + E_3}
\left[\begin{array}{ccc|c}
1 & 1 & 1 & 6 \\
0 & 4 & -1 & 5 \\
0 & 0 & -2 & -6
\end{array}\right]
$$

As is seen, the matrix now becomes the upper triangular matrix and the unknowns can be solved by backward-substitution.

In general, a system of $n$ linear equations is given by

$$
\begin{bmatrix}
a_{11} & a_{12} & \cdots & a_{1n} \\
a_{21} & a_{22} & \cdots & a_{2n} \\
a_{31} & a_{32} & \cdots & a_{3n} \\
\vdots & \vdots & \ddots & \vdots \\
a_{n1} & a_{n2} & \cdots & a_{nn}
\end{bmatrix}
\begin{bmatrix}
x_1 \\
x_2 \\
x_3 \\
\vdots \\
x_n
\end{bmatrix}
=
\begin{bmatrix}
b_1 \\
b_2 \\
b_3 \\
\vdots \\
b_n
\end{bmatrix}
$$

Writing it in the augmented matrix gives

$$
\left[
\begin{array}{cccc|c}
a_{11} & a_{12} & \cdots & a_{1n} & b_1 \\
a_{21} & a_{22} & \cdots & a_{2n} & b_2 \\
a_{31} & a_{32} & \cdots & a_{3n} & b_3 \\
\vdots & \vdots & \ddots & \vdots & \vdots \\
a_{n1} & a_{n2} & \cdots & a_{nn} & b_n
\end{array}
\right]
$$

We first eliminate $a_{i1}$ with $i = 2, 3, \cdots, n$ by multiplying the first row by $a_{i1}/a_{11}$ and adding the multiplication result to the $i$th row. Consequently, we have

$$
\left[
\begin{array}{cccc|c}
a_{11} & a_{12} & \cdots & a_{1n} & b_1 \\
0 & a_{22}^1 & \cdots & a_{2n}^1 & b_2^1 \\
0 & a_{32}^1 & \cdots & a_{3n}^1 & b_3^1 \\
\vdots & \vdots & \ddots & \vdots & \vdots \\
0 & a_{n2}^1 & \cdots & a_{nn}^1 & b_n^1
\end{array}
\right]
$$

The superscript 1 indicates that the coefficients are modified after level 1 elimination. We repeat a similar process to eliminate all elements in the lower triangle to transform $A$ into the upper triangular form. Finally, we use backward substitution to find the solution of the problem.

In some cases, we would like to solve several problems involving the same coefficient matrix but with different right-hand sides as illustrated below:

$$
\begin{array}{l|l}
x_1 + x_2 + x_3 = 1 & x_1 + x_2 + x_3 = -2 \\
2x_1 - x_2 + 3x_3 = 4 & 2x_1 - x_2 + 3x_3 = 5 \\
3x_1 + 2x_2 - 2x_3 = -2 & 3x_1 + 2x_2 - 2x_3 = 1
\end{array}
$$

Even though the right-hand sides are different, the same coefficient matrix will be manipulated when we apply Gaussian elimination to each system. This observation leads us to write the augmented matrix as follows

$$
\left[
\begin{array}{ccc|cc}
1 & 1 & 1 & 1 & -2 \\
2 & -1 & 3 & 4 & 5 \\
3 & 2 & -2 & -2 & 1
\end{array}
\right]
$$

and implement the Gaussian elimination algorithm to perform elementary row operations simultaneously on each system for efficiency:

```
/*----------------------------------------------------------
API Name
    apiGaussNoPivot

Description
    It solves a linear system via Gaussian elimination without pivoting.

Signature
    void apiGaussNoPivot(
```

```
                    std::vector<vector<double>> &aug_mat, apiError &rc)

   INPUT:
      aug_mat   augment matrix (appending right sides to the matrix)
   OUTPUT:
      aug_mat   right side of the augment matrix stores the solutions

History

   Y.M. Li     03/10/2013 : Creation date
-----------------------------------------------------------------*/
#include "MyHeader.h"

void apiGaussNoPivot(std::vector<vector<double>> &aug_mat,apiError &rc)
{
   int      i, j, k, n_row, n_col;
   double   dMultiplier;

   rc = api_OK;
   n_row = (int)aug_mat.size();
   n_col = (int)aug_mat[0].size();

   // Apply Gaussian eliminations to the augmented matrix so
   // that the matrix becomes the upper triangular matrix
   for (k=0; k<n_row-1; k++)
   {
      if (fabs(aug_mat[k][k]) < zerol_tol)
      {
         rc = api_DIVIDEBYZERO;
         goto wrapup;
      }

      for (i=k+1; i<n_row; i++)
      {
         // Multiply the kth row by the multiplier and add to
         // the ith row to make a[i][k]=0 (i=k+1, k+2, ...)
         dMultiplier = - aug_mat[i][k] / aug_mat[k][k];
         for (j=k; j<n_col; j++)
            aug_mat[i][j] += dMultiplier * aug_mat[k][j];
      }
   }

   // Backward substitution
   for (k=n_row-1; k>=0; k--)
   {
      if (fabs(aug_mat[k][k]) < zero_tol)
      {
```

```
        rc = api_DIVIDEBYZERO;
        goto wrapup;
    }
    for (i=n_row; i<n_col; i++)
    {
        for (j=k+1; j<n_row; j++)
            aug_mat[k][i] -= aug_mat[k][j] * aug_mat[j][i];
        aug_mat[k][i] /= aug_mat[k][k];
    }
}

wrapup:

    return;
}
```

The Gaussian elimination roughly requires $n^3/3$ multiplications and divisions to transform the matrix to an upper triangular matrix and $n(n+1)/2$ multiplications and divisions for backward substitutions. In essence, it is an $O(n^3)$ algorithm.

It is noted that two-dimensional STL vector is used to store the argument matrix whose initialization is done in the main driver as follows:

```
// Local variables to call the testing function:
apiError      rc = api_OK;
int           i, j, n_row, n_col;
vector<vector<double>> aug_mat, aug_mat_save;

fscanf_s(infile, "%d", &n_row);
fscanf_s(infile, "%d", &n_col);
aug_mat_save.resize(n_row);
for (i=0; i<n_row; i++)
    aug_mat_save[i].resize(n_col);

for (i=0; i<n_row; i++)
{
    for (j=0; j<n_col; j++)
        fscanf_s(infile, "%lf",  &aug_mat_save[i][j]);
}

// Invoke the function
tStart = clock();

for (nIter=0; nIter < nLoops; nIter++)
{
    aug_mat = aug_mat_save;
    apiGaussNoPivot(aug_mat, rc);
    if (rc)
```

```
    {
        printf("*** rc = %d at nIter = %d\n", rc, nIter);
        goto wrapup;
    }
    else if (nIter != nLoops - 1)
    {
        //  If it is not the last iteration, delete memory
        //  that was allocated by the function being called.
        ;
    }
}

tFinish = clock();
duration = (double)(tFinish - tStart) / CLOCKS_PER_SEC;
printf("\nCPU time = %lf seconds for %d iteration.\n",
                                    duration, nLoops);

if (rc == api_OK)
{
    for (j=n_row; j<n_col; j++)
    {
        fprintf(outfile, "\n");
        for (i=0; i<n_row; i++)
        {
            fprintf(outfile, "%.10e\n", aug_mat[i][j]);
        }
    }
}
```

## 6.2   Gaussian elimination with partial pivoting

The Gaussian elimination method discussed previously is simple to implement. However, it can be numerically unstable in solving, for example, the following system of linear equations using four-digit arithmetic with rounding

$$E_1 : \qquad 0.001x_1 + 2.000x_2 + 3.000x_3 = 1.000$$
$$E_2 : \qquad -1.000x_1 + 3.712x_2 + 4.623x_3 = 2.000$$
$$E_3 : \qquad -2.000x_1 + 1.072x_2 + 5.643x_3 = 3.000$$

To eliminate $x_1$ from $E_2$ and $E_3$, we need to multiply $E_1$ by $1.000/0.001 = 1000$ and $2.000/0.001 = 2000$; then add to $E_2$ and $E_2$ respectively. Writing the result in the augmented matrix gives

$$\begin{bmatrix} 0.001 & 2.000 & 3.000 & 1.000 \\ 0 & 2004 & 3005 & 1002 \\ 0 & 4001 & 6006 & 2003 \end{bmatrix}$$

We then multiply the second row by $4001/2004 = 1.997$ and add to the third row to eliminate $x_2$

$$\begin{bmatrix} 0.001 & 2.000 & 3.000 & \bigm| & 1.000 \\ 0 & 2004 & 3005 & \bigm| & 1002 \\ 0 & 0 & 5.000 & \bigm| & 2.000 \end{bmatrix}$$

Using the backward substitution, we obtain the solutions

$$x_1 = -0.400, \quad x_2 = -0.0998, \quad x_3 = 0.4000$$

which is very different from the correct solutions:

$$x = (-0.4904, -0.0510, 0.3675)^T.$$

The inaccuracy is caused by dividing a large number by a selected small pivot element 0.001. The disparity in the magnitude of the multiplier has introduced roundoff error, which ruined the approximation of the correct result. The accuracy can be improved if the system is rewritten in the following order:

$$E_1: \qquad -2.000x_1 + 1.072x_2 + 5.643x_3 = 3.000$$
$$E_2: \qquad -1.000x_1 + 3.712x_2 + 4.623x_3 = 2.000$$
$$E_3: \qquad 0.001x_1 + 2.000x_2 + 3.000x_3 = 1.000$$

The new arrangement minimizes the numerical instability incurred by dividing a large number by a small one, which is the idea of Gaussian elimination with pivoting.

The Gaussian elimination with partial pivoting is performed by finding the largest element at the first column. Assume that the largest element appears at $a_{p1}$. We then exchange the first row with the $p$th row so that new $a_{11}$ is the largest at the first column. Next, we multiply the first row by the multiplier $-a_{i1}/a_{11}$ and add to $i$th row to make $a_{i1} = 0$ $(i = 2, 3, \cdots, n)$. This process is repeated for the second, third, $\cdots$, and $n$th column until the matrix is transformed to the upper triangular matrix. The implementation of Gaussian elimination with partial pivoting is listed below:

```
/*------------------------------------------------------------
API Name
   apiGaussPPivot

Description
   It solves a linear system via Gaussian elimination
   with partial pivoting.

Signature
   void apiGaussPPivot(
               std::vector<vector<double>> &aug_mat, apiError &rc)

   INPUT:
       aug_mat   augment matrix (appending right sides to the matrix)
   OUTPUT:
```

```
        aug_mat    right side of the augment matrix stores the solutions

History

    Y.M. Li       03/10/2013 : Creation date
-------------------------------------------------------------------*/
#include "MyHeader.h"

void apiGaussPPivot(std::vector<vector<double>> &aug_mat, apiError &rc)
{
    int     i, i_p, j, k, n_row, n_col;
    double  pivot, dMultiplier;

    rc = api_OK;
    n_row = (int)aug_mat.size();
    n_col = (int)aug_mat[0].size();

    // Apply Gaussian eliminations to the augmented matrix so that
    // the matrix becomes the upper triangular matrix
    for (k=0; k<n_row-1; k++)
    {
        // Find the larger pivot element
        pivot = 0.0;
        for (i=k; i<n_row; i++)
        {
            if (fabs(pivot) < fabs(aug_mat[i][k]))
            {
                pivot = aug_mat[i][k];
                i_p = i;
            }
        }

        if (fabs(pivot) < zero_tol)
        {
            rc = api_DIVIDEBYZERO;
            goto wrapup;
        }

        // Check if row exchange is needed
        if (i_p != k)
        {
            for (j=0; j<n_col; j++)
            {
                pivot = aug_mat[i_p][j];
                aug_mat[i_p][j] = aug_mat[k][j];
                aug_mat[k][j] = pivot;
            }
        }
```

```
      }

      for (i=k+1; i<n_row; i++)
      {
          // Multiply the kth row by the multiplier and add to
          // the ith row to make a[i][k]=0 (i=k+1, k+2, ...)
          dMultiplier = - aug_mat[i][k] / aug_mat[k][k];
          for (j=k; j<n_col; j++)
              aug_mat[i][j] += dMultiplier * aug_mat[k][j];
      }
  }

  // Backward substitution
  for (k=n_row-1; k>=0; k--)
  {
      for (i=n_row; i<n_col; i++)
      {
          for (j=k+1; j<n_row; j++)
              aug_mat[k][i] -= aug_mat[k][j] * aug_mat[j][i];
          aug_mat[k][i] /= aug_mat[k][ k];
      }
  }

wrapup:

  return;
}
```

By performing partial pivoting, we ensures that $|a_{ii}| \geq |a_{ji}|$, so the multiplier $|a_{ij}/a_{ii}|$ is always less or equal to 1 and the algorithm has favorable error propagation characteristics. For this reason, Gaussian elimination with partial pivoting is actually used in real world computation. This is especially true for systems that are well-balanced, i.e., all elements along any given raw $a_{i1}, a_{i2}, \cdots, a_{in}$ are all of the same order of magnitudes.

## 6.3   Gauss-Jordan elimination with full pivoting

If pivoting elements are searched along both columns and rows, Gaussian elimination is less susceptible to roundoff, but the increase in stability comes at the cost of more complex programming and an increase in work associated with searching and data movement. In this section, we shall discuss Gauss-Jordan elimination with full pivoting – a variant of Gaussian elimination.

The goal of Gauss-Jordan elimination is to transform the coefficient matrix into a *diagonal matrix*, and the zeros are introduced into the matrix one column at a time. We work to eliminate the elements both above and below the diagonal element of a given column in one pass through the matrix. The general procedure for Gauss-Jordan elimination can be summarized as follows:

1. Write the augmented matrix for the system of linear equations.

2. Assume that we are at the $i$th row $(i = 1, \cdots, n)$. Find the largest pivot of matrix $A$. If necessary, perform row and column exchanges so that the pivot element in $A$ is $a_{ii}$.

3. Divide the $i$th row by the pivot $a_{ii}$ so that the diagonal element is 1.

4. For each other row $j$, add $-a_{ji}$ times row $i$ to row $j$ so that all the elements, except for $a_{ii}$, at column $i$ are set to 0.

5. The next pivot is then found and the procedure repeated until $A$ becomes the diagonal or *identity* matrix. When this is accomplished, the right-hand side becomes the solution set.

With full pivoting, things get a bit complicated because of row and column swaps on $A$. These operations change the correspondence between the columns of $A$ and the solution set. In other words, this interchange scrambles the order of the rows in the solution. If we do this, we will need to unscramble the solution by restoring the rows to their original order. Unfortunately, all this makes the code very opaque - but it's a worthwhile tradeoff.

The Gauss-Jordan elimination method requires roughly $n^3/2$ and is more expensive than Gaussian elimination, but it can be used to compute the inverse matrix. This can be done by augmenting the square matrix with the identity matrix of the same dimensions. When the original matrix is transformed to an identity matrix, the solution is the inverse matrix.

The implementation of Gauss-Jordan elimination is given below.

```
/*------------------------------------------------------------
API Name
    apiGaussJordan

Description
    It solves a linear system via Gauss-Jordan elimination method.
    This API can also be used to compute an inverse matrix by
    augmenting the square matrix with the identity matrix of
    the same dimensions.


Signature
    void apiGaussJordan(
            std::vector<vector<double>> &aug_mat, apiError &rc)

    INPUT:
        aug_mat    augment matrix (appending right sides to the matrix)
    OUTPUT:
        aug_mat    right side of the augment matrix stores solutions
```

```
History

    Y.M. Li      03/10/2013 : Creation date
---------------------------------------------------------------*/
#include "MyHeader.h"

void apiGaussJordan(
        std::vector<vector<double>> &aug_mat, apiError &rc)
{
    int     i, j, k, jj, n_row, n_col, i_p;
    double  pivot, bidon;
    vector<int> j_p;

    rc = api_OK;
    n_row = (int)aug_mat.size();
    n_col = (int)aug_mat[0].size();
    j_p.resize(n_col);

    for (k=0; k<n_row; k++)
    {
        // Find the pivot for level k elimination:
        pivot = 0.0;
        for (i=k; i<n_row; i++)
        {
            for (j=0; j<n_row; j++)
            {
                if (fabs(pivot) < fabs(aug_mat[i][j]))
                {
                    pivot = aug_mat[i][j];
                    i_p = i;
                    j_p[k] = j;
                }
            }
        }

        if (fabs(pivot) < zero_tol)
        {
            rc = api_DIVIDEBYZERO;
            goto wrapup;
        }

        if (i_p != k)
        {
            // Swapping rows. Note column swap is done at next block
            for (j=0; j<n_col; j++)
            {
```

```
              bidon = aug_mat[i_p][j];
              aug_mat[i_p][j] = aug_mat[k][j];
              aug_mat[k][j] = bidon;
          }
      }

      for (j=0; j<n_col; j++)
        aug_mat[k][j] /= pivot;

      // Level k elimination to ensure aug_mat(i,j_p)=0 for i!=k
      for (i=0; i<k; i++)
      {
          bidon = -aug_mat[i][j_p[k]];
          for (j=0; j<n_col; j++)
            aug_mat[i][j] += bidon * aug_mat[k][j];
      }
      for (i=k+1; i<n_row; i++)
      {
          bidon = -aug_mat[i][j_p[k]];
          for (j=0; j<n_col; j++)
            aug_mat[i][j] += bidon * aug_mat[k][j];
      }
  }

// Adjust the order of results. It could be done by swapping rows
// so that the resulting matrix is a unit matrix. For efficiency,
// however, we adjust the order of results based on the indices.
for (k=0; k<n_row; k++)
{
    for (i=k+1; i<n_row; i++)
    {
        if (j_p[k] > j_p[i])
        {
            /// Swapping indices and results
            for (j=n_row; j<n_col; j++)
            {
                bidon = aug_mat[k][j];
                aug_mat[k][j] = aug_mat[i][j];
                aug_mat[i][j] = bidon;
            }
            jj = j_p[k];
            j_p[k] = j_p[i];
            j_p[i] = jj;
        }
    }
}
```

```
wrapup:

    return;
}
```

Gauss-Jordan elimination's principal strength is that it is a very stable method or at least as stable as any other direct method. However, it is approximately three times slower that the best alternative technique for solving a single linear set when the inverse matrix is not desired. For inverting a matrix, Gauss-Jordan elimination is about as efficient as any other method. However, it is usually not a good idea to compute the inverse matrix purely for the solution $x = A^{-1}b$ because it is inefficient and may have large roundoff errors. If we come along later with an additional right-hand side vector, we can multiply it by the inverse matrix, of course. This does give an answer, but one that is quite susceptible to roundoff error, not nearly as good as if the new vector had been included with the set of right-hand side vectors in the first instance.

## 6.4   Eigenvalue and eigenvector

The word "eigen" is from the German word for "characteristic", and so this section could also be called "Characteristic values and characteristic vectors". However, the terms "Eigenvalues" and "Eigenvectors" are most commonly used.

In studying plane geometry transformation, it is known that

$$\begin{bmatrix} \cos\theta & -\sin\theta \\ \sin\theta & \cos\theta \end{bmatrix} \begin{bmatrix} x \\ y \end{bmatrix}$$

rotates a vector $v = (x, y)^T$ about the $z$-axis by an angle $\theta$. In general, all vectors of dimension $n$ change directions when they are multiplied by a square matrix $A$. However, certain exceptional vectors are in the same direction as $Ax$. Those vectors are the *eigenvectors*. Since an eigenvector has the same direction as $Ax$, there exists a non-zero number $\lambda$ such that $Ax = \lambda x$. The number $\lambda$ is an *eigenvalue* that tells us whether the special vector $x$ is stretched, shrunk, reversed, or left unchanged when it is multiplied by $A$.

The determination of the eigenvalues and eigenvectors of a system is extremely important in physics and engineering, where it is equivalent to *matrix diagonalization* (a matrix that only has entries on the diagonal) and arises in common applications such as stability analysis, the physics of rotating bodies (e.g., principal moments of inertia), small oscillations of vibrating systems, and least squares approximation, to name a few.

We now discuss how eigenvalues and eigenvectors are computed. From $Ax = \lambda x$, we have $(A - \lambda I)x = 0$ with $I$ being the identity matrix. The so-called *characteristic polynomial* of $A$ is defined by

$$p(\lambda) = \det(A - \lambda I).$$

It is not difficult to see that $p$ is a polynomial of degree $n$ in $\lambda$ and consequently has, at most, $n$ distinct zeros. For $x \neq 0$, the zeros of $p(\lambda)$ (or the roots of $p(\lambda) = 0$) are then the eigenvalues or the *characteristic values* of the matrix $A$.

As an example, look at $\det(A - \lambda I)$:

$$A = \begin{bmatrix} 0.8 & 0.3 \\ 0.2 & 0.7 \end{bmatrix} \quad \det \begin{bmatrix} 0.8 - \lambda & 0.3 \\ 0.2 & 0.7 - \lambda \end{bmatrix} = \lambda^2 - \frac{3}{2}\lambda + \frac{1}{2} = (\lambda - 1)(\lambda - \frac{1}{2})$$

Therefore, the matrix $A$ has two eigenvalues $\lambda = 1$ and $\lambda = 1/2$. To find the eigenvector corresponding to $\lambda$, we simply solve the system of linear equations $(A - \lambda I)\boldsymbol{x} = \boldsymbol{0}$. Let $\boldsymbol{x} = (x_1, x_2)^T$ and $\lambda = 1$. Then, $(A - \lambda I)\boldsymbol{x} = \boldsymbol{0}$ gives us

$$\begin{bmatrix} 0.8 - 1 & 0.3 \\ 0.2 & 0.7 - 1 \end{bmatrix} \begin{bmatrix} x_1 \\ x_2 \end{bmatrix} = \begin{bmatrix} -0.2 & 0.3 \\ 0.2 & -0.3 \end{bmatrix} \begin{bmatrix} x_1 \\ x_2 \end{bmatrix},$$

from which we obtain the duplicate equations

$$-0.2x_1 + 0.3x_2 = 0,$$
$$0.2x_2 - 0.3x_2 = 0.$$

If we let $x_1 = t$, then $x_2 = \frac{2}{3}t$. Therefore, the eigenvector corresponding to $\lambda = 1$ is

$$\boldsymbol{x} = \begin{bmatrix} x_1 \\ x_2 \end{bmatrix} = t \begin{bmatrix} 1 \\ 2/3 \end{bmatrix}$$

When $t$ changes, we get different eigenvectors, indicating that eigenvectors are not unique but instead are multiples of $\binom{1}{2/3}$. The collection of all eigenvectors with the same eigenvalue forms the *eigenspace* of $A$, and $\binom{1}{2/3}$ is a basis of the eigenspace corresponding to $\lambda = 1$.

Similarly, another eigenvector can be found by letting $\lambda = 1/2$, i.e.,

$$\begin{bmatrix} 0.8 - 0.5 & 0.3 \\ 0.2 & 0.7 - 0.5 \end{bmatrix} \begin{bmatrix} x_1 \\ x_2 \end{bmatrix} = \begin{bmatrix} 0.3 & 0.3 \\ 0.2 & 0.2 \end{bmatrix} \begin{bmatrix} x_1 \\ x_2 \end{bmatrix}.$$

This gives two equations:

$$0.3x_1 + 0.3x_2 = 0$$
$$0.2x_2 + 0.2x_2 = 0$$

Consequently, the eigenvector corresponding to $\lambda = 1/2$ is

$$\boldsymbol{x} = \begin{bmatrix} x_1 \\ x_2 \end{bmatrix} = t \begin{bmatrix} 1 \\ -1 \end{bmatrix}$$

What makes these two eigenvectors so special? It is readily checked that $A$ scales and rotates most vectors but only scales eigenvectors. That is, eigenvectors lie on lines that are unmoved by $A$. We state two important properties of eigenvectors without proof:

- If the eigenvalues of matrix $A$ are all different, then the corresponding eigenvectors are linearly independent.

- If $A$ is *symmetric* (i.e., $a_{ij} = a_{ji}$), then all eigenvalues are real, and eigenvectors corresponding to different eigenvalues must be orthogonal to each other. Furthermore, in this case there will exist $n$ linearly independent eigenvectors for $A$ so that $A$ will be diagonalizable.

## 6.5   Power method for eigenpair

It is not so difficult to solve eigenvalue and eigenvector problems when the matrix is $2 \times 2$ or $3 \times 3$. However, it is non-trivial for a matrix of higher dimension. In applications, eigenvalue and eigenvector problems are usually solved numerically by the iteration method.

The *power method* is an iterative technique used to determine the dominant eigenvalue of a matrix – that is, the eigenvalue with the largest magnitude. One useful feature of the power method is that it produces not only an eigenvalue, but also an associated eigenvector. Although we only found one eigenvector, we found a very important eigenvector because many real world applications are primarily interested in the dominant eigenpair.

To apply the power method, we assume that the $n \times n$ matrix $A$ has $n$ eigenvalues $\lambda_1, \lambda_2, \cdots, \lambda_n$ with associated eigenvectors $v_1, v_2 \cdots, v_n$ that are linearly independent. Moreover, we assume that $A$ has precisely one eigenvalue, $\lambda_1$, that is the largest in magnitude, i.e.,

$$|\lambda_1| > |\lambda_2| \geq \cdots \geq |\lambda_n| \geq 0.$$

If $x_0$ is any vector in $\mathbb{R}^n$, we can construct $n$ vectors as follows

$$x_1 = Ax_0,$$
$$x_2 = Ax_1 = A^2 x_0,$$
$$\cdots$$
$$x_k = Ax_{k-1} = A^k x_0,$$
$$\cdots$$

Since the eigenvectors $v_1, v_2 \cdots, v_n$ are linearly independent, we can represent $x_0$ as a linear combination of vector $v_i$:

$$x_0 = \alpha_1 v_1 + \alpha_2 v_2 + \cdots + \alpha_n v_n.$$

Consequently, we have

$$x_k = A^k x_0 = \sum \alpha_i A^k v_i.$$

Since $v_i$ are eigenvectors, we have $A^k v_i = \lambda_i^k v_i$ and thus

$$x_k = A^k x_0 = \alpha_1 \lambda_1^k v_1 + \alpha_2 \lambda_2^k v_2 + \cdots + \alpha_n \lambda_n^k v_n$$
$$= \lambda_1^k \left[ \alpha_1 v_1 + \sum_{i=2}^{n} \alpha_i \left( \frac{\lambda_i}{\lambda_1} \right)^k v_i \right] = \lambda_1^k [\alpha_1 v_1 + \varepsilon_k].$$

The fact that $\lambda_1$ has the largest magnitude guarantees that $|\lambda_i/\lambda_1| < 1$ $(i = 2, 3, \cdots, n)$. Accordingly, $\lim_{k \to \infty} \varepsilon_k = 0$ and

$$\lim_{k \to \infty} \frac{x_k}{\lambda_1^k} = \alpha_1 v_1.$$

When $k$ is sufficiently large, we have

$$\boldsymbol{x}_k \approx \alpha_1 \lambda_1^k \boldsymbol{v}_1,$$

indicating that $\boldsymbol{x}_k$ is an approximation of the dominant eigenvector $\boldsymbol{v}_1$. Denoting the $i$th component of $\boldsymbol{x}_k$ by $(\boldsymbol{x}_k)_i$, the dominant eigenvalue is thus approximated by

$$\lambda_1 \approx \frac{(\boldsymbol{x}_k)_i}{(\boldsymbol{x}_{k-1})_i}.$$

The eigenvalues of

$$A = \begin{bmatrix} 0.8 & 0.3 \\ 0.2 & 0.7 \end{bmatrix}$$

were computed in the previous section; they are $\lambda_1 = 1$ and $\lambda_2 = 1/2$. We now use the power method to compute the dominant eigenvalue $\lambda_1$. We start with an arbitrary non-zero vector $\boldsymbol{x}_0 = (1, 1)^T$:

$$\boldsymbol{x}_1 = A\boldsymbol{x}_0 = \begin{bmatrix} 0.8 & 0.3 \\ 0.2 & 0.7 \end{bmatrix} \begin{bmatrix} 1 \\ 1 \end{bmatrix} = \begin{bmatrix} 1.1 \\ 0.9 \end{bmatrix}$$

$$\boldsymbol{x}_2 = A\boldsymbol{x}_1 = \begin{bmatrix} 0.8 & 0.3 \\ 0.2 & 0.7 \end{bmatrix} \begin{bmatrix} 1.1 \\ 0.9 \end{bmatrix} = \begin{bmatrix} 1.15 \\ 0.85 \end{bmatrix}$$

$$\boldsymbol{x}_3 = A\boldsymbol{x}_2 = \begin{bmatrix} 0.8 & 0.3 \\ 0.2 & 0.7 \end{bmatrix} \begin{bmatrix} 1.15 \\ 0.85 \end{bmatrix} = \begin{bmatrix} 1.175 \\ 0.825 \end{bmatrix}$$

$$\boldsymbol{x}_4 = A\boldsymbol{x}_3 = \begin{bmatrix} 0.8 & 0.3 \\ 0.2 & 0.7 \end{bmatrix} \begin{bmatrix} 1.175 \\ 0.825 \end{bmatrix} = \begin{bmatrix} 1.1875 \\ 0.8125 \end{bmatrix}$$

$$\boldsymbol{x}_5 = A\boldsymbol{x}_4 = \begin{bmatrix} 0.8 & 0.3 \\ 0.2 & 0.7 \end{bmatrix} \begin{bmatrix} 1.1875 \\ 0.8125 \end{bmatrix} = \begin{bmatrix} 1.19375 \\ 0.80625 \end{bmatrix}$$

$$\boldsymbol{x}_6 = A\boldsymbol{x}_5 = \begin{bmatrix} 0.8 & 0.3 \\ 0.2 & 0.7 \end{bmatrix} \begin{bmatrix} 1.19375 \\ 0.80625 \end{bmatrix} = \begin{bmatrix} 1.196875 \\ 0.803125 \end{bmatrix}$$

$$\boldsymbol{x}_7 = A\boldsymbol{x}_6 = \begin{bmatrix} 0.8 & 0.3 \\ 0.2 & 0.7 \end{bmatrix} \begin{bmatrix} 1.196875 \\ 0.803125 \end{bmatrix} = \begin{bmatrix} 1.1984375 \\ 0.8015624 \end{bmatrix}$$

If we stop after seven iterations, $\lambda_1$ is then approximated by either

$$\lambda_1 \approx \frac{(\boldsymbol{x}_7)_1}{(\boldsymbol{x}_6)_1} = \frac{1.1984375}{1.196875} \approx 1.0013 \quad \text{or} \quad \lambda_1 \approx \frac{(\boldsymbol{x}_7)_2}{(\boldsymbol{x}_6)_2} = \frac{0.8015624}{0.803125} \approx 0.99805.$$

In this particular case, both are good approximations of $\lambda_1 = 1$. In other cases, some components of $\boldsymbol{x}_k$ are zeros or near zeros. To avoid numerical instability, we usually choose a reciprocal of the largest component of $\boldsymbol{x}_k$ as a scaling factor to scale $\boldsymbol{x}_k$ such that the *maximum norm* $\|\boldsymbol{x}_k\|_\infty = 1$. In vector algebra, the most widely-used norms of vector $\boldsymbol{x} = (x_1, x_2, \cdots, x_n)^T$ are

$$\|\boldsymbol{x}\|_2 = \sqrt{x_1^2 + x_2^2 + \cdots x_n^2}$$
$$\|\boldsymbol{x}\|_\infty = \max |x_i| \quad (i = 1, \cdots, n)$$

with $\|x\|_2$ being called the *Euclidian norm* of vector $x$ since it represents the usual notion of distance from the origin.

Denoting the largest component of $x_k$ by $(x_k)_p$, $\lambda_1$ is then computed as

$$\lambda_1 \approx \frac{(x_{k+1})_p}{(x_k)_p}.$$

Since $x_k$ is normalized to 1, we have $(x_k)_p = 1$ and hence $\lambda_1 \approx (x_{k+1})_p$, which avoids division by zero or a very small number.

Before implementation, we need to consider a termination condition. An iteration loop should be terminated when either of the following two conditions is met:

- Result converges. In our case, we check $\|x_{k+1} - x_k\|_\infty < \varepsilon$.

- The maximum number of iterations is reached.

Finally, we would like to normalize the converged eigenvector to the unit vector in the sense of the Euclidian norm, i.e., $\|x_k\|_2 = 1$, since it describes the direction in the Euclidean coordinate system. The implementation of the power method is listed below:

```
/*------------------------------------------------------------------
API Name
    apiEigenByPower

Description
    It computes the dominant eigenvalue and eigenvector
    of a square matrix A via power method.

Signature
    void apiEigenByPower(std::vector<vector<double>> &Amat,
                         double tol, double &eigenValue,
                         std::vector<double> &eigenVector,
                         apiError &rc)

    INPUT:
        Amat            square matrix
        tol             convergency tolerance
    OUTPUT:
        eigenValue      the dominant eigenvalue
        eigenVector     the dominant eigenvector

History

    Y.M. Li     03/10/2013 : Creation date
------------------------------------------------------------------*/
#include "MyHeader.h"
```

```
void apiEigenByPower(std::vector<vector<double>> &Amat,
                     double tol, double &eigenValue,
                     std::vector<double> &eigenVector, apiError &rc)
{
#define max_num 100
   int             id, i, j, k, n;
   double          temp, dValue, dError;
   vector<double> x_saved, x_k;

   // Initialize memory
   rc = api_OK;
   n = (int)eigenVector.size();
   x_saved.resize(n);
   x_k.resize(n);

   // Normalize input vector so that max(x[i])=1
   temp = fabs(eigenVector[0]);
   id = 0;
   for (i=1; i<n; i++)
   {
      if (temp < fabs(eigenVector[i]))
      {
         id = i;
         temp = fabs(eigenVector[i]);
      }
   }
   for (i=0; i<n; i++)
      x_saved[i] = eigenVector[i] / temp;

   for (k=0; k<max_num; k++)
   {
      for (i=0; i<n; i++)
      {
         x_k[i] = 0.0;
         for (j=0; j<n; j++)
            x_k[i] += Amat[i][j] * x_saved[j];
      }
      dValue = x_k[id];

      // Normalize transformed vector
      temp = fabs(x_k[0]);
      id = 0;
      for (i=1; i<n; i++)
      {
         if (temp < fabs(x_k[i]))
         {
            id = i;
```

```
            temp = fabs(x_k[i]);
        }
    }
    if (temp < zero_tol)
    {
        rc = api_DIVIDEBYZERO;
        goto wrapup;
    }
    for (i=0; i<n; i++)
        x_k[i] /= temp;

    // Chck if convergency is reached
    dError = fabs(x_k[0] - x_saved[0]);
    for (i=1; i<n; i++)
    {
        if (dError < fabs(x_k[i] - x_saved[i]))
            dError = fabs(x_k[i] - x_saved[i]);
    }
    if (dError < tol)
    {
        eigenValue = dValue;
        // Normalize the eigenvector to (Euclidian) unit vector
        temp = 0.0;
        for (i=0; i<n; i++)
            temp += x_k[i] * x_k[i];
        temp = sqrt(temp);
        for (i=0; i<n; i++)
            eigenVector[i] = x_k[i] / temp;
        goto wrapup;
    }

    // Assign data for next iteration
    x_saved = x_k;
}

// Did not converge
rc = api_EXCEEDMAXITERATION;

wrapup:

    return;
}
```

It is noted that **eigenVector** is used as both an input and output argument. It stores the initial guessing vector when the program starts and then the converged eigenvector when the program ends.

The power method computes the largest eigenvalue and the corresponding eigenvector.

In many applications, we are often interested in either the largest or the smallest eigenvalue and associated eigenvector. In the case where the smallest eigenvector is desired, we can inverse the matrix $A$ and apply the power method to $A^{-1}$ to get the largest eigenvalue for $A^{-1}$ and hence the smallest for $A$. This is known as the *inverse power method*.

The inverse power method may also be modified to refine the eigenvalue and compute the corresponding eigenvector when an approximating eigenvalue $q$ is known from other methods. Suppose the matrix $A$ has eigenvalues $\lambda_1, \cdots, \lambda_n$ with linearly independent eigenvectors $v_1, \cdots, v_n$. The eigenvalues of $(A - qI)^{-1}$ are

$$\frac{1}{\lambda_1 - q}, \quad \frac{1}{\lambda_2 - q}, \quad \cdots, \quad \frac{1}{\lambda_n - q}$$

whose corresponding eigenvectors are still $v_1, v_2, \cdots, v_n$. When $\lambda_j \approx q$, then $1/(\lambda_j - q)$ is the dominant eigenvalue and so is the solution of the power method.

## 6.6 Summary

In this chapter, we looked at the most fundamental methods for solving linear systems, namely the Gaussian elimination without, with partial, and with full pivoting. In real world applications, Gaussian elimination without pivoting is rarely used. The pivoting techniques are used to minimize the effects of roundoff error, which can dominate the solution. It is recommended to use partial and full pivoting for most problems since they decrease the effects of roundoff error without adding much extra computation. The Gauss-Jordan elimination method discussed in this chapter is not only numerically stable but can also be used to compute the inverse matrix – provided that the matrix is inventible.

Gaussian elimination methods are fundamental and easy to implement. But they are not the only methods used to solve linear systems. With minor modification Gaussian elimination may be used to factorize the matrix $A$ into the lower ($L$) and upper ($U$) triangular matrices. Once the matrix factorization is completed, the solution to $Ax = LUx = b$ is found by first letting $y = Ux$ and solving $Ly = b$ for $y$. After $y$ is found by the forward-substitution process, the upper-triangular system $Ux = y$ is solved for $x$ by backward substitution. This process is often called $LU$ or *Doolittle* factorization. A square matrix is *symmetric* if $a_{ij} = a_{ji}$ and is *positive definite* if $x^T Ax > 0$. Factorizations take a simpler form when the matrix $A$ is symmetric and positive definite. For example, the *Choleski factorization* has a unique factorization of the form $A = LL^T$, where $L$ is the lower triangular matrix. Because of this symmetric property, the Choleski factorization works almost as twice fast as $LU$ does.

Gaussian elimination is an $O(n^3)$ algorithm, which can be very expensive when $n$ is large. Depending on the properties of the matrix, Gaussian elimination or matrix factorization methods are modified to improve performance. For example, when a *piecewise* polynomial curve known as the *spline* curve is used to interpolate a large amount of data points, the matrix has mostly zero elements. Such matrix is known as *banded matrix*. The Gaussian elimination and the factorization algorithms can be considerably simplified in the case of a banded matrix because of a large number of zeros that appear in these matrices in regular patterns.

In this chapter, we discussed the use of the power method to approximate the dominant eigenvalue of a matrix. If the matrix is invertible, the power method can also be used to find the smallest eigenvalue and corresponding eigenvector through determination of the dominant eigenvalue of inverse matrix. The inverse power method may also be modified to refine the eigenvalue and compute the corresponding eigenvector when an approximating eigenvalue is known from another method. The power method is simple to understand and implement. However, its use in real world computation is limited. The QR decomposition algorithm is more widely used to find all eigenvalues and eigenvectors. It is the basis of all modern eigenpair computation, including MATLAB. The QR algorithm can be seen as a more sophisticated variation of the power method. Recall that the power method repeatedly multiplies $A$ by a single vector, normalizing after each iteration. The vector converges to an eigenvector of the largest eigenvalue. Instead, the QR algorithm works with a complete basis of vectors. By using the Gram-Schmidt process, we factorize the matrix

$$A = A_1 = Q_1 R_1$$

into a product of an orthogonal matrix $Q_1$ (i.e., $Q_1^T Q_1 = I$) and a positive (i.e., with all positive entries along the diagonal) upper triangular matrix $R_1$. If $A$ is nonsingular, then this factorization is unique. Next, multiply the two factors together *in the wrong order*. The result is the new matrix

$$A_2 = R_1 Q_1.$$

We then factorize $A_2$ in order to produce $A_3$

$$A_2 = Q_2 R_2 \quad \rightarrow \quad A_3 = R_2 Q_2.$$

The astonishing fact is that, for many matrices $A$, the iterates $A_k$ converge to an upper triangular matrix whose diagonal entries are the eigenvalues of $A$. For each eigenvalue, the corresponding eigenvector can be computed by solving the appropriate homogeneous linear system, or by applying the shifted inverse power method. The QR algorithm can be found in most numerical analysis text books.

# Chapter 7

# Design Reusable Code

When interviewing candidates with computer science major, one of the questions I usually ask is how to design reusable code. Referring to question 6 in the preface, candidates were asked to find the roots of $f(x) = x^3 + 2x - 2$ in $[0, 1]$ and $f(x) = \sin(x)$ in $[2, 4]$ based on the presented bisection method with minimum implementation efforts. I was surprised to find that many candidates, including those who were working on their master degrees in computer science, failed to give satisfactory answers. For this reason, I would like to devote a full chapter to discuss the basic techniques for creating reusable code.

Code reuse is the idea that a partial computer program written at one time can be, should be, or is being used in another program written at a later time. The reuse of programming code is a common technique that attempts to save time and energy by reducing redundant work. Design and implementation of reusable code always involves some level of *modularization*. Modular programming is the approach where the application code is broken into several subsystems or subfunctions, each of which has the potential to be reused in other projects. For example, the bisection method requires an evaluation of a polynomial function to find the root of $f(x) = x^3 + 2x - 2$. By modularizing a polynomial evaluation method and implementing it in `apiHornerEval`, we do not have to rewrite the polynomial evaluation method when implementing the bisection method; we simply call the modularized evaluation API as follows (It was originally implemented in chapter 5):

```
double apiBisection(int ndeg, double *pA,
          double a, double b, double tol)
{
    double f_a, f_b, f_mid, x_mid;

    // Terminate condition
    x_mid = 0.5 * (a + b);
    apiHornerEval(ndeg, pA, x_mid, f_mid);
    if (fabs(f_mid) < tol)
        return x_mid;
```

```
    // Recuce the complexity via recursion
    apiHornerEval(ndeg, pA, a, f_a);
    apiHornerEval(ndeg, pA, b, f_b);
    if (f_a * f_mid < 0.0)
        return apiBisection(ndeg, pA, a, x_mid, tol);
    else if (f_a * f_mid > 0.0)
        return apiBisection(ndeg, pA, x_mid, b, tol);
    else
        return api_INCONSISTENT;
}
```

Modularization of code is essential to designing reusable code. However, modularization alone is insufficient to answer the question of how to find the roots of $f(x) = x^3 + 2x - 2$ in $[0, 1]$ and $f(x) = \sin(x)$ in $[2, 4]$ with minimum implementation efforts. The primary goal in this chapter is to answer this question by writing a generic, extensible, and reusable code through *callback* functions.

A great breakthrough in reusability is, however, the widespread use of *object-oriented programming*. Concepts such as *inheritance* and *polymorphism* provide the mechanisms necessary to develop reusable and extensible code. Through inheritance with polymorphism, programmers can extend an existing functionality by modifying (especially overriding) an existing method. Besides discussion of callback functions, we will also demonstrate in this chapter how the object oriented programming technique can help us design and implement the bisection method capable of solving any function with minimum code implementation.

## 7.1   Integration

In chapter 5, the algorithm `apiCurveLength` is implemented to compute the arc length of a specific function

$$f(x) = \frac{x^3}{6} + \frac{1}{2x}.$$

If we want to compute a definite integral of a different function, we may use the existing API `apiCurveLength` as a template and save it under a different name. We then modify `myEavl` to evaluate the integrand of the new integration. Everything else stays the same. The problem with this approach is that we would create many integration programs even though the majority of the code is the same. If a bug is found in the implementation of Gauss-Legendre quadrature, we would have to fix the bug in every copied function. This is obviously a painful and wasteful process, which should be avoided if possible.

Referring to the implementation of `apiCurveLength`, it should be noted that, except for `myEavl`, the implementation of Gauss-Legendre quadrature is independent of a particular function. We would naturally ask whether it is possible to implement `myEavl` inside the caller function where a specific function is defined rather than in the callee and instruct the callee to use `myEavl` defined in the caller. This is achievable in C/C++ by passing a *function pointer* to the callee function so that the callee function can call the function defined in the caller function. By using a function pointer, we can implement a generic Gauss-Legendre integration without `myEval` in a separate file. When users want to call it to compute a definite integration of any specific function, they simply implement `myEval` for that function and pass the function pointer to the generic Gauss-Legendre integration method. Before going into detail about a function pointer, let's review again the C/C++ pointer.

A pointer in C/C++ is a special variable that holds the address of another variable. The following code fragment illustrates how we can assign the address of a variable to a pointer of the same type and then access the content of the variable.

```
double    pi = 3.14159265;
double    *ptr; // declare a pointer whose type is "double"

ptr = &pi;   // assign the address of variable "pi" to a pointer.

// Print the content of the pointer in two ways
printf("%lf\n", *ptr);
printf("%lf\n", ptr[0]);
```

Our next example shows how the address of dynamically-allocated heap memory is passed to a callee function so that the callee can access the memory block allocated by the caller.

```
void apiMultiplyByFactor(double scale, int n, double *pA)
{
    int    i;
    for (i=0; i<n; i++)
    {
        pA[i] *= scale;
    }
}

void main(void)
{
    int       i, n = 10;
    double    *pDblArray = NULL;

    // Allocate heap memory
    pDblArray = new double[n];
    if (pDblArray)
    {
        // Initialize the array
        for (i=0; i<n; i++)
        {
            pDblArray[i] = (double) i;
        }

        // Multiply the content in each memory cell by 5
        apiMultiplyByFactor(5.0, n, pDblArray);
```

```
      delete [] pDblArray;
   }
}
```

It should be noted that `pDblArray` is a pointer of type `double` and is used to hold the entry address of dynamically-allocated heap memory. When passing it to the callee `apiMultiplyByFactor`, we purposely use a different name (i.e., `pA`) in the callee function to indicate that the name of the pointer is not important as long as it has the same type `double`.

With basic knowledge about C/C++ pointer, we can now discuss a function pointer. Similar to program variables, the addresses of functions or subroutines are also stored within the program's memory address. Therefore, we can declare a function pointer of the **same type** and assign the address of the function to it. By passing the function pointer to the callee function, this function can be called from the callee function via the function pointer (just like the memory allocated in `main` can be accessed by `apiMultiplyByFactor` in the above example). As this function is not defined in the callee but in the caller function, it is thus referred to as a *callback* function.

To better understand a callback function, let's design and implement a generic Gauss-Legendre quadrature algorithm `apiIntegration`. First, we type the following at the command line:

```
D:\ArtProgram\test>getvcproj Integration
```

This creates a new Visual C/C++ project with the desired settings in the destination folder `D:\ArtProgram\test`. Since it is easier to modify existing routines with similar functionalities than to create them from scratch, we copy `apiCurveLength.cpp` and `mnCurveLength.cpp` to the `test` folder as the templates. Copying a source file and test driver to the current directory can be done by typing the scripts at the command line as follows:

```
 D:\ArtProgram\test>getsrcfl CurveLength
 D:\ArtProgram\test>getmnfl CurveLength
```

We then rename the source and main driver respectively to `apiIntegration.cpp` and `mnIntegration.cpp`. By now we should have the following four files in the `test` folder:

```
apiIntegration.cpp
mnIntegration.cpp
mnIntegration.vcxproj
mnIntegration.vcxproj.filters
```

We can now open this project to modify the source and main driver. The Gauss-Legendre integration method requires the evaluation of a function at the given variable value. Accordingly, we define the prototype of `myEval` to be

```
double myEval(double x)
```

Since the function pointer of `myEval` will be passed into the Gauss-Legendre integration method, the prototype of `apiIntegration` is defined as follows

```
void apiIntegration(double a, double b, double tol,
                    double (*userEvalFunct)(double), //function pointer
                    double &dValue, apiError &rc)
```

The function pointer `userEvalFunct` has the same type (or signature) as `myEval`: it takes a `double` as input and returns a `double` to the caller. It should be noted that the name `userEvalFunct` is arbitrary as long as it has the same signature as `myEval`. With the use of a function pointer, we can implement the generic Gauss-Legendre integration method as follows:

```
/*----------------------------------------------------------------
API Name
    apiIntegration

Description
    It is a generic numerical integration API that computes a definite
    integral of any function in [a, b] via Gauss-Legendre quadrature.
    To call this function, users have to implement a callback
    function that evaluates the function at a given parameter.

Signature
    void apiIntegration(double a, double b, double tol,
                        double (*userEvalFunct)(double),
                        double &dValue, apiError &rc)

    INPUT:
        a, b            integral interval [a, b]
        tol             convergency tolerance
        userEvalFunct   callback function pointer
    OUTPUT:
        dValue          the integral value
        rc              error code: api_OK if no error

History

    Y.M. Li     03/10/2013 : Creation date
----------------------------------------------------------------*/
#include "MyHeader.h"

void apiIntegration(double a, double b, double tol,
                    double (*userEvalFunct)(double),
                    double &dValue, apiError &rc)
{
    int     i, k, n, num_roots[2] = {8, 10};
    double  *pRoots = NULL, *pA = NULL;
    double  alpha, beta, x, d[2], f_i[10];
```

```
double    dLeft, dRight;

// Compute approximate value at n=8 and 10
rc = api_OK;
alpha = (b - a) / 2.0;
beta =  (a + b) / 2.0;
for (k=0; k<2; k++)
{
    n = num_roots[k];
    apiGetGaussLdgRtWts(n, pRoots, pA, rc);
    if (rc != api_OK)
        goto wrapup;

    d[k] = 0.0;
    for (i=0; i<n; i++)
    {
        x = alpha * pRoots[i] + beta;
        f_i[i] = userEvalFunct(x);
    }

    for (i=0; i<n/2; i++)
    {
        d[k] += f_i[i] * pA[i];
        d[k] += f_i[n-1-i] * pA[i];
    }

    d[k] *= alpha;
}

// Terminate condition
if (fabs(d[1] - d[0]) < tol)
{
    dValue = d[1];
    goto wrapup;
}

// Reduce the complexity by halving the interval
x = 0.5 * (a + b);
apiIntegration(a, x, tol, userEvalFunct, dLeft, rc);
if (rc != api_OK)
    goto wrapup;
apiIntegration(x, b, tol, userEvalFunct, dRight, rc);
if (rc != api_OK)
    goto wrapup;

// Combine the results
dValue = dLeft + dRight;
```

```
wrapup:

    return;
}
```

As long as the caller provides a respective evaluation method, the above implementation is flexible enough to compute any definite integration. Besides using the associated main driver to run and explore the above implementation, we can also simplify the implementation of `apiCurveLength` to call the generic function `apiIntegration`:

```
/*-------------------------------------------------------------------
API Name
    apiCurveLength

Description
    It computes the curve (or girth) length of a particular
    function via Gauss-Legendre quadrature.

Signature
    void apiCurveLength(double a, double b, double tol,
                        double &dValue, apiError &rc)

    INPUT:
      a, b      integral interval [a, b]
      tol       convergency tolerance
    OUTPUT:
      dValue    the integral value
      rc        error code: api_OK if no error

History

    Y.M. Li      03/10/2013 : Creation date
-------------------------------------------------------------------*/
#include "MyHeader.h"

static double myEval(double x)
{
    double xx, dy;
    xx = x * x;
    dy = 0.5 * (xx - 1.0/xx);
    return sqrt(1.0 + dy * dy);
}

void apiCurveLength(double a, double b, double tol,
                    double &dValue, apiError &rc)
{
    apiIntegration(a, b, tol, myEval, dValue, rc);
```

}

It was said that the name of pointer is not important as long as it has the same type (or signature). Therefore, it is absolutely fine to name the evaluation function `myEval` in the caller function and pass it to the callee as `userEvalFunct`.

The example presented in this section has one simple callback function. In the next section, we will see that it is perfectly fine to have more than one callback function when necessary.

## 7.2   Double integral

Numerical integration for a single variable can be extended to compute multiple integrals. In this section, we discuss how to expand the algorithm to compute a double integral through the use of two callback functions. Afterwards, it is straightforward to extend the approach to triple or even higher dimensional integrals.

Consider a function of two variables $f(u, v)$. The definite integral is denoted by

$$\int \int_D f(u, v) \, du \, dv,$$

where $D$ is the domain of $f$ in the $u$-$v$ plane. If $D$ is defined by a rectangle $[a, b] \times [c, d]$, the above integral is written as

$$\int_a^b \int_c^d f(u, v) \, du dv.$$

As an example, we assume that $f(u, v) = u^2 v$ and $D = [0, 1] \times [0, 2]$. Then, the exact solution of the double integral is

$$\int_0^1 \int_0^2 u^2 v \, du \, dv = \int_0^1 \left( \int_0^2 u^2 v \, dv \right) du = \int_0^1 \left( u^2 \frac{v^2}{2} \Big|_{v=0}^{v=2} \right) du$$

$$= \int_0^1 2u^2 \, du = \frac{2u^3}{3} \Big|_0^1 = \frac{2}{3}.$$

The double integral is done by first integrating the inner integral with respect to $v$, treating $u$ as a constant. The final answer is obtained by integrating the outer integral with respect to $u$. A numerical solution to a double integral is also performed in two steps: computing the inner and then the outer integral. Let us rewrite the double integral as

$$\int_a^b \int_c^d f(u, v) \, du \, dv = \int_a^b \left( \int_c^d f(u, v) \, dv \right) du = \int_a^b g(u) \, du.$$

Referring to section 5.3, the Gauss-Legendre quadrature requires the evaluation of an integrand at the roots of a Legendre polynomial of degree $n$. Since Legendre roots $t_i$

are confined in $[-1, 1]$, we have to reparametrize $g(u)$ by

$$u(t) = \frac{1}{2}[(b - a)t + (a + b)]$$

such that $t \in [-1, 1]$. It is readily checked that $u = a$ and $b$ when $t = -1$ and $1$ respectively. This permits us to compute $g(u)$ by the Gaussian-Legendre quadrature as follows:

$$\int_a^b g(u) \, du = \frac{b - a}{2} \int_{-1}^1 g(u(t)) dt \approx \frac{b - a}{2} \sum_{i=1}^n A_i g(u_i),$$

where $u_i = u(t_i)$ and $A_1, A_2, \cdots, A_n$ are the weights for the Gauss-Legendre quadrature. The inner integral $g(u_i)$ is computed using again the Gauss-Legendre quadrature by treating $u_i$ as a constant

$$g(u_i) = \int_c^d f(u_i, v) \, dv \approx \frac{d - c}{2} \sum_{j=1}^n A_j f(u_i, v_j),$$

where $v_j$ is computed using the following reparametrization:

$$v_j = \frac{1}{2}[(d - c)t_j + (c + d)], \quad j = 1, 2, \cdots, n.$$

The implementation of the Gauss-Legendre quadrature is listed below:

```
/*-----------------------------------------------------------
API Name
    apiIntegrationDbl

Description
    It is a generic numerical integration API that computes a
    definite double integral of any function in [a, b]x[c, d]
    via Gauss-Legendre quadrature. To call this function,
    users have to implement the following callback function

        double (*userEval)(double, double)

    to evaluate the integrand at the given (u, v).

Signature
    void apiIntegrationDbl(
                double (*userEval)(double, double),
                double a, double b, double c, double d,
                double &dValue, apiError &rc)

    INPUT:
        a, b      integral interval [a, b]
        c, d      integral interval [c, d]
    OUTPUT:
        dValue    the integral value
```

```
        rc          error code: api_OK if no error

History

    Y.M. Li      03/10/2013 : Creation date
------------------------------------------------------------------*/
#include "MyHeader.h"

void apiIntegrationDbl(double (*userEval)(double, double),
                       double a, double b, double c, double d,
                       double &dValue, apiError &rc)
{
#define numLgdRoots 10

    int      i, j, k;
    double   u, v, result, alpha, beta, lambda, gamma;
    double   g_u[numLgdRoots], f[numLgdRoots];
    double   *pRoots=NULL, *pA = NULL;

    rc = api_OK;
    alpha = (b - a) / 2.0;
    beta =  (a + b) / 2.0;
    lambda = (d - c) / 2.0;
    gamma =  (c + d) / 2.0;
    apiGetGaussLdgRtWts(numLgdRoots, pRoots, pA, rc);
    if (rc != api_OK)
          goto wrapup;

    for (i=0; i<numLgdRoots; i++)
    {
        // Compute f(u_i, v_j) with j=0, 1,...,n-1
        u = alpha * pRoots[i] + beta;
        for (j=0; j<numLgdRoots; j++)
        {
            v = lambda * pRoots[j] + gamma;
            f[j] = userEval(u, v);
        }

        // Compute g(u_i) = sum of A_j * f(u_i, v_j)
        result = 0.0;
        for (k=0; k<numLgdRoots/2; k++)
        {
            result += f[k] * pA[k];
            result += f[numLgdRoots-1-k] * pA[k];
        }
        g_u[i] = lambda * result;
    }
```

```
    // Compute the final result: sum of A_i * g(u_i)
    result = 0.0;
    for (i=0; i<numLgdRoots/2; i++)
    {
        result += g_u[i] * pA[i];
        result += g_u[numLgdRoots-1-i] * pA[i];
    }
    dValue = alpha * result;

wrapup:

    return;
}
```

It should be noted that an array is used to store $g(u_i)$, and the final result is computed in a separate and reduced **for** loop. This is because the Gauss-Legendre weights are symmetric; hence, only half of them were stored in the global table in **MyHeader.h**. As will be seen later on, both the array for $g(u_i)$ and the separate loop can be eliminated. However, this makes the code relatively harder to understand.

We can now call **apiIntegrationDbl** to compute

$$\int_0^1 \int_0^2 u^2 v \, du \, dv$$

by implementing the callback function in a main driver as follows:

```
double myEval(double u, double v)
{
    return u * u * v;
}
```

With the help of a callback function, **apiIntegrationDbl** is able to compute a definite double integral over a rectangular domain $D = [a, b] \times [c, d]$. In reality, however, most of the domains are not rectangular but a region bounded by two curves (referring to figure 7.1):

$$D = \{(u, v) \mid a \leq u \leq b, \, h_1(u) \leq v \leq h_2(u)\}.$$

In this case, the integral is

$$\int \int_D f(u, v) \, du \, dv = \int_a^b \int_{h_1(u)}^{h_2(u)} f(u, v) \, du \, dv.$$

To solve it numerically, another callback function (say, **Eval_c_d**) is required to compute $c = h_1(u)$ and $d = h_2(u)$ at each $u_i$. Accordingly, we need to modify the declaration of **apiIntegrationDbl** to have two callback functions, **userEval** and **Eval_c_d**, so the API can perform the required computation. The modified implementation is

```
/*-----------------------------------------------------------
API Name
    apiIntegrationDbl

Description
    It is a generic numerical integration API that computes a
    definite double integral of any function over a domain via
    Gauss-Legendre quadrature. The domain may be defined by
    either [a,b]x[c,d] or two curves. To call this function,
    users have to implement two required callback functions
    to perform the specific evaluations:

    1) The callback function
            double (*userEval)(double, double)
       evaluates f(u, v).
    2) The callback function
          void (*Eval_c_d)(double, double &, double&)
       computes the interval [c_i, d_i] for v at any u_i.

Signature
    void apiIntegrationDbl(
                double (*userEval)(double, double),
                void (*Eval_c_d)(double, double &, double&),
                double a, double b,
                double &dValue, apiError &rc)

    INPUT:
       a, b      integral interval [a, b]
    OUTPUT:
       dValue    the integral value
       rc        error code: api_OK if no error

History

    Y.M. Li      03/10/2013 : Creation date
-------------------------------------------------------------*/
#include "MyHeader.h"

void apiIntegrationDbl(double (*userEval)(double, double),
                       void (*Eval_c_d)(double, double &, double&),
                       double a, double b,
                       double &dValue, apiError &rc)
{
#define numLgdRoots 10

    int      i, j, k;
    double   u, v, c, d, alpha, beta, lambda, gamma;
```

```
    double    g_i, result, f[numLgdRoots];
    double    *pRoots=NULL, *pA = NULL;

    rc = api_OK;
    alpha = (b - a) / 2.0;
    beta =   (a + b) / 2.0;
    apiGetGaussLdgRtWts(numLgdRoots, pRoots, pA, rc);
    if (rc != api_OK)
        goto wrapup;

    dValue = 0.0;
    for (i=0; i<numLgdRoots; i++)
    {
        // Compute f(u_i, v_j) with j=0, 1,..., n-1
        u = alpha * pRoots[i] + beta;
        Eval_c_d(u, c, d);
        lambda = (d - c) / 2.0;
        gamma =  (c + d) / 2.0;
        for (j=0; j<numLgdRoots; j++)
        {
            v = lambda * pRoots[j] + gamma;
            f[j] = userEval(u, v);
        }

        // Compute g(u_i) = sum of A_j * f(u_i, v_j)
        result = 0.0;
        for (k=0; k<numLgdRoots/2; k++)
        {
            result += f[k] * pA[k];
            result += f[numLgdRoots-1-k] * pA[k];
        }
        g_i = lambda * result;
        if (i < numLgdRoots/2)
            dValue += g_i * pA[i];
        else
            dValue += g_i * pA[numLgdRoots - i - 1];
    }
    dValue *= alpha;

wrapup:

    return;
}
```

It is noted that the need for the array g_u is eliminated, and $\sum A_i g(u_i)$ is combined in one loop. For a demonstration, let's implement a main driver to compute

$$\int\int_D 4uv - v^3 \, du \, dv$$

with $D$ being bound by $h_1(u) = u^3$ and $h_2(u) = \sqrt{u}$ as shown below.

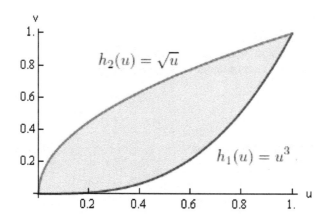

Figure 7.1: Integration domain bounded by two curves

For each fixed $u_i$, the lower and upper bounds for

$$\int_{c_i}^{d_i} f(u_i, v) dv$$

are determined by $c_i = h_1(u_i) = u_i^3$ and $d_i = h_2(u_i) = \sqrt{u_i}$. Therefore, the two callback functions in the main driver are

```
double myEval(double u, double v)
{
    return 4.0 * u * v - pow(v, 3);
}


void Eval_c_d(double u, double &c, double &d)
{
    c = pow(u, 3);
    d = sqrt(u);
}
```

and apiIntegrationDbl is called as follows

```
    apiIntegrationDbl(myEval, Eval_c_d, 0.0, 1.0, dValue, rc);
```

The exact solution is $55/156$ and the numerical solution is

```
  dValue = 0.35256410256410253;
```

which is accurate with respect to the machine epsilon.

It should be pointed out that we used a fixed number of Legendre polynomials to compute a double integral for simplicity. In real world computing, a tolerance should be given as the input to test the convergence as we did for a single variable integral.

So far, all of our callback functions are simple in terms of input and output arguments. In chapter 8, we shall discuss how to pass complex data structures of different types between the caller and callee to solve more complex applications.

## 7.3 Inheritance and polymorphism

Object-oriented programming (OOP) has been around for many decades and is taught as a core course in computer science. Many candidates I have interviewed knew the terminologies *data abstraction, encapsulation, polymorphism,* and *inheritance.* When asked to demonstrate their knowledge and skill to design a bisection method that is capable of finding a root of different functions (referring to question 6 given in the preface), however, very few of them sent back a satisfactory solution.

It appears to me that there is a gap between academic training and real world computing. For example, mammals (or people) are often used in many text books to teach inheritance and polymorphism. Engineering students are taught how mammals form a base class and how dogs and cats are derived from mammals and thus form the derived classes. The need for inheritance and polymorphism sounds very artificial and may fail to draw students' attention to the topic and may even cause their resistance to the idea. Therefore, when asked to use inheritance with polymorphism to design a bisection method that can be used to solve any function, candidates had trouble connecting the dots between what they have learned in the classroom and real engineering applications.

It is beyond the scope of this section to discuss OOP in detail. Instead, we will focus on inheritance and polymorphism. In particular, we will use the bisection method as an example to show how a reusable code can be implemented via inheritance with polymorphism. In C++ programming, inheritance allows one data type to acquire properties of other data types. Inheritance from a base class may be declared as *public, protected,* or *private.* This access specifier determines whether unrelated and derived classes can access the inherited public and protected members of the base class. Inheritance allows code to be reused between related types. Polymorphism enables one common interface for many implementations and for objects to act differently under different circumstances. By this definition, method or operator *overloading* is a form of polymorphism or "ad-hoc" polymorphism, since it allows methods to have the same method name but different signatures and implementations. For example, the following two classes were defined in **myHeader.h** to store 2D and 3D positions.

```
class GPosition2d
{
public:
   double  x;
   double  y;
};

class GPosition
{
```

```
public:
    double   x;
    double   y;
    double   z;
};
```

We may define the following two methods to compute the Euclidian distance in 2D and 3D coordinates:

```
double GDistance2d(GPosition2d &p1, GPosition2d &p2)
{
    double dx, dy;
    dx = p2.x - p1.x;
    dy = p2.y - p1.y;
    return sqrt(dx * dx + dy * dy);
}


double GDistance3d(GPosition &p1, GPosition &p2)
{
    double dx, dy, dz;
    dx = p2.x - p1.x;
    dy = p2.y - p1.y;
    dz = p2.z - p1.z;
    return sqrt(dx * dx + dy * dy + dz * dz);
}
```

Since the two methods have different argument data types, the C++ method overloading mechanism allows us to use the same name for different signatures. Accordingly, we have

```
double GDistance(GPosition2d &p1, GPosition2d &p2)
{
    double dx, dy;
    dx = p2.x - p1.x;
    dy = p2.y - p1.y;
    return sqrt(dx * dx + dy * dy);
}


double GDistance(GPosition &p1, GPosition &p2)
{
    double dx, dy, dz;
    dx = p2.x - p1.x;
    dy = p2.y - p1.y;
    dz = p2.z - p1.z;
    return sqrt(dx * dx + dy * dy + dz * dz);
}
```

Overloading a method allows us to logically call the same method regardless of the types of data we are passing in, which helps us remember what a procedure does as opposed to having to come up with several new names.

It is also possible to overload an operator. We will use the dot and cross product of two vectors as an example to discuss operators overloading. In mathematics, the dot product of two vectors $v_1 = (x_1, y_1, z_1)$ and $v_2 = (x_2, y_2, z_2)$ yields a scalar value of

$$v_1 \cdot v_2 = x_1 x_2 + y_1 y_2 + z_1 z_2.$$

The cross product of these two vectors defines a new vector that is perpendicular to both $v_1$ and $v_2$:

$$v_1 \times v_2 = \begin{vmatrix} i & j & k \\ x_1 & y_1 & z_1 \\ x_2 & y_2 & z_2 \end{vmatrix}.$$

By default, operator % is used to find the remainder of the division of one number by another and * is used to perform multiplication of integers and doubles. It is possible to overload these two operators to perform the dot- and cross-product of two vectors respectively as follows:

```
double operator%(GVector &V1, GVector &V2)
{
    return (V1.x * V2.x + V1.y * V2.y + V1.z * V2.z);
}

GVector operator*(GVector &V1, GVector &V2)
{
    GVector V;
    V.x = V1.y * V2.z - V1.z * V2.y;
    V.y = V1.z * V2.x - V1.x * V2.z;
    V.z = V1.x * V2.y - V1.y * V2.x;
}
```

Accordingly, we can use these two overloaded operators to perform the dot- and cross-product of two vectors as follows:

```
double  dotP = V1 % V2;
GVector crossV = V1 * V2;
```

Overloading a method or an operator enables one common name or operator for many implementations. For the purpose of code extensibility and reusability, this type of "ad hoc" polymorphism will not help. We are looking for the polymorphism that is often achieved by method *overriding*, which is not the same as method overloading. Method overriding is where a subclass replaces the implementation of one or more of its parent methods.

Referring to section 5.2, it is noted that we did not explicitly specify any particular function when presenting the bisection method. The method becomes functional dependency only when it is used to find the root of a particular function. For example, the following bisection implementation finds a root of a canonical polynomial function at the given interval $[a, b]$:

```
double apiBisection(int ndeg, double *pA,
          double a, double b, double tol)
{
    double f_a, f_b, f_mid, x_mid;

    // Terminate condition
    x_mid = 0.5 * (a + b);
    apiHornerEval(ndeg, pA, x_mid, f_mid);
    if (fabs(f_mid) < tol)
        return x_mid;

    // Recuce the complexity via recursion
    apiHornerEval(ndeg, pA, a, f_a);
    apiHornerEval(ndeg, pA, b, f_b);
    if (f_a * f_mid < 0.0)
        return apiBisection(ndeg, pA, a, x_mid, tol);
    else if (f_a * f_mid > 0.0)
        return apiBisection(ndeg, pA, x_mid, b, tol);
    else
        return -1.0; // Need error.
}
```

The implementation is not general enough to find the root of, say, $\sin(x)$ because apiHornerEval works only for polynomials. It is fine to use again a callback function rather than apiHornerEval to design a reusable bisection method. In this section, however, we shall explore how to use the OOP technique to design reusable code. Since the bisection method is universal to all functions, we should implement it in the base class so that all derived classes have access to this method. The declaration of the base class in MyHeader.h is

```
class CBisection
{
public:

    // pure virtual function to be implemented by derived class
    virtual double EvaluateFunc(double x) = 0;

    double ComputeRoot(double a, double b, double tol)
    {
        double f_a, f_b, f_mid, x_mid;

        // Terminate condition
        x_mid = 0.5 * (a + b);
        f_mid = this->EvaluateFunc(x_mid);
        if (fabs(f_mid) < tol)
            return x_mid;

        // Recuce the complexity via recursion
```

```
    f_a = this->EvaluateFunc(a);
    f_b = this->EvaluateFunc(b);
    if (f_a * f_mid < 0.0)
        return ComputeRoot(a, x_mid, tol);
    else
        return ComputeRoot(x_mid, b, tol);
    };
};
```

The method `ComputeRoot` is a generic implementation of a bisection algorithm. The method `EvaluateFunc` is declared as a *pure virtual* function by placing = 0 at the end of its declaration, indicating that the derived class must implement it. It is left for the derived classes to do so because the implementation of `EvaluateFunc` varies with respect to different applications. A pure virtual function is also known as an *abstract function* and a C++ class with a pure virtual function is known as an *abstract class*. An abstract class cannot be used to instantiate an object and serves only as an *interface* that describes the behavior or capabilities of a C++ class without committing to a particular implementation of that class.

It is noted that we did not declare a constructor and destructor since we do not have any specific data need to be initialized. Some compilers will implicitly define default ones if no explicit constructor and destructor are defined.

With the above base class, we can implement a derived class to solve any specific question with minimal coding effort. For example, to find a solution of $\sin x = 0$ in the given interval $[a, b]$, we first define the `CSineRoot` class whose parent class is the base class `CBisection`. Since a derived class inherits both data and member functions from a parent class, `CSineRoot` class has access to the generic bisection method `ComputeRoot` defined in the parent class. The only thing we need to do inside the derived class is to implement the pure virtual function `EvaluateFunc` to evaluate $\sin x$:

```
// A class to find x such that sin(x) = 0
class CSineRoot : public CBisection
{
public:
    // Implementation of pure virtual function
    double EvaluateFunc(double x)
    {
        return sin(x);
    }
};
```

Then, the root of $\sin x$ is computed by creating an instance of `CSineRoot` class and calling the bisection method as follows:

```
CSineRoot   objSin;
x = objSine.ComputeRoot(a, b, tol);
```

Similarly, to find a root of the polynomial function

$$f(x) = \sum_{i=0}^{n} a_i x^i,$$

we derive the CPolynomialRoot class from the base class CBisection. Inside this derived class, we implement the constructor to properly setup polynomial information, the destructor to free allocated memory, and the pure virtual function to evaluate the polynomial:

```
// A class to find x such that a polynomial function f = 0
class CPolynomialRoot : public CBisection
{
private:
    int       m_ndeg;
    double    *m_pA;

public:
    // Use constructor to initialize polynomial
    CPolynomialRoot(int ndeg, double *pA)
    {
        m_ndeg = ndeg;
        m_pA = new double[ndeg + 1];
        memcpy(m_pA, pA, (ndeg + 1) * sizeof(double));
    };

    // Destructor is responsible to delete memory
    ~CPolynomialRoot()
    {
        if (m_pA)
            delete [] m_pA;
    }

    // Implementation of pure virtual function
    double EvaluateFunc(double x)
    {
        double f;
        apiHornerEval(m_ndeg, m_pA, x, f);
        return f;
    }
};
```

Accordingly, the root of $f(x) = x^3 + 2x - 2$ in $[a, b]$ is computed by creating an instance of CPolynomialRoot class and calling the bisection method as follows:

```
double         A[4] = {-2.0, 2.0, 0.0, 1.0};
CPolynomialRoot objCubic(3, A);
x = objCubic.ComputeRoot(a, b, tol);
```

With inheritance and polymorphism mechanisms, the implementation of the bisection method for any specific function is reduced to implementing the virtual function EvaluateFunc that evaluates this particular function. The generic bisection method itself is not rewritten in derived classes but repeatedly reused by derived classes.

It is noted that the implementation of ComputeRoot was done inside the class definition. By default, member functions implemented (not just declared) in the class definition are implicitly inline. There are two disadvantages in doing so. Firstly, most functions can have very large definitions. Mixing the definition and the implementation details makes the class harder to manage and work with. Secondly, excessive inlining will degrade compiling time and increase an executable size. C++ provides a way to separate the definition portion of the class from the implementation portion. This is done by defining the function outside of the class definition using the scope resolution operator ::. This scope resolution operator allows a programmer to define the functions somewhere else. We thus implement the ComputeRoot method outside the class definition in apiBisectionObj.cpp as follows:

```
/*-----------------------------------------------------------
API Name
    apiBisectionObj

Description
    Implementation of CBisection::ComputeRoot method that finds
    the root of any function in the given interval [a, b].

Signature
    double CBisection::ComputeRoot(double a, double b, double tol)

    INPUT:
      a, b          defines the interval where the root is
      tol           convergency tolerance
    OUTPUT:
      return the root of function

History

    Y.M. Li     03/10/2013 : Creation date
-----------------------------------------------------------*/
#include "MyHeader.h"

double CBisection::ComputeRoot(double a, double b, double tol)
{
    double f_a, f_b, f_mid, x_mid;

    // Terminate condition
    x_mid = 0.5 * (a + b);
    f_mid = this->EvaluateFunc(x_mid);
    if (fabs(f_mid) < tol)
```

```
        return x_mid;

    // Recuce the complexity via recursion
    f_a = this->EvaluateFunc(a);
    f_b = this->EvaluateFunc(b);
    if (f_a * f_mid < 0.0)
        return ComputeRoot(a, x_mid, tol);
    else
        return ComputeRoot(x_mid, b, tol);
}
```

As usual, `apiBisectionObj.cpp` will be saved in the `src` folder and built into `FunctDLL`. We learned in section 4.1 that we need to provide the `linker` with information about function exporting. The so-called standard C linkage was used in `FunctDLL.def` to make all functions accessible. For exporting a method in C++ class, we usually have to use either a decorated name in `FunctDll.def` or the following Microsoft recommended protocol:

```
__declspec(dllexport) type __cdecl
```

We modify the class definition as follows to export the method `ComputeRoot`:

```
class CBisection
{
public:

    // pure virtual function to be implemented by derived class
    virtual double EvaluateFunc(double x) = 0;

    __declspec(dllexport) double __cdecl ComputeRoot(
                    double a, double b, double tol);
};
```

To export all public data members and member functions in a class, the keyword must appear to the left of the class name as follows:

```
class __declspec(dllexport) CBisection
{
public:

    // pure virtual function to be implemented by derived class
    virtual double EvaluateFunc(double x) = 0;

    double ComputeRoot(double a, double b, double tol);
};
```

The following main driver `mnBisectionObj.cpp` is implemented to compute the root of $\sin(x) = 0$ and $f(x) = x^3 + 2x - 2 = 0$ in the interval $[a, b]$ (note that $a$, $b$ and the convergency tolerance are read in from `BisectionObj.d1`).

```
#include "MyHeader.h"

int main(int argc, char* argv[])
{
    ⋮
    int      nIter, nLoops = atoi(argv[2]);
    double   duration;
    clock_t  tStart, tFinish;


    // Local variables to call the testing function:

    // A class to find x such that sin(x) = 0
    class CSineRoot : public CBisection
    {
    public:
        // Implementation of pure virtual function
        double EvaluateFunc(double x)
        {
            return sin(x);
        }
    };

    // A class to find x such that a polynomial function f = 0
    class CPolynomialRoot : public CBisection
    {
    private:
        int      m_ndeg;
        double   *m_pA;

    public:
        // Use constructor to initialize polynomial
        CPolynomialRoot(int ndeg, double *pA)
        {
            m_ndeg = ndeg;
            m_pA = new double[ndeg + 1];
            memcpy(m_pA, pA, (ndeg + 1) * sizeof(double));
        };

        // Destructor is responsible to delete memory
        ~CPolynomialRoot()
        {
            if (m_pA)
                delete [] m_pA;
        }

        // Implementation of pure virtual function
```

```
        double EvaluateFunc(double x)
        {
            double f;
            apiHornerEval(m_ndeg, m_pA, x, f);
            return f;
        }
    };

    apiError        rc = api_OK;
    int             ndeg = 3;
    double          A[4] = {-2.0, 2.0, 0.0, 1.0};
    double          a, b, x, tol;

    CSineRoot           objSine;
    CPolynomialRoot     objCubic(ndeg, A);

    // Read interval and tolerance
    fscanf_s( infile, "%lf", &a);
    fscanf_s( infile, "%lf", &b);
    fscanf_s( infile, "%lf", &tol);

    // Invoke the function
    tStart = clock();

    for (nIter=0; nIter < nLoops; nIter++)
    {
        x = objCubic.ComputeRoot(a, b, tol);
        fprintf(outfile, "root for P(x) = 0 is: %.15e\n", x);

        x = objSine.ComputeRoot(a, b, tol);
        fprintf(outfile, "root for sin(x) = 0 is: %.15e\n", x);
    }

    tFinish = clock();
    duration = (double)(tFinish - tStart) / CLOCKS_PER_SEC;
    printf("\nCPU time = %lf sec for %d iteration.\n", duration,nLoops);

    if (infile)
        fclose(infile);
    if (outfile)
        fclose(outfile);
    return rc;
}
```

In this section, we used a very simple example to illustrate how an OOP technique (in particular, the *inheritance with polymorphism*) can be used to design reusable code. With the implementation of the base class CBisection, it takes minimal effort to implement a program to compute a root of a particular function. Both function pointers and OOP techniques can be used to design and implement reusable code. However, inheritance with polymorphism is applicable only to functions implemented as classes. This limits its use in developing computational software, as most numerical methods are more naturally and efficiently implemented via functional programming.

## 7.4 Summary

In our local Costco wholesale store, cashiers who handle most transactions are honorably listed on a white board for their productivity. In the early days of software development, a developer's productivity was similarly measured proportionally by the quantity of code he or she wrote. Someone who appears to be writing a lot of code must be working diligently. But we learned some time ago that productivity should not be solely measured by lines of code. Lots of code certainly indicate activity, but activity does not necessarily correlate with progress and quality. Studies have found that an average application contains anywhere from 20 to 250 bugs per 1,000 lines of code! This metric is known as *defect density*. We can draw a major conclusion from this data: fewer lines of code mean fewer defects. By using the same code repeatedly by every programmer in every project, errors will be identified and eliminated at an early stage. Therefore, the reuse of source code is an important technique and has been encouraged and practiced in every software house. Its general purpose is to reduce unnecessary coding, which ultimately reduces project development time and money.

Callback functions are very powerful techniques for code reuse. In computer programming, a callback is executable code that is passed as an argument to other code. It allows a lower-level software layer to call a function defined in a higher-level layer. Several examples were presented in this chapter to demonstrate the need for callback functions in designing reusable code. Another good example of code reuse via a function pointer is the implementation of **qsort** (short for *QuickSort*) found in the C/C++ standard library. The QuickSort algorithm was developed in 1960 by a British computer scientist Tony Hoare while in Soviet Union as a visiting student. It is a divide-and-conquer algorithm and widely regarded as an efficient sorting algorithm. On average, it makes $O(n \log n)$ comparisons to sort $n$ elements. The idea is to pick any element of the array as the pivot element **pe**. By exchanging the elements, the array can be arranged so that all elements to the right of **pe** are greater than or equal to **pe**. Also, all elements to the left of **pe** are less than or equal to **pe**. Now the same method is applied to sort each of the smaller arrays on either side of **pe** via recursive calls. The recursion terminates when the length of the array becomes less than 2. To make QuickSort flexible to sort a one-dimensional array of integer, double, or any data structure, the Standard C/C++ implementation of QuickSort uses a callback function so that callers can provide their own callback methods to sort integer, double, or a particular element in data structure. The declaration of **qsort** is

```
void qsort(void *pArray, size_t num, size_t size,
           int (*compar)(const void *elem1, const void *elem2));
```

The caller is responsible to implement the callback function **compar** such that it returns a negative, zero, positive number if the data in **elem1** is less, equal to, or greater than data in **elem2** respectively. A pointer to **void** type (specified as **void** *) is called the void pointer. Variables of this type are pointers to data of an *unspecified* or a *universal* or *generic* type. Through the use of void pointers, we can pass generic data type to the callback function to compare. The use of void pointers will be discussed in detail in the next chapter.

Inheritance with polymorphism is an alternative to the callback function in designing reusable and extensible code. However, it is available only in object-oriented programming languages such as C++, C#, and Java. When new objects are created, they can inherit the data attributes or variables from their classes and all classes above them in the class hierarchy. Because a method is procedural code, when an object inherits methods, it is inheriting the programming code associated with the method. Polymorphism is the ability of different objects to receive the same message and respond in different ways. Polymorphism enables the programmer to concentrate on the common operations that are applied to objects of all the classes in a hierarchy. The general processing capabilities can be separated from any code that is specific to each class. Those general portions of the code can accommodate new classes without modification. An example was given in this chapter to illustrate how a generic computation can be implemented in the base class and inherited in a derived class to extend the functionality, which is often achieved via overriding virtual or pure virtual (abstract) functions.

# Chapter 8

# Reusable Solver for Nonlinear Systems

In mathematics, a nonlinear system is any problem in which the equations to be solved cannot be written as a linear combination of the unknown variables. Fluid and plasma mechanics, gas dynamics, elasticity, relativity, chemical reactions, combustion, ecology, biomechanics, and many, many other phenomena are all governed by inherently nonlinear equations. Nonlinear equations are usually more difficult to solve than linear equations and often require some problem-specific knowledge. In practice, a system of nonlinear equations is often solved by linearizing the equations and solving them iteratively via, for example, Newton's method and its variations.

In chapter 6, we studied a system of $n$ linear equations and implemented Gaussian elimination with partial pivoting and Gauss-Jordan with full pivoting methods to solve a generic system of linear equations of the following form:

$$\begin{bmatrix} a_{11} & a_{12} & \cdots & a_{1n} \\ a_{21} & a_{22} & \cdots & a_{2n} \\ a_{31} & a_{32} & \cdots & a_{3n} \\ \vdots & \vdots & \ddots & \vdots \\ a_{n1} & a_{n2} & \cdots & a_{nn} \end{bmatrix} \begin{bmatrix} x_1 \\ x_2 \\ x_3 \\ \vdots \\ x_n \end{bmatrix} = \begin{bmatrix} b_1 \\ b_2 \\ b_3 \\ \vdots \\ b_n \end{bmatrix}$$

We are out of luck when it comes to a system of nonlinear equations, as each system may have a completely different representation. For example, one system may consist of polynomial functions such as

$$x_1^2 - x_2^2 + 2x_2 = 0,$$
$$2x_1 + x_2^2 - 6 = 0.$$

Another system has a combination of different transcendental functions such as

$$\ln(x_1^2 + x_2^2) - \sin(x_1 x_2) = \ln 2 + \ln \pi,$$
$$e^{x_1 - x_2} + \cos(x_1 x_2) = 0.$$

The use of function pointers alone is not enough to implement a generic solver for nonlinear systems. We have to learn how to pass data that defines a particular system among the caller, callee, and callback function. Therefore, this chapter is a continued study of reusable code through implementation of a non-linear system solver.

## 8.1   Newton's method for one variable

A one-dimensional root-finding problem is a special and simple case of solving a system of nonlinear equations. The bisection method discussed in section 5.2 is a robust algorithm to find a root of a one-variable equation. Though conceptually clear, the bisection method has one significant drawback: it has only linear convergence and hence is slow. A good method for root finding converges *quadratically*, that is, the number of accurate digits doubles at every iteration!

Newton's method is one of the most powerful and well-known numerical methods for solving a root-finding problem. When a good estimation of root is available, it has quadratic convergence. There are many ways of introducing Newton's method. If we only want an algorithm, we can consider the technique geometrically, as is often done in calculus. In this section, an alternative means of introducing Newton's method is based on Taylor's expansion.

Assume that $f(x)$ is at least twice differentiable in $[a, b]$ and has a root $p$ in this interval. Let $x_0$ be a good estimation of the root $p$. Then, the Taylor expansion at $x_0$ is

$$f(x) = f(x_0) + f'(x_0)(x - x_0) + \frac{f''(\xi)}{2}(x - x_0)^2,$$

where $\xi$ lies between $x$ and $x_0$. Since $f(p) = 0$, this equation with $x = p$ gives

$$0 = f(x_0) + f'(x_0)(p - x_0) + \frac{f''(\xi)}{2}(p - x_0)^2. \qquad (8.1.1)$$

Newton's method is derived by assuming that since $|p - x_0|$ is small, the term involving $(p - x_0)^2$ is much smaller, so

$$0 \approx f(x_0) + f'(x_0)(p - x_0).$$

Solving for $p$ gives

$$p \approx x_0 - \frac{f(x_0)}{f'(x_0)}.$$

This sets the stage for Newton's method, which starts with an initial approximation $x_0$ and generates the sequence $\{x_i\}_{i=0}^{\infty}$, by

$$x_{i+1} = x_i - \frac{f(x_i)}{f'(x_i)} \quad i = 1, 2, \cdots \qquad (8.1.2)$$

The iterations terminate when the following criterion is met:

$$|f(x_{i+1})| < \varepsilon.$$

To prove that Newton's method converges quadratically, define the error at the $i$th iteration to be $e_i = p - x_i$. From the Taylor expansion, (8.1.1) we have

$$-\frac{f(x_i)}{f'(x_i)} = e_i + \frac{f''(\xi)}{2f'(x_i)}e_i^2.$$

Then,

$$e_{i+1} = p - x_{i+1} = p - \left( x_i - \frac{f(x_i)}{f'(x_i)} \right)$$

$$= e_i - \left( e_i + \frac{f''(\xi)}{2f'(x_i)}e_i^2 \right)$$

$$= -\frac{f''(\xi)}{2f'(x_i)}e_i^2 = C \times e_i^2.$$

When $f'(x_i) \neq 0$, we say that Newton's method has quadratic convergence since $e_{i+1}$ is equal to $e_i^2$ multiplied by a constant $C$. In plain English, if the error at the $i$th iteration is $10^{-3}$, we expect the new error at the $(i+1)$th iteration to be $10^{-6}$ multiplied by a constant.

We now discuss the implementation of Newton's method. It is noted that our discussion of Newton's method is independent of any particular function as far as the function is differentiable. This implies that we can design a reusable Newton's method for solving a root-finding problem. In the previous chapter, we learned that there are two ways to achieve this goal: callback functions and inheritance with polymorphism. Since this book focuses on numerical computations and it is more natural to implement algorithms as functions instead of object-oriented classes, a callback function will be used to implement Newton's method:

```
/*-------------------------------------------------------------
API Name
    apiNewtonOneVar

Description
    It finds the root of a function via Newton's method. A good initial
    estimation of root is often required to have a convergent solution.
    Users have to implement the callback function

        void (*userEval)(double x, double &f, double &f1)

    that evaluates the function value (i.e., f) and first
    derivative (i.e., f1)   at x.

Signature
    void apiNewtonOneVar(double x0, double tol,
                    void (*userEval)(double x, double &f,
                                        double &f1),
                    double &x, double &f, apiError &rc)
```

```
    INPUT:
       x0              initial estimation
       tol             convergency tolerance
       userEval        callback function
    OUTPUT:
       x               the root
       f               function value evaluated at x
       rc              error code: api_OK if no error

History

    Y.M. Li      03/27/2013 : Creation date
---------------------------------------------------------------------*/
#include "MyHeader.h"

void apiNewtonOneVar(double x0, double tol,
                     void (*userEval)(double x, double &f,
                                                double &f1),
                     double &x, double &f, apiError &rc)
{
    int         i;
    double      xi, fi, f1;

    rc = api_EXCEEDMAXITERATION;
    xi = x0;
    for (i=0; i<20; i++)
    {
       userEval(xi, fi, f1);
       if (fabs(fi) < tol)
       {
          rc = api_OK;
          x = xi;
          f = fi;
          break;
       }

       if (fabs(f1) < zero_tol)
       {
          rc = api_DIVIDEBYZERO;
          break;
       }
       xi -= fi / f1;
    }
}
```

We use the same example for **apiBisection** to test the above implementation: finding
the root of the cubic polynomial function

$$f(x) = x^3 - 5x^2 - 2x + 10$$

in the interval $[1, 3]$ with the convergency tolerance being $10^{-10}$. The code fragment of the testing main driver, mnNewtonOneVar.cpp, is listed below:

```
void myNewtonEval(double x, double &f, double &f1)
{
   f = pow(x, 3) - 5.0 * x * x - 2.0 * x + 10.0;
   f1 = 3.0 * x * x - 10.0 * x - 2.0;
}


// Implementation of mnNewtonOneVar.cpp
int main(int argc, char* argv[])
{
    :
    :
   x0 = 0.5 * (a + b);
   apiNewtonOneVar(x0, tol, myNewtonEval, x, f, rc);
    :
    :
}
```

By setting $x_0 = 0.5(a + b) = 2$, it takes 5 iterations to reach the following results:

```
x = 1.414213562373095e+000
f(x) = -1.776356839400251e-015
```

For the same test case, we would need 37 recursions for apiBisection to reach the following coarser results:

```
x = 1.414213562369696e+000
f(x) = 3.447553353908006e-011
```

Obviously, Newton's method converges much faster than the bisection method. However, Newton's method may diverge if the initial estimation is not sufficiently close to the true solution. In practice, the bisection method is used to find a reasonably good estimation, and Newton's method is deployed to refine the root to achieve a higher order of accuracy at the quadratic convergency speed.

## 8.2    Passing void data between function calls

Provided that the calling function implements a callback function to evaluate $f$ and $f'$ at the given $x$, apiNewtonOneVar should be generic enough to find the root of any smooth, one-variable function. However, the implementation of the callback function may require some information to be passed among the caller, callee, and the callback function. To understand this, let us look at the test driver mnNewtonOneVar implemented in the previous section. Every line of code in myNewtonEavl was hard-coded, which means that this main driver can only be used for testing this specific polynomial. Since a test driver reflects how an application may call an API, the limitation found in the test driver indicates the same restriction in a real world application.

It is not an issue for a test driver to open an input file and read generic polynomial information from the data file. The problem here is how to pass the polynomial information to the callback function myNewtonEval. As the name suggests, the callback function myNewtonEval is called by the callee (i.e., apiNewtonOneVar), not the caller (i.e., the test driver). Since the callee does not have the polynomial information stored in the caller, it cannot convey such information to the callback function. For this reason, polynomial coefficients in myNewtonEval were hard-coded. Such a problem is solvable if the required information is passed to apiNewtonOneVar and then to the callback function, which in turn requires us to add two more input arguments to the function declarations:

```
void apiNewtonOneVar(int ndeg, double *pA, double x0, double tol,
                     void (*userEval)(int ndeg, double *pA, double x,
                                      double &f, double &f1),
                     double &x, double &f, apiError &rc)
```

It should be noted that ndeg is the degree of the polynomial and *pA is an array that stores polynomial coefficients. This approach is fine when apiNewtonOneVar is intended to find only the root of a polynomial function. If it is designed for applications more than just a polynomial, it is preferable to use a void pointer so that different sets of data can be passed among the caller, callee, and callback function. The void data type means *undefined* or *unspecified*. Accordingly, a void pointer points to an object of unspecified type and can thus be used as a "generic" data pointer. For information retrieval, the void pointer can later be *casted* explicitly to the pointer of a specific data type. By introducing a pointer to void data type, Newton's method is re-implemented as follows:

```
void apiNewtonOneVar(void *pData, double x0, double tol,
                     void (*userEval)(void *pData, double x,
                                      double &f, double &f1),
                     double &x, double &f, apiError &rc)
{
    int         i;
    double      xi, fi, f1;

    rc = api_EXCEEDMAXITERATION;
    xi = x0;
    for (i=0; i<20; i++)
    {
        userEval(pData, xi, fi, f1);
        if (fabs(fi) < tol)
        {
            rc = api_OK;
            x = xi;
            f = fi;
            break;
        }

        if (fabs(f1) < zero_tol)
```

```
    {
        rc = api_DIVIDEBYZERO;
        break;
    }
    xi -= fi / f1;
  }
}
```

By using the pointer void *, we are able to pass generic data among the caller, callee, and callback function to achieve a high level of reusability. To illustrate how this is accomplished, let us implement a generic method that finds the root of any polynomial function at the given interval $[a, b]$. This function calls apiBisection with a coarse tolerance to get a reasonably good estimation of the root and then calls apiNewtonOneVar to refine it.

```
/*-----------------------------------------------------------------
API Name
    apiFndPolynomialRoot

Description
    It finds the root of a polynomial function in the
    given interval [a, b]

Signature
    void apiFndPolynomialRoot(int ndeg, double *pA, double a, double b,
                    double tol, double &x, double &f, apiError &rc)

    INPUT:
        ndeg          degree of polynomial function
        pA            array that stores coefficients of polynomial
        tol           convergence accuracy
        a, b          defines the solution interval [a, b]
    OUTPUT:
        x             the root
        f             polynomial value at x, i.e., f(x)
        rc            error code: api_OK if no error

History

    Y.M. Li     03/27/2013 : Creation date
-------------------------------------------------------------------*/
#include "MyHeader.h"

static void myEval(void *pData, double x, double &f, double &f1)
{
    int       ndeg;
    double    *pA;
```

```
   // casting the pointer
   pA = (double *)pData;

   // Retrieve polynomial information
   ndeg = (int)pA[0];

   // Increment pointer so pA[0] is now a_0 (the constant term)
   pA++;

   apiHornerEval(ndeg, pA, x, f, &f1);
}

void apiFndPolynomialRoot(int ndeg, double *pA, double a, double b,
                  double tol, double &x, double &f, apiError &rc)
{
   int            i;
   double         x0;
   vector<double> polyInfo;

   rc = api_OK;
   x0 = apiBisection(ndeg, pA, a, b, 0.1);

   // Pack polynomial information in polyInfo:
   polyInfo.resize(ndeg + 2);
   polyInfo[0] = ndeg;
   for (i=0; i<=ndeg; i++)
      polyInfo[1+i] = pA[i];

   // Cast polyInfo to the (void *) pointer to call Newton's method:
   apiNewtonOneVar((void *)&polyInfo[0], x0, tol, myEval, x, f, rc);
}
```

As seen above, `myEavl` is not hard-coded to evaluate a specific polynomial function. It is implemented to evaluate any polynomial function. It receives the polynomial information indirectly via the callee function `apiNewtonOneVar`.

I will give another example to demonstrate how the "generic" data type has maximized the reusability of `apiNewtonOneVar`. In computer-aided geometric design, one of the most commonly-used geometric operations is to find the *minimum distance* between a point and a curve. The minimum distance API is also used to compute the parameter of a parametric curve from a known point. For simplicity, we will consider how to find the minimum distance between a point and an ellipse. In high school, we learned that an ellipse centered at $(x_0, y_0)$ may be represented parametrically as

$$x(t) = x_0 + a\cos(t)$$
$$y(t) = y_0 + b\sin(t)$$

where $a$ and $b$ are the semi-major and semi-minor axes that are parallel to the $x$- and $y$-axis respectively. The angular parameter $t$ is measured counter-clockwise from the major axis. If the semi-major and semi-minor axes are not parallel to the $x$- and $y$-axis as shown in figure 8.1, then an ellipse in generic parametric form is given by

$$x(t) = x_0 + a\cos(t)\cos(\phi) - b\sin(t)\sin(\phi)$$
$$y(t) = y_0 + a\cos(t)\sin(\phi) + b\sin(t)\cos(\phi)$$

where $\phi$ is the angle between the $x$-axis and the major axis of the ellipse.

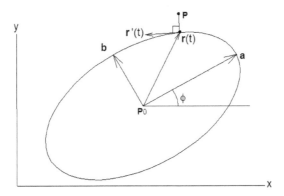

Figure 8.1: Minimum distance between point and ellipse

In computer graphics and computer-aided geometric design, a parametric curve is often represented as a *vector-valued* function for simplicity and easy manipulation (e.g., transformation and evaluation). By using vectors to represent the major and minor axes of an ellipse (see figure 8.1), we can write a generic ellipse in vector-valued parametric form as

$$\boldsymbol{r}(t) = \boldsymbol{p}_0 + \boldsymbol{a}\cos(t) + \boldsymbol{b}\sin(t), \tag{8.2.1}$$

where $\boldsymbol{p}_0 = (x_0, y_0)$, $\boldsymbol{a} = (x_a, y_a)$, and $\boldsymbol{b} = (x_b, y_b)$. Given an arbitrary point $\boldsymbol{p}$, the squared distance to the ellipse

$$g(t) = \|\boldsymbol{r}(t) - \boldsymbol{p}\|^2$$

is minimized (or maximized) if $g'(t) = 0$, which is equivalent to finding $t$ such that

$$f(t) = [\boldsymbol{r}(t) - \boldsymbol{p}] \cdot \boldsymbol{r}'(t) = 0.$$

The above relation indicates that the minimum (or maximum) distance occurs at $t$ such that $[\boldsymbol{r}(t) - \boldsymbol{p}]$ is perpendicular to the tangent of curve evaluated at $t$. For an ellipse, there are two parameters $t_1$ and $t_2$ such that $f(t_1) = f(t_2) = 0$, with one being the minimum distance parameter and the other being the maximum distance parameter.

If Newton's method is used to find the root of $f(t) = 0$, we need to solve the following equation iteratively

$$t_{i+1} = t_i - \frac{f(t_i)}{f'(t_i)}$$

where

$$f'(t) = \boldsymbol{r}'(t) \cdot \boldsymbol{r}'(t) + [\boldsymbol{r}(t) - \boldsymbol{p}] \cdot \boldsymbol{r}''(t).$$

From equation (8.2.1), it is readily obtained the first and second derivatives of the ellipse:

$$r'(t) = -a\sin(t) + b\cos(t),$$
$$r''(t) = -(a\cos(t) + b\sin(t)) = p_0 - r(t).$$

Newton's method requires a good estimation of the solution. We now discuss how to determine the initial estimation. Projecting the vector $(p - p_0)$ onto the major and minor axis gives respectively:

$$(p - p_0) \cdot \frac{a}{\|a\|} \quad \text{and} \quad (p - p_0) \cdot \frac{b}{\|b\|}.$$

Accordingly, the angle between the major axis and the vector $(p - p_0)$ is given by

$$\theta = \arctan\left(\frac{(p - p_0) \cdot \dfrac{a}{\|a\|}}{(p - p_0) \cdot \dfrac{b}{\|b\|}}\right). \tag{8.2.2}$$

If it is a circle (a special case of ellipse when $\|a\| = \|b\|$), the minimum distance parameter $t_0$ is the same as $\theta$. If it is not a circle, we may still use equation (8.2.2) to compute the initial estimation and to call Newton's method for a refined solution.

Having discussed the underling mathematics, we implement the minimum distance algorithm as follows. Please note that the operator % denotes the dot-product of two vectors, and GDistance computes the distance between two points, which was discussed in the previous chapter.

```
/*-------------------------------------------------------------------
API Name
    apiDminPtEllipse

Description
    It computes the minimum distance between a point
    and an ellipse.

Signature
    void apiDminPtEllipse(GPosition2d p0, GVector2d &a, GVector2d &b,
                          GPosition2d &pt, double tol, double &dmin,
                          double &t, GPosition2d &pjpt, apiError &rc)

    INPUT:
        p0          center of ellipse
        a           major axis
        b           minor axis
        pt          an arbitrary point
        tol         accuracy tolerance
    OUTPUT:
```

```
        dmin      minimum distance
        t         minimum distance parameter
        pjpt      point on ellipse such that |p - pjpt| is minimized
        rc        error code: api_OK if no error

History

    Y.M. Li     04/27/2013 : Creation date
------------------------------------------------------------------*/
#include "MyHeader.h"

typedef struct{
    GPosition2d *p0;
    GVector2d   *a;
    GVector2d   *b;
    GPosition2d *pt;
} EllipInfo;


static void myEval(void *pData, double t, double &f, double &f1)
{
    GVector2d   r, r1, r2, r_p;
    EllipInfo   *pInfo;

    // casting the pointer
    pInfo = (EllipInfo *)pData;

    // Evaluate the point on ellipse
    r.x = pInfo->p0->x + pInfo->a->x * cos(t) + pInfo->b->x * sin(t);
    r.y = pInfo->p0->y + pInfo->a->y * cos(t) + pInfo->b->y * sin(t);

    // Evaluate the first derivative of ellipse
    r1.x = -pInfo->a->x * sin(t) + pInfo->b->x * cos(t);
    r1.y = -pInfo->a->y * sin(t) + pInfo->b->y * cos(t);

    // Evaluate the second derivative of ellipse
    r2.x = pInfo->p0->x - r.x;
    r2.y = pInfo->p0->y - r.y;

    r_p.x = r.x - pInfo->pt->x;
    r_p.y = r.y - pInfo->pt->y;

    f = r_p % r1;
    f1 = r1 % r1 + r_p % r2;
}


void apiDminPtEllipse(GPosition2d p0, GVector2d &a, GVector2d &b,
```

```
                        GPosition2d &pt, double tol, double &dmin,
                        double &t, GPosition2d &pjpt, apiError &rc)
{
    double      t0, d0, f, cos_t, sin_t, majRadius, minRadius;
    GVector2d   P0;
    EllipInfo   ellip_info;

    rc = api_OK;
    P0.x = pt.x - p0.x;
    P0.y = pt.y - p0.y;
    majRadius = sqrt(a % a);
    minRadius = sqrt(b % b);

    // Estimate the initial solution t0:
    cos_t = P0 % a / majRadius;
    sin_t = P0 % b / minRadius;
    t0 = atan2(sin_t, cos_t);

    // Evaluate ellipse based on t0
    pjpt.x = p0.x + a.x * cos(t0) + b.x * sin(t0);
    pjpt.y = p0.y + a.y * cos(t0) + b.y * sin(t0);
    d0 = GDistance(pt, pjpt);

    // Setup data for callback function
    ellip_info.a = &a;
    ellip_info.b = &b;
    ellip_info.p0 = &p0;
    ellip_info.pt = &pt;

    // Refine the solution
    apiNewtonOneVar((void *)&ellip_info, t0, tol, myEval, t, f, rc);
    if (rc == api_OK)
    {
        pjpt.x = p0.x + a.x * cos(t) + b.x * sin(t);
        pjpt.y = p0.y + a.y * cos(t) + b.y * sin(t);
        dmin = GDistance(pt, pjpt);
        if (dmin > d0 + tol)
        {
            // Readers are encouraged to explore a way
            // to reset t0 to call Newtons method
            rc = api_NOSOLUTION;
        }
    }
}
```

In the above implementation, a structure was defined and created to store the center, major, and minor axis of the ellipse as well as the given point from which the distance is measured. This structure was cast as void * to convey the required information among the caller, callee, and callback function. It is possible to use a `double` array to store all information as we did in the first example (i.e., implementation of `apiFndPolynomialRoot`). But we chose a structure to emphasize that we could cast not only an array but also a structure/class to the `void` pointer.

Two examples in this section demonstrated how the use of "generic" data type maximized the reusability of Newton's method. Through the `void` pointer, we were able to pass various data among the caller, callee, and callback function to solve two completely different sets of problems. It should be pointed out that the above implementation was for the purpose of understanding the design of reusable code. For this reason, we wanted to keep the implementation as simple as possible and hence did not address the case where the initial estimation did not yield the solution.

## 8.3 Newton's method for multiple variables

Newton's method discussed previously can be expanded to solve a system of nonlinear equations. In general, a system of nonlinear equations has the form

$$f_1(x_1, x_2, \cdots, x_n) = 0,$$
$$f_2(x_1, x_2, \cdots, x_n) = 0,$$
$$\vdots$$
$$f_n(x_1, x_2, \cdots, x_n) = 0,$$

where each function $f_i$ maps a vector $\mathbf{x} = (x_1, x_2, \cdots, x_n)^T$ of the $n$-dimensional space $\mathbb{R}^n$ into the real line $\mathbb{R}$. For convenience we can think of $(x_1, x_2, \cdots, x_n)$ as a vector $\boldsymbol{x}$ and $(f_1, f_2, \cdots, f_n)$ as a vector-valued function $\boldsymbol{F}$. With this notation, we can write the above system of equations simply as:

$$\boldsymbol{F}(\boldsymbol{x}) = \boldsymbol{0}.$$

Accordingly, $\boldsymbol{F}$ is a mapping from $\mathbb{R}^n$ into $\mathbb{R}^n$, and the functions $f_1, f_2, \cdots, f_n$ are the coordinate functions of $\boldsymbol{F}$. Our task now becomes finding a vector that makes the vector function equal to the zero vector.

In the single variable case, Newton's method was derived by considering the linear approximation of the function $f$ at the initial guess $x_0$. From calculus, the following is the linear approximation of $\boldsymbol{F}$ at the initial estimation $\boldsymbol{x}^{(0)}$ for vectors and vector-valued functions:

$$\boldsymbol{F}(\boldsymbol{x}) \approx \boldsymbol{F}(\boldsymbol{x}^{(0)}) + J(\boldsymbol{x}^{(0)})(\boldsymbol{x} - \boldsymbol{x}^{(0)}).$$

Here $J(\boldsymbol{x}^{(0)})$ is an $n \times n$ *Jacobian* matrix whose entries are the various partial derivatives of the components of $F$. Specifically:

$$J(x) = \begin{pmatrix} \dfrac{\partial f_1}{\partial x_1}(x) & \dfrac{\partial f_1}{\partial x_2}(x) \cdots & \dfrac{\partial f_1}{\partial x_n}(x) \\[2mm] \dfrac{\partial f_2}{\partial x_1}(x) & \dfrac{\partial f_2}{\partial x_2}(x) \cdots & \dfrac{\partial f_2}{\partial x_n}(x) \\[1mm] \vdots & & \\[1mm] \dfrac{\partial f_n}{\partial x_1}(x) & \dfrac{\partial f_n}{\partial x_2}(x) \cdots & \dfrac{\partial f_n}{\partial x_n}(x) \end{pmatrix},$$

With initial estimation $x^{(0)}$, Newton's method for nonlinear systems is given by

$$x^{(k+1)} = x^{(k)} - J^{-1}\left(x^{(k)}\right) F\left(x^{(k)}\right) \qquad (k = 0, 1, 2, \cdots) \qquad (8.3.1)$$

It is noted that $x^{(0)}$ is the initial estimation, and $x^{(k)}$ is the result of the $k^{\text{th}}$ iteration. Newton's method is generally expected to give a quadratic convergence, provided that a sufficiently accurate starting value is known and that the inverse of Jacobian matrix $J^{-1}(x)$ exists. The weakness in Newton's method arises from the need to compute derivatives and inverse the matrix $J(x)$ at each iteration step. In practice, explicit computation of $J^{-1}(x)$ is avoided by performing the operation in a two-step manner. First, let $y = x^{(k)} - x^{(k+1)}$. The vector $y$ is found by solving the following linear system:

$$J\left(x^{(k)}\right) y = F\left(x^{(k)}\right).$$

Then, the new approximation, $x^{(k+1)}$, is obtained by subtracting $y$ from $x^{(k)}$.

With the initial estimation of $x$, Newton's method is outlined below:

Step 1: Allocate and initialize memory for $F$ (n doubles) and $J$ (n $\times$ n doubles).

Step 2: While ($k <$ max_iteration) do Steps 3 – 7

   Step 3: Calculate $F$ and $J$.

   Step 4: If $||F||_\infty < \delta$, terminate the loop and output the results ($\delta$ is the given tolerance).

   Step 5: Solve the $n \times n$ linear system $J(x)y = F(x)$.

   Step 6: If $||y||_\infty < \varepsilon$, terminate as no changes can be made ($\varepsilon$ is the machine tolerance).

   Step 7: Set $x = x - y$ and $k = k + 1$.

Step 8: Set error code to api_EXCEEDMAXITERATION due to exceeding the maximum number of iterations.

The implementation of Newton's method is independent of any particular system of nonlinear equations except for Step 3, where it evaluates $F$ and $J$. Similar to the implementation of apiNewtonOneVar, a callback function and a pointer to void data type will be used to achieve a high level of reusability. Consequently, the implementation of Newton's method for a multi-variable system is:

```
/*----------------------------------------------------------------
API Name
   apiNewtonMultiVar

Description
   It solves a non-linear system via Newton iteration method.
   Users have to implement the following callback function

      apiError (*userEvalFunct)(void *pUserData, double *X,
                                double *F, double *Jmat)

   that evaluates the system and Jacobian matrix at X -- the
   estimation of solutions.

Signature
   void apiNewtonMultiVar(
           apiError (*userEvalFunct)(void *, double *,
                                     double *, double *),
              void *pUserData, double tol, int n,
              double *X, double *F, apiError &rc)

   INPUT:
      pUserData   undefined data structure for passing information
      tol         convergency tolerance
      n           number of unknowns
      X           collection of estimations
   OUTPUT:
      X           collection of solutions
      F           function values (less than tol if converging)

History

   Y.M. Li     03/10/2013 : Creation date
----------------------------------------------------------------*/
#include "MyHeader.h"


void apiNewtonMultiVar(
        apiError (*userEvalFunct)(void *,
           double *, double *, double *),
        void *pUserData, double tol, int n,
        double *X, double *F, apiError &rc)
{
   int            i, j, k, max_num_iter = 20;
   vector<double> Jmat, sol;

   // Allocate memory for solutions and Jacobian matrix
```

```cpp
    Jmat.resize(n * n);
    sol.resize(n);

    // Iteration loops
    for (k=0; k<max_num_iter; k++)
    {
        rc = userEvalFunct(pUserData, X, F, &Jmat[0]);
        if (rc != api_OK)
            goto wrapup;

        for (j=0; j<n; j++)
        {
            if (fabs(F[j]) > tol)
            {
                rc = api_NOSOLUTION;
                break;
            }
        }
        if (rc == api_OK)
        {
            // Convergence has been reached
            goto wrapup;
        }

        if (n == 2)
        {
            double det;

            det = Jmat[0] * Jmat[3] - Jmat[1] * Jmat[2];
            if (fabs(det) > zero_tol)
            {
                sol[0] = (F[0] * Jmat[3] - F[1] * Jmat[1]) / det;
                sol[1] = (F[1] * Jmat[0] - F[0] * Jmat[2]) / det;
            }
        }
        else
        {
            // Solve linear system for new solutions
            vector<vector<double>> aug_mat;

            aug_mat.resize(n);
            for (i=0; i<n; i++)
            {
                aug_mat[i].resize(n+1);
                for (j=0; j<n; j++)
                    aug_mat[i][j] = Jmat[i*n+j];
                aug_mat[i][n] = F[i];
```

```
        }
        apiGaussPPivot(aug_mat, rc);
        if (rc != api_OK)
            goto wrapup;

        for (i=0; i<n; i++)
            sol[i] = aug_mat[i][n];
    }

    // Terminate if sol is too small:
    rc = api_NOSOLUTION;
    for (j=0; j<n; j++)
    {
        if (fabs(sol[j]) > machine_epsilon)
        {
            rc = api_OK;
            break;
        }
    }
    if (rc != api_OK)
        break;

    // Update the variables for next iteration:
    for (j=0; j<n; j++)
        X[j] -= sol[j];
    }

wrapup:

    return;
}
```

We now implement a test driver to solve the following system of polynomial equations:

$$f_1(x_1, x_2) = x_1^2 - x_2^2 + 2x_2,$$
$$f_2(x_1, x_2) = 2x_1 + x_2^2 - 6.$$

The graph of two functions is shown in figure 8.2. Newton's method requires a good estimation of the solution. In general, the more variables we have, the harder it is to find a good initial guess. In practice, this may be overcome by using physically reasonable assumptions about the possible values of a solution, i.e., take advantage of mathematic and engineering knowledge of the problem. For example, solving the above system of non-linear equations is geometrically a problem of finding the intersections of two algebraic curves in certain intervals. Assume that $-3 \le x_1, x_2 \le 3$. By sampling and plotting enough points on both functions, we may sketch the graph of two functions as shown in figure 8.2.

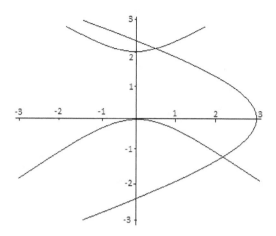

Figure 8.2: Graph of two polynomial curves

By looking at the graph, we guess that the two intersections are roughly at $(1.0, 2.5)$ and $(2.5, -1.5)$. We take these two points as an initial guess of the solution to create two testing files: NewtonMultiVar.d1 and NewtonMultiVar.d2. We then implement the driver as follows:

```
// Callback function
apiError myNewtonEval(void *pDataStruct, double *X,
                           double *F, double *Jmat)
{
    // Evaluate functions
    F[0] = X[0] * X[0] - X[1] * X[1] + 2.0 * X[1];
    F[1] = 2.0 * X[0] + X[1] * X[1] - 6.0;

    // Compute Jacobian matrix
    Jmat[0] = 2.0 * X[0]; // df1/dx1
    Jmat[1] = -2.0 * X[1] + 2.0; // df1/dx2

    Jmat[2] = 2.0;   // df2/dx1
    Jmat[3] = 2.0 * X[1]; // df2/dx2

    return api_OK;
}

int main(int argc, char* argv[])
{
    :
    :

    // Local variables to call the testing function:
    double      tol, X[2], F[2];
    apiError    rc = api_OK;
```

```
fscanf_s(infile, "%lf  %lf", &X[0], &X[1]);
fscanf_s(infile, "%lf", &tol);

// Invoke the function
tStart = clock();

for (nIter=0; nIter < nLoops; nIter++)
{
    apiNewtonMultiVar(myNewtonEval, NULL, tol, 2, X, F, rc);
    if (rc)
    {
        printf("*** rc = %d at nIter = %d\n", rc, nIter);
        goto wrapup;
    }
}

tFinish = clock();
    ⋮
}
```

Save and run this program. With respect to the initial guess of $(1.0, 2.5)$ and $(2.5, -1.5)$, Newton's method finds converging solutions in only 3 iterations. The results are:

$$(x_1, x_2) = (0.62520409521, 2.1793558245),$$
$$(x_1, x_2) = (2.1095119193, -1.3345321882).$$

It should be pointed out that the callback function was hard-coded without using *pDataStruct. Readers are encouraged to generalize it for any system of polynomial equations by using *pDataStruct. Later in this chapter, we shall present more application examples that rely on *pDataStruct to setup different nonlinear systems to call apiNewtonMultiVar.

In computer aided geometric design, polynomial curves and surfaces are frequently used to model geometric objects such as telephone handsets, human bodies, cars, and airplanes. In CAD software companies, developers are constantly challenged to solve complex curve/curve, curve/surface, and surface/surface intersection problems. It is impractical to sketch the graph of polynomial equations to find an initial guess of the solution as it depends on graphing capability and human interactions. Recall the seventh question given in the preface where candidates were asked to outline a way to solve curve/curve intersection problems. A feasible approach would be to bisect the solid and dashed curves and save halved segments (or intervals) in two binary trees as shown in figure 8.3. It is assumed that the solid curve is defined in the interval $[a, b]$ and dashed curve in $[c, d]$. After the first subdivision, the left- and right-halved solid curves are defined respectively in $[a, b/2]$ and $[b/2, b]$. The intervals of both solid and dashed curves are continuously halved when the subdivision process is repeated.

When the segment is almost linear with respect to the given tolerance, we call the line/line intersection routine to obtain an intersection point of two approximating lines.

This intersection point is then used as a good estimation for `apiNewtonMultiVar` to refine the solution at a much faster convergency speed. Since the two curves intersect at multiple places, we need to transverse two binary trees to make sure we have checked every halved segment. To optimize the computation, *range boxes* (or *rectangular bounding boxes*) are often used to filter out the halved segments whose range boxes do not intersect each other.

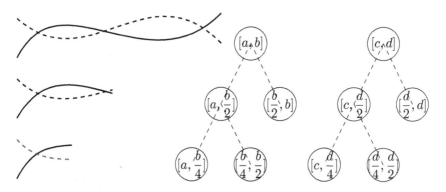

Figure 8.3: Each node stores the halved candidate curve

A brute force solution to this problem is to stroke each curve and save the stroking points into two arrays. It then loops through two arrays to create lines from two adjacent stroking points and to call the line/line intersection routine. Such an approach is an $O(n^2)$ method and should be avoided by all means.

## 8.4   Steepest descent method

Newton's method for solving nonlinear systems has a very fast convergence speed once a sufficiently accurate estimation is known. When a poor estimation is given, it often diverges. In practice, a good estimation can be obtained by the bisection method when the system has two variables (or two-dimension). It is much harder, if not impossible, to obtain a global convergence via bisection in higher dimensions! In this section, we will discuss the *Steepest Descent* algorithm. This method converges slowly to the solution, but it will often converge even for poor initial estimations. When sufficient accurate estimations are obtained, Newton's method is used to refine the solutions at a very fast convergence speed.

Let us define a mapping $g : \mathbb{R}^n \to \mathbb{R}$. The connection between the minimization of $g$ from $\mathbb{R}^n$ to $\mathbb{R}$ and the solutions of a system of nonlinear equations is due to the fact that the system has a solution at $\boldsymbol{x} = (x_1, x_2, \cdots, x_n)^T$ precisely when the function $g$ defined by

$$g(x_1, x_2, \cdots, x_n) = \sum_{i=0}^{n} f_i^2$$

has the minimal value 0. By introducing $g$, we translate the multidimensional search into a sequence of searches in one dimension and hence avoid complex searches in multiple dimensions.

The Steepest descent is also known as the *gradient descent*. From vector calculus, it is known that, for $g : \mathbb{R}^n \to \mathbb{R}$, the gradient of $g$ at $\boldsymbol{x}$ is denoted $\nabla g$ whose components are the partial derivatives of $g$. That is:

$$\nabla g(\boldsymbol{x}) = \left( \frac{\partial g}{\partial x_1}, \frac{\partial g}{\partial x_2}, \cdots, \frac{\partial g}{\partial x_n} \right)^T$$

The gradient of a function gives the direction of steepest increase (uphill). Thus a natural minimization algorithm is to go in the direction opposite the gradient (downhill) by a certain amount. Let's evaluate $g$ at the initial estimation $\boldsymbol{x}$ and denote it by $g_1$. Since $-\nabla g$ is the steepest descent direction, we expect to obtain a smaller $g$ if we evaluate it at

$$\boldsymbol{x}^{(3)} = \boldsymbol{x} - a_3 \nabla g(\boldsymbol{x}).$$

Different $a_3$ results in different $g_3 = g(\boldsymbol{x}^{(3)})$. To derive the optimized step length $a_3$, we use the quadratic interpolation method that is outlined as follows:

Step 1: Find $a_3 \in (0, 1)$ such that $g_3 < g(\boldsymbol{x})$. This is done by assigning $a_3 = 1$ and repeatedly reducing it by half until $g_3 < g(\boldsymbol{x})$ or $a_3$ is too small.

Step 2: Take $a_2 = a_3/2$ and set $\boldsymbol{x}^{(2)} = \boldsymbol{x} - a_2 \nabla g(\boldsymbol{x})$.

Step 3: Evaluate $g$ at $\boldsymbol{x}^{(2)}$ and denote the result by $g_2$.

Step 4: Set $a_0 - 0.5(a_2 - h_1/h_3)$ with

$h_1 = (g_2 - g_1)/a_2,$

$h_2 = (g_3 - g_2)/(a_3 - a_2),$

$h_3 = (h_2 - h_1)/a_3.$

Note these values are derived from quadratic interpolation at three points $(0, g)$, $(a_3, g_3)$, and $(a_2, g_2)$.

Step 5: Compute the critical point $\boldsymbol{x}^{(0)} = \boldsymbol{x} - a_0 \nabla g(\boldsymbol{x})$ and $g_0 = g(\boldsymbol{x}^{(0)})$.

Step 6: Select $a$ from $\{a_0, a_3\}$ so that $g = g(\boldsymbol{x} - a\nabla g(\boldsymbol{x})) = \min\{g_0, g_1\}$.

Step 7: Terminate and output $\boldsymbol{x}$ if $g < 0.1$.

Step 8: Set $\boldsymbol{x} = \boldsymbol{x} - a\nabla g(\boldsymbol{x})$ and $g_1 = g$. Go to Step 1.

The implementation of Steepest Descent is listed below:

```
/*-------------------------------------------------------------
API Name
    apiSteepDescent


Description
```

It improves the estimated solutions of a non-linear
system via Steepest Descent algorithm. It is used in
conjunction with Newton iteration method to solve the
non-linear system. The callback function

```
    apiError (*userEvalFunct)(void *pUserData, double *X,
                              double *F, double *Jmat)
```

evaluates the system and Jacobian matrix at X.

Signature
```
    void apiSteepDescent(apiError (*userEvalFunct)(
                void *, double *, double *, double *),
                void *pUserData, int n, double *X,
                double *F, apiError &rc)
```

```
    INPUT:
        *userEvalFunct  function pointer
        pUserData       data structure required to build system
        tol             convergency tolerance
        n               number of unknowns
        X               collection of estimations
    OUTPUT:
        X               improved collection of estimations
        F               function values evaluated at X
```

History

```
    Y.M. Li     03/10/2013 : Creation date
-----------------------------------------------------------------*/
#include "MyHeader.h"

void apiSteepDescent(apiError (*userEvalFunct)(
                void *, double *, double *, double *),
                void *pUserData, int n, double *X,
                double *F, apiError &rc)
{
    int        i, j, k;
    double     tol = 0.1, d, g0, g1, g2, g3;
    double     a0, a2, a3, h1, h2, h3;
    vector<double> xi, dG, Jmat;

    rc = api_OK;
    xi.resize(n);
    dG.resize(n);
    Jmat.resize(n * n);
```

```
// Evaluate functions and derivatives at given values
rc = userEvalFunct(pUserData, X, F, &Jmat[0]);
if (rc)
   goto wrapup;
g1 = 0.0;
for (i=0; i<n; i++)
   g1 += F[i] * F[i];
if (g1 < tol)
   return;

// Loop to refine the roots based on Steepest Descent Algorithm
for (k=0; k<20; k++)
{
   // Compute the normalized gradient of g=sum(f_i * f_i)
   for (i=0; i<n; i++)
   {
      dG[i] = 0.0;
      for (j=0; j<n; j++)
         dG[i] += Jmat[j*n+i] * F[j];
      dG[i] *= 2.0;
   }
   d = 0.0;
   for (i=0; i<n; i++)
      d += dG[i] * dG[i];
   d = sqrt(d);
   if (d < machine_epsilon)
      goto wrapup; // No improvement can be made
   for (i=0; i<n; i++)
      dG[i] /= d;

   // Derive a3 along gradient so (x - a3 * dG) yields smaller g3
   g3 = 2.0 * g1;
   a3 = 1.0;
   while (g3 > g1)
   {
      if (a3 < 0.1 * tol)
         goto wrapup; // No improvement can be made

      a3 *= 0.5;
      for (i=0; i<n; i++)
         xi[i] = X[i] - a3 * dG[i];
      rc = userEvalFunct(pUserData, &xi[0], F, &Jmat[0]);
      if (rc)
         goto wrapup;
      g3 = 0.0;
      for (i=0; i<n; i++)
         g3 += F[i] * F[i];
```

```
    if (fabs(g3) < tol)
    {
        for (i=0; i<n; i++)
            X[i] = xi[i];
        goto wrapup; // converged
    }
}


// Compute g2 between g1 and g3
a2 = 0.5 * a3;
for (i=0; i<n; i++)
    xi[i] = X[i] - a2 * dG[i];
rc = userEvalFunct(pUserData, &xi[0], F, &Jmat[0]);
if (rc)
    goto wrapup;
g2 = 0.0;
for (i=0; i<n; i++)
    g2 += F[i] * F[i];


// Using quadratic interpolation to find a0
h1 = (g2 - g1) / a2;
h2 = (g3 - g2) / (a3 - a2);
h3 = (h2 - h1) / a3;
a0 = 0.5 * (a2 - h1/h3);


for (i=0; i<n; i++)
    xi[i] = X[i] - a0 * dG[i];
rc = userEvalFunct(pUserData, &xi[0], F, &Jmat[0]);
if (rc)
    goto wrapup;
g0 = 0.0;
for (i=0; i<n; i++)
    g0 += F[i] * F[i];


// Choose smaller of a0 and a3 as our new estiJmations
if (g0 < g3)
{
    for (i=0; i<n; i++)
        X[i] = X[i] - a0 * dG[i];
}
else
{
    for (i=0; i<n; i++)
        X[i] = X[i] - a3 * dG[i];
}


rc = userEvalFunct(pUserData, X, F, &Jmat[0]);
```

```
    if (rc)
        goto wrapup;
    g0 = 0.0;
    for (i=0; i<n; i++)
        g0 += F[i] * F[i];

    if (fabs(g0) < tol)
        goto wrapup; // Converged
    g1 = g0;
}
```

```
wrapup:

    return;
}
```

In the next section, we will demonstrate how the Steepest Descent method helps in solving a system of nonlinear equations. Let us now modify the implementation of `apiNewtonMultiVar` to add a call to the **SteepDescent** method before the iteration loop as shown below:

```
void apiNewtonMultiVar(apiError (*userEval)(
                void *, double *, double *, double *),
                void *pUserData, double tol, int n,
                double *X, double *F, apiError &rc)
{
    int               i, j, k, max_num_iter = 20;
    vector<double> Jmat, sol;

    // Allocate memory for solutions and Jacobian matrix
    Jmat.resize(n * n);
    sol.resize(n);

    apiSteepDescent(userEvalFunct, pUserData, n, X, F, rc);

    // Iteration loops
    for (k=0; k<max_num_iter; k++)
    {
        rc = userEvalFunct(pUserData, X, F, &Jmat[0]);
        :
    }
}
```

## 8.5  Design power lines

The need to solve a system of nonlinear equations arises in many engineering and scientific applications. As an example, we consider modeling a catenary curve, which may find its application in designing power lines. Based on Webster dictionary, a *catenary* is the curve assumed by a cord of uniform density and cross-section that is perfectly flexible but not capable of being stretched and that hangs freely from two fixed points. In the real world, we can find many catenary examples such as spider webs and power lines as shown in figure 8.4.

Figure 8.4: A power line is an example of catenary curve

Mathematically, a catenary curve is the graph of a hyperbolic cosine function that has the following generic form:

$$y(x) = u \cosh\left(\frac{x - v}{u}\right) + \beta \tag{8.5.1}$$

where $u$, $v$, and $\beta$ are three constants to be determined by the boundary conditions of the problem. Usually these conditions include two points from which the cable is being suspended plus either the length of the cable, clearance height, or sag value. We will discuss these three common boundary conditions in subsequent sections.

### 8.5.1  Power line by length

Assume the two points are given by $p_1 = (x_1, y_1)$ and $p_2 = (x_2, y_2)$. Substituting them into equation (8.5.1) gives

$$y_1 = u \cosh\left(\frac{x_1 - v}{u}\right) + \beta, \tag{8.5.2}$$

$$y_2 = u \cosh\left(\frac{x_2 - v}{u}\right) + \beta. \tag{8.5.3}$$

In addition to the above two equations, we will need one more equation to form a system of three equations with three unknowns. Since the cable length $L$ is given, the third equation would be the arc length of catenary curve, i.e.,

$$L = \int_{x_1}^{x_2} \sqrt{1 + y'(x)^2}\,dx.$$

Since

$$y'(x) = u\sinh\left(\frac{x-v}{u}\right)\left(\frac{1}{u}\right) = \sinh\left(\frac{x-v}{u}\right),$$

we have

$$L = \int_{x_1}^{x_2} \sqrt{1 + \sinh^2\left(\frac{x-v}{u}\right)}\, dx = \int_{x_1}^{x_2} \cosh\left(\frac{x-v}{u}\right) dx$$

$$= u\int_{x_1}^{x_2} \cosh\left(\frac{x-v}{u}\right) d\left(\frac{x-v}{u}\right) = u\sinh\left(\frac{x-v}{u}\right)\Big|_{x_1}^{x_2}$$

$$= u\left[\sinh\left(\frac{x_2-v}{u}\right) - \sinh\left(\frac{x_1-v}{u}\right)\right] \tag{8.5.4}$$

Equations (8.5.2), (8.5.3), and (8.5.4) form a system of nonlinear equations. The solution to the three unknowns is nontrivial. There are numerous research papers about a system of non-linear equations. Here, Newton's method is used since it converges very fast when sufficiently good estimations of solutions are available. Let's rewrite equations (8.5.2), (8.5.3), and (8.5.4) in the following forms:

$$f_1 = u\cosh\left(\frac{x_1-v}{u}\right) + \beta - y_1 = 0$$

$$f_2 = u\cosh\left(\frac{x_2-v}{u}\right) + \beta - y_2 = 0 \tag{8.5.5}$$

$$f_3 = u\left[\sinh\left(\frac{x_2-v}{u}\right) - \sinh\left(\frac{x_1-v}{u}\right)\right] - L = 0$$

Differentiating the above three equations with respect to $u$, $v$, and $\beta$ gives

$$\frac{\partial f_1}{\partial u} = \cosh\left(\frac{x_1-v}{u}\right) - \frac{x_1-v}{u}\sinh\left(\frac{x_1-v}{u}\right)$$

$$\frac{\partial f_1}{\partial v} = -\sinh\left(\frac{x_1-v}{u}\right)$$

$$\frac{\partial f_1}{\partial \beta} = 1$$

$$\frac{\partial f_2}{\partial u} = \cosh\left(\frac{x_2-v}{u}\right) - \frac{x_2-v}{u}\sinh\left(\frac{x_2-v}{u}\right)$$

$$\frac{\partial f_2}{\partial v} = -\sinh\left(\frac{x_2-v}{u}\right)$$

$$\frac{\partial f_3}{\partial \beta} = 1$$

$$\frac{\partial f_3}{\partial u} = \sinh\left(\frac{x_2-v}{u}\right) - \sinh\left(\frac{x_1-v}{u}\right)$$
$$- \frac{1}{u}\left[(x_2-v)\cosh\left(\frac{x_2-v}{u}\right) - (x_1-v)\cosh\left(\frac{x_1-v}{u}\right)\right]$$

$$\frac{\partial f_3}{\partial v} = \cosh\left(\frac{x_1-v}{u}\right) - \cosh\left(\frac{x_2-v}{u}\right)$$

$$\frac{\partial f_3}{\partial \beta} = 0$$

Those partial derivatives are the entries of Jacobian matrix of the following form

$$
J = \begin{pmatrix}
\dfrac{\partial f_1}{\partial u} & \dfrac{\partial f_1}{\partial v} & \dfrac{\partial f_1}{\partial \beta} \\[2mm]
\dfrac{\partial f_2}{\partial u} & \dfrac{\partial f_2}{\partial v} & \dfrac{\partial f_2}{\partial \beta} \\[2mm]
\dfrac{\partial f_3}{\partial u} & \dfrac{\partial f_3}{\partial v} & \dfrac{\partial f_3}{\partial \beta}
\end{pmatrix}
$$

Then, Newton iteration to find a better solution $(u^{(k+1)}, v^{(k+1)}, \beta^{(k+1)})^T$ from the previous result $(u^{(k)}, v^{(k)}, \beta^{(k)})^T$ is given below:

$$
\begin{pmatrix} u^{(k+1)} \\ v^{(k+1)} \\ \beta^{(k+1)} \end{pmatrix} = \begin{pmatrix} u^{(k)} \\ v^{(k)} \\ \beta^{(k)} \end{pmatrix} - J^{-1} \times \begin{pmatrix} f_1(u^{(k)}, v^{(k)}) \\ f_2(u^{(k)}, v^{(k)}) \\ f_3(u^{(k)}, v^{(k)}) \end{pmatrix} \qquad (k = 0, 1, 2, \cdots)
$$

where $J^{-1}$ is the inverse of the Jacobian matrix evaluated at $(u^{(k)}, v^{(k)}, \beta^{(k)})^T$. We terminate the iteration when $f_1, f_2, f_3$ are smaller than the given distance tolerance.

It seems that we are ready to implement a callback function that takes input $x$ and returns function values $F(x)$ and Jacobian matrix $J(x)$. However, we are not. Referring to equation (8.5.5), construction of the nonlinear system depends on coordinates of two poles and the cable length. Such information is available only in the caller function. To be able to pass such information to the callback function indirectly via apiNewtonMultiVar, we need to make use of void *pUserData pointer. We first use an array to store $p_1 = (x_1, y_1)$, $p_2 = (x_2, y_2)$, and the length $L$ in the calling function. We then cast this array to void and pass it to the callee apiNewtonMultiVar. When the callee calls the callback function, it passes this void pointer to the callback function implemented at the same level and same time as the caller function was written. Therefore, the developer has the knowledge of how to cast the void pointer to the intended data type for information retrieval. Accordingly, the implementation of power line by length is given below:

```
// Callback function for apiNewtonMultiVar
static apiError myEvalByLength(void *pDataStruct, double *X,
                               double *F, double *Jmat)
{
    double   x1, x2, y1, y2, L;
    double   ch1, ch2, sh1, sh2, *pData;

    // Retrieve information
    pData = (double *)pDataStruct;
    x1 = pData[0];
    y1 = pData[1];
    x2 = pData[2];
    y2 = pData[3];
    L  = pData[4];

    // Evaluate functions:
```

```
ch1 = cosh((x1 - X[1]) / X[0]);
ch2 = cosh((x2 - X[1]) / X[0]);
sh1 = sinh((x1 - X[1]) / X[0]);
sh2 = sinh((x2 - X[1]) / X[0]);

F[0] = X[0] * ch1 + X[2] - y1;
F[1] = X[0] * ch2 + X[2] - y2;
F[2] = X[0] * (sh2 - sh1) - L;

// Compute Jacobian matrix
Jmat[0] = ch1 - (x1 - X[1]) * sh1 / X[0]; // df1/du
Jmat[1] = -sh1; // df1/dv
Jmat[2] = 1.0;  // df1/db

Jmat[3] = ch2 - (x2 - X[1]) * sh2 / X[0]; // df2/du
Jmat[4] = -sh2; // df2/dv
Jmat[5] = 1.0;  // df2/db

Jmat[6] = sh2 - sh1 - (ch2 * (x2 -X[1]) - ch1 * (x1 - X[1])) / X[0];
Jmat[7] = ch1 - ch2;  // df3/dv
Jmat[8] = 0.0;  // df3/db

    return api_OK;
} // End of myEvalByLength

void apiPowerLineByLength(
            GPosition2d &pt1, GPosition2d &pt2, // Input
            double L, double tol, double *X,    // Input

            double& u, double& v, double& beta, // Output
            apiError &rc) // Output
{
    double   pData[5], F[3];

    // Store cable length and coordinates
    rc = api_OK;
    pData[0] = pt1.x;
    pData[1] = pt1.y;
    pData[2] = pt2.x;
    pData[3] = pt2.y;
    pData[4] = L;

    apiNewtonMultiVar(myEvalByLength, pData, tol, 3, X, F, rc);
    if (rc == api_OK)
    {
        u = X[0];
        v = X[1];
```

```
        beta = X[2];
    }
}
```

Given the cable length $L = 150$ and coordinates of two poles $(-50, 100)$ and $(60, 120)$, we make the following wild estimation of the solution:

```
    X[0] = X[1] = X[2] = 1.0;
```

With the help of the Steepest Descent API, the final solution converges quickly as indicated below:

```
X = (3.9728980628e+001  -3.2892736331e-001  2.4959068203e+001)
F = (0.0000000000e+000  0.0000000000e+000  0.0000000000e+000)
```

By commenting out the call to Steepest Descent API, many of the provided test cases would diverge if the initial estimations are not good enough.

## 8.5.2   Power line by height

Overhead power lines have some strict guidelines for height clearances over streets, sidewalks, alleys, roads, and driveways. The National Electrical Code mandates acceptable clearances for power lines to keep the public safe from coming into contact with them. Assume that we are given coordinates of two poles and the lowest clearance height $H$. In addition to equations (8.5.2) and (8.5.3), we need to derive the third equation to solve the three unknowns $u$, $v$, and $\beta$. The lowest point occurs at either one of the end points or a local extremum at which

$$y'(x) = u \sinh\left(\frac{x-v}{u}\right)\left(\frac{1}{u}\right) = \sinh\left(\frac{x-v}{u}\right) = 0.$$

This, in turn, means that

$$\frac{x-v}{u} = 0 \quad \Longleftrightarrow \quad x = v.$$

Therefore, at $x = v$ the power line needs to have a clearance height $H$ (i.e., $y = H$ at $x = v$). Accordingly, we have

$$y(x) = u \cosh\left(\frac{x-v}{u}\right) + \beta \quad \overset{x=v}{\Longrightarrow} \quad H = u + \beta.$$

Replacing $\beta = H - u$ in equations (8.5.2) and (8.5.3), we obtain two equations for two unknowns:

$$y_1 = u \cosh\left(\frac{x_1 - v}{u}\right) + H - u,$$

$$y_2 = u \cosh\left(\frac{x_2 - v}{u}\right) + H - u.$$

Let

$$f(u, v) = u \cosh\left(\frac{x_1 - v}{u}\right) + H - y_1 - u = 0,$$

$$g(u, v) = u \cosh\left(\frac{x_2 - v}{u}\right) + H - y_2 - u = 0.$$

Differentiating $f$ and $g$ with respect to $u$ and $v$ gives

$$f_u = \cosh\left(\frac{x_1 - v}{u}\right) - \frac{x_1 - v}{u} \sinh\left(\frac{x_1 - v}{u}\right) - 1$$

$$f_v = \sinh\left(\frac{x_1 - v}{u}\right)$$

$$g_u = \cosh\left(\frac{x_2 - v}{u}\right) - \frac{x_2 - v}{u} \sinh\left(\frac{x_2 - v}{u}\right) - 1$$

$$g_v = \sinh\left(\frac{x_2 - v}{u}\right)$$

Accordingly, $u$ and $v$ can be solved by using the Newton iteration method given in equation (8.3.1). When $u$ and $v$ have been obtained, the third unknown is given by $\beta = H - u$. The implementation is given below:

```
// Callback function for apiNewtonMultiVar
static apiError myEvalByHeight(void *pDataStruct, double *X,
                               double *F, double *Jmat)
{
    double   x1, x2, y1, y2, h, ch1, ch2, sh1, sh2, *pData;

    pData = (double *)pDataStruct;
    x1 = pData[0];
    y1 = pData[1];
    x2 = pData[2];
    y2 = pData[3];
    h  = pData[4];

    ch1 = cosh((x1 - X[1]) / X[0]);
    ch2 = cosh((x2 - X[1]) / X[0]);
    sh1 = sinh((x1 - X[1]) / X[0]);
    sh2 = sinh((x2 - X[1]) / X[0]);
    F[0] = X[0] * ch1 + h - y1 - X[0];
    F[1] = X[0] * ch2 + h - y2 - X[0];

    Jmat[0] = ch1 - ((x1 - X[1]) * sh1 / X[0]) - 1.0;
    Jmat[1] = -sh1;
    Jmat[2] = ch2 - ((x2 - X[1]) * sh2 / X[0]) - 1.0;
    Jmat[3] = -sh2;

    return api_OK;
```

```
} // End of myEvalByHeight


void apiPowerLineByHeight(
            GPosition2d &pt1, GPosition2d &pt2,
            double h, double tol, double X[],

            double& u, double& v, double& beta,
            apiError &rc)
{
   double  pData[5], F[2];

   // Store coordinates and height clearance
   rc = api_OK;
   pData[0] = pt1.x;
   pData[1] = pt1.y;
   pData[2] = pt2.x;
   pData[3] = pt2.y;
   pData[4] = h;

   apiNewtonMultiVar(myEvalByHeight, pData, tol, 2, X, F, rc);
   if (rc == api_OK)
   {
      u = X[0];
      v = X[1];
      beta = h - u;
   }
}
```

Given the following information:

```
H = 5.45289245290322380e+001
pt1 = (-55, 100)
pt2 = (55, 100)
tol = 1.0e-10
initial guess: X[0] = X[1] = 1.0
```

we obtain the following converged result:

```
X[0] = 39.116968962325089
X[1] = 1.7824818004027050e-015


F[0] = -1.4210854715202004e-014
F[1] = -1.4210854715202004e-014
```

## 8.5.3   Power line by sag

In some other cases, the power line needs to be restricted to have a specific sag value at
the middle between two poles as shown below.

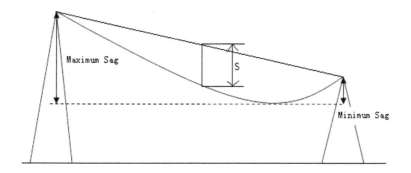

Figure 8.5: Sag value at middle is known

If two poles are connected by a straight line, the coordinate at the middle of this line is

$$\left( \frac{x_1 + x_2}{2}, \frac{y_1 + y_2}{2} \right).$$

The $y$-coordinate of the cable is computed by equation (8.5.1). At $(x_1 + x_2)/2$, the $y$-coordinate can also be determined by

$$\frac{y_1 + y_2}{2} - S.$$

Therefore, we have

$$\frac{y_1 + y_2 - 2S}{2} = u \cosh\left( \frac{x_1 + x_2 - 2v}{2u} \right) + \beta. \tag{8.5.6}$$

Subtracting equation (8.5.3) from (8.5.2) gives $f(u, v)$, and subtracting the above equation from (8.5.2) gives $g(u, v)$ as follows:

$$f(u, v) = \cosh\left( \frac{x_2 - v}{u} \right) - \cosh\left( \frac{x_1 - v}{u} \right) - \frac{y_2 - y_1}{u} = 0$$

$$g(u, v) = \cosh\left( \frac{x_1 - v}{u} \right) - \cosh\left( \frac{x_1 + x_2 - 2v}{2u} \right) - \frac{y_1 - y_2 + 2S}{2u} = 0$$

Differentiating $f$ and $g$ with respect to $u$ and $v$ gives

$$f'_u = -\frac{1}{u^2}\left[ \sinh\left( \frac{x_2 - v}{u} \right)(x_2 - v) - \sinh\left( \frac{x_1 - v}{u} \right)(x_1 - v) - (y_2 - y_1) \right]$$

$$f'_v = -\frac{1}{u}\left[ \sinh\left( \frac{x_2 - v}{u} \right) - \sinh\left( \frac{x_1 - v}{u} \right) \right]$$

$$g'_u = -\frac{1}{u^2}\left[ \sinh\left( \frac{x_1 - v}{u} \right)(x_1 - v) - \left( \frac{y_1 - y_2 + 2S}{2} \right) \right.$$
$$\left. - \sinh\left( \frac{x_1 + x_2 - 2v}{2u} \right)\left( \frac{x_1 + x_2 - 2v}{2} \right) \right]$$

$$g'_v = \frac{1}{u}\left[ \sinh\left( \frac{x_1 + x_2 - 2v}{2u} \right) - \sinh\left( \frac{x_1 - v}{u} \right) \right]$$

Thus, $u$ and $v$ can be solved by using the Newton iteration method given in equation (8.3.1). When $u$ and $v$ have been obtained, the third unknown $\beta$ can be solved via equation (8.5.2). The implementation is given below:

```
static apiError myEvalBySag(void *pDataStruct, double *X,
                            double *F, double *Jmat)
{
    double    x1, x2, y1, y2, S, ch1;
    double    ch2, ch3, sh1, sh2, sh3, *pData;

    pData = (double *)pDataStruct;
    x1 = pData[0];
    y1 = pData[1];
    x2 = pData[2];
    y2 = pData[3];
    S  = pData[4];

    ch1 = cosh((x1 - X[1]) / X[0]);
    ch2 = cosh((x2 - X[1]) / X[0]);
    ch3 = cosh((x1 + x2 - 2.0 * X[1]) / (2.0 * X[0]));

    sh1 = sinh((x1 - X[1]) / X[0]);
    sh2 = sinh((x2 - X[1]) / X[0]);
    sh3 = sinh((x1 + x2 - 2.0 * X[1]) / (2.0 * X[0]));

    F[0] = ch2 - ch1 - (y2 - y1) / X[0];
    F[1] = ch1 - ch3 - (y1 - y2 + 2.0 * S) / (2.0 * X[0]);

    Jmat[0] = (sh2 * (x2 - X[1]) - sh1 * (x1 - X[1])
                  - (y2 - y1)) / (-X[0] * X[0]);
    Jmat[1] = (sh2 - sh1)/ (-X[0]);
    Jmat[2] = (sh1 * (x1 - X[1]) - 0.5 * sh3 * (x1 + x2 - 2.0*X[1])
                  - 0.5 * (y1 - y2 + 2.0 * S)) / (-X[0] * X[0]);
    Jmat[3] = (sh3 - sh1) / X[0];

    return api_OK;
} // End of myEvalBySag

void apiPowerLineBySag(
            GPosition2d &pt1, GPosition2d &pt2, // Input
            double S, double tol, double *X,    // Input

            double& u, double& v, double& beta, // Output
            apiError &rc) // Output
{
    double    pData[5], F[2];

    // Store coordinates and sag value
```

```
    rc = api_OK;
    pData[0] = pt1.x;
    pData[1] = pt1.y;
    pData[2] = pt2.x;
    pData[3] = pt2.y;
    pData[4] = S;

    apiNewtonMultiVar(myEvalBySag, pData, tol, 2, X, F, rc);
    if (rc == api_OK)
    {
        u = X[0];
        v = X[1];
        beta = pt1.y - u * cosh((pt1.x - v) / u);
    }
}
```

Given the following information:

```
pt1 = (-50.0  130.0)
pt2 = (100.0   80.0)

S = 30.0
tol 1.0e-10

initial guess: X[0] = X[1] = 1.0
```

we obtain the following converged result:

```
X[0] = 102.47703171588701
X[1] = 55.823047438640231


F[0] = 7.7604589421298442e-014
F[1] = 4.8849813083506888e-015
```

## 8.5.4 Integration of three designs

In previous sections, we discussed how to design power lines with respect to three common options. Solutions to all options are based on solving three different systems of nonlinear equations. With reusable Newton's method, we can obtain the solutions without rewriting Newton's method for each case regardless of the differences among the three systems. Since all three algorithms are closely related, we integrate them into a single API called **apiPowerLine** whose prototype and description are:

```
/*------------------------------------------------------------
API Name
    apiPowerLine


Description
```

It determines three values: u, v, and beta
that are required to design a power line.

Signature
```
    void apiPowerLine(GPosition2d &pt1, GPosition2d &pt2,
                      int nFlag, double dValue, double tol, double *X,
                      double &u, double &v, double &bete, apiError &rc)
```

```
    INPUT:
        pt1, pt2         coordinates of two poles
        nFlag, dValue    dValue is Length, height, sag if nFlag is 1, 2, 3.
        tol              convergency tolerance
        X                array to store initial guess
    OUTPUT:
        u, v, beta       three unknowns to be determined
        rc               error code: api_OK if no error
```

History

```
    Y.M. Li     03/15/2013 : Creation date
----------------------------------------------------------------*/
```


The complete source file, test drive, and six test cases are available to readers who purchased this book.


## 8.6   Summary

In the previous chapter, we studied how to design and implement extensible and reusable code with the help of callback functions and inheritance with polymorphism. In this chapter, we expanded our techniques by introducing the (void *) pointer. If a pointer's type is void *, the pointer can point to any variable that is not declared with the const or volatile keyword. When needed, a void pointer can be converted into any other type of data pointer (including C/C++ structures) by explicit casting. This provides a flexible way to pass data among the caller, callee, and the callback function. However, pointers to void are not type-safe, and their use is discouraged in managed C++ in Microsoft .Net Framework (referring to chapter 10 for more detail).

Nonlinear problems are of interest to engineers, physicists and mathematicians because most physical systems are inherently nonlinear in nature. For this reason, we chose nonlinear systems to continue our study in designing extensible and reusable code. Newton's method is a powerful tool in solving a system of nonlinear equations. However, it is not always easy to determine starting values that will lead to a solution, and the method is comparatively expensive as a Jacobian matrix must be computed and an $n \times n$ linear system that involves this matrix must be solved. In practice, quasi-Newton methods such as *Broyden's method* are also used for solving a large system of nonlinear equations. These methods replace the Jacobian matrix in Newton's method with an approximation matrix that is updated at each iteration. Consequently, these methods reduce the amount of computations at each step without significantly degrading the speed of convergence. Detailed discussions about quasi-Newton methods can usually be found in numerical analysis books.

# Chapter 9

# Least Squares Approximation

Galileo Galilei (1564-1642) said, "The universe cannot be read until we have learned the language and become familiar with the characters in which it is written. It is written in mathematical language, and the letters are triangles, circles and other geometrical figures, without which means it is humanly impossible to comprehend a single word. Without these, one is wandering about in a dark labyrinth." Carl Friedrich Gauss (1777-1855), who is credited with developing the fundamentals of the basis for least squares analysis at the age of eighteen, referred to mathematics as "the Queen of the Sciences." Over a century later, mathematics is still seen throughout the world as an essential tool in many fields, including natural science, engineering, medicine, economics, and social science. In his speech *"10 Lessons of an MIT Education,"* Prof. Gian-Carlo Rota told the MIT Alumni Association that mathematics is still the queen of the sciences, and "MIT is one huge applied mathematics department; you can find applied mathematicians in practically every department at MIT except mathematics."

Unfortunately, not every software developer realizes the importance of mathematics. It is not uncommon for developers to search for answers online when developing algorithms. After reading some articles or postings, they think that they understand the problem and known how to solve it. This often leads to insufficient, if not incorrect, implementations. In this chapter, I will give some examples that may look simple but actually require developers to scratch their heads and dig deep into their memory for mathematics they learned in high schools and colleges. I hope that readers will see how mathematics plays an important role in software development when working on these examples and that they will be motivated to do more math on their own before implementing any algorithms.

In many applications such as linear regression, reverse engineering, image processing, metrology, and computer aided geometric modeling, we often want to find the best fit line, circle, and plane to the given data. Solutions to these problems are commonly studied in *point cloud* computing. A point cloud refers to a collection of points obtained by digitizing devices such as a 3D laser scanner. These 3D points typically represent the external surface of a geometric object. Point clouds are used for many purposes, including feature recognition, reverse engineering, and metrology inspection. For example, a manufactured part may be laser scanned to obtain a collection of points. The point cloud is then aligned and compared with a CAD model to check for differences. These differences can be displayed as color maps that give a visual indicator of the deviation between the manufactured part and the CAD model. Geometric dimensions and tolerances can also be extracted directly from the point cloud.

While point clouds can be rendered and inspected, they are usually not directly usable in most CAD applications. They often need to be converted to triangle meshes or approximated by polynomial curves and surfaces. This process is commonly known as *reverse engineering*. It is beyond the scope of this chapter to discuss how to approximate a point cloud by, for example, spline curves and surfaces. Instead, we shall focus on four fundamental methods: approximating a point cloud by line, circle, arc, and plane. By understanding the techniques described in this chapter, readers should know where to look for more information to solve their own point cloud computation problems.

## 9.1   Least Squares Line

Given a collection of points, it is often desirable to know whether these points can be represented by a straight line. To achieve this goal, we first find the "best fit" line for the data points and then compute the deviation between the line and the points. If the largest deviation is less than the given tolerance, the point cloud is said to degenerate to a straight line.

A line is uniquely defined by two distinct points. When there are more than two points, the *least squares approximation* is often used to find the best fit line, although other approximation methods are also used. The process of attempting to fit a linear model to observed data is known as *linear regression* in statistics. Searching online for *"least squares"* or *"best fit"* line, one is most likely to find the method described in this section.

A line not perpendicular to the $x$-axis may be represented either explicitly as $y = kx + c$ or implicitly as $y - kx - c = 0$. Assume this line is used to approximate the given set of points $p_i$ $(i = 1, 2, \cdots, n)$. Then, the squared error with respect to $p_i = (x_i, y_i)$ is $(y_i - kx_i - c)^2$. Accordingly, the sum of squared errors is

$$\mathcal{E} = \sum_{i=1}^{n}(y_i - kx_i - c)^2. \tag{9.1.1}$$

From calculus it is known that $\mathcal{E}$ is minimized if

$$\frac{\partial \mathcal{E}}{\partial k} = 2\sum_{i=0}^{n}(y_i - kx_i - c)x_i = 0$$

$$\frac{\partial \mathcal{E}}{\partial c} = 2\sum_{i=0}^{n}(y_i - kx_i - c) = 0 \tag{9.1.2}$$

The above equations may alternatively be represented as

$$a_{00}k + a_{01}c = b_0$$
$$a_{10}k + a_{11}c = b_1 \tag{9.1.3}$$

where,

$$a_{00} = \sum x_i^2, \quad a_{01} = \sum x_i, \quad b_0 = \sum x_i y_i$$
$$a_{10} = \sum x_i, \quad a_{11} = n, \quad b_1 = \sum y_i$$

Since it is assumed that the line is not perpendicular to the $x$-axis, we have

$$\begin{vmatrix} a_{00} & a_{01} \\ a_{10} & a_{11} \end{vmatrix} \neq 0.$$

Therefore,

$$k = \frac{\begin{vmatrix} b_0 & a_{01} \\ b_1 & a_{11} \end{vmatrix}}{\begin{vmatrix} a_{00} & a_{01} \\ a_{10} & a_{11} \end{vmatrix}}, \quad c = \frac{\begin{vmatrix} a_{00} & b_0 \\ a_{10} & b_1 \end{vmatrix}}{\begin{vmatrix} a_{00} & a_{01} \\ a_{10} & a_{11} \end{vmatrix}}.$$

If the line is perpendicular to the $x$-axis, we may represent it as $x = \bar{k}y + \bar{c}$. Accordingly, we can solve the following linear system of equations to obtain optimized $\bar{k}$ and $\bar{c}$

$$\bar{a}_{00}\bar{k} + \bar{a}_{01}\bar{c} = \bar{b}_0$$

$$\bar{a}_{10}\bar{k} + \bar{a}_{11}\bar{c} = \bar{b}_1$$

where,

$$\bar{a}_{00} = \sum y_i^2, \quad \bar{a}_{01} = \sum y_i, \quad \bar{b}_0 = \sum x_i y_i$$
$$\bar{a}_{10} = \sum y_i, \quad \bar{a}_{11} = n, \quad \bar{b}_1 = \sum x_i$$

In actual implementation, it is recommended to compare both determinants

$$\begin{vmatrix} a_{00} & a_{01} \\ a_{10} & a_{11} \end{vmatrix} \quad \text{and} \quad \begin{vmatrix} \bar{a}_{00} & \bar{a}_{01} \\ \bar{a}_{10} & \bar{a}_{11} \end{vmatrix}$$

and choose the method that has the larger absolute value of a determinant to avoid numerical noise. When the given points sit far away from the origin, numerical noise can further be reduced by transforming the points such that the *centroid* (or the mass of center) coincides with the origin.

Referring to equation (9.1.2), $\dfrac{\partial \mathcal{E}}{\partial c} = 0$ indicates

$$\sum y_i - k \sum x_i - \sum c = 0 \quad \Longrightarrow \quad c = \frac{\sum y_i}{n} - k\frac{\sum x_i}{n} = y_c - kx_c$$

which implies that the best fit line passes through the centroid $(x_c, y_c)$. Therefore, $c = 0$ if we translate all points such that the centroid $(x_c, y_c)$ coincides with the origin of the coordinate system. Such translation is done by subtracting $(x_c, y_c)$ from all points. Denoting $\bar{x}_i = x_i - x_c$ and $\bar{y}_i = y_i - y_c$, the error equation (9.1.1) becomes

$$\mathcal{E} = \sum_{i=1}^{n} (\bar{y}_i - k\bar{x}_i)^2.$$

$\mathcal{E}$ is minimized if $\dfrac{d\mathcal{E}}{k} = 0$, which yields

$$\sum_{i=1}^{n} \bar{x}_i \bar{y}_i - k \sum_{i=1}^{n} \bar{x}_i^2 = 0 \quad \Longleftrightarrow \quad k = \frac{\sum_{i=1}^{n} \bar{x}_i \bar{y}_i}{\sum_{i=1}^{n} \bar{x}_i^2}.$$

If a line is represented by $\bar{x} - \bar{k}\bar{y} = 0$, the slope of the best fit line can similarly be computed as

$$\bar{k} = \frac{\sum_{i=1}^{n} \bar{x}_i \bar{y}_i}{\sum_{i=1}^{n} \bar{y}_i^2}.$$

The following implementation chooses the larger denominator for numerical stability:

```
/*------------------------------------------------------------------
API Name
    apiBestFitLineV1

Description
    Given a collection of points, it computes a best fit line.
    The least squares error is measured along y-axis.

Signature
    void apiBestFitLineV1(std::vector<GPosition2d> &points,
                          GPosition2d &pt, GVector2d &dirV,
                          apiError &rc)

    INPUT:
      points    collection of points
    OUTPUT:
      pt        point on the best fit line
      dirV      direction vector of the best fit line
      rc        error code: api_OK if not error.

History

    Y.M. Li      03/10/2013 : Creation date
-----------------------------------------------------------------*/
#include "MyHeader.h"

void apiBestFitLineV1(std::vector<GPosition2d> &points,
        GPosition2d &pt, GVector2d &dirV, apiError &rc)
{
    int       i, n;
    double    sum_xx, sum_yy, sum_xy, x_i, y_i, k, temp;

    // Compute the center of mass:
    rc = api_OK;
    n = (int)points.size();
```

```
    pt.x = pt.y = 0.0;
    for (i=0; i<n; i++)
    {
        pt.x += points[i].x;
        pt.y += points[i].y;
    }
    pt.x /= n;
    pt.y /= n;

    // Transform points and compute summations
    sum_xx = sum_yy = sum_xy = 0.0;
    for (i=0; i<n; i++)
    {
        x_i = points[i].x - pt.x;
        y_i = points[i].y - pt.y;
        sum_xx += x_i * x_i;
        sum_yy += y_i * y_i;
        sum_xy += x_i * y_i;
    }

    if (sum_xx < machine_epsilon && sum_yy < machine_epsilon)
    {
        rc = api_NOSOLUTION;
        goto wrapup;
    }
    if (sum_xx > sum_yy)
    {
        k = sum_xy / sum_xx;
        // Line direction vector is (1/sqrt(1+k^2), k/sqrt(1+k^2):
        temp = 1.0 + k * k;
        dirV.x = 1.0 / sqrt(temp);
        dirV.y = k * dirV.x;
    }
    else
    {
        k = sum_xy / sum_yy;
        // Line direction vector is (k/sqrt(1+k^2), 1/sqrt(1+k^2)):
        temp = 1.0 + k * k;
        dirV.y = 1.0 / sqrt(temp);
        dirV.x = k * dirV.y;
    }

wrapup:

    return;
}
```

In many applications such as computer graphics and computer-aided design, a line is often represented in *vector-valued parametric form* as

$$p(t) = p_0 + tv,$$

where $p_0$ is a point on the line, $v$ the direction vector, and $t$ the arc length parameter. For this reason, the line slope is converted to the direction vector in the above implementation.

The algorithm described above is readily available online, and the implementation of the algorithm is straightforward. Without doing math, many developers may think that they have found the best fit line and hence fail to realize that the obtained least squares line is the "best fit" to data points only in the given coordinate system because the error measurements are done vertically as shown in figure 9.1 (a). If the coordinate system is rotated by some angle, this line may not be the best fit to the data points. Such behavior is known as *non-invariant* under coordinate rotation. In computer-aided geometric modeling and many other applications, it is often desirable to have a property that is *invariant* under coordinate transformations. To find the best fit line that is invariant under coordinate rotations, we need to measure a distance from any point to the line orthogonally as shown in figure 9.1 (b), which is the shortest (or Euclidean) distance.

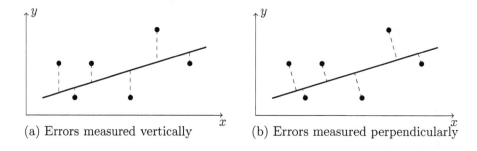

(a) Errors measured vertically          (b) Errors measured perpendicularly

Figure 9.1: Best fit lines

The best fit line obtained by measuring error orthogonally will be discussed in a later section.

## 9.2   Least squares circle

Fitting a circle to given points in a plane is a problem that arises in many application areas such as computer graphics, image processing, computer numerical controlled (CNC) machining, metrology, and statistics. The orthogonal least squares circle is a non-linear problem that is often solved by first approximating the model by a linear one to obtain initial estimation and then refining the solution via, for example, the Gauss-Newton algorithm. In this section, we will not discuss the non-linear least squares circle but a quasi-orthogonal "best fit" circle that can be solved via linear least squares approximation.

Writing a circle in a general form gives

$$x^2 + y^2 + 2ax + 2by + c = 0. \tag{9.2.1}$$

By factorizing the above equation we have

$$(x + a)^2 + (y + b)^2 - (a^2 + b^2 - c) = 0.$$

Hence, it is readily seen that the center of the circle is $(-a, -b)$, and the radius is $r = \sqrt{a^2 + b^2 - b}$. If this circle is used to approximate a collection of points, then the shortest distance from $p_i = (x_i, y_i)$ to the circle is

$$\left| \sqrt{(x_i + a)^2 + (y_i + b)^2} - r \right|.$$

Consequently, the squared distance is

$$(x_i + a)^2 + (y_i + b)^2 - 2r\sqrt{(x_i + a)^2 + (y_i + b)^2} + r^2,$$

which leads to solving a system of non-linear equations. It is noted that

$$r = \sqrt{(x_i + a)^2 + (y_i + b)^2}$$

when $p_i$ lies on the circle. To avoid solving a non-linear least squares problem, we may measure the deviation from $p_i$ to the circle as

$$\left| \left( \sqrt{(x_i + a)^2 + (y_i + b)^2} \right)^2 - r^2 \right| = \left| x_i^2 + y_i^2 + 2ax_i + 2by_i + c \right|.$$

Accordingly, the sum of squared errors is given by

$$\mathcal{E} = \sum_{i=1}^{n} (x_i^2 + y_i^2 + 2ax_i + 2by_i + c)^2.$$

From calculus, $\mathcal{E}$ is minimized if

$$\frac{\partial \mathcal{E}}{\partial a} = 0, \quad \frac{\partial \mathcal{E}}{\partial b} = 0, \quad \frac{\partial \mathcal{E}}{\partial c} = 0.$$

Explicitly, we need to solve

$$2\sum_{i=1}^{n} x_i^2 a + 2\sum_{i=1}^{n} x_i y_i b + \sum_{i=1}^{n} x_i c + \sum_{i=1}^{n} (x_i^2 + y_i^2) x_i = 0$$

$$2\sum_{i=1}^{n} x_i y_i a + 2\sum_{i=1}^{n} y_i^2 b + \sum_{i=1}^{n} y_i c + \sum_{i=1}^{n} (x_i^2 + y_i^2) y_i = 0$$

$$2\sum_{i=1}^{n} x_i a + 2\sum_{i=1}^{n} y_i b + nc + \sum_{i=1}^{n} (x_i^2 + y_i^2) = 0$$

Let

$$a_{00} = 2\sum x_i^2, \qquad a_{01} = 2\sum x_i y_i, \qquad a_{02} = \sum x_i, \qquad b_0 = -\sum(x_i^2 + y_i^2)x_i$$

$$a_{10} = a_{01}, \qquad a_{11} = 2\sum y_i^2, \qquad a_{12} = \sum y_i, \qquad b_1 = -\sum(x_i^2 + y_i^2)y_i$$

$$a_{20} = 2a_{02}, \qquad a_{21} = 2a_{12}, \qquad a_{22} = n, \qquad b_2 = -\sum(x_i^2 + y_i^2).$$

Then, the least squares circle is obtained by solving the following system of linear equations:

$$\begin{bmatrix} a_{00} & a_{01} & a_{02} \\ a_{10} & a_{11} & a_{12} \\ a_{20} & a_{21} & a_{22} \end{bmatrix} \begin{bmatrix} a \\ b \\ c \end{bmatrix} = \begin{bmatrix} b_0 \\ b_1 \\ b_2 \end{bmatrix}. \qquad (9.2.2)$$

The obtained best fit circle is invariant under coordinate rotations. The implementation of least squares circle is listed below.

```
/*--------------------------------------------------------------------
API Name
    apiBestFitCircle

Description
    Given a collection of points, it computes a best fit circle.

Signature
    void apiBestFitCircle(std::vector<GPosition2d> &points,
                          GPosition2d &center, double &radius,
                          apiError &rc)

    INPUT:
      points    collection of points
    OUTPUT:
      center    center of circle
      radius    radius of circle
      rc        error code: api_OK if not error.

History

    Y.M. Li     03/10/2013 : Creation date
----------------------------------------------------------------*/
#include "MyHeader.h"

void apiBestFitCircle(std::vector<GPosition2d> &points,
        GPosition2d &center, double &radius, apiError &rc)
{
    int        i, n;
    double     x_c, y_c, x_i, y_i, xx, xy, yy;
    double     temp, a, b, c;
    vector<vector<double>> aug_mat;
```

```
// Initialize STL vector
rc = api_OK;
n = (int)points.size();
aug_mat.resize(3);
for (i=0; i<3; i++)
{
   aug_mat[i].resize(4);
}

// Compute centroid
x_c = points[0].x;
y_c = points[0].y;
for (i=1; i<n; i++)
{
   x_c += points[i].x;
   y_c += points[i].y;
}
x_c /= n;
y_c /= n;

// Solve linear least squares approximation
for (i=0; i<n; i++)
{
   x_i = points[i].x - x_c;
   y_i = points[i].y - y_c;
   xx = x_i * x_i;
   xy = x_i * y_i;
   yy = y_i * y_i;

   aug_mat[0][0] += xx;
   aug_mat[0][1] += xy;
   aug_mat[0][2] += x_i;
   aug_mat[1][1] += yy;
   aug_mat[1][2] += y_i;

   temp = xx + yy;
   aug_mat[0][3] -= temp * x_i;
   aug_mat[1][3] -= temp * y_i;
   aug_mat[2][3] -= temp;
}

aug_mat[0][0] *= 2.0;
aug_mat[0][1] *= 2.0;
aug_mat[1][1] *= 2.0;
aug_mat[1][0] = aug_mat[0][1];
aug_mat[2][0] = 2 * aug_mat[0][2];
```

```
aug_mat[2][1] = 2 * aug_mat[1][2];
aug_mat[2][2] = n;

apiGaussPPivot(aug_mat, rc);
if (rc == api_OK)
{
    a = aug_mat[0][3];
    b = aug_mat[1][3];
    c = aug_mat[2][3];
    radius = sqrt(a * a + b * b - c);
    center.x = x_c - a;
    center.y = y_c - b;
}
}
```

When the given points are far away from the origin, it is recommended to transform the points to the local coordinate system whose origin coincides with the center of mass of $n$ points. The data file BestFitCircle.d1 was obtained by stroking a circle centered at $(0, 0)$ with the radius being 0.5 units. These points were rounded to the third decimal place and then purposely moved far away from the origin by the translation vector $(2 \times 10^5, 10^5)$. Therefore, the best fit circle should be centered at $(2 \times 10^5, 10^5)$ with the radius being roughly 0.5 units with three decimal places. Executing the above program with BestFitCircle.d1 gives the following expected results:

```
center = (2.000000000012346e+005, 1.000000000000000e+005)
radius = 4.999678963300172e-001
```

But if we did not transform the points such that the centroid coincides with the origin, the least squares circle would be a very poor approximation to the points due to numerical instability.

## 9.3   Least squares arc with endpoints constraints

Referring to Figure 9.2, a planar plate has been cut by a circular cutter. In computer-aided geometric modeling, such geometric operation is modeled by a Boolean subtraction between a cylinder and the plate. In theory, the intersection curve should be a circular arc. In practice, however, it may have to be represented by a non-circular curve when the cylinder axis is not truly perpendicular to the plate due to numerical noise. In exporting/importing this model for manufacture, it is desirable to represent the cutting path by a circular arc. One possible approach is to stroke the curve to obtain enough sampling points and apply the least squares approximation outlined in the previous section to create the best fit circle. It is then trimmed to obtain the best circular arc (referring to chapter 10 for detail). To have a continuous outer profile (or path) of the plate, the trimmed arc has to interpolate two end points $p_1$ and $p_n$, which is not guaranteed by the method discussed in the previous section. Therefore, a new approximation method needs to be developed to meet the requirement.

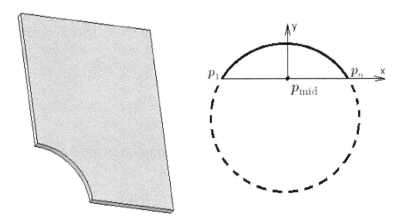

Figure 9.2: Plate cut by circular cutter

Requiring the best fit circle to interpolate two end points $p_1 = (x_1, y_1)$ and $p_n = (x_n, y_n)$ means the circle equation has to meet the following two conditions:

$$x_1^2 + y_1^2 + 2x_1 a + 2y_1 b + c = 0$$
$$x_n^2 + y_n^2 + 2x_n a + 2y_n b + c = 0$$

Recall the fifth question in the preface where candidates were asked what went wrong in deriving the best fit arc. With the added two constraints, we need to eliminate two variables and solve for one. However, the approach given in the preface failed to do so.

In this section, we will discuss how to create a best fit circle that interpolates the endpoints. To simplify the equation and minimize numerical noise, we first compute the mid-point of $(x_1, y_1)$ and $(x_n, y_n)$ and then transform the given points to the new coordinates system whose origin is at the mid-point $p_{mid}$. The transformation is

$$\bar{x}_i = x_i - x_{mid}$$

$$\bar{y}_i = y_i - y_{mid}$$

We then rotate the chord defined by $(x_1, y_1)$ and $(x_n, y_n)$ so that it coincides with the $x$-axis as shown in Figure 9.2. The rotation angle is determined by

$$\theta = -\arctan\left(\frac{y_n - y_1}{x_n - x_1}\right).$$

Therefore, the rotation transformation is

$$\hat{x}_i = \bar{x}_i \cos\theta - \bar{y}_i \sin\theta$$

$$\hat{y}_i = \bar{x}_i \sin\theta + \bar{y}_i \cos\theta$$

After transformation, the circle would be symmetric to the $y$-axis and, hence, $a$ in equation (9.2.1) is zero. Accordingly, we have

$$\hat{x}^2 + \hat{y}^2 + 2b\hat{y} + c = 0. \tag{9.3.1}$$

It is also known that $\hat{y}_1$ and $\hat{y}_n$ are zeros in the new coordinate system. By plugging in $(\hat{y}_1, \hat{x}_1)$ (or $(\hat{y}_n, \hat{x}_n)$) into equation (9.3.1), we have $c = -\hat{x}_1^2$ (or $c = -\hat{x}_n^2$) (i.e., the circle interpolates the endpoints). Therefore, our task boils down to find $b$ so that the circle best fits the remaining points in a least squares sense. Let

$$\mathcal{E}(b) = \sum_{i=1}^{n} \left( \hat{x}_i^2 + \hat{y}_i^2 + 2\hat{y}_i b + c \right)^2$$

Minimizing the summation of squared errors is equivalent to solving $\dfrac{d\mathcal{E}}{db} = 0$, i.e.,

$$2 \sum_{i=1}^{n} \left( \hat{x}_i^2 + \hat{y}_i^2 + 2\hat{y}_i b + c \right) \hat{y}_i = 0.$$

The above equation is met if

$$b = -\frac{\displaystyle\sum_{i=1}^{n} (\hat{x}_i^2 + \hat{y}_i^2 + c)\hat{y}_i}{2 \displaystyle\sum_{i=1}^{n} \hat{y}_i^2}.$$

Consequently, the center of the circular arc is $(0, -b)$, and the radius is $\sqrt{b^2 - c}$. It should be pointed out that the obtained center of circle is defined in the new coordinate system. Therefore, we need to transform it back to the original coordinate system:

$$x_c = x_{\text{mid}} - b\sin(\theta)$$

$$y_c = y_{\text{mid}} - b\cos(\theta)$$

The implementation of least squares arc is listed below.

```
/*-----------------------------------------------------------------
API Name
    apiBestFitArc

Description
    Given a collection of points, it computes a best fit arc
    that interpolates the start and end points.

Signature
    void apiBestFitArc(std::vector<GPosition2d> &points,
                       GPosition2d &center, double &radius,
                       apiError &rc)

    INPUT:
        points    collection of points
    OUTPUT:
        center    center of arc
```

```
        radius    radius of arc
        rc        error code: api_OK if not error.

History

    Y.M. Li     03/10/2013 : Creation date
------------------------------------------------------------------*/
#include "MyHeader.h"

void apiBestFitArc(std::vector<GPosition2d> &points,
                   GPosition2d &center,
                   double &radius, apiError &rc)
{
    int      i, n;
    double   x_i, y_i, x_mid, y_mid, dx, dy;
    double   theta, bid1, bid2, sin_theta, cos_theta, b, c;
    vector<vector<double>> aug_mat;

    // Check if two endpoints coincide
    rc = api_OK;
    n = (int)points.size();
    dx = points[n-1].x - points[0].x;
    dy = points[n-1].y - points[0].y;
    bid1 = sqrt(dx * dx + dy * dy);
    if (bid1 < 1,0e-6)
    {
        rc = api_INVALIDARG;
        goto wrapup;
    }

    // Compute transformation
    x_mid = 0.5 * (points[0].x + points[n-1].x);
    y_mid = 0.5 * (points[0].y + points[n-1].y);
    theta = -atan2(points[n-1].y-points[0].y,points[n-1].x-points[0].x);
    sin_theta = sin(theta);
    cos_theta = cos(theta);
    bid1 = bid2 = 0.0;
    for (i=0; i<n; i++)
    {
        dx =  points[i].x - x_mid;
        dy =  points[i].y - y_mid;
        x_i = dx * cos_theta - dy * sin_theta;
        y_i = dx * sin_theta + dy * cos_theta;
        if (0 == i)
            c = -x_i * x_i;
        bid1 += (x_i * x_i + y_i * y_i + c) * y_i;
        bid2 += y_i * y_i;
```

```
    }

    if (bid2 < zero_tol)
    {
        // It may happen if all points are coincident
        rc = api_INVALIDARG;
        goto wrapup;
    }

    b = -bid1 / (2.0 * bid2);
    radius = sqrt(fabs(b * b - c));

    // Transform the center back to original coordinate system
    center.x = x_mid - b * sin_theta;
    center.y = y_mid - b * cos_theta;

wrapup:

    return;
}
```

## 9.4   Least squares approximation

In this section, we generalize the least squares approximation and derive the so-called *normal equations* to solve least squares approximation problems. Let's consider the least squares line again. Rewriting the line equation $y = kx + b$ in matrix form gives

$$\begin{bmatrix} x & 1 \end{bmatrix} \begin{bmatrix} k \\ b \end{bmatrix} = (y).$$

Given $n$ points $p_i = (x_i, y_i)$, we have $n$ equations for two unknowns $k$ and $b$

$$\begin{bmatrix} x_1 & 1 \\ x_2 & 1 \\ \vdots & \vdots \\ x_n & 1 \end{bmatrix} \begin{bmatrix} k \\ b \end{bmatrix} = \begin{bmatrix} y_1 \\ y_2 \\ \vdots \\ y_n \end{bmatrix},$$

which is over-determined. In general, a linear system $Ax = b$ is said to be *over-determined* if $A$ is a matrix of $n \times m$, where $n > m$. In this case, we usually do not have an exact solution for $x$. The best we can do is to minimize the *residual* or error $E = Ax - b$. When $\|E\|$ is minimized, the solution $\hat{x}$ is a least squares solution of $Ax = b$.

To find $\hat{x}$, we minimize the norm of residual squared

$$\|E\|^2 = \|Ax - b\|^2 = x^T A^T Ax - 2b^T Ax + b^T b$$

where $A^T$, $x^T$ and $b^T$ are transpose of $A$, $x$, and $b$ respectively. The norm of squared residual is minimized by setting the gradient with respect to $x$ to zero:

$$\nabla \|E\|^2 = 2A^T A x - 2A^T b = 0$$

which gives us the *normal equations* $A^T A x = A^T b$. In other words, the least squares solution for $\hat{x}$ can be obtained by simply solving a system of linear equations (i.e., the normal equations).

We will now look at how to find the least squares line via solving normal equations. Writing a line $kx + c = y$ in matrix form gives

$$\begin{bmatrix} x & 1 \end{bmatrix} \begin{bmatrix} k \\ c \end{bmatrix} = y.$$

Given $n$ points, we have

$$A = \begin{bmatrix} x_1 & 1 \\ x_2 & 1 \\ \vdots & \vdots \\ x_n & 1 \end{bmatrix}, \quad x = \begin{bmatrix} k \\ b \end{bmatrix}, \quad b = \begin{bmatrix} y_1 \\ y_2 \\ \vdots \\ y_n \end{bmatrix}.$$

Thus,

$$A^T A = \begin{bmatrix} x_1 & x_2 & \cdots & x_n \\ 1 & 1 & \cdots & 1 \end{bmatrix} \begin{bmatrix} x_1 & 1 \\ x_2 & 1 \\ \vdots & \vdots \\ x_n & 1 \end{bmatrix} = \begin{bmatrix} \sum x_i^2 & \sum x_i \\ \sum x_i & n \end{bmatrix}$$

$$A^T b = \begin{bmatrix} x_1 & x_2 & \cdots & x_n \\ 1 & 1 & \cdots & 1 \end{bmatrix} \begin{bmatrix} y_1 \\ y_2 \\ \vdots \\ y_n \end{bmatrix} = \begin{bmatrix} \sum x_i y_i \\ \sum y_i \end{bmatrix}$$

which matches (9.1.3). As another example, we write circle equation (9.2.1) in the matrix form:

$$\begin{bmatrix} 2x & 2y & 1 \end{bmatrix} \begin{bmatrix} a \\ b \\ c \end{bmatrix} = -(x^2 + y^2).$$

Given $n$ points, we have

$$A^T A = \begin{bmatrix} 2x_1 & 2x_2 & \cdots & 2x_n \\ 2y_1 & 2y_2 & \cdots & 2y_n \\ 1 & 1 & \cdots & 1 \end{bmatrix} \begin{bmatrix} 2x_1 & 2y_1 & 1 \\ 2x_2 & 2y_2 & 1 \\ \vdots & \vdots & \vdots \\ 2x_n & 2y_n & 1 \end{bmatrix} = \begin{bmatrix} 4\sum x_i^2 & 4\sum x_i y_i & 2\sum x_i \\ 4\sum x_i y_i & 4\sum y_i^2 & 2\sum y_i \\ 2\sum x_i & 2\sum y_i & n \end{bmatrix}$$

$$A^T b = - \begin{bmatrix} 2x_1 & 2x_2 & \cdots & 2x_n \\ 2y_1 & 2y_2 & \cdots & 2y_n \\ 1 & 1 & \cdots & 1 \end{bmatrix} \begin{bmatrix} x_1^2 + y_1^2 \\ x_2^2 + y_2^2 \\ \vdots \\ x_n^2 + y_n^2 \end{bmatrix} = - \begin{bmatrix} 2\sum (x_i^2 + y_i^2) x_i \\ 2\sum (x_i^2 + y_i^2) y_i \\ \sum (x_i^2 + y_i^2) \end{bmatrix}$$

which matches (9.2.2) after cancelling the factor 2 in the first and second row. The approach we just discussed is the most direct way of solving a linear least squares problem, as it avoids direct computation of partial derivatives and tedious algebraic manipulations. This is especially desirable in consideration that it is not uncommon to have tens of thousands of data points and a few hundred variables. For the case of best fit line, $A$ is simple so that $A^T A$ and $A^T b$ are readily derived. When the dimension of matrix $A$ becomes high, $A^T A$ and $A^T b$ are usually computed via a matrix multiplication program (e.g., `apiAtAMatrix`).

As will be seen in subsequent sections, we may encounter the case in which $A^T A x = 0$. Obviously, the minimum is archived when $x = 0$, but this is uninteresting. Therefore, we repose the problem by constraining the solution so it only considers vectors $x$ of some fixed length, e.g., $\|x\| = 1$. We can solve this constrained least squares problem using the Lagrange multipliers by finding the $x$ that minimizes

$$A^T A x + \lambda x = 0$$

which says that $x$ is an eigenvector of $A^T A$. Since $A^T A$ is symmetric, all eigenvalues are real. If $A^T A$ is also positive definite, then all eigenvalues are real and positive. A matrix $B$ is *positive definite* if $x^T B x > 0$ for all non-zero column vector $x$. It is noted that

$$x^T (A^T A) x = (x^T A^T)(A x) = (A x)^T (A x).$$

Since $A x$ gives a transformed vector, $(A x)^T (A x)$ is equivalent to the dot product of the same vector and, hence, $(A x)^T (A x) > 0$. Accordingly, $A^T A$ is positive definite, and all the eigenvalues of $A^T A$ are positive, and the eigenvector with smallest eigenvalue is thus the desired solution of least squares approximation.

## 9.5 Orthogonal least squares line

The least squares line obtained in section one is the "best fit" line to data only in the given coordinate system because the error measurements are done along the $y$-axis. If the coordinate system is rotated by some angle, this line may no longer be the best fit to the data points. In this section, we will discuss how to obtain the least squares line that is invariant under coordinate transformation.

A line in the general (or standard) form is written as $\bar{a} x + \bar{b} y - \bar{c} = 0$, where $\bar{a}$ and $\bar{b}$ are not both zero. The shortest distance from any point $p_i = (x_i, y_i)$ to the line is

$$d = \frac{\bar{a} x_i + \bar{b} y_i - \bar{c}}{\sqrt{\bar{a}^2 + \bar{b}^2}}.$$

Since $\sqrt{\bar{a}^2 + \bar{b}^2} \neq 0$, we can divide $\bar{a}$, $\bar{b}$, and $\bar{c}$ by $\sqrt{\bar{a}^2 + \bar{b}^2}$ to obtain the *normalized line*

$$ax + by - c = 0, \tag{9.5.1}$$

where $\sqrt{a^2 + b^2} = 1$ and $a$ and $b$ are the components of a unit vector that is perpendicular to the line. Accordingly, the shortest distance from $p_i$ to the normalized line is

$d_i = ax_i + by_i - c$. If all points are transformed such that the center of mass coincides with the origin, the least squares line passes through the origin and hence $c = 0$. In this case, the above normalized line reduces to $ax + by = 0$ or in matrix form

$$\begin{bmatrix} x & y \end{bmatrix} \begin{bmatrix} a \\ b \end{bmatrix} = 0.$$

Given $n$ points, we have

$$\begin{bmatrix} x_1 & y_1 \\ x_2 & y_2 \\ \vdots & \vdots \\ x_n & y_n \end{bmatrix} \begin{bmatrix} a \\ b \end{bmatrix} = 0$$

which is the form $A^T A \boldsymbol{x} = \boldsymbol{0}$ that can only be solved via computation of eigenvalues and eigenvectors. Since $A$ is very simple, we compute $A^T A$ manually here:

$$A^T A = \begin{bmatrix} x_1 & x_2 & \cdots & x_n \\ y_1 & y_2 & \cdots & y_n \end{bmatrix} \begin{bmatrix} x_1 & y_1 \\ x_2 & y_2 \\ \vdots & \vdots \\ x_n & y_n \end{bmatrix} = \begin{bmatrix} \sum \bar{x}_i^2 & \sum \bar{x}_i \bar{y}_i \\ \sum \bar{x}_i \bar{y}_i & \sum \bar{y}_i^2 \end{bmatrix}.$$

The above $2 \times 2$ matrix has two eigenvalues $\lambda_1$ and $\lambda_2$ and two corresponding eigenvectors $\boldsymbol{n}_1 = (a_1, b_1)$ and $\boldsymbol{n}_2 = (a_2, b_2)$. As was discussed in the previous section, the eigenvector associated with the smaller eigenvalue defines the best fit line. Assume that $\lambda_1 > \lambda_2$. Then, $\boldsymbol{n}_1$ and $\boldsymbol{n}_2$ define the normal direction of the worst and best fit line respectively. Since $\boldsymbol{n}_1$ and $\boldsymbol{n}_2$ are mutually orthogonal, $\boldsymbol{n}_1$ is the normal direction of the worst fit line but the tangent direction of the best fit line. Therefore, the tangent direction of the best fit line is the eigenvector associated with the larger eigenvalue that can be found via apiEigenByPower developed in chapter 6.

The best fit line obtained via orthogonal least squares approximation is invariant under any coordinate rotation. In other words, this line best fits the data in both the least-squares and geometric sense. The implementation to compute the orthogonal least squares line is listed below:

```
/*------------------------------------------------------------
API Name
    apiBestFitLine

Description
    Given a collection of points, it computes a best fit line.
    The least squares error is measured orthogonal to the line.

Signature
    void apiBestFitLine(std::vector<GPosition2d> &points,
                        GPosition2d &pt, GVector2d &dirV,
                        apiError &rc)
```

```
    INPUT:
       points    collection of points
    OUTPUT:
       pt        point on the best fit line
       dirV      direction vector of the best fit line
       rc        error code: api_OK if not error.

History

    Y.M. Li      03/10/2013 : Creation date
----------------------------------------------------------------*/
#include "MyHeader.h"

void apiBestFitLine(std::vector<GPosition2d> &points,
       GPosition2d &pt, GVector2d &dirV, apiError &rc)
{
    int              i, n;
    double           x, y, eigenValue;
    vector<double> eigenVector;
    vector<vector<double>> Amat;

    // Initialize memory
    rc = api_OK;
    n = (int)points.size();
    Amat.resize(2);
    for (i=0; i<2; i++)
       Amat[i].resize(2);
    eigenVector.resize(2);

    pt.x = pt.y = 0.0;
    for (i=0; i<n; i++)
    {
       pt.x += points[i].x;
       pt.y += points[i].y;
    }
    pt.x /= n;
    pt.y /= n;

    for (i=0; i<n; i++)
    {
       x = points[i].x - pt.x;
       y = points[i].y - pt.y;
       Amat[0][0] += x * x;
       Amat[0][1] += x * y;
       Amat[1][1] += y * y;
    }
    Amat[1][0] = Amat[0][1];
```

```
eigenVector[0] = 1.0;
apiEigenByPower(Amat, machine_epsilon, eigenValue, eigenVector, rc);
if (rc != api_OK)
    goto wrapup;

dirV.x = eigenVector[0];
dirV.y = eigenVector[1];

wrapup:

    return;
}
```

Again, the line is represented by the centroid point `pt` and tangent direction vector `dirV`.

It is simpler to solve a linear least squares problem via its normal equation because a direct computation of partial derivatives is avoided. Otherwise, we have to write the sum of squared distance as

$$\mathcal{E} = \sum_{i=1}^{n}(ax_i + by_i)^2$$

and solve the following equations:

$$\frac{\partial \mathcal{E}}{\partial a} = 2\sum_{i=0}^{n}(ax_i + by_i)x_i = 0$$

$$\frac{\partial \mathcal{E}}{\partial b} = 2\sum_{i=0}^{n}(ax_i + by_i)y_i = 0$$

By some algebraic manipulations, we can write the above two equation in matrix form as

$$\begin{bmatrix} \sum \bar{x}_i^2 & \sum \bar{x}_i\bar{y}_i \\ \sum \bar{x}_i\bar{y}_i & \sum \bar{y}_i^2 \end{bmatrix} \begin{bmatrix} a \\ b \end{bmatrix} = \begin{bmatrix} g_{00} & g_{01} \\ g_{10} & g_{11} \end{bmatrix} \begin{bmatrix} a \\ b \end{bmatrix} = 0.$$

The above system has a trivial solution $a = b = 0$. For non-trivial solutions we need to find $\lambda$ such that

$$\begin{bmatrix} g_{00} & g_{01} \\ g_{10} & g_{11} \end{bmatrix} \begin{bmatrix} a \\ b \end{bmatrix} = \lambda \begin{bmatrix} a \\ b \end{bmatrix},$$

which is an eigenvalue problem.

## 9.6 Least squares plane

Similar to the least squares line, we may write a plane as $z = \bar{a}x + \bar{b}y + \bar{c}$ and minimize

$$\mathcal{E} = \sum_{i=1}^{n}(\bar{a}x_i + \bar{b}y_i + \bar{c} - z_i)^2$$

to obtain a simple least squares plane. Since the errors are measured along the direction of $z$-axis, this "best fit" plane is not invariant under coordinate rotation. In this section, we are concerned only with the orthogonal least squares plane.

A plane in 3D space is defined with *normal vector* $\boldsymbol{n}$ (a vector that is perpendicular to the plane) and an arbitrary point on the plane. For our purpose, we describe a plane as an equation in the form $\bar{a}x + \bar{b}y + \bar{c}z + \bar{d} = 0$. If $\bar{a}$, $\bar{b}$, $\bar{c}$, and $\bar{d}$ are divided by $\sqrt{\bar{a}^2 + \bar{b}^2 + \bar{c}^2}$ and denoted respectively by $a$, $b$, $c$, and $d$, we obtain the normalized plane

$$ax + by + cz + d = 0$$

where $a$, $b$, and $c$ furnish the components of plane normal. Since $\sqrt{a^2 + b^2 + c^2} = 1$, the plane normal $\boldsymbol{n} = (a, b, c)$ is a unit vector. The shortest distance from an arbitrary point $\boldsymbol{p}_i = (x_i, y_i, z_i)$ to the normalized plane is

$$d_i = |ax_i + by_i + cz_i + d|.$$

A plane is uniquely defined by three non-collinear points. If more than three points are given, the approximation process is sought to find the best fit plane. Before proceeding, we want to show that the best fit plane passes through the center of mass. Let

$$\mathcal{E} = \sum_{i=1}^{n}(ax_i + by_i + cz_i + d)^2.$$

From multi-variable calculus, it is known that the following condition has to be met for the best fit plane

$$\frac{\partial \mathcal{E}}{\partial d} = 0,$$

which is equivalent to

$$a\sum_{i=1}^{n} x_i + b\sum_{i=1}^{n} y_i + c\sum_{i=1}^{n} z_i + \sum_{i=1}^{n} d = 0.$$

Therefore, the best fit plane passes through the center of mass $(x_c, y_c, z_c)$ because

$$-d = a\frac{\sum x_i}{n} + b\frac{\sum y_i}{n} + c\frac{\sum z_i}{n} = ax_c + by_c + cz_c.$$

Transforming all given points such that the center of mass coincides with the origin reduces the normalized plane to $ax + by + cz = 0$ or, in matrix form,

$$\begin{bmatrix} x & y & z \end{bmatrix} \begin{bmatrix} a \\ b \\ c \end{bmatrix} = 0.$$

Accordingly, the normal equations are

$$(A^T A)\boldsymbol{n} = \begin{bmatrix} x_1 & x_2 & \cdots & x_n \\ y_1 & y_2 & \cdots & y_n \\ z_1 & z_2 & \cdots & z_n \end{bmatrix} \begin{bmatrix} x_1 & y_1 & z_1 \\ x_2 & y_2 & z_2 \\ \vdots & \vdots & \vdots \\ x_n & y_n & z_n \end{bmatrix} \begin{bmatrix} a \\ b \\ c \end{bmatrix} = \boldsymbol{0}$$

With some algebraic computations, we have

$$(A^T A)\boldsymbol{n} = \begin{bmatrix} g_{00} & g_{01} & g_{02} \\ g_{10} & g_{11} & g_{12} \\ g_{20} & g_{21} & g_{22} \end{bmatrix} \begin{bmatrix} a \\ b \\ c \end{bmatrix} = \boldsymbol{0}$$

where

$$g_{00} = \sum_{i=1}^{n} \bar{x}_i^2, \qquad g_{01} = \sum_{i=1}^{n} \bar{x}_i \bar{y}_i, \qquad g_{02} = \sum_{i=1}^{n} \bar{x}_i \bar{z}_i,$$

$$g_{10} = g_{01}, \qquad g_{11} = \sum_{i=1}^{n} \bar{y}_i^2, \qquad g_{12} = \sum_{i=1}^{n} \bar{y}_i \bar{z}_i,$$

$$g_{20} = g_{02}, \qquad g_{21} = g_{12}, \qquad g_{22} = \sum_{i=1}^{n} \bar{z}_i^2.$$

This is again an eigenvalue problem. $A^T A$ is symmetric and positive definite, so it has three non-negative eigenvalues that define three eigenvectors $\boldsymbol{n}_k = (a_k, b_k, c_k)$ ($k = 1, 2, 3$) that are mutually orthogonal. The eigenvector defined by the smallest eigenvalue is the normal of the best fitting plane. Recall that `apiEigenByPower` is designed to find the largest eigenvalue. It is readily proven that the smallest eigenvalue and corresponding eigenvector can be obtained by applying the power method to the inverse matrix $G^{-1}$. The implementation is given below:

```
/*------------------------------------------------------------
API Name
    apiBestFitPlane

Description
    Given a collection of points, it computes a best fit plane.
    The least squares error is measured orthogonal to the plane.

Signature
    void apiBestFitPlane(std::vector<GPosition> &points,
            GPosition &pt, GVector &dirV, apiError &rc)

    INPUT:
        points    collection of points
    OUTPUT:
        pt        a point on the best fit plane
        dirV      normal direction of the plane
        rc        error code: api_OK if not error.

History

    Y.M. Li    03/10/2013 : Creation date
------------------------------------------------------------*/
#include "MyHeader.h"
```

```
void apiBestFitPlane(std::vector<GPosition> &points,
        GPosition &pt, GVector &dirV, apiError &rc)
{
    int             i, j, n;
    double          x, y, z, eigenValue;
    vector<double> eigenVector;
    vector<vector<double>> Amat;
    vector<vector<double>> aug_mat;

    // Initialize memory
    rc = api_OK;
    n = (int)points.size();
    Amat.resize(3);
    for (i=0; i<3; i++)
        Amat[i].resize(3);
    eigenVector.resize(3);

    // Compute center of mass
    pt.x = pt.y = pt.z = 0.0;
    for (i=0; i<n; i++)
    {
        pt.x += points[i].x;
        pt.y += points[i].y;
        pt.z += points[i].z;
    }
    pt.x /= n;
    pt.y /= n;
    pt.z /= n;

    for (i=0; i<n; i++)
    {
        x = points[i].x - pt.x;
        y = points[i].y - pt.y;
        z = points[i].z - pt.z;
        Amat[0][0] += x * x;
        Amat[0][1] += x * y;
        Amat[0][2] += x * z;
        Amat[1][1] += y * y;
        Amat[1][2] += y * z;
        Amat[2][2] += z * z;
    }
    Amat[1][0] = Amat[0][1];
    Amat[2][0] = Amat[0][2];
    Amat[2][1] = Amat[1][2];

    // Compute the inverse matrix
```

```
aug_mat.resize(3);
for (i=0; i<3; i++)
{
    aug_mat[i].resize(6);
    for (j=0; j<3; j++)
    {
        aug_mat[i][j] = Amat[i][j];
    }
    aug_mat[i][3+i] = 1.0;
}
apiGaussJordan(aug_mat, rc);
if (rc != api_OK)
    goto wrapup;
for (i=0; i<3; i++)
{
    for (j=0; j<3; j++)
        Amat[i][j] = aug_mat[i][3+j];
}

// Get the eigenvalue and eigenvector
eigenVector[2] = 1.0;
apiEigenByPower(Amat, machine_epsilon, eigenValue, eigenVector, rc);
if (rc != api_OK)
    goto wrapup;

dirV.x = eigenVector[0];
dirV.y = eigenVector[1];
dirV.z = eigenVector[2];

wrapup:

    return;
}
```

If an API is available to compute all three eigenvalues and corresponding eigenvectors, then the given 3D points are planar, linear, or coincident if one, two, or all of the three eigenvalues are zeros respectively. If all three eigenvalues are non-zero and equal, then the given points are symmetric (e.g., points from a sphere surface).

## 9.7  Summary

In the age of the internet, one can virtually find any information he or she wants. I have seen numerous cases in which developers search online for algorithms and implement them without a thorough grasp of the underlying math. As a result, their implementations are either insufficient or wrong. To draw readers' attention to this common problem, we presented the least squares line, circle, and plane to illustrate why a "simple and straightforward" application may not have such simple math behind.

Without doing the math, developers may simply implement the posted online algorithms without knowing the obtained "best fit" line and plane are coordinate system dependent. If their intention is to obtain the least squares line and plane that is invariant under coordinate transformations, they should actually look for the orthogonal or *total* least squares approximation that minimizes the sum of Euclidian geometric distance. In this case, they will find that the underlying math is then not so simple, and the information about it is not readily available online.

The orthogonal least squares line and plane are obtained via solving the eigenvalues and eigenvectors problems. The API `apiPowerMethod` is designed to find the dominant eigenvalue and associated eigenvector. In real world applications, the QR decomposition algorithm is often used to find all eigenvalues and eigenvectors.

By understanding the least squares line, circle, and plane intuitively, we expanded the technique to a generic linear least squares approximation and derived the normal equations. It is the most direct way of solving a linear least squares problem, as it avoids direct computation of partial derivatives and tedious algebraic manipulations. It should be pointed out that normal equations and QR decomposition only work for full-ranked matrices. If a matrix is rank-deficient, *singular value decomposition* (SVD) is usually used to solve least squares approximation problems, which is considered to be numerically more stable but computationally more expensive algorithm. A simple example to get a singular or rank-deficient matrix is to sample points from a line that passes through the origin and to use these points to compute the least squares line. In this case, all equations are linearly dependent, which results in a rank-deficiency matrix.

The linear least squares approximation is widely used in many fields. The technique and implementation skill learned in this chapter lay a good foundation for readers to solve their own application problems.

# Chapter 10

# Data Visualization

CAD/CAM have revolutionized much of the engineering design and manufacturing processes in the world and eliminated some traditional disciplines. For example, engineering drawing was one of the core curriculums for many engineering majors prior to the birth of computer-aided design and drafting systems. In today's world, many engineering students in universities do not learn manual drafting techniques; instead they learn how to use CAD systems to design components and generate engineering drawings from computerized models. The days of using protractors and compasses to create drawings are gone for good.

If asked to describe what a CAD system is in a few words, I would say it is essentially a collection of sophisticated tools that are exposed to users via graphical user interface (GUI) for creating, visualizing, and manipulating data. Visualization is essential to CAD systems because it allows designers and engineers to collaborate and to accurately see what the product is really going to look like throughout the entire design process. Without the data visualization capability, a CAD system is not that much different from a pocket calculator.

Data visualization is mainly studied in computer graphics. It is beyond the scope of this book to discuss graphics programming in detail. Instead, we will focus on how to develop a simple Windows-based application that calls our least squares approximation APIs and displays the end result on the screen.

## 10.1 Overview of windows application

In the early days, programmers depended on Win32 API to develop Windows-based 32-bit applications. Although Win32 API gives developers maximum control, it is difficult to master. A basic action such as opening a window or adding some text, a few buttons, or other controls can require lengthy coding. It can take months or even years to learn how to master event handlers and all other techniques necessary to build a full-featured application. In the early 1990s, Microsoft released the *Microsoft Foundation Class (MFC) Library* in C++ that wraps big portions of the Windows Win32 API in C++ classes. The MFC library brings Windows programming down to the average programmer. It uses an object-oriented model that eliminates much of the tedium and exacting detail of the Win32 API, yet it still offers most of the power needed to create full-featured Windows programs. MFC uses a model-view-controller pattern to separate programs into more manageable pieces. The Visual C++ resource editors, MFC AppWizard and ClassWizard significantly reduce the time needed to write code that is specific to a particular application. For example, the resource editor creates a header file that contains assigned values for #define constants. AppWizard generates skeleton code for an entire application, and ClassWizard generates prototypes and function bodies for message handlers.

In 1995, Sun Microsystems, a company best known for its high-end UNIX workstations, released the Java programming language. Sun describes Java as a *"simple, object-oriented, distributed, interpreted, and dynamic language."* It is true that Java is simple to learn, as it removed or streamlined the area where programmers have had difficulty or that have been the largest source of bugs. For example, we will not find pointers in Java, nor will we find overloaded operators. To an experienced C/C++ programmer, these omissions may be difficult to get used to, but to beginners or programmers who have worked in other languages, they make the Java language far easier to learn. Furthermore, memory management in Java is automatic, which avoids memory leaking that is common to all levels of programmers. Java applications are typically compiled to *bytecode* (.class file) that can run on any *Java virtual machine (JVM)* regardless of computer architecture. For these reasons, Java is one of the most popular programming languages in use, particularly for client-server web applications, with a reported 10 million users.

Microsoft saw the challenge from Java and started the development of the .NET Framework in the late 1990s, originally under the name of *Next Generation Windows Services.* By late 2000, the first beta versions of .NET 1.0 were released. It includes a large library and provides language interoperability (each language can use code written in other languages) across several programming languages. Programs written for the .NET Framework execute in a software environment (as contrasted to a hardware environment), known as the *Common Language Runtime (CLR)*, an application virtual machine that provides services such as security, memory management, and exception handling. The class library and the CLR together constitute the .NET Framework. With .Net Framework, applications are usually written in *managed code* that has its execution managed by the .NET Framework Common Language Runtime. Managed code may be implemented in $C^{\#}$, J#, Microsoft Visual Basic .NET, or managed C++. All of these languages share a unified set of class libraries and can be encoded into an *Intermediate Language (IL)*. A runtime-aware compiler compiles the IL into native executable code within a managed execution environment that ensures type safety, array bound and index checking, exception handling, and garbage collection. It is said that, by using managed code and compiling in this managed execution environment, developers can avoid many typical programming mistakes that lead to security holes and unstable applications. Also, many unproductive programming tasks are automatically taken care of, such as type safety checking, memory management, and destruction of unneeded objects.

The MFC library is implemented with unmanaged C++ and, hence, is not directly compatible with .Net Framework. *Windows Forms* (or *WinForms* for short) is the name given to the graphical application programming interface included as a part of Microsoft .NET Framework, providing access to native Microsoft Windows interface elements by wrapping the extant Windows API in managed code. Windows Forms is for creating Microsoft Windows applications on the .NET Framework. This framework provides a modern, object-oriented, extensible set of classes. With Windows Forms, developers are able to create a rich client application that can access a wide variety of data sources and provide data-display and data-editing facilities using Windows Forms controls.

*Windows Presentation Foundation (WPF)* is a graphics platform included in Microsoft .NET Framework 3.0 and later versions. It is a next-generation presentation system for building Windows client applications with visually stunning user experiences. We can create a wide range of both stand-alone and browser-hosted applications that incorporate documents, media, 2D and 3D graphics, and animations. In essence, WPF has the following advantages:

- WPF offers additional programming enhancements for Windows client application development. One obvious enhancement is the ability to develop an application using both *markup* and *code-behind*. The *Extensible Application Markup Language (XAML)* (markup) is usually used to implement the appearance of an application while managed programming languages (code-behind) are used to implement its behavior. This separation of appearance and behavior makes the development of windows-based applications more efficient because designers can implement an application's appearance simultaneously with developers who are implementing the application's behavior.

- XAML opens up a world of possibilities for collaboration, because many graphics design tools understand the XAML format.

- WPF changes how we do graphics programming. It integrates three basic Windows elements – text, controls, and graphics – into a single programming model and puts these three elements in the same element tree in the same manner. Without WPF, developing a graphics application would involve a number of different technologies, ranging from GDI/GDI+ for 2D graphics to Direct3D or OpenGL for 3D graphics. WPF, on the other hand, is designed as a single model for graphics application development, providing seamless integration between such services within an application. Similar constructs can be used for creating animations, data binding, and 3D models.

- When creating a UI, developers arrange their controls by location and size to form a layout. A key requirement of any layout is to adapt to changes in window size and display settings. Rather than forcing developers to write the code to adapt a layout in these circumstances, WPF provides a first-class, extensible layout system for application developers. The cornerstone of the layout system is relative positioning, which increases the ability to adapt to changing window and display conditions. WPF manages a layout using different containers. Each container has its own layout logic – some stack elements together, others arrange them in a grid of invisible cells, and so on. WPF includes several layout controls:

| Name | Description |
|---|---|
| StackPanel | Places elements in a horizontal or vertical stack. This layout container is typically used for small sections of a larger, more complex window. |
| WrapPanel | Places elements in a series of wrapped lines. In horizontal orientation, the WrapPanel lays items out in a row from left to right and then onto subsequent lines. In vertical orientation, the WrapPanel lays out items in a top-to-bottom column and then uses additional columns to fit the remaining items. |
| DockPanel | Aligns elements against an entire edge of the container. |
| Grid | Arranges elements in rows and columns according to an invisible table. This is one of the most flexible and commonly-used layout containers. |
| UniformGrid | Places elements in an invisible table but forces all cells to have the same size. This layout container is used infrequently. |
| Canvas | Allows elements to be positioned absolutely using fixed coordinates. This layout container is the most similar to traditional Windows Forms, but it doesn't provide anchoring or docking features. As a result, it's an unsuitable choice for a resizable window unless you're willing to do a fair bit of work. |

Enough has been said about WPF. Two simple examples will be given to illustrate how XAML is used to design the appearance of applications. The first example is to create a browser-based application that draws and stacks three shapes in a grid. Save the following code as `DrawShapes.xaml` in any folder:

```
<Page
  xmlns="http://schemas.microsoft.com/winfx/2006/xaml/presentation"
  xmlns:x="http://schemas.microsoft.com/winfx/2006/xaml"
  WindowTitle="Draw sahpes"
  Title="Draw shapes">
  <Grid>
    <StackPanel>
      <TextBlock Text="Ellipse:" Margin="5"/>
      <Ellipse Width="150" Height="70"  Fill="yellow" Stroke="Black"/>

      <TextBlock Text="Rectangle without fillet:" Margin="5"/>
      <Rectangle Width="150" Height="70" Fill="red" Stroke="Black"/>

      <TextBlock Text="Rectangle with fillet of radius 20:"Margin="5"/>
      <Rectangle Width="150" Height="70" RadiusX="20" RadiusY="20"
                 Fill="blue" Stroke="Black"/>
    </StackPanel>
  </Grid>
```

```
</Page>
```

Double click `DrawShapes.xaml`, and Microsoft's Internet Explorer will display the specified shapes as follows:

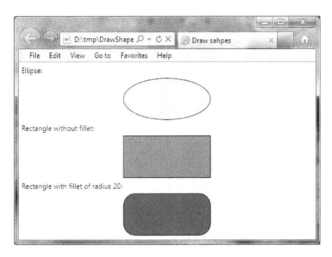

Figure 10.1: Draw simple shapes via XAML

This is a simple markup-only, browser-based application since no C$^\#$or .Net VB code has been involved. Our second example is creating a `Canvas` inside the `Grid` with the background of rich-looking gradient color (from light-blue to blue). A `DrawLine` button is also placed inside the `Grid` at the top-right corner with (20,20) margin measured from the top-right corner. Save the following markup code as `DrawLine.xaml` in any folder.

```
<Page xmlns="http://schemas.microsoft.com/winfx/2006/xaml/presentation"
   xmlns:x="http://schemas.microsoft.com/winfx/2006/xaml"
   WindowTitle="Button in mixed layout" Height="400" Width="600">
  <Grid x:Name="myGrid">
   <Canvas x:Name="myCanvas" ClipToBounds="True">
   <Canvas.Background>
      <LinearGradientBrush StartPoint="0,0" EndPoint="0,1">
      <LinearGradientBrush.GradientStops>
      <GradientStop Color="LightBlue" Offset="0"/>
      <GradientStop Color="Blue" Offset="1"/>
      </LinearGradientBrush.GradientStops>
      </LinearGradientBrush>
   </Canvas.Background>
   </Canvas>
   <Button Content="DrawLine" Height="23" HorizontalAlignment="Right"
               Margin="0,20,20,0" Name="button1"
               VerticalAlignment="Top" Width="75"/>
  </Grid>
</Page>
```

Double click `DrawLine.xaml`, and Microsoft's Internet Explorer will display the browser-based application as follows:

Figure 10.2: Create a browser-based application via XAML

Clicking the `DrawLine` button does nothing because no "code-behind" has been implemented to handle the button clicking event. We will not implement the event handler for this case because WPF and `WinForm` are part of .Net Framework that works with managed code such as $C^{\#}$, Microsoft Visual Basic .NET, or managed C++.

Throughout this book, all of our algorithms have been implemented in conventional C/C++ (or unmanaged C/C++ code in Microsoft's term) to make them workable for any platform. Consequently, we will not be able to call these APIs from WPF and `WinForm` without considerable effort. For this reason, MFC is chosen to implement our Windows-based application that displays the best fit line, circle, and arc via GDI interface.

## 10.2  Create MFC application template

The MFC library uses an object-oriented model that eliminates much of the tedium and exacting detail of the Win32 API, yet it still offers most of the power needed to create full-featured Windows programs. As a matter of fact, most commercially available windows-based CAD systems have been developed using the MFC library. This section is designed to familiarize readers with the basics of MFC library through creation of an MFC application template with customized GUIs.

So far, all algorithms have been implemented as console applications. For a console application, the only absolute requirement is a function named `main`. The operating system calls **main** when we run the program, and from that point on, we implement our application and can use any programming structure we want. If an application program needs to get user keystrokes, for example, it calls an appropriate I/O function such as **getchar**. When the Windows operating system launches a program, it calls the program's **WinMain** function. An essential difference between a console program and a program written for Windows is that a console program calls the operating system to get user input, but a Windows-based program processes user input via *messages* from the operating system. Messages in Windows are strictly defined and apply to all programs. For example, a **WM_CREATE** message is sent when a window is being created; a **WM_LBUTTONDOWN** message is sent when the user presses the left mouse button. All messages have two 32-bit parameters that convey information such as cursor coordinates, key code, and so forth. Windows sends **WM_COMMAND** messages to the appropriate window in response to user menu choices, dialog button clicks, and so on. Command message parameters vary depending on the window's menu layout.

Message mapping in MFC provides an efficient way to direct Windows messages to an appropriate C++ object instance. In the implementation (.cpp) file that defines the member functions for our class, start the message map with the **BEGIN_MESSAGE_MAP** macro, then add macro entries for each of our message-handler functions, and complete the message map with the **END_MESSAGE_MAP** macro. Although message-map macros are important, we generally won't have to use them directly. As will be seen later, this is because the **Properties** window automatically creates message-map entries in our source files when we use it to associate message-handling functions with messages. Any time we want to edit or add a message-map entry, we can use the **Properties** window to achieve so.

Besides the difference in handling user input, console and windows based applications handle output/display also differently. Many console programs write directly to the video memory and the printer port. The disadvantage of this technique is the need to supply driver software for every video board and every printer model. Windows introduced a layer of abstraction called the *Graphic Device Interface (GDI)*. Windows provides the video and printer drivers, so the application program does not need to know the type of video card and printer attached to the system. Instead of addressing the hardware, the application program calls GDI functions that reference a data structure called *device content (DC)*. Windows maps the device content structure to a physical device and issues the appropriate input/output instruction. In essence, applications based on the Microsoft Win32 API do not access graphics hardware directly. Instead, GDI interacts with device drivers on behalf of the applications.

Having discussed the major differences between a console and windows-based application, it is time for us to create an MFC application template. Let's start Visual Studio 2010 and click **File->New->Project** to bring up the **New Project** dialog box. Select **Visual C++->MFC->MFC Application** in the **Templates** pane to open the wizard. Define the application settings such as path and project name using the MFC Application Wizard as shown in figure 10.3. Click **OK** to bring up an application wizard. Let's select **Single document** for application type and **MFC standard** for project style as illustrated in figure 10.4.

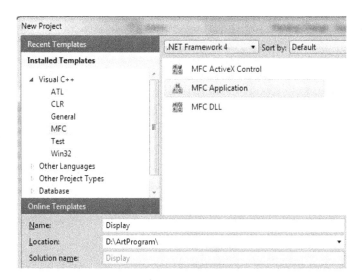

Figure 10.3: Create a project for MFC application

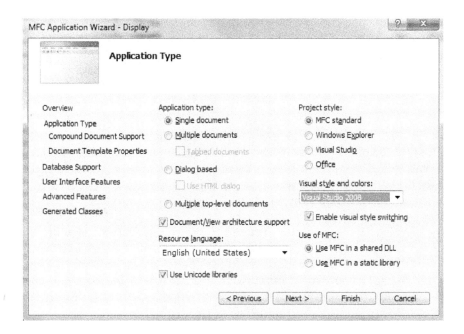

Figure 10.4: Create a single document MFC application

MFC makes it easy to work with both single-document interface (SDI) and multiple-document interface (MDI) applications. SDI applications allow only one open document frame window at a time. MDI applications allow multiple document frame windows to be open in the same instance of an application. An MDI application has a window within which multiple MDI child windows, which are frame windows themselves, can be opened, each containing a separate document. In some applications, the child windows can be of different types, such as chart windows and spreadsheet windows. In that case, the menu bar can change as MDI child windows of different types are activated. In our case, SDI application is good enough.

Repeatedly click Next until we reach Advanced Features. Then, deselect every checkbox and click Finish as shown in figure 10.5.

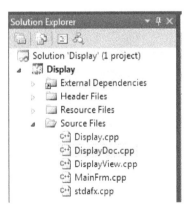

Figure 10.5: Deselect all advanced features

Five *.cpp source files will be added into the project as indicated in figure 10.6.

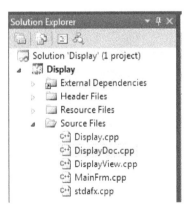

Figure 10.6: Source files created by wizards

Among these five source files, we are mainly interested in DisplayView.cpp in which event handling, message mapping, and drawing activities will be implemented. At this stage, we can, without any coding, compile and press F5 to run the project, which brings up a familiar windows document application with File, Edit, view, and Help entries on the menu-bar and a few icons on the toolbar as shown below.

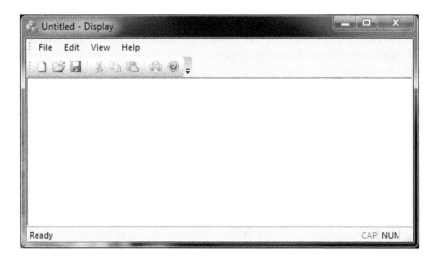

Figure 10.7: Appearance of MFC application

As seen above, MFC Application Wizard has eased the burden for us to design and add basic features to a new MFC application. The framework defines the skeleton of an application and supplies standard user-interface implementations that can be placed onto the skeleton. As a programmer, our job is to fill in the rest of the skeleton, which are those things that are specific to our application.

We now look how to add the following three customized icons to the toolbar:

BestLine,
BestCircle,
BestArc.

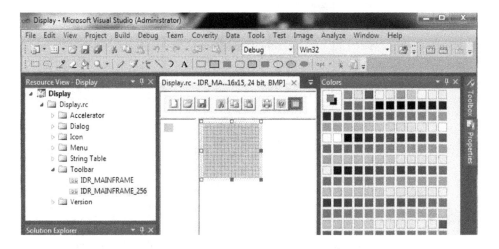

Figure 10.8: Invoke Toolbar utility

These three icons are GUIs for users to interact with the application to create the best fit line, circle, or arc. With Microsoft Visual Studio IDE, we can use the resource editor to create and edit menus, dialog boxes, custom controls, accelerator keys, bitmaps, icons, cursors, strings, and version resources. To see how it works, click `View->Resource View` on the project's menu-bar to bring up `Resource View` and place it on the left pane as shown in figure 10.9. Expand the `Toolbar` folder and double click `IDR_MAINFRAME_256` to bring up the toolbar recourse file `Display.rc`. Click the gray, rectangle box after the question mark icon on the toolbar (referring to figure 10.8). Then select a proper tool on the `Image editor` toolbar to create three bitmap images to represent the best fit line, circle, and arc icons as shown in figure 10.9. It should be pointed out that software companies usually use more advanced image editing tools to create the rich and nice-looking bitmap images for toolbar icons.

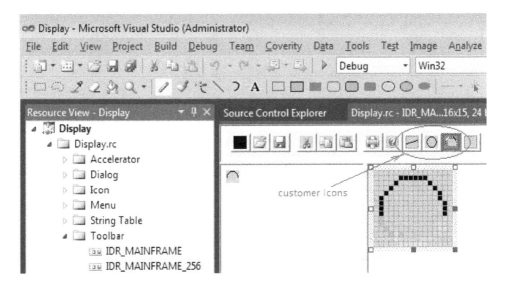

Figure 10.9: Design customized command icons

Save, compile, and run the project. We now should see three new icons on the toolbar (screenshot is not provided). Stop the application so that we can continue our implementation. If `Display.rc` is not active in the `Toolbar` editor window, double click `IDR_MAINFRAME_256` from `Resource View` pane to make it active. Then, double click the best fit line icon to bring up `Properties` window of the `Toolbar Editor` as shown in figure 10.10. Type `ID_BestLine` for ID name and *"Best Fit Line: Click the left mouse button to generate points, then the right button to create best fit line"* for `Prompt` (referring to figure 10.10). The description for this command will be displayed on the `status bar`. We similarly name `ID_BestCircle` and `ID_BestArc` for the other two icons and provide informative prompt text strings.

Save, compile, and run the project. When the application is running, moving the mouse cursor to each icon triggers display of text string on the `status bar` at the bottom of the application document. The prompt string helps users take required actions.

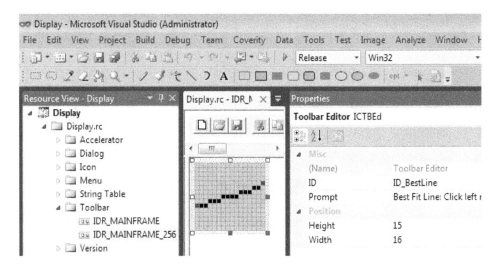

Figure 10.10: Add prompt text string

We are done with GUI design. It is time to explore how MFC `Class Wizard` assists us to add a message handler (a member function that handles Windows messages) to a class and map Windows messages to the message handler. On the project menu-bar, click `Project->Class Wizard`. In the popup `MFC Class Wizard` dialog box, select `CDisplayView` for `Class name` and browse down to find `ID_BestLine` in `Object IDs`. Then, click the `Add Handler` button to add `COMMAND` and also `UPPDATE_COMMAND_UI` as illustrated in figure 10.11.

Figure 10.11: Add command ID

Click the `Apply` button, which will add the required declarations to the header file `DisplayView.h`, the corresponding entries to `Message Map`, and the following stub member function bodies to the class's implementation file `DisplayView.cpp`:

```
void CDisplayView::OnBestline()
{
    // TODO: Add your command handler code here
}
```

```
void CDisplayView::OnUpdateBestline(CCmdUI *pCmdUI)
{
    // TODO: Add your command update UI handler code here
}
```

Based on the above skeleton code bodies, we can implement or edit our message handler code later. We need to repeat similar processes for ID_BestCircle and ID_BestArc.

We also need to add the left and right mouse-button click entries and methods to DisplayView.cpp. On the project menu-bar, click Project->Class Wizard. In the popup MFC Class Wizard dialog box, select Messages and browse down to find WM_LBUTTONDOWN and click Add Handler (referring to figure 10.11). Next, browse down to find WM_RBUTTONUP and click Add Handler.

We are done with the design and implementation of application template. Let's open DisplayView.cpp to see what MFC Class Wizard has done to this .cpp file. We will immediately notice that all macro entries for our message-handler functions have been added to the message map as seen below:

```
BEGIN_MESSAGE_MAP(CDisplayView, CView)
    ON_WM_RBUTTONUP()
    ON_COMMAND(ID_BestLine, &CDisplayView::OnBestline)
    ON_UPDATE_COMMAND_UI(ID_BestLine, &CDisplayView::OnUpdateBestline)
    ON_WM_LBUTTONDOWN()
    ON_COMMAND(ID_BestArc, &CDisplayView::OnBestarc)
    ON_UPDATE_COMMAND_UI(ID_BestArc, &CDisplayView::OnUpdateBestarc)
    ON_COMMAND(ID_BestCircle, &CDisplayView::OnBestcircle)
    ON_UPDATE_COMMAND_UI(ID_BestCircle,&CDisplayView::OnUpdateBestcircle)
END_MESSAGE_MAP()
```

Scrolling down the source file, we will also notice that all message-handler stub member function bodies have been created and are waiting for us to add our code to handle specific events. For example, the left mouse button down message-handler function body is created as

```
void CDisplayView::OnLButtonDown(UINT nFlags, CPoint point)
{
    // TODO: Add your message handler code here and/or call default
}
```

In the next section we shall do the actual implementation for message mapping, event handling, and drawing activities.

## 10.3   Implementation of event handlers

In the previous section, we showed how MFC helped us build a windows-based application with customized GUIs. In this section, we will do the actual implementation to handle a specific event such as BestFitLine button clicking, left mouse button down, right mouse button up, etc. The main tasks are outlined below:

1. Make BestLine an active icon by default. When users click a different icon, disable the active one and enable the clicked one.

2. Click the left mouse button to generate points and store them in STL vector.

3. Draw a tiny circle at each clicked place to indicate where the point is. This is accomplished by calling the GDI function via an MFC wrapper API.

It helps to understand the implementation with the above tasks in mind. Prior to the actual implementation, however, we have to include MyHeader.h in this project so that STL vector, GPosition2d, and other structures are exposed. This may be done by adding #include "MyHeader.h" in each .cpp file. Alternatively, we may simply add it in stdafx.h since this standard system header file is included in each .cpp file. We then need to add the path D:\ArtProgram\include in the field of Addtional Include Directories in project's configuration properties settings (referring to Figure 4.8 in Chapter 4) so the compiler knows where to look for MyHeader.h. We can now start our implementation. Open DisplayView.h to add the following member variables:

```
public:
    double          m_scale;
    CRect           m_clientRect;
    int             m_fitOption;
    bool            m_bDrawCurve;
    vector<GPosition2d> m_gPoints;
```

The variable m_clientRect stores the size of the active document in pixels and is used to determine a transformation between the *device* and *world* coordinates. The device coordinate is given in pixels, and the origin is at the top-left corner with the *y*-direction pointing downward (the so-called *left-hand coordinate system*). The world coordinate often refers to the coordinate system used by applications and is measured in either metric or imperial units. Its origin can be anywhere but is often at the bottom-left corner with the *x*-axis pointing rightward and the *y*-axis pointing upward (the so-called *right-hand coordinate system*). The variable m_fitOption takes three values: 1, 2, and 3 corresponding to the best fit line, circle, and arc. The variable m_bDrawCurve indicates whether it is ready to draw a curve. Finally, m_gPoints collects all points generated by repeatedly clicking the left mouse button. Open DisplayView.cpp and initialize the variables inside the constructor as follows:

```
CDisplayView::CDisplayView()
{
    m_scale = 1.0;
    m_clientRect.left = 0;
    m_clientRect.top = 0;
```

```
    m_clientRect.bottom = 400;
    m_clientRect.right = 800;
    m_fitOption = 1;
    m_bDrawCurve = false;
}
```

The constructor is called when the executable is invoked. At this time, the application window (or the client window) has not been brought up. Therefore, the exact window size is unknown, and m_clientRect is initialized by some reasonable guessing values. It will be correctly reset when the application window shows up.

When the BestLine icon is clicked, the OnBestline method will be called. Inside this method, we initialize the variables as follows:

```
void CDisplayView::OnBestline()
{
    // TODO: Add your command handler code here
    m_fitOption = 1;
    m_bDrawCurve = false;
    m_gPoints.clear();
    Invalidate();
}
```

A call to Invalidate sends out a WM_PAINT message, which, in turn, triggers the paint method to refresh and repaint the document. Since we have cleaned m_gPoints and set m_bDrawCurve to false, the effect of Invalidate is to erase what has been drawn previously in the screen. This is important because users need a fresh screen to experiment with the best fit line when they click the BestLine icon.

Next, we add implementation to

```
void CDisplayView::OnUpdateBestline(CCmdUI *pCmdUI)
{
    // TODO: Add your command update UI handler code here
    if (m_fitOption == 1)
        pCmdUI->SetCheck(1);
    else
        pCmdUI->SetCheck(0);
}
```

This method is called whenever a toolbar icon is clicked or a screen is resized. It is responsible to set the BestLine icon active or inactive, depending on the value of m_fitOption. We need to add similar implementations for BestCircle and BestArc:

```
void CDisplayView::OnBestcircle()
{
    // TODO: Add your command handler code here
    m_fitOption = 2;
    m_bDrawCurve = false;
    m_gPoints.clear();
```

```
        Invalidate();
}


void CDisplayView::OnUpdateBestcircle(CCmdUI *pCmdUI)
{
        // TODO: Add your command update UI handler code here
        if (m_fitOption == 2)
            pCmdUI->SetCheck(1);
        else
            pCmdUI->SetCheck(0);
}


void CDisplayView::OnBestarc()
{
        // TODO: Add your command handler code here
        m_fitOption = 3;
        m_bDrawCurve = false;
        m_gPoints.clear();
        Invalidate();
}


void CDisplayView::OnUpdateBestarc(CCmdUI *pCmdUI)
{
        // TODO: Add your command update UI handler code here
        if (m_fitOption == 3)
            pCmdUI->SetCheck(1);
        else
            pCmdUI->SetCheck(0);
}
```

As was said at the beginning of this section, data points are generated by clicking the left mouse button. The point sending to OnLButtonDown specifies the $x$- and $y$-coordinate of the cursor. These coordinates are always relative to the upper-left corner of the window (i.e., the device coordinates). Therefore, conversions between the device and world coordinates are required. If both the device and world coordinate use the pixel unit, the conversion is simply:

$$x_{\mathrm{wd}} = x_{\mathrm{dc}},$$
$$y_{\mathrm{wd}} = y_{\mathrm{dc\_max}} - y_{\mathrm{dc}},$$

which transforms the origin from top-left to bottom-left corner and from a left-hand to right-hand coordinate system. If the world coordinate is measured in a different unit, then the ratio of a pixel on the client window to the corresponding distance on the world coordinate has to be determined. By taking this ratio, known as *scaling factor* or *scale*, into consideration, the conversion formula is

$$x_{\mathrm{wd}} = x_{\mathrm{dc}}/\mathrm{scale},$$
$$y_{\mathrm{wd}} = (y_{\mathrm{dc\_max}} - y_{\mathrm{dc}})/\mathrm{scale}.$$

For simplicity, we set `m_scale=1` for now in our implementation:

```
void CDisplayView::DCToWorld(CPoint &cPoint, GPosition2d &gPoint)
{
    gPoint.x = cPoint.x / m_scale;
    gPoint.y = (m_clientRect.bottom - cPoint.y ) / m_scale;
}
```

```
void CDisplayView::WorldToDC(GPosition2d &gPoint, CPoint &cPoint)
{
    cPoint.x = (int)(gPoint.x * m_scale);
    cPoint.y = (int)(m_clientRect.bottom - gPoint.y * m_scale);
}
```

Since the above two methods are customized functions, we have to declare their signatures inside the class of `CDisplayView` in `DisplayView.h`:

```
public:
    void DCToWorld(CPoint &cPoint, GPosition2d &gPoint);
    void WorldToDC(GPosition2d &gPoint, CPoint &cPoint);
```

We now implement the `OnLButtonDown` method that handles the left-mouse-button clicking event. The basic tasks are:

- Convert the mouse position to the world coordinate when the left button is down.

- Add the converted mouse position to `m_gPoints`.

- Send a `WM_PAINT` message via a call to `Invalidate` so that circles can be drawn at collected mouse positions.

Accordingly, the implementation is:

```
void CDisplayView::OnLButtonDown(UINT nFlags, CPoint point)
{
    // TODO: Add your message handler code here and/or call default
    if (!m_bDrawCurve)
    {
        GPosition2d gPoint;
        DCToWorld(point, gPoint);
        m_gPoints.push_back(gPoint);
        Invalidate();
    }
}
```

`Invalidate` sends a message to the `CDisplayView::OnDraw` method that overrides the virtual function `CView::OnDraw`. It is called by the framework to perform screen display, printing, and print preview. In our case, `CDisplayView::OnDraw` will draw tiny red circles on the screen to indicate mouse clicking positions.

```
void CDisplayView::OnDraw(CDC* pDC)
{
    // TODO: add draw code for native data here
    int     i;
    CPoint  cPoint;
    CPen    redPen;

    GetClientRect(m_clientRect); // Reset client window size

    // Draw collected points in red circles.
    // Pen style is solid and width is 2 pixels.
    redPen.CreatePen(PS_SOLID, 2, RGB(225, 0, 0));
    pDC->SelectObject(&redPen);
    for (i=0; i<(int)m_gPoints.size(); i++)
    {
        WorldToDC(m_gPoints[i], cPoint);

        // Draws an ellipse specified by a bounding Rectangle:
        pDC->Ellipse(CRect(cPoint.x-3, cPoint.y-3,
                           cPoint.x+3, cPoint.y+3));
    }
}
```

The class of a device-context (CDC) object provides member functions for working with a device context, such as a display or printer, as well as members for working with a display context associated with the client area of a window. All drawing is done through the member functions of a CDC object. The class provides member functions for device-context operations, working with type-safe graphics device interface (GDI) object selection and drawing tools to draw simple shapes such as lines, rectangles, ellipses, polygons, and so on. Explanations of these graphics methods can be readily found on the Microsoft Developer Network (MSDN) website. For example, googling "CDC ellipse MSND" will lead us to the MSDN website with detailed explanations of two signatures of CDC::Ellipse. The MSDN website has been the important reference resource for professional programmers who develop Windows applications.

Save and compile the project. Press F5 to start windows application. When the application window shows up, we can click the left mouse button. With each click, a red circle will be drawn instantly.

## 10.4   Draw line, circle, and arc

Data points are generated by repeatedly clicking the left mouse button while moving the mouse around. When enough points have been collected (the number of points should be greater than 2), we need to send out the WM_PAINT message to tell CDisplayView::OnDraw to draw the best fit curve. This is done by clicking the right mouse button. The implementation of OnRButtonUp method is:

```
void CDisplayView::OnRButtonUp(UINT /* nFlags */, CPoint point)
{
    if (m_gPoints.size() > 2)
    {
        m_bDrawCurve = true;
        Invalidate();
    }
}
```

Before implementing `CDisplayView::OnDraw` to draw the best fit curve, we need to add our dynamic linking library to the project so that the least squares approximation APIs can be called. Let's create a new folder `Lib` under `Display` project in the `Solution Explore` pane (referring to section 4.2 for detail). Highlight `Lib` and click the right mouse button to add `FunctDLL_d.lib` and `FunctDLL_r.lib`. It is important to exclude `FunctDLL_r.lib` from building a `Debug` code and `FunctDLL_d.lib` from `Release` mode (referring to figure 4.14).

We now consider how to draw a curve. In computer graphics and computer-aided geometric design, curves are often represented parametrically. For example, a vector-valued parametric line is given by

$$r(t) = p + tv,$$

where $p$ is an arbitrary point on the line, $v$ is the direction vector, and $t \in (-\infty, +\infty)$ is the arc length parameter. For any given $t$, evaluation of the above equation yields a unique point on the line. For the convenience of programming, we may define a data structure to store a finite line as

```
typedef struct{
    GPosition2d   m_point; // arbitrary point on the line
    GUnitVector2d m_dirV;  // direction vector
    double        m_start; // start parameter of finite line
    double        m_end;   // end parameter of finite line
} GLine2d;
```

Similarly, a vector-valued parametric ellipse is given by

$$r(t) = c + \cos(t)a + \sin(t)b,$$

where $c$ is the center of the ellipse, $a$ and $b$ are the semi-major and semi-minor axes of the ellipse, and $t \in [0, 2\pi]$ is the angular parameter in radian. When the lengths of $a$ and $b$ are the same, an ellipse degenerates to a circle. Accordingly, we may use the following data structure to store both an ellipse and a circle:

```
typedef struct{
    GPosition2d m_center;    // center of ellipse
    GVector2d   m_majorAxis; // semi-major axis
    double      m_minorMajorRatio;
} GEllipse2d;
```

Since a semi-minor axis can be derived from the semi-major axis and the ratio of the lengths of minor and major axes, the above representation saves memory usage by omitting the semi-minor axis.

We can go on and on discussing parametric representations of all kinds of curves and surfaces, associated structures for these curves and surfaces, and implementation of supporting algorithms that include point-stroking, transformation, evaluation, etc. Since not every reader is interested in curve and surface modeling if he or she does not want to work in gaming and CAD/CAM industries, we will not go into detail about parametric representation of a line, circle, arc, B-spline curve, etc. Besides, covering such information needs a book, not a section. Interested readers may refer to my online book *Java Graphics Programming* at www.infogoaround.org or any published computer graphics and geometric modeling book.

If we had defined data structures to support parametric representations of all curves and implemented a generic API to stroke points on these curves, the display of a parametric curve would simply be rendered by drawing a bunch of lines that connect the obtained stroking points. Omission of such information makes our implementation of `Display` application relatively tedious.

We first consider how to draw a line. Given the data points, `apiBestFitLine` returns a point `pt` on the best fit line and the line direction `dirV`. Such information is only good to define an infinite line. Addtional information is required to draw a finite line on the screen. Referring to the following figure, the dot-product of displacement vector $(p_i - p)$ and the direction unit vector `dirV` yields the signed distance from $p$ to the projection point $p_{proj}$.

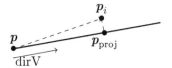

Figure 10.12: Project a point onto a line

Denoting this dot-product by parameter $t$, we can loop through each point to compute the corresponding parameter

$$t_i = (p_i - p) \cdot v,$$

where $v$ is the direction unit vector. By recording the smallest and largest parameters: $t_{min}$ and $t_{max}$, we can compute the start and end points of the best fit line as follows:

$$p_{start} = p + t_{min} v \quad \text{and} \quad p_{end} = p + t_{max} v.$$

The start and end points are sufficient for us to draw a finite line that best fits the collected points.

Drawing a circle is straightforward. However, it requires several special functions to properly draw a circular arc – the trimmed circle. We start with the implementation of an API that computes an angle of a circle from the given point.

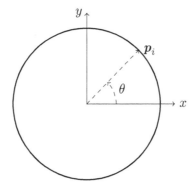

Figure 10.13: Evaluation of a circle

Referring to figure 10.13, an angle, which is the parameter of parametric circle, is *always* measured counter-clockwise from the major axis (i.e., the $x$-axis in the above figure) to avoid getting a negative parameter. It can be computed in the following code list:

```
/*-----------------------------------------------------------------
API Name
    apiGetAngleFromPoint

Description
    It computes the angular parameter of a circle from a given point

Signature
    double apiGetAngleFromPoint(GPosition2d &center, GPosition2d& pt)

    INPUT:
        center      center of the circle
        pt          point that is either on or near the circle
    OUTPUT:
        returns the angular parameter associated with the given point

History

    Y.M. Li    03/10/2013 : Creation date
-------------------------------------------------------------*/
#include "MyHeader.h"

double apiGetAngleFromPoint(GPosition2d &center, GPosition2d& pt)
{
    double      dx, dy, angle;
    dx = pt.x - center.x;
```

```
      dy = pt.y - center.y;
      angle = atan2(dy, dx);
      if (angle < 0)
          angle += 2.0 * GPI;
      return angle;
}
```

With this API, we can determine the start and end angle of the arc that corresponds to the first and last clicked point. Besides the start and end angle, we also need to know the orientation of an arc that indicates how the point on the arc flows when moving from $p_0$ towards $p_n$. Therefore, an arc can have a clockwise or counter-clockwise orientation as shown below. If the orientation is messed up, the arc will be drawn incorrectly. It should be noted that, to avoid getting negative angular parameter, the angle parameter of an arc is always measured counter-clockwise from the major axis as illustrated below. This counter-clockwise measurement of angle parameter has nothing to do with the orientation of the arc.

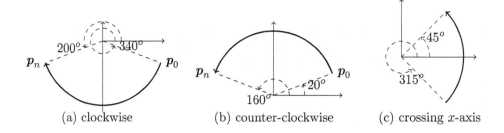

(a) clockwise            (b) counter-clockwise            (c) crossing x-axis

Figure 10.14: Different orientation of arc

Though tricky, it is possible to determine the correct orientation of the fitting arc. We first compute the starting and ending angles (i.e., $\theta_0$ and $\theta_n$) that correspond to $p_0$ and $p_n$. We then take a middle point in an array of collected mouse points and compute the corresponding angle $\theta$. If the fitting arc is counter-clockwise oriented as illustrated in figure 10.14 (b), we have $\theta_0 < \theta < \theta_n$ because parametric angle is always measured counter-clockwise from the major axis. If $\theta_n < \theta < \theta_0$ (referring to figure 10.14 (a)), the fitting arc is clockwise oriented. It should be noted that, when an arc crosses the major axis as shown in (c), the parametric interval is broken into two: $[315^o, 360^o]$ and $[0^o, 45^o]$. Because of these configurations, it is not very straightforward to implement an algorithm that detects whether the given arc parameter is in the parametric interval. We purposely break the implementation into several **if-else** blocks to make the code more understandable:

```
/*-------------------------------------------------------------
API Name
    apiIsParInRange

Description
    It checks if the given angle is in the valid angular parametric
    interval. Note: angles are always measured counter clockwise
```

```
      regardless arc orientation.

Signature
      bool apiIsParInRange(double u_beg, double u_end,
                           bool bCounterClock, double u)

      INPUT:
         u_beg            starting parameter
         u_end            ending parameter
         bCounterClock    true if it is counter-clock oriented
         u                angular parameter to be checked
      OUTPUT:
         returns true if it is in the interval

History

      Y.M. Li      03/10/2013 : Creation date
------------------------------------------------------------------*/
#include "MyHeader.h"

bool apiIsParInRange(double u_beg, double u_end,
                     bool bCounterClock, double u)
{
   double   twoPI, tol;
   bool     isInside = false, bCrossAxis = false;

   tol - 1.0e-8;
   twoPI = 2.0 * GPI;
   if (bCounterClock)
   {
      if (u_end < u_beg)
         bCrossAxis = true;
   }
   else if (u_end > u_beg)
   {
      bCrossAxis = true;
   }

   if (!bCrossAxis)
   {
      if (bCounterClock)
      {
         if (u > u_beg - tol && u < u_end + tol)
            isInside = true;
      }
      else
      {
```

```
            if (u > u_end - tol && u < u_beg+ tol)
                isInside = true;
        }
    }
    else
    {
        if (bCounterClock)
        {
            if (u > u_beg- tol && u < twoPI + tol ||
                u > 0 && u < u_end + tol)
                isInside = true;
        }
        else
        {
            if (u < u_beg + tol && u > 0 ||
                u > u_end - tol && u < twoPI + tol)
                isInside = true;
        }
    }

    return isInside;
}
```

In `apiStrokeCircle`, the number of stroking points is determined based on the full sweep angle $2\pi$. For the case of arc (i.e., the trimmed circle), the sweep angle is no longer $2\pi$ and has to be determined properly. The computation of the sweep angle is not simply the difference of start and end angles. Referring to figure 10.14, the sweep angle for (c) is $90°$ and is determined by taking into consideration that the arc crosses the major-axis (i.e., the $x$-axis).

```
/*----------------------------------------------------------------
API Name
    apiGetSweepAngle

Description
    It computes the sweep angle of an arc based on the given
    radius, start and end angles, as well as orientation.

Signature
    double apiGetSweepAngle(double radius, double startAngle,
                      double endAngle, bool bCounterClock)

    INPUT:
        radius          radius of arc
        startAngle
        endAngle
        bCounterClock   true if it is counter-clock oriented
    OUTPUT:
```

```
        returns the sweep angle

History

    Y.M. Li      03/10/2013 : Creation date
--------------------------------------------------------------------*/
#include "MyHeader.h"

double apiGetSweepAngle(double radius, double startAngle,
                        double endAngle, bool bCounterClock)
{
   double    tol, sweepAngle, twoPI = 2.0 * GPI;

   tol = 1.0e-5 / radius;
   if (fabs(fabs(endAngle - startAngle)-twoPI) < tol)
   {
      sweepAngle = 2.0 * GPI;
   }
   else
   {
      if (bCounterClock)
      {
         if (startAngle < endAngle)
            sweepAngle = endAngle - startAngle;
         else
            sweepAngle = twoPI - (startAngle - endAngle); //Cross axis
      }
      else
      {
         if (startAngle > endAngle)
            sweepAngle = startAngle - endAngle;
         else
            sweepAngle = twoPI - (endAngle - startAngle); //Cross axis
      }
   }
   return sweepAngle;
}
```

The method to stroke a circular arc is the same as the one used to stroke a circle except that the sweep angle is not $2\pi$ and has to be determined by calling the above API. Because of the similarity of the two APIs, let us copy **apiStrokeCircle.cpp** and save it as **apiStrokeArc.cpp**. We then modify it as follows to stroke a circular arc:

```
/*------------------------------------------------------------
API Name
   apiStrokeArc

Description
```

It strokes an arc with respect to the chord-height tolerance.

Signature
```
   void apiStrokeArc(GPosition2d &center, double radius, double tol
            double startAngle, double endAngle, bool bCounterClock,
            std::vector<GPosition2d>& pStrkPts,   apiError &rc)
```

    INPUT:
       center           center of circle
       radius           radius of circle
       startAngle
       endAngle
       bCounterClock    true if arc orientation is counter clockwise
       tol              chord-height tolerance
    OUTPUT:
       pStrkPts         STL vector that stores stroking points
       apiError         error code: api_OK if no error

History

    Y.M. Li      03/01/2013 : Creation date
```
------------------------------------------------------------------*/
#include "MyHeader.h"

void apiStrokeArc(GPosition2d &center, double radius, double tol
            double startAngle, double endAngle, bool bCounterClock,
            std::vector<GPosition2d>& pStrkPts,   apiError &rc)
{
   int          i, nStrkPts;
   double       sweepAngle, delta, sin_delta, cos_delta;

   // Initialize data and determine the number of stroking points
   rc = api_OK;
   delta = 2.0 * acos(1.0 - tol / radius);
   sweepAngle = apiGetSweepAngle(radius, startAngle,
                          endAngle, bCounterClock);
   nStrkPts = 2 + (int)(sweepAngle / delta);
   delta = sweepAngle / (nStrkPts - 1);
   if (!bCounterClock)
      delta = -delta;
   pStrkPts.resize(nStrkPts);

   // Loop to compute stroking points on the arc centered at (0,0)
   sin_delta = sin(delta);
   cos_delta = cos(delta);
   pStrkPts[0].x = radius * cos(startAngle);
   pStrkPts[0].y = radius * sin(startAngle);
```

```
for (i=1; i<nStrkPts; i++)
{
    pStrkPts[i].x = pStrkPts[i-1].x * cos_delta -
                    pStrkPts[i-1].y * sin_delta;
    pStrkPts[i].y = pStrkPts[i-1].y * cos_delta +
                    pStrkPts[i-1].x * sin_delta;
}

// Translate the points based on the given center
for (i=0; i<nStrkPts; i++)
{
    pStrkPts[i].x += center.x;
    pStrkPts[i].y += center.y;
}
}
```

It should be pointed out that it is possible to combine two APIs, apiStrokeCircle and apiStrokeArc into a single API to stroke both the circle and arc with startAngle, endAngle, and bCounterClock being the optional input arguments. However, we keep them separated to make each API more readable.

All the functions we just implemented need to be added to our dynamic-link library and exported properly so that they can be accessed by our windows-based application. We have implemented all necessary supporting functions and are ready to modify CDisplayView::OnDraw to render the line, circle, and arc. With added comments, the implementation is mostly self-explanatory and descriptions of GDI functions (e.g., pDC->SelectObject, pDC->Ellipse, pDC->LineTo, etc.) can be readily found on the MSDN website:

```
void CDisplayView::OnDraw(CDC* pDC)
{
    // TODO: add draw code for native data here
    int       i;
    CPoint    cPoint;
    CPen      blackPen, redPen;

    GetClientRect(m_clientRect);

    // Pen style is solid and width is 1 pixel for
    // the black pen and 2 pixels for the red pen:
    blackPen.CreatePen(PS_SOLID, 1, RGB(0, 0, 0));
    redPen.CreatePen(PS_SOLID, 2, RGB(225, 0, 0));

    // Draw collected points with red pen:
    pDC->SelectObject(&redPen);
    for (i=0; i<(int)m_gPoints.size(); i++)
    {
        WorldToDC(m_gPoints[i], cPoint);
```

```
    // Draws a circle specified by a bounding Rectangle:
    pDC->Ellipse(CRect(cPoint.x-3, cPoint.y-3,
                       cPoint.x+3, cPoint.y+3));
}

if (m_bDrawCurve && m_gPoints.size() > 2)
{
    // Draw line, circle, or arc
    apiError    rc = api_OK;
    double      tol = 0.5 / m_scale;
    GPosition2d pt, pt_min, pt_max;
    GVector2d   dirV;

    // Draw line, circle, or arc with black pen:
    pDC->SelectObject(&blackPen);

    if (m_fitOption == 1)
    {
        double      dx, dy, d, dmin = 1.0e+10, dmax = 0.0;
        apiBestFitLine(m_gPoints, pt, dirV, rc);
        if (rc != api_OK)
            return;

        // Compute the start and end point of the finite line:
        dx = m_gPoints[0].x - pt.x;
        dy = m_gPoints[0].y - pt.y;
        dmin = dmax = dx * dirV.x + dy *dirV.y;
        for (i=1; i<(int)m_gPoints.size(); i++)
        {
            dx = m_gPoints[i].x - pt.x;
            dy = m_gPoints[i].y - pt.y;
            d = dx * dirV.x + dy *dirV.y;
            if (d > dmax)
                dmax = d;
            else if (d <dmin)
                dmin = d;
        }
        pt_min.x = pt.x + dmin * dirV.x;
        pt_min.y = pt.y + dmin * dirV.y;
        WorldToDC(pt_min, cPoint);
        pDC->MoveTo(cPoint.x, cPoint.y);

        pt_max.x = pt.x + dmax * dirV.x;
        pt_max.y = pt.y + dmax * dirV.y;
        WorldToDC(pt_max, cPoint);
        pDC->LineTo(cPoint.x, cPoint.y);
```

```
   }
   else if (m_fitOption == 2)
   {
      double    dRadius;
      vector<GPosition2d> pStrkPts;

      apiBestFitCircle(m_gPoints, pt, dRadius, rc);
      if (rc != api_OK)
         return;
      apiStrokeCircle(pt, dRadius, tol, pStrkPts, rc);
      if (rc != api_OK)
         return;

      WorldToDC(pStrkPts[0], cPoint);
      pDC->MoveTo(cPoint.x, cPoint.y);
      for (i=1; i<(int)pStrkPts.size(); i++)
      {
         WorldToDC(pStrkPts[i], cPoint);
         pDC->LineTo(cPoint.x, cPoint.y);
      }
   }
   else if (m_fitOption == 3)
   {
      int       n;
      double    dRadius, startAngle, endAngle, angle;
      bool      bCounterClock = true;
      vector<GPosition2d> pStrkPts;

      apiBestFitArc(m_gPoints, pt, dRadius, rc);
      if (rc != api_OK)
         return;

      // Determine start/end angle and orientation
      n = m_gPoints.size();
      startAngle = apiGetAngleFromPoint(pt, m_gPoints[0]);
      endAngle = apiGetAngleFromPoint(pt, m_gPoints[n-1]);
      angle = apiGetAngleFromPoint(pt, m_gPoints[n/2]);
      if (!apiIsParInRange(startAngle,endAngle,bCounterClock,angle))
         bCounterClock = false;

      apiStrokeArc(pt, dRadius, startAngle, endAngle,
                   bCounterClock, tol, pStrkPts, rc);
      if (rc != api_OK)
         return;

      WorldToDC(pStrkPts[0], cPoint);
      pDC->MoveTo(cPoint.x, cPoint.y);
```

```
    for (i=1; i<(int)pStrkPts.size(); i++)
    {
        WorldToDC(pStrkPts[i], cPoint);
        pDC->LineTo(cPoint.x, cPoint.y);
    }
  }
 }
}
```

It is noted that the tolerance used for stroking a circle or an arc is defined as $0.5/m\_scale$. If both the world and device coordinate units are pixel, then $m\_scale=1$ and 0.5 stands for "half pixel". Otherwise, the tolerance for the world coordinate is the half pixel divided by the scaling factor.

We are done with all required implementations! Save and compile this project. The application can be run by either pressing F5, double clicking `Display.exe`, or invoking the executable from the command line. By clicking one of three customized icons on the tool bar, we can experiment with the corresponding fitting method and visualize the result. Figure 10.15 illustrates the result of best fit arc. By design, the best fit arc interpolates the start and end point and approximates the remaining points in a least squares sense.

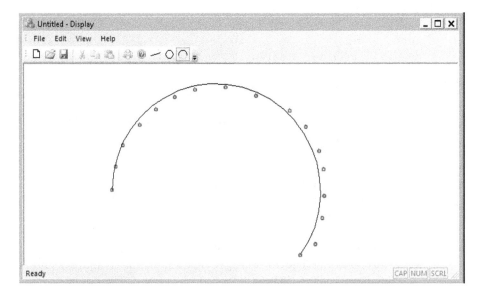

Figure 10.15: Best fit arc

## 10.5   Display user data

The windows-based application we just created is good for "show-off" or casual demos but is of little practical use. In real world applications, we usually want to display our own data sets, not some randomly-clicked point cloud. Recall how our main drivers for console applications were designed: each driver opens a specific input file defined via the command-line arguments, reads input data through I/O methods, and calls an associated function to run a test case. For a windows-based application, an input file is usually browsed and selected via the Explorer-style `File Open` dialog box (referring to figure 10.16). By using Explorer-style common dialogs, we give users a consistent and comfortable experience across different programs. We will thus discuss in this section how to add the `File Open` dialog box into our application so that we can browse a file and open it for display. As will be seen later, this seemingly difficult task is readily accomplished with MFS `ClassWizard`. With a slight modification, the code discussed in this section can also be used for a familiar `File Save As` operation.

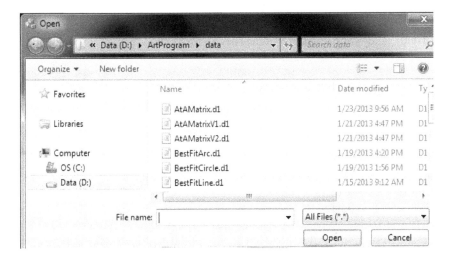

Figure 10.16: File Open dialog box

Let us start our `Display` application from the Visual Studio environment by pressing F5 in debug mode. When the application window shows up, click `File->Open` to bring up a `File Open` dialog as shown in figure 10.16. This is MFC's default appearance of the `File Open` dialog box. Do not open any file or close or cancel the dialog box. Instead, go back to Visual Studio and click from main menu bar `Debug->Break All` to halt the execution and break into the debugger. At the `Call Stack` window, find `CWinApp::OnFileOpen()` and double click it, which leads us to the following method:

```
void CWinApp::OnFileOpen()
{
    ENSURE(m_pDocManager != NULL);
    m_pDocManager->OnFileOpen();
}
```

`CWinApp` is a base class from which we derive a windows application object, and the member function `CWinApp::OnFileOpen` in the base class can be overridden by derived classes. The purpose of this section is to override this method with our own implementation of `OnFileOpen` in `CDisplayView` class.

Stop the application. On the project menu-bar, click `Project->Class Wizard`. In the popup `MFC Class Wizard` dialog box, select `CDisplayView` for `Class name` and browse down to find `ID_FILE_OPEN` (referring to Figure 10.11); highlight it and click the `Add Handlers` button. Consequently, the following macro entry will be added to message map:

```
ON_COMMAND(ID_FILE_OPEN, &CDisplayView::OnFileOpen)
```

The `CDisplayView::OnFileOpen` method body will also be created. Let us open `DisplayView.cpp` and add the following code to override the default implementation of the `OnFileOpen` method in `CWinApp` class:

```
void CDisplayView::OnFileOpen()
{
    // TODO: Add your command handler code here
    CFileDialog fileDlg(TRUE);

    if (fileDlg.DoModal() == IDOK)
    {
        ;
    }
}
```

An instance of `CFileDialog` is created by its constructor with one parameter `TRUE`, indicating to create a `File Open` dialog box. If it is set to `FALSE`, the `File Save As` dialog box will be constructed. Save the change, compile the project, and press `F5` to start the program. When the application window shows up, click `File->Open` to bring up the `File Open` dialog box that looks similar to Figure 10.16. When browsing a folder as we usually do with Windows Explorer, we notice that files of different types are all shown in the file list box. Our purpose is to select specific types of data files (e.g., files with these extensions `.txt`, `.d*`, `.o*`, and `.n*`) so that they can be rendered on the screen. We thus naturally ask whether MFC provides filters for the `File Open` dialog. The answer is "YES." As indicated below, the `CFileDialog` constructor takes several optional (or default) parameters to control how the `File Open` dialog box behaves.

```
explicit CFileDialog(
    BOOL bOpenFileDialog,
    LPCTSTR lpszDefExt = NULL,
    LPCTSTR lpszFileName = NULL,
    DWORD dwFlags = OFN_HIDEREADONLY | OFN_OVERWRITEPROMPT,
    LPCTSTR lpszFilter = NULL,
    CWnd* pParentWnd = NULL,
    DWORD dwSize = 0
);
```

The descriptions of these optional parameters are

*bOpenFileDialog*

> Set to TRUE to construct a File Open dialog box or FALSE to construct a File Save As dialog box.

*lpszDefExt*

> The default filename extension. If the user does not include an extension in the Filename edit box, the extension specified by `lpszDefExt` is automatically appended to the filename. If this parameter is `NULL`, no file extension is appended.

*lpszFileName*

> The initial filename that appears in the filename edit box. If `NULL`, no filename initially appears.

*dwFlags*

> A combination of one or more flags that allows you to customize the dialog box. The default bitwise value indicates "Hides the Read Only check box" and "Causes the Save As dialog box to generate a message box if the selected file already exists. The user must confirm whether to overwrite the file."

*lpszFilter*

> A series of string pairs that specifies filters you can apply to the file. If you specify file filters, only the selected files will appear in the Files list box.

*pParentWnd*

> A pointer to the file dialog-box object's parent or owner window.

*dwSize*

> The size of the `OPENFILENAME` structure. This value is dependent on the operating system version. The default size of 0 means that the MFC code will determine the proper dialog box size to use based on the operating system version on which the program is run.

To control what types of files appear in the File list box, we need only the optional parameter `szFilters`. By the rule of optional parameters, however, we need to specify all default arguments that appear in front of `szFilters` as:

```
void CDisplayView::OnFileOpen()
{
    // TODO: Add your command handler code here
    TCHAR szFilters[]=
      _T("My Files (*.txt;*.d*;*.o*;*.n*)|*.txt;*.d*;*.o*;*.n*|")
      _T("All Files (*.*)|*.*||");
    CFileDialog fileDlg(TRUE, NULL, NULL, OFN_EXPLORER, szFilters);

    if (fileDlg.DoModal() == IDOK)
    {
        ;
    }
}
```

The `OFN_EXPLORER` flag tells the system to use the specified template to create a dialog box that is a child of the default Explorer-style dialog box. Two sets of string pairs are used as file filters. The first pair ensures that only those files whose suffixes are

```
.txt; *.d*; *.o*; *.n*
```

will be shown in the File list box. The second pair ensures that all files will be shown
on the File list box. When executing the program, we can select either My Files or
All Files (*.*) filter option as indicated below.

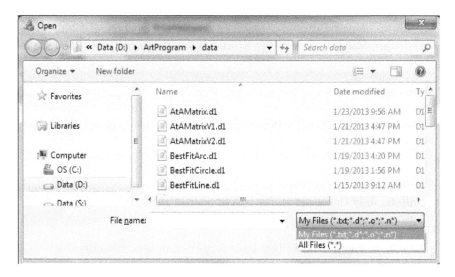

Figure 10.17: File open dialog with filter

After an instance of CFileDialog has been constructed, call the DoModal member
function to display the above dialog box. The user can either enter the path and file name
or browse the folder to find the desired file. DoModal returns a flag, indicating whether
the user has selected the OK (IDOK) or the Cancel (IDCANCEL) button. If DoModal
returns IDOK, we can use CFileDialog's public member function GetPathName to obtain
the selected filename and its path and then use such information to open the input file
to read input data. Let's expand the implementation of CDisplayView::OnFileOpen
to achieve this goal:

```
void CDisplayView::OnFileOpen()
{
    // TODO: Add your command handler code here
    TCHAR szFilters[]=
        _T("My Files (*.txt;*.d*;*.o*;*.n*)|*.txt;*.d*;*.o*;*.n*|")
        _T("All Files (*.*)|*.*||");
    CFileDialog fileDlg(TRUE, NULL, NULL, OFN_EXPLORER, szFilters);

    if (fileDlg.DoModal() == IDOK)
    {
        FILE    *infile=NULL;
        CString  pathName = fileDlg.GetPathName();

        _wfopen_s(&infile, pathName, _T("r"));
```

```
    if (infile)
    {
        int       i, n;
        m_gPoints.clear();
        fscanf_s(infile, "%d", &n);
        m_gPoints.resize(n);
        for (i=0; i<n; i++)
        {
            fscanf_s(infile,"%lf %lf",&m_gPoints[i].x,&m_gPoints[i].y);
        }
        fclose(infile);
    }

    m_bDrawCurve = TRUE;
    OnInitialUpdate(); // Triger to draw curves
    }
}
```

We use _wfopen_s instead of fopen_s because pathName is stored in CSting rather than char string. Save the changes, compile the project, and run the program. By browsing and opening, for example, D:\ArtProgram\data\BestFitLine.d1, we expect the data points and the best fit line to be drawn properly on the screen. It is, however, not the case due to the mismatch of two coordinate systems. Referring to the DCToWorld and WorldToDC methods implemented in the previous section, we assumed that both the world and device coordinate systems use a pixel as a unit. Furthermore, data points were generated by clicking the left mouse button while moving the cursor around the client windows, which indicates that all points are visible. The data points stored in a text file usually do not use a pixel as a unit, and also the world coordinate system may not necessarily overlap with the device coordinate system as shown below.

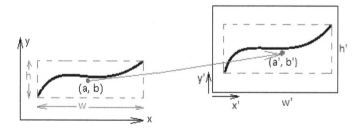

Figure 10.18: Mapping between world and screen coordinate systems

Therefore, two transformations are usually required to move a curve in the $(x, y)$ to $(x', y')$ coordinate system:

1. Scaling transformation: since two coordinate systems use different units, a scaling factor needs to be determined. Assume that the available draw area in the $(x', y')$ coordinate system is $w' \times h'$. Our purpose is to maximally fit the image in the $(x, y)$ coordinate system to the drawing area defined by $w' \times h'$. Assume the

maximum width and height of the image in $(x, y)$ coordinate system is $(w, h)$.
Then,
$$\text{xScale} = w'/w \quad \text{and} \quad \text{yScale} = h'/h.$$

To leave some margin in the drawing area, we take

```
0.8 * min(xSvale, yScale)
```

as the scaling factor.

2. Translation: Compute the center of the image in $(x, y)$ system and the center of the drawing area in the $(x', y')$ coordinate system. Denoting two centers by $(a, b)$ and $(a', b')$, the translation vector is defined as

$$\boldsymbol{v} = (a' - a, b' - b).$$

With the above two transformations in mind, we can now complete the implementation of `OnFileOpen` as follows:

```
void CDisplayView::OnFileOpen()
{
    // TODO: Add your command handler code here
    TCHAR szFilters[]=
        _T("My Files (*.txt;*.d*;*.o*;*.n*)|*.txt;*.d*;*.o*;*.n*|")
        _T("All Files (*.*)|*.*||");
    CFileDialog fileDlg(TRUE, NULL, NULL, OFN_EXPLORER, szFilters);

    if (fileDlg.DoModal() == IDOK)
    {
        FILE      *infile=NULL;
        CString   pathName = fileDlg.GetPathName();

        _wfopen_s(&infile, pathName, _T("r"));
        if (infile)
        {
            int       i, n;
            LONG      dx, dy;
            double    xmin, xmax, ymin, ymax, xScale, yScale;
            GPosition2d pt_mid_scrn, pt_mid_wd;
            CPoint      cPt;

            m_gPoints.clear();
            fscanf_s(infile, "%d", &n);
            m_gPoints.resize(n);
            for (i=0; i<n; i++)
            {
                fscanf_s(infile, "%lf %lf", &m_gPoints[i].x,
                                            &m_gPoints[i].y);
            }
```

```
            fclose(infile);

            // Determine the scaling factor
            xmin = xmax = m_gPoints[0].x;
            ymin = ymax = m_gPoints[0].y;
            for (i=1; i<n; i++)
            {
                if (xmin > m_gPoints[i].x)
                    xmin = m_gPoints[i].x;
                else if (xmax < m_gPoints[i].x)
                    xmax = m_gPoints[i].x;

                if (ymin > m_gPoints[i].y)
                    ymin = m_gPoints[i].y;
                else if (ymax < m_gPoints[i].y)
                    ymax = m_gPoints[i].y;
            }

            dx = m_clientRect.right - m_clientRect.left;
            dy = m_clientRect.bottom - m_clientRect.top;
            xScale = dx / (xmax - xmin);
            yScale = dy / (ymax - ymin);
            m_scale = 0.8 * min(xScale, yScale);

            cPt.x = m_clientRect.left + dx / 2;
            cPt.y = m_clientRect.top + dy / 2;
            DCToWorld(cPt, pt_mid_scrn);
            pt_mid_wd.x = xmin + 0.5 * (xmax - xmin);
            pt_mid_wd.y = ymin + 0.5 * (ymax - ymin);

            m_translation.x = pt_mid_scrn.x - pt_mid_wd.x;
            m_translation.y = pt_mid_scrn.y - pt_mid_wd.y;
            m_bDrawCurve = TRUE;
            OnInitialUpdate(); // Triger to draw curves
        }
    }
}
```

We also need to modify the WorldToDC method to take the translation into consideration:

```
void CDisplayView::WorldToDC(GPosition2d &gPoint, CPoint &cPoint)
{
    GPosition2d pt;
    pt.x = gPoint.x + m_translation.x;
    pt.y = gPoint.y + m_translation.y;
    cPoint.x = (int)(pt.x * m_scale);
    cPoint.y = (int)(m_clientRect.bottom - pt.y * m_scale);
}
```

We are now ready to play with the windows-based application `Display`. When the `BestLine` icon is active, we can either click mouse buttons to generate a best fit line or open an existing data file (e.g., `BestFitLine.d2`) to display the data points as tiny red circles and the best fit line in black color as shown in figure 10.19. Similarly, when the `BestCircle` or `BestArc` icon is active, we can open corresponding data files to visualize the input and output results.

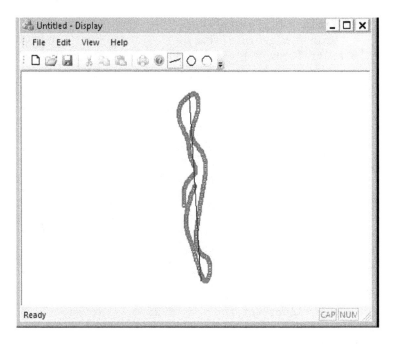

Figure 10.19: Best fit line to customer data points

## 10.6  Summary

We have seen how the MFC Application Wizard and Class Wizard simplify our work in developing a windows-based application. Though a very simple application program, it does provides hands-on experience in Windows programming and gives a glimpse of how sophisticated CAD systems are developed. Most GUIs in windows-based CAD systems have historically been built with native Win32 APIs and MFC. Therefore, the hands-on experience and MFC knowledge gained in this chapter will certainly help readers not only shorten the learning curve when working in a software company that develops windows-based applications, but also develop their own windows-based applications.

Coordinate transformations play an essential role in data visualization. Geometric 2D and 3D transformations used in computer graphics are mappings from one coordinate system to the other. They play a central role in model construction and visualization. For example, tools such as rotating, zooming, and mirroring an image found in most CAD systems are all based on geometric transformations. In this chapter, we studied only limited 2D transformations that are necessary to map images in the world coordinate to the device coordinate (e.g., the client window of our `Display` application). General discussions about 2D and 3D transformations can be found in most computer graphics books. Readers can also find such information in my online book, *Java Graphics Programming*, at www.infogoaround.org. After becoming comfortable with coordinate transformations, readers can expand this Display tool to include commonly-used commands such as `zoom-in`, `drag`, `rotate`, etc. as shown below. This is the tool I developed at work to visualize and manipulate geometric entities saved in the internal format known only by the internal math functions.

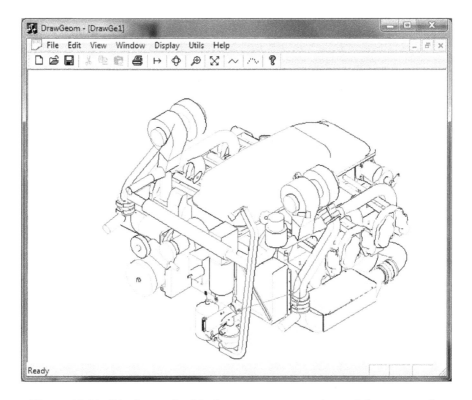

Figure 10.20: Display tool with drag, rotate, zoom-in, and fit commands.

It should be pointed out that the transformations we used in this chapter did not take into consideration the so-called *pixel aspect ratio*, which is the ratio between the width and height of each pixel. We assumed that most modern computers have squared pixels. If this is not the case, the aspect ratio may be critical when users try to draw a figure with symmetric shape such as circles and squares.

Microsoft is constantly evolving its core technologies. To keep up the pace, developers in software industry are constantly learning and renewing their knowledge and skills. Win32 and MFC have traditionally been the primary choice for windows-based applications developed with unmanaged C/C++. With the introduction of Microsoft .Net framework, developers are implementing applications in managed code such as $C^{\#}$ and .Net VB. For this reason, Windows Forms and Windows Presentation Foundation are gaining popularity in developing windows-based applications.

In our example, display of line, circle, and arc is rendered via Microsoft's Graphics Device Interface. The GDI provides functions for drawing points, lines, rectangles, polygons, ellipses, bitmaps, and text. For 3D rendering, Microsoft DirectX is preferred over GDI as its *High Level Shading Language (HLSL)* is capable of doing vertex, geometry, and pixel (or fragment) shading. DirectX has also a well-defined set of graphics processing unit (GPU) functionality.

# Chapter 11

# Parallel Programming

Parallel computing is a discipline of computer science that deals with the system architecture and software issues related to the concurrent execution of applications. The interest in parallel computing dates back to the late 1950s but had been primarily confined to a few franchise industries (IBM, Honeywell, etc.) and leading research universities (University of Illinois at Urbana-Champaign, Caltech, MIT, and Carnegie Mellon). Today it is emerging as a prevalent computing paradigm due to the semiconductor industry's shift to multi-core processors. Most desktop and laptop systems now ship with dual-core, quad-core, or even six-core chips. Chip manufacturers have begun to increase overall processing performance by adding additional CPU cores. The reason is that increasing performance through parallel processing can be far more energy-efficient than increasing microprocessor clock frequencies. In a world that is increasingly mobile and energy conscious, this has become essential.

As multi-core processors bring parallel computing to mainstream customers, the key challenge in computing today is transitioning the software industry to parallel programming. Parallel programs are usually harder to write than sequential ones. A program that is divided into multiple concurrent tasks is more difficult to write, due to the necessary synchronization and communication that need to take place between those tasks. There are multiple models for constructing parallel programs. At a very high level, there are two basic models: *multiple-program multiple-data* (MPMD) and *single-program multiple-data* (SPMD). In the MPMD model, each processor executes a different program ("multiple-program") with the different programs working in tandem to process different data ("multiple-data"). In the SPMD model, the same program runs on each processor ("single-program") but each program instance processes different data ("multiple-data"). In this chapter, we are concerned with the SPMD model.

The two most common implementations of the SPMD model are the *Message Passing Interface* (MPI) and *Open Multi-Processing* (OpenMP). In MPI, the program is started on all processors. The program is responsible for distributing data among processors, and then each processor processes its section of the data, communicating among themselves as needed. MPI provides the user with a programming model where processes communicate with other processes by calling library routines to send and receive messages. The advantage of the MPI programming model is that the user has complete control over data distribution and process synchronization, permitting the optimization data locality and workflow distribution. The disadvantage is that existing sequential applications require a considerable amount of restructuring for a parallelization based on MPI. OpenMP provides a *fork-and-join* execution model (see figure 11.1) in which a program begins execution as a single process or thread. This thread executes sequentially until a parallelization directive for a parallel region is found. At this time, the thread creates a team of threads and becomes the *master thread* of the new team. All threads execute the statements until the end of the parallel region. Work-sharing directives are provided to divide the execution of the enclosed code region among the threads. All threads need to synchronize at the end of parallel constructs. The advantage of OpenMP is that an existing code can be easily parallelized by placing OpenMP directives around time-consuming loops that do not contain data dependence, leaving the source code largely unchanged. Furthermore, parallelism directives can be added incrementally, which is ideal for beginners. The disadvantage is that it is not easy for the user to optimize workflow and memory access. In this chapter, we focus on OpenMP.

## 11.1   OpenMP overview

Have computers stopped getting faster?  If we looked only at the clock speeds of microprocessor chips, we might well think so.  Chip makers have struggled to design CPUs that run much faster than about 3.5 GHz due to thermodynamic limits in current semiconductor process technologies (e.g., wasted energy in the form of heat). The highest clock speed microprocessor ever sold commercially to date is found inside IBM's zEnterprise 196 mainframe, which was introduced in July, 2010. Its cores run continuously at 5.2 GHz. Due to physical limitations, the major CPU vendors have shifted their attention away from ramping up clock speeds to adding parallelism support with multi-core processors that can handle different tasks simultaneously. This seems like pretty good news. Yet, for most tasks, it is not. That is because the majority of software is traditionally designed to run on a single-core chip; in other words, it is designed to do only one thing at a time. It requires broad collaborations across industry and academia to create families of technologies that work together to bring the power of parallel computing to future mainstream applications. Most of the major vendors of concurrent computers were involved in both MPI and OpenMP along with researchers from universities, government laboratories, and industry. The changes will affect the entire industry – from consumers to hardware manufacturers and from the entire software development infrastructure to application developers who rely upon it.

OpenMP helps FORTRAN and C/C++ developers create multi-threaded applications with minimal and manageable changes in their serial code. Unlike MPI that is most suited for a system with multiple processors and multiple memory (e.g., a cluster of computers with their own local memory), OpenMP is designed for shared memory systems like the ones we have in our desktop and laptop computers. In computer hardware, shared memory refers to a large block of random access memory that can be accessed by several different central processing units (CPUs) in a multiple-processor computer system.

OpenMP is an explicit (not automatic) programming model, offering the programmer full control over parallelization. It uses the so-called *fork-join* model of parallel execution as shown below:

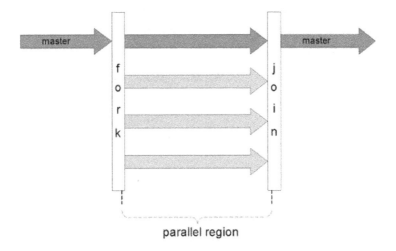

parallel region

Figure 11.1: OpenMP: The fork-join model

All OpenMP begins as a single process known as the master thread. It executes sequentially until the first *parallel region* construct is encountered. The master thread then creates (or *spawns*) a team of parallel threads. The statements in the program that are enclosed by the parallel region construct are then executed in parallel among the various team threads. When the team threads complete the statements in the parallel region construct, they synchronize and terminate, leaving only the master thread.

OpenMP designers have developed a platform-independent set of compiler `pragma directives`, `function calls`, and `environment variables` that explicitly instruct the compiler how and where to insert threads into the application. Many of them will be discussed in subsequent sections.

## 11.2 Specify parallelism

OpenMP has been available since Visual Studio 2005. Although OpenMP version 3.0 has been available since May, 2008, both Visual Studio 2010 and 2012 support only OpenMP version 2.0 that was released in 2002. It is hoped that future Visual Studio releases will support OpenMP version 3.0 or newer (OpenMP version 4.0 was released in July, 2013).

To be able to experiment with OpenMP, we need to do the following two things:

- Include <omp.h> in the source file or global header file `MyHeader.h`.

- Enable OpenMP compiler switch in Project Properties as illustrated below. Since all of our functions will be built into DLLs, we need to enable OpenMP compiler switch for the FunctDLL project and the application project. Please note this has to be done in both debug and release modes.

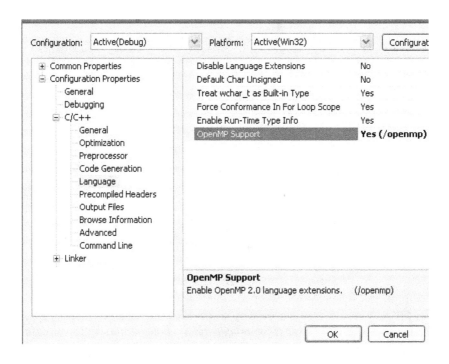

Figure 11.2: Enabling OpenMP for Visual C++

Let's write a short program to illustrate how OpenMP constructs a parallel regions and spawns a team of threads for parallel computing:

```
#include "MyHeader.h"
#include <omp.h>

void main()
{
    printf("Multi-thread computing starts here:\n\n");
    #pragma omp parallel
    {
        printf("Hello from thread %d\n", omp_get_thread_num());
    }
    printf("\nMulti-thread computing ends here.\n");
}
```

The parallel region in the above example is constructed by using the **pragma** directive. In C/C++ programming language, **pragma** has long been used by developers as a *preprocessor directive* to access compiler-specific preprocessor extensions. A common use of **pragma** is the #pragma once directive to speedup compilation because it asks the compiler to include a header file only once, no matter how many times it has been imported. Each implementation of C and C++ supports some features unique to its host machine or operating system. Some programs, for instance, need to exercise precise control over the memory areas where data is placed or to control the way certain functions receive parameters. The `#pragma` directives provide a way for each compiler to offer machine- and operating-system-specific features while retaining overall compatibility with the C and C++ languages. The OpenMP `pragma` directs the compiler to parallelize sections of code. All OpenMP `pragms` begin with `#pragma omp`. As with any `pragma`, these directives are ignored by compilers that do not support the feature.

Now, let us compile and run the above short program at the command prompt. If your computer has at least a dual-core processor, you should see more than one "Hello" line being printed at the command prompt. My laptop has eight threads (Core i7) and, hence, prints eight "Hello's."

```
Multi-thread computing starts here:

Hello from thread 0
Hello from thread 7
Hello from thread 6
Hello from thread 5
Hello from thread 3
Hello from thread 4
Hello from thread 2
Hello from thread 1


Multi-thread computing ends here.
```

The program begins as a single process known as the master thread. It executes the first print statement "Multi-thread computing starts here:" sequentially until it reaches the parallel region constructed with `#pragma omp parallel`. The master thread then creates a team of available threads. The "Hello" print statement enclosed by the parallel region construct is executed in parallel among all available threads. When the team threads complete the statements in the parallel region construct, they synchronize and terminate, leaving only the master thread to execute the last print statement "Multi-thread computing ends here."

This simple example was created to show how OpenMP's fork-join model behaves. In practice, we should not construct a parallel region to perform redundant work as the above program does. The parallelism is usually constructed by using more than one `pragmas` directive along with optional directive clauses to *share* (not to duplicate) the workload among available threads. The general syntax is:

```
#pragma omp <directive> [clause ...]
```

The directives we will use include: `parallel`, `for`, `section`, `ordered`, `critical`, etc. These directives specify either work-sharing or synchronization constructs and will be discussed in this and subsequent sections. The OpenMP clauses are optional modifiers of the directives and affect the behavior of the directives. The OpenMP clauses we will come across are mostly for task scheduling and data sharing. The data sharing attribute clauses include `private`, `firstprivate`, `lastprivate`, and `reduction`. They are mainly used to manage data environment to avoid data race conditions.

To demonstrate how OpenMP helps us construct a parallel region to share the workload, we start by considering the circle stroking algorithm discussed in section 3.3 of chapter 3. If we do not care about the performance, the circle stroking method may be implemented as follows:

```
#include "MyHeader.h"

void apiStrokeCircleV2(GPosition2d &center, double radius, double tol,
                   std::vector<GPosition2d>& pStrkPts, apiError &rc)
{
    int         i, nStrkPts;
    double      delta;

    // Determine the number of stroking points
    rc = api_OK;
    delta = 2.0 * acos(1.0 - tol / radius);
    nStrkPts = 2 + (int)(2.0 * GPI / delta);
    delta = 2.0 * GPI / (nStrkPts - 1);
    pStrkPts.resize(nStrkPts);

    // Loop to compute stroking points
    for (i=0; i<nStrkPts; i++)
    {
        pStrkPts[i].x = center.x + radius * cos(i * delta);
        pStrkPts[i].y = center.y + radius * sin(i * delta);
    }
}
```

As is seen above, the computation of the $i$th stroking point is independent of the $(i-1)$th stroking point. Therefore, stroking points do not have to be computed sequentially. We can thus parallelize `apiStrokeCircleV2` as follows:

```
#include "MyHeader.h"
#include <omp.h>

void apiStrokeCircleV2(GPosition2d &center, double radius, double tol,
                   std::vector<GPosition2d>& pStrkPts, apiError &rc)
{
    int         i, nStrkPts;
    double      delta;

    // Determine the number of stroking points
    rc = api_OK;
    delta = 2.0 * acos(1.0 - tol / radius);
    nStrkPts = 2 + (int)(2.0 * GPI / delta);
    delta = 2.0 * GPI / (nStrkPts - 1);
```

```
pStrkPts.resize(nStrkPts);

// Loop to compute stroking points
#pragma omp parallel
{
    #pragma omp for
    for (i=0; i<nStrkPts; i++)
    {
        pStrkPts[i].x = center.x + radius * cos(i * delta);
        pStrkPts[i].y = center.y + radius * sin(i * delta);
    }
}
```

Two OpenMP directives were used in the above implementation. The first directive `#pragma omp parallel` tells the compiler that the structured block of code should be executed in parallel on multiple threads. The second directive `#pragma omp for` is a work-sharing directive that tells OpenMP that, when called from a parallel region, the `for` loop should have its iterations divided among the thread team. Assuming that four threads are available and `nStrkPts=100`. Then, the iterations of the loop may get allocated such that processor 1 gets iterations 1-25, processor 2 gets iterations 26-50, processor 3 gets iterations 51-75, and processor 4 gets iterations 76-100. It should be pointed out, however, that the iterations may not be divided exactly as it is suggested here. But it neither concerns us nor can we do anything about it. One thing that is not explicit in this program is a *barrier* synchronization at the end of the parallel region. All threads will pause there until the last thread is complete. It should also be pointed out that, without the second directive `#pragma omp for`, each thread would execute the *full* `for` loop. Accordingly, the program would run much slower than if compiled by a single thread..

My computer has four cores and eight hyper threads. Compiling and running the above parallel implementation, we would expect it to significantly outperform the one without parallelism. In reality, it is only 2 times faster. This is because multi-threaded executables often incur longer startup times, so they can actually run much slower than if compiled by a single thread. Based on Microsoft's article, multi-threading computation may not be appropriate if the `for` loop block runs less than 15 ms. Therefore, it is important to understand and evaluate the workload before adding parallelism.

In section 3.3, we developed a very fast algorithm to stroke a circle. The `for` loop code fragment is as follows:

```
sin_delta = sin(delta);
cos_delta = cos(delta);
pStrkPts[0].x = radius; pStrkPts[0].y = 0.0;
for (i=1; i<nStrkPts; i++)
{
    pStrkPts[i].x = pStrkPts[i-1].x * cos_delta -
                    pStrkPts[i-1].y * sin_delta;
```

```
        pStrkPts[i].y = pStrkPts[i-1].y * cos_delta +
                        pStrkPts[i-1].x * sin_delta;
}
```

The computation of a new stroking point depends on the result of the previous one. Therefore, the above code has to be executed sequentially, which indicates that the `for` loop region is not suitable for parallel programming. Even so, it still runs faster than the one that repeatedly calls sin and cos with parallelism.

## 11.3   OpenMP runtime routines

In the previous section, we saw how multi-threading may improve the performance of a program. However, we should not expect to speed up the execution by $m$ times when running a program parallelized using OpenMP on an $m$ processor computer for the following main reasons:

- It may have $m$ times the computation power, but the memory bandwidth usually does not scale up $m$ times. Quite often, the original memory path is shared by multiple processors, and performance degradation may be observed when they compete for the shared memory bandwidth.

- Multi-threaded executables often incur longer startup times.

- A large part of the program may not be parallelized by OpenMP, which means that the theoretical upper limit of speedup is limited according to Amdahl's law. For example, if, for a given problem size, a parallelized implementation of an algorithm can run 12% of the algorithm's operations arbitrarily quickly (while the remaining 88% of the operations are not parallelizable), Amdahl's law states that the maximum speedup of the parallelized version is $1/(10.12) = 1.136$ times as fast as the non-parallelized implementation.

- Barrier synchronization at the end of the work sharing construct incurs a performance overhead (It can be suppressed by using the optional clause `nowait` if it is safe to do so).

For these reasons, we may not need to consume all available threads, leaving no room for other applications running concurrently. The number of threads used to share the `for` loop iterations can be controlled by calling OpenMP runtime routine. For example, the following code fragment sets 4 threads to construct the parallel region:

```
// Loop to compute stroking points
omp_set_num_threads(4);
#pragma omp parallel
{
    #pragma omp for
    for (i=0; i<nStrkPts; i++)
    {
        pStrkPts[i].x = center.x + radius * cos(i * delta);
        pStrkPts[i].y = center.y + radius * sin(i * delta);
```

```
      }
  }
```

It should be pointed out that a call to runtime routines may be combined with `#pragma` directive as

```
  #pragma omp parallel num_threads(4)
  {
      #pragma omp for
      for (i=0; i<nStrkPts; i++)
      {
          pStrkPts[i].x = center.x + radius * cos(i * delta);
          pStrkPts[i].y = center.y + radius * sin(i * delta);
      }
  }
```

OpenMP runtime routines are used primarily to set and retrieve information about the environment. We will encounter more OpenMP runtime routines in the subsequent sections. There are also APIs for certain types of synchronization. In order to call the OpenMP runtime routines, the program must include the OpenMP header file `omp.h` so that the compiler recognizes the signatures of these runtime routines.

OpenMP provides a number of runtime routines that can be used to obtain information about threads in the program. Some commonly used routines are:

- `omp_get_num_procs()` - Returns the number of processors that are available to the program

- `omp_get_num_threads()` - Returns the number of threads in the current team. In a sequential section of the program, this method returns 1.

- `omp_get_thread_num()` - Returns the current thread ID.

- `omp_set_num_threads(int)` - Specifies the number of threads used in subsequent parallel sections.

In addition, OpenMP provides a number of lock routines that can be used for thread synchronization.

## 11.4  Data scope and race condition

In writing parallel programs, understanding what data is shared and what is private becomes very important not only for performance, but also for correct operation. Shared variables are shared by all the threads in the thread team. Thus, a change of any shared variable in one thread becomes visible to all the threads in the parallel region. Private variables, on the other hand, have private copies made for each thread in the thread team, so changes made in one thread are not visible to the other threads. *Caution about the use of structure/class where C/C++ pointers are member variables*: modifications to the contents of the pointer in a private copy of the structure/class may still be visible to other threads due to the fact that the pointer points to the same memory address.

We will discuss it in detail later. By default, all the variables in a parallel region are shared with some exceptions such as `for` loop index and locally-defined variables.

To understand how data scope may affect parallel programming, we consider the evaluation of the trigonometric function $\sin x$ at $n$ points (i.e., computing $\sin x_i$ for $i = 0, 1, \cdots, n-1$). The need arises when we want to plot the graph of $\sin x$. Trigonometric functions are widely available across programming languages and platforms. To gain great performance, many CPU architectures have a built-in instruction for sin. My implementation of $\sin x$ is solely for illustrating the use of OpenMP. It does not reflect how trigonometric functions are implemented by the standard C/C++ library.

Expanding $\sin x$ via the Maclaurin series gives:

$$\sin x = x - \frac{x^3}{3!} + \frac{x^5}{5!} - \frac{x^7}{7!} + \cdots = \sum_{i=0}^{\infty} \frac{(-1)^i}{(2i+1)!} x^{2i+1}.$$

It is noted that the $i$th term is equal to the $(i-1)$th term multiplied by

$$\frac{x^2}{i(i-1)}$$

with the sign negated. So, the evaluation of $\sin x$ can be done with minimal arithmetic operations as outlined below:

1. Assign $x$ to the intermediate variable `term` and set $f = 0$ and $i = 3$.

2. Perform `f += term`.

3. Multiply `term` by $x^2/(i(i-1))$ and negate its sign.

4. Increment $i$ by 2 and go to step 2 to repeat the process until convergence is reached.

We now consider the termination condition. Let

$$P_n(x) = \sum_{i=0}^{n} \frac{(-1)^i}{(2i+1)!} x^{2i+1}.$$

If $|P_n(x) - P_{n-1}(x)| < \varepsilon$, the polynomial $P_n(x)$ converges to the series with respect to $\varepsilon$. Since $P_n(x) - P_{n-1}(x)$ yields the last term of $P_n(x)$, we can simply check `term` for convergence. Evaluation of $\sin x$ at $n$ evenly spaced $x$-value is implemented as

```
#include "MyHeader.h"

void apiEvalSine(int numPts, double *pValues)
{
    int       i, n;
    double    x, xx, f, term, delta;

    delta = 2.0 * GPI / (numPts - 1);
```

```
for (n=0; n<numPts; n++)
{
    x = n * delta;
    i = 3;
    f = 0.0;
    term = x;
    xx = x * x;
    while (true)
    {
        f += term;
        if (fabs(term) < DBL_EPSILON)
        {
            pValues[n] = f;
            break;
        }
        term = -term * xx / (i * (i - 1));
        i += 2;
    }
}
}
```

Save it as apiEvalSine.cpp and create EvalSine.d1 for only one data entry 100, which means the evaluation of $\sin x$ at 100 evenly-spaced $x$-value in the interval $[0, 2\pi]$. We then compile and run it to generate the EvalSine.o1 file. We now construct the parallel region to spread iterations of for loop among available threads, which should be

```
#include "MyHeader.h"

void apiEvalSine(int numPts, double *pValues)
{
    int         i, n;
    double      x, xx, f, term, delta;

    delta = 2.0 * GPI / (numPts - 1);
    #pragma omp parallel
    {
        #pragma omp for
        for (n=0; n<numPts; n++)
        {
            x = n * delta;
            i = 3;
            f = 0.0;
            term = x;
            xx = x * x;
            while (true)
            {
                f += term;
                if (fabs(term) < DBL_EPSILON)
```

```
        {
            pValues[n] = f;
            break;
        }
        term = -term * xx / (i * (i - 1));
        i += 2;
    }
  }
 }
}
```

Compiling and running the above implementation at the command line, we will see

```
D:\ArtProgram\test>mntest EvalSine 1 1

 Processing data file EvalSine.d1 ...

CPU time = 0.000000 seconds for 1 iteration.
          *** Results differ from previous ones.
```

Occasionally, it may say "Results match previous ones." In this case, we run it again and will, for sure, see the difference warning. How can this happen by simply declaring parallelism in the working code? It is noted that, except for loop index i, all variables are global to the **for** loop and, hence, are shared by all threads. Thus, a change of the shared variable in one thread becomes visible to all the threads in the parallel region. Assume thread 1 is executing the **while** loop with some fixed $x$ value. Concurrently, thread 2 is modifying the $x$ value and, hence, affects the evaluation of thread 1. This is known as data *race conditions* that arise in software when separate processes or threads of execution depend on some shared state. Operations upon shared states are critical sections that must be mutually exclusive. Failure to do so opens up the possibility of corrupting the shared state. Race conditions are notoriously difficult to reproduce and debug since the end result is nondeterministic and highly dependent on the relative timing between interfering threads. In a given instance, for example, the variables might "win the race" in the order that happens to make the program function correctly. Just because a program works once doesn't mean that it will always work. When it is run the next time, some other variables may win the race, which causes the program to fail. Furthermore, problems occurring in production systems can therefore disappear when running in debug mode, when additional logging is added, or when attaching a debugger – a phenomenon often referred to as a *Heisenbug*. It is therefore highly preferable to avoid race conditions in the first place by thoughtful design and implementation instead of fixing problems afterwards.

One possible fix is to declare shared variables as private via the **private** clause:

```
void apiEvalSine(int numPts, double *pValues)
{
    int      i, n;
    double   x, xx, f, term, delta;
```

```
delta = 2.0 * GPI / (numPts - 1);
#pragma omp parallel
{
    #pragma omp for private (i, x, xx, f, term)
    for (n=0; n<numPts; n++)
    {
        x = n * delta;
        i = 3;
        f = 0.0;
        term = x;
        xx = x * x;
        while (true)
        {
            f += term;
            if (fabs(term) < DBL_EPSILON)
            {
                pValues[n] = f;
                break;
            }
            term = -term * xx / (i * (i - 1));
            i += 2;
        }
    }
}
```

Accordingly, changes made in one thread are not visible to the other threads. The `private` clause used in our example does not initialize the variables when new copies are created for each thread. This is fine because the private copies of i, x, xx, f, term are properly set at each iteration inside the `for` loop. If we do want to initialize a copied variable to the value of its global (or shared) varibale before entering the parallel region, we need to use the `firstprivate` clause. There is also the `lastprivate` clause that will assign a shared variable the value of the *last iteration* before leaving the parallel region. To understand it, we look at the following example:

```
void main()
{
    int     i;
    double  x = 0.0;

    #pragma omp parallel num_threads(4)
    {
        #pragma omp for lastprivate (x)
        for (i=1; i<=12; i++)
        {
            x = (double)i;
            printf("x = %lf, thread = %d\n", x, omp_get_thread_num());
        }
```

```
   }

   printf("\nThe global x = %lf\n", x);
}
```

Running the above program at the command prompt gives

```
   x = 1.000000, thread = 0
   x = 2.000000, thread = 0
   x = 3.000000, thread = 0
   x = 10.000000, thread = 3
   x = 11.000000, thread = 3
   x = 12.000000, thread = 3
   x = 4.000000, thread = 1
   x = 5.000000, thread = 1
   x = 6.000000, thread = 1
   x = 7.000000, thread = 2
   x = 8.000000, thread = 2
   x = 9.000000, thread = 2
```

```
   The global x = 12.000000
```

It is noted that that the global or shared variable $x$ is not 9.0 but 12.0. This is because 12 would be the last iteration result if the program is run sequentially. Therefore, the *last iteration* should be understood to be the iteration that would be performed last in a serial execution of the code. Depending on the load balance and execution environment of the various threads, this "last iteration" may be completed before some of the other iterations are completed, but a **lastprivate** variable's value does not become valid in the enclosing context until the entire OpenMP loop is complete. If the **lastprivate** is replaced by **private** in the above program, the last print statement will print

```
   The global x = 0.000000
```

because the global $x$ was initialized to zero by compiler and has not been assigned any new value during the execution. Computation performed inside the **for** loop is done to the private copy of $x$ and is lost when the OpenMP loop is complete.

An alternative solution to make shared variables invisible to different threads is to move the declaration of variables inside the **for** loop so that these variables become local and, hence, automatically private as shown below:

```
void apiEvalSine(int numPts, double *pValues)
{
   int          n;
   double       delta;

   delta = 2.0 * GPI / (numPts - 1);
   #pragma omp parallel
   {
      #pragma omp for
```

```
        for (n=0; n<numPts; n++)
        {
            int      i;
            double   x, xx, f, term;
            x = n * delta;
            i = 3;
            f = 0.0;
            term = x;
            xx = x * x;
            while (true)
            {
                f += term;
                if (fabs(term) < DBL_EPSILON)
                {
                    pValues[n] = f;
                    break;
                }
                term = -term * xx / (i * (i - 1));
                i += 2;
            }
        }
    }
}
```

Our example has one simple for loop. Accordingly, it is not very difficult to identify
what variables need to be declared as private. In real world programming, however,
the for loop block may contain quite a few operations. In this case, it becomes
increasingly difficult to properly manage the scope of all variables inside the for loop.
My recommendation is to make a sub-function out of the block so that the code is
modularized and the for loop is simplified as shown below:

```
#include "MyHeader.h"

static void evalOneSine(double x, double &f)
{
    int      i;
    double   xx, term;

    i = 3;
    f = 0.0;
    term = x;
    xx = x * x;
    while (true)
    {
        f += term;
        if (fabs(term) < DBL_EPSILON)
            break;
        term = -term * xx / (i * (i - 1));
```

```
        i += 2;
    }
}

void apiEvalSine(int numPts, double *pValues)
{
    int         n;
    double      delta;

    delta = 2.0 * GPI / (numPts - 1);
    #pragma omp parallel
    {
        #pragma omp for
        for (n=0; n<numPts; n++)
        {
            evalOneSine(n * delta, pValues[n]);
        }
    }
}
```

All variables in the implementation of $\sin x$ are readily privatized. In practice, however, we may have to deal with global data declared in other functions. For example, a distance tolerance is used in a CAD system to determine whether a point lies on a surface, whether two curves are endpoint connected, etc. Since different CAD systems may use different distance tolerances, it is necessary for us to change our default system tolerance so that we can import and thus heal foreign models. To do so, we declare the distance tolerance as a *static variable* and provide GetDistanceTolerance and SetDistanceTolerance to get or modify its value. Since this static variable is visible to all threads, there will be a data race condition. This kind of problems can be solved by replacing the following declaration

```
    static double dist_tol = 1.0e-6;
```

with the following:

```
    thread_local double dist_tol = 1.0e-6;
```

By default, the variable dist_tol is still static but each thread will have its own copy of the static variable.

Making variables private does not solve all race problems. A common example is to have a summation in the for loop. When working on the best fit line, circle, and plane in chapter 9, we had to compute the centroid of discreet points so that we can transform all points to a local coordinate system. The centroid of $n$ points is computed as

$$x_c = \frac{\sum_{i=1}^{n} x_i}{n}, \quad y_c = \frac{\sum_{i=1}^{n} y_i}{n}, \quad z_c = \frac{\sum_{i=1}^{n} z_i}{n}.$$

Such computations can be implemented as

```
/*-----------------------------------------------------------------
API Name
    apiCenterOfPoints

Description
    It computes the center of mass of discrete points

Signature
    void apiCenterOfPoints(std::vector<GPosition2d> &points,
                                        GPosition2d &center)

    INPUT:
      points    collection of points
    OUTPUT:
      center    centroid

History

    Y.M. Li      03/10/2013 : Creation date
------------------------------------------------------------------*/
#include "MyHeader.h"

void apiCenterOfPoints(std::vector<GPosition> &points,
                                    GPosition &center)
{
    int       i, n;
    double    xSum, ySum, zSum;

    n = (int)points.size();
    xSum = ySum = zSum = 0.0;

    for (i=0; i<n; i++)
    {
        xSum += points[i].x;
        ySum += points[i].y;
        zSum += points[i].z;
    }

    center.x = xSum / n;
    center.y = ySum / n;
    center.z = zSum / n;
}
```

Save, compile, and run this program with **CenterOfPoints.d1** that contains 1151 points. It is noted that xSum, ySum, and zSum are shared variables. If the **for** loop is parallelized, all threads will race to update these three scalar variables and, hence, may produce an unpredictable result. If these variables are declared to be private, each thread will get their own copies of the variables. Accordingly, the race condition seems to be solved. However, it is not for two reasons:

- Local copies are destroyed when threads complete their assigned work.

- Local copies hold partial summation results. These results need to be combined
  to generate a correct result.

OpenMP solves this kind of problems by providing the following **reduction** clause:

```
reduction(operator : variable list)
```

A private copy for each list variable is created for each thread, but the values of the
local copies will be summarized (reduced) into a global shared variable. This is very
useful if a particular operation (specified in operator for this particular clause) on a
data type that runs iteratively so that its value at a particular iteration depends on its
value at a prior iteration. Basically, the steps that lead up to the operational increment
are parallelized, but the threads gather up and wait before updating the data type,
then increment the data type in order so as to avoid the racing condition. With the
OpenMP **reduction** clause, the centroid API is parallelized correctly as follows:

```
void apiCenterOfPoints(std::vector<GPosition> &points,
                                     GPosition &center)
{
    int      i, n;
    double   xSum, ySum, zSum;

    n = (int)points.size();
    xSum = ySum = zSum = 0.0;

    #pragma omp parallel
    {
        #pragma omp for reduction(+ : xSum,ySum,zSum)
        for (i=0; i<n; i++)
        {
            xSum += points[i].x;
            ySum += points[i].y;
            zSum += points[i].z;
        }
    }

    center.x = xSum / n;
    center.y = ySum / n;
    center.z = zSum / n;
}
```

Variables in the **reduction** clause must have a scalar arithmetic data type. For this
reason, xSum, ySum, and zSum were used instead of GPosition.

It is stated in many OpenMP tutorials and documents that all variables in a parallel
region are shared by default, with some exceptions such as **for** loop index and locally-
defined variables. What has not been mentioned explicitly is the scope of nested loop

indices. By assuming all indices of nested loops are private, we can parallelize the multiplication of matrices as follows:

```
void apiAtAMatrixV1(int n, int m, double **pA, double **pAtA)
{
    int     i, j, k;

    #pragma omp parallel
    {
        #pragma omp for
        for (i=0; i<m; i++)
        {
            for (j=0; j<m; j++)
            {
                pAtA[i][j] = 0.0;
                for (k=0; k<n; k++)
                {
                    pAtA[i][j] += pA[k][i] * pA[k][j];
                }
            }
        }
    }
}
```

Compiling and running the above code with saved data cases, we will find that the program either crashes or generates bad data. When it comes to parallelize the nested for loops with OpenMP, the loop indices may or may not be private, depending on the programming languages used. In FORTRAN, each thread gets a private copy of the loop index for any loops nested inside the main loop. In C/C++, nested loop indices are not automatically "privatized." By default, only the outer for loop index is private, and all sequential loop indices are shared. Therefore, the above implementation created data race conditions and, hence, caused a failure. Data race conditions can be avoided by explicitly declaring j and k to be private as follows

```
void apiAtAMatrixV1(int n, int m, double **pA, double **pAtA)
{
    int     i, j, k;

    #pragma omp parallel
    {
        #pragma omp for private (j, k)
        for (i=0; i<m; i++)
        {
            for (j=0; j<m; j++)
            {
                pAtA[i][j] = 0.0;
                for (k=0; k<n; k++)
                {
                    pAtA[i][j] += pA[k][i] * pA[k][j];
```

```
            }
          }
        }
      }
}
```

In practice, it is always a good idea to explicitly declare the scope of all variables if we are not sure the scope of these variables. It is noted that we did not use the `reduction` clause for

```
    pAtA[i][j] += pA[k][i] * pA[k][j];
```

because there is no data race condition when the outer loop is divided among the available threads.

Multiplication of two matrices has three nested `for` loops. It is, in general, a cubic or $O(n^3)$ algorithms. When $n$ is large, multiplication of matrices is costly. Therefore, it makes sense to parallelize the nested loops to improve the performance. Three real application data cases have been selected to test the program. The matrix size of `AtAMatrixV1.d3` is $8863 \times 49$. It takes 0.239 seconds to run the program with this case in debug without parallelism as opposed to 0.079 seconds with parallelism. The performance may be further improved by using OpenMP 3.0 or a higher version since the `collapse` clause has been added to support nested loops. It combines closely-nested loops into one, which is equivalent to parallelizing all nested loops. Unfortunately, Microsoft Visual C++ 2010 and 2012 support only OpenMP 2.0 standard.

## 11.5   Load balance

Load balancing (i.e., the division of work among threads) is among the most important attributes for parallel application performance. It ensures that the processors are busy most, if not all, of the time. Without a balanced load, some threads may finish significantly before others, leaving processor resources idle and wasting performance opportunities. OpenMP, by default, assumes that all loop iterations consume the same amount of time. This assumption leads OpenMP to distribute the iterations of the loop among the threads in roughly equal amounts. If some threads complete their tasks, they will pause until the last thread finishes before leaving the parallel region due to implicit barrier synchronization at the end of the parallel region. This obviously degrades the overall performance. OpenMP designers foresaw the need of explicit synchronization and task scheduling. They provided a rich set of clauses so developers can best tune the synchronization and task scheduling in their applications. In this section, we will discuss some of these features.

Referring to the `apiEvalSine` algorithm, it is known that the Maclaurin series of $\sin x$ converges faster when $x$ is near zero. When iterations of `for` loop are evenly divided among available threads, some threads will complete sooner than others. In our case, it is safe that threads completing assigned work can proceed without waiting for all threads in the team to finish. Therefore, we can add the optional clause `nowait` to suppress implicit barrier synchronization at the end of the parallel region and, hence, improve the performance.

```
void apiEvalSine(int numPts, double *pValues)
{
    int         i;
    double      delta;

    delta = 2.0 * GPI / (numPts - 1);
    #pragma omp parallel
    {
        #pragma omp for nowait
        for (i=0; i<numPts; i++)
        {
            evalOneSine(i * delta, pValues[i]);
        }
    }
}
```

Load balancing can also be conveyed to OpenMP on the parallel construct via the schedule clause. OpenMP offers the schedule clause with a set of predefined iteration scheduling strategies to specify how (and when) the assignment of iterations to threads is done. The syntax is

```
#pragma omp parallel for schedule(type [, chunk size])
```

Four different loop scheduling types can be provided to OpenMP. They are

**static** Divides the loop into equal-sized chunks or as possible in the case where the number of loop iterations is not evenly divisible by the number of threads multiplied by the chunk size. By default, the chunk size is loop / number of threads.

**dynamic** Uses an internal work queue to give a chunk-sized block of loop iterations to each thread. When a thread is finished, it retries the next block of loop iterations from the top of the work queue. By default, chunk size is 1. Be careful when using this scheduling type because of the extra overhead required.

**guided** Similar to dynamic scheduling, but the chunk size starts off large and shrinks in an effort to reduce the amount of time threads have to go to the work-queue to get more work. The optional chunk parameter specifies the minimum chunk to use. By default, the chunk size is approximately the loop count / number of threads.

**runtime** The scheduling decision is deferred until runtime by the environment variable OMP_SCHEDULE. It is illegal to specify a chunk size for this clause.

It is not an easy task even for an experienced programmer to choose the appropriate assignment of loop iterations to threads. For example, apiEvalSine repeatedly calls evalOneSine in the for loop. Depending on the value of i * alpha, evalOneSine converges in different speeds. It is thus natural to think that dynamic scheduling would be more suitable in this case because, when a thread completes its assignment, it goes to the work-queue to get more work. Based on my test on `apiEvalSine`, it performs the worst with default dynamic `chunk` size as shown below:

```
void apiEvalSine(int numPts, double *pValues)
{
    int         i;
    double      delta;

    delta = 2.0 * GPI / (numPts - 1);
    #pragma omp parallel
    {
        #pragma omp for schedule(dynamic)
        for (i=0; i<numPts; i++)
        {
            evalOneSine(i * delta, pValues[i]);
        }
    }
}
```

The poor performance may be due to the fact that `evalOneSine` takes an insignificant time in comparison to the scheduling overhead in determining the work share. In practice, it is recommended to perform various timing tests and choose the one that has the best overall performance.

## 11.6   Synchronization

The advantage of parallel programming is that the workload is shared among available threads. However, some applications that are parallel are partially constrained by the sequential nature. In this case, it is necessary to synchronize one thread with another thread to impose some ordering in the sequence of actions of the threads. OpenMP synchronization is the process through which data dependency is observed in parallel computing. OpenMP supplies two types of synchronization to help in many different situations.

One type is implied barrier synchronization. At the end of each parallel region is an implied barrier synchronization of all threads within the parallel region. A barrier synchronization requires all threads to reach that point before any can proceed beyond it. As was demonstrated in the previous section, the implied barrier synchronization can be removed by adding `nowait` clause. The `nowait` clause on the work-sharing directive indicates that the threads do not have to synchronize at the end of the `for` loop.

Another type is explicit barrier synchronization. Explicit synchronization is specified by the user to manage order or data dependencies. Synchronization is a form of interprocess communication and as such can greatly impact program performance. In general, best performance is achieved by minimizing the synchronization requirements (explicit and implicit) of a program. For this reason OpenMP provides a rich set of synchronization features so developers can best tune the synchronization in an application.

Common synchronization clauses include

barrier: each thread waits until all of the other threads of a team have reached this
point. A work-sharing construct has an implicit barrier synchronization at the
end.

nowait: specifies that threads completing assigned work can proceed without waiting
for all threads in the team to finish. In the absence of this clause, threads encounter
a barrier synchronization at the end of the work sharing construct will wait for
other threads to finish.

ordered: the structured block is executed in the order in which iterations would be
executed in a sequential loop.

critical: the enclosed code block will be executed by only one thread at a time,
and not simultaneously executed by multiple threads. It is often used to protect
shared data from race conditions.

atomic: the memory update (write, or read-modify-write) in the next instruction will
be performed atomically. It does not make the entire statement atomic; only the
memory update is atomic. A compiler might use special hardware instructions for
better performance than when using critical.

We shall cover ordered, critical, and atomic in this section.

Referring to apiStrokeCircleV2 implemented at the beginning of this chapter, stroking
points are added to STL vector via index operation because the memory of pStrkPts
has been allocated via a call to resize in advance. It is fairly common that the size of
array is unknown in advance. In this case, it is unfeasible to resize the STL vector
prior to the for loop. It is better to use push_back to add elements to STL vector
since its size can grow or shrink automatically. Let's copy apiStrokeCircleV2 to
apiStrokeCircleV3 and modify it so that pStrkPts is not resized in advance:

```
void apiStrokeCircleV3(GPosition2d &center, double radius, double tol,
                       std::vector<GPosition2d>& pStrkPts, apiError &rc)
{
    int        i, nStrkPts;
    double     delta;

    // Determine the number of stroking points
    rc = api_OK;
    delta = 2.0 * acos(1.0 - tol / radius);
    nStrkPts = 2 + (int)(2.0 * GPI / delta);
    delta = 2.0 * GPI / (nStrkPts - 1);

    // Loop to compute stroking points
    #pragma omp parallel
    {
        #pragma omp for
```

```
      for (i=0; i<nStrkPts; i++)
      {
         GPosition2d pt;
         pt.x = center.x + radius * cos(i * delta);
         pt.y = center.y + radius * sin(i * delta);
         pStrkPts.push_back(pt);
      }
   }
}
```

Since developers have no control over how iterations are divided and executed in each thread, stroking points will not be sequentially added to `pStrkPts` based on the above implementation. This is a problem for many applications (e.g., display) since they usually require stroking points to be saved sequentially. OpenMP provides `ordered` directive to specify that iterations of the enclosed loop will be executed in the same order as if they were executed on a serial processor. The `ordered` directive must be within the dynamic extent of a `for` or `parallel for` construct with an `ordered` clause such as shown below:

```
void apiStrokeCircleV3(GPosition2d &center, double radius, double tol,
                  std::vector<GPosition2d>& pStrkPts, apiError &rc)
{
   int         i, nStrkPts;
   double      delta;

   // Determine the number of stroking points
   rc = api_OK;
   delta = 2.0 * acos(1.0 - tol / radius);
   nStrkPts = 2 + (int)(2.0 * GPI / delta);
   delta = 2.0 * GPI / (nStrkPts - 1);

   // Loop to compute stroking points
   #pragma omp parallel
   {
      #pragma omp for ordered
      for (i=0; i<nStrkPts; i++)
      {
         GPosition2d pt;
         pt.x = center.x + radius * cos(i * delta);
         pt.y = center.y + radius * sin(i * delta);
         #pragma omp ordered
         {
            // This block will be executed in sequential order
            pStrkPts.push_back(pt);
         }
      }
   }
}
```

When data is forced to save sequentially, there is a considerable performance drawback since threads will need to wait before executing their chunk of iterations if previous iterations have not been finished yet. For example, it takes 0.1 seconds to run the executable for 10,000 times when OpenMP is disabled. When OpenMP is enabled with `ordered` directive, it takes 0.32 seconds to do the same work. Construct of parallelism for the above case is inappropriate as the execution time of

```
for (i=0; i<nStrkPts; i++)
{
    GPosition2d pt;
    pt.x = center.x + radius * cos(i * delta);
    pt.y = center.y + radius * sin(i * delta);
}
```

is insignificant. It makes sense to construct parallelism with the `ordered` directive only when the computation inside the `for` loop is very demanding, as illustrated below

```
#pragma omp parallel
{
    #pragma omp for ordered
    for (i=0; i<n; i++)
    {
        {
            // Heavy computation is involved here

            :
        }

        #pragma omp ordered
        {
            // This block will be executed in sequential order

            :
        }
    }
}
```

In general, the `ordered` directive should be used only if it is absolutely necessary, and it must be used as follows:

- It must appear within the extent of `omp for` or `omp parallel for` construct containing an ordered clause.

- It applies to the statement block immediately following it. Statements in that block are executed in the same order in which iterations are executed in a sequential loop.

- An iteration of a loop must not execute the same `omp ordered` directive more than once.

We will give one more example concerning synchronization. Long before commercial memory tools such as `BoundsChecker` were available, we had developed a memory tool to catch memory leaks, memory scratch (i.e., accessing memory beyond defined size), and use of uninitialized memory. This tool has played a vital role in developing clean and reliable computational functions. As a matter of fact, we have not seen a single incident where a memory leak was caught by other commercial tools but not by our own. Our memory tool can be summarized as follows:

- When users call memory allocation, we allocate two more cells so that we can put a special flag at the beginning and end of the allocated memory block. The memory address is also saved in a global `list`.

- When users call memory free, we check if the allocated memory still has the added two flags to make sure users did not scratch the memory. We then delete this memory and remove the address from our `list`.

- When a session ends, we check if all allocated memory addresses have been removed from the `list`. If not, we have memory leaks.

Since the `list` that tracks memory allocations and deallocations is global data, it is not thread-safe because each thread races to update the counter and the content of the `list`. One of the remedies for this problem is blocking the critical region of code to ensure this blocked region is executed one thread at a time. This can be done by using the `critical` directive with optional section name to mark the critical region as follows:

```
   ⋮
#pragma omp critical (optional name)
{
    // The following code fragment is executed one thread at a time:
    Memlist.list[Memlist.number] = address; // store memory address
    Memlist.number++; // update the counter
}
   ⋮
```

If a thread is currently executing inside a critical region and another thread reaches that critical region and attempts to execute it, the newcomer will be blocked until the active thread exits that critical region. A critical region is often used to protect shared data from race conditions. By doing so, however, it will degrade the performance and, hence, diminish the advantage of parallel programming. The optional section name may be used when declaring a critical region. It is a global identifier, and no two threads can run critical sections (anywhere in the program) with the same global identifier name at the same time.

Besides the `critical` directive, OpenMP provides also the `atomic` directive. It specifies that a specific memory location must be updated atomically rather than letting multiple threads attempt to write to it. In essence, this directive provides a mini-CRITICAL section.

## 11.7   Non-loop parallelism

Up to now, OpenMP parallelism has been used for sharing the workload of iterative `for` loop, but it also supports non-iterative work-sharing construct that breaks work into separate and discrete sections such that each section is to be executed by a thread. This is done by using the OpenMP `sections` directive and best understood by an example. Consider `apiIntegration` developed in chapter 7. Instead of reserving a big chunk of stack memory to store Legendre roots and Gauss-Legendre weights for various degrees, we perform a half-cut via recursion to compute definite integrals at reduced intervals. This API serves as a good example to show how `sections` may be used to parallelize recursive calls:

```
void apiIntegration(double a, double b, double tol,
                    double (*userEvalFunct)(double),
                    double &dValue, apiError &rc)
{
   apiError rc1 = api_OK, rc2 = api_OK;
   int      i, k, n, num_roots[2] = {8, 10};
   double   *pRoots = NULL, *pA = NULL;
   double   alpha, beta, x, d[2], f_i[10];
   double   dLeft, dRight;

   // Compute approximate value at n=8 and 10
   rc = api_OK;
   alpha = (b - a) / 2.0;
   beta =  (a + b) / 2.0;
   for (k=0; k<2; k++)
   {
      n = num_roots[k];
      apiGetGaussLdgRtWts(n, pRoots, pA, rc);
      if (rc != api_OK)
         goto wrapup;

      d[k] = 0.0;
      for (i=0; i<n; i++)
      {
         x = alpha * pRoots[i] + beta;
         f_i[i] = userEvalFunct(x);
      }

      for (i=0; i<n/2; i++)
      {
         d[k] += f_i[i] * pA[i];
         d[k] += f_i[n-1-i] * pA[i];
      }

      d[k] *= alpha;
   }
```

```
    // Terminate condition
    if (fabs(d[1] - d[0]) < tol)
    {
        dValue = d[1];
        goto wrapup;
    }

    // Reduce the complexity by halving the interval
    x = 0.5 * (a + b);
    #pragma omp parallel sections
    {
        #pragma omp section
        apiIntegration(a, x, tol, userEvalFunct, dLeft, rc1);

        #pragma omp section
        apiIntegration(x, b, tol, userEvalFunct, dRight, rc2);
    }

    if (rc1 != api_OK || rc2 != api_OK)
    {
        rc = rc1 != api_OK ? rc1 : rc2;
        goto wrapup;
    }

    // Combine the results
    dValue = dLeft + dRight;

wrapup:

    return;
}
```

Note that this example uses the shorthand #pragma omp parallel sections in a way analogous to #pragma omp parallel for. If you prefer, you can place #pragma omp sections within a parallel region as a stand-alone directive. In the above example, the first #pragma creates a parallel region of sections. Each section is preceded by the directive #pragma omp section and is given to a single thread in the thread team. Both sections in the parallel region are handled concurrently with each parallel section calling apiIntegration recursively.

When creating a parallel region via the #pragma omp parallel for directive, it is our job to ensure that the for loop is thread-safe and can be executed concurrently by multi-thread. In constructing a non-loop parallel region, we are also responsible for ensuring that each section is independent of the other sections so that they can be executed in parallel. If the sections update shared resources without synchronizing access to those resources, the results are undefined.

Recursive calls are supported with parallel regions and, in this case, specifically with parallel sections. However, there are a few things to note about the above implementation. Firstly, it is wrong to call the runtime routine to set the maximum of threads for the parallel region as follows:

```
// Reduce the complexity by halving the interval
x = 0.5 * (a + b);
omp_set_num_threads(4);
#pragma omp parallel sections
{
    #pragma omp section
    apiIntegration(a, x, tol, userEvalFunct, dLeft, rc1);

    #pragma omp section
    apiIntegration(x, b, tol, userEvalFunct, dRight, rc2);
}
```

This is because `omp_set_num_threads` should only be called in serial regions. When `apiIntegration` is called first time, it is not yet parallelized. Therefore, it is fine to call `omp_set_num_threads` before this statement:

```
#pragma omp parallel sections
```

But as soon as it steps into a next level of recursion, the whole program becomes parallelized. Consequently, it generates the following runtime error when running in the debug mode:

```
User Error 1001: omp_set_num_threads should only
                 be called in serial regions.
```

If there is a need to set a particular number of threads for parallel region, we call `omp_set_num_threads` outside `apiIntegration` in, for example, the main driver.

Secondly, the recursion may spawn more threads than the number of physical cores if nested parallelism is enabled. In general, the performance of our application will degrade if the number of thread exceeds the number of processors. We can turn off nested parallelism by calling the runtime routine `omp_set_nested` with 0 as an input argument.

The next thing to note is that `rc1` and `rc2` were used to catch any computation error. But error checking was placed outside the parallel region because it is not allowed to `break` or `goto wrapup` in a parallel region.

Finally, it may not be a good practice to use OpenMP `sections` for deep recursion because it can significantly degrade the performance even if nested parallelism is disabled. For illustration, we parallelize the QuickSort method as follows:

```
/*------------------------------------------------------------------
API Name
    apiQuickSort
```

Description
    It sorts an array of double in ascending order. This
    program is created to test OpenMP sections directive.

Signature
    void apiQuickSort(std::vector<double> &x)

    INPUT/OUTPUT:
        x               array of doubles

History

    Y.M. Li      08/10/2013 : Creation date
------------------------------------------------------------------*/
```cpp
#include "MyHeader.h"
#include <omp.h>

static int findPartition(double *x, int left, int right)
{
    int i = left, j = right;
    double  tmp;
    double pivot = x[(left + right) / 2];

    while (i <= j)
    {
        while (x[i] < pivot)
            i++;
        while (x[j] > pivot)
            j--;

        if (i <= j)
        {
            tmp = x[i];
            x[i] = x[j];
            x[j] = tmp;
            i++;
            j--;
        }
    }
    return i;
}

void QuickSort(double *x, int left, int right)
{
    int pivodID = findPartition(x, left, right);
```

```
   #pragma omp parallel
   {
      #pragma omp sections nowait
      {
         #pragma omp section
         if (left < pivodID - 1)
         {
            QuickSort(x, left, pivodID - 1);
         }

         #pragma omp section
         if (pivodID < right)
         {
            QuickSort(x, pivodID, right);
         }
      }
   }
}

void apiQuickSort(std::vector<double> &x)
{
   if (!x.empty())
   {
      int n_left = 0, n_right = (int)x.size() - 1;
      omp_set_nested(0);
      omp_set_num_threads(2);
      QuickSort(&x[0], n_left, n_right);
   }
}
```

The above parallelized program runs $3 \sim 4$ times slower than the non-parallelized version. Here, we set the number of threads to 2 and found no noticeable difference by setting numbers of threads between 2 and the number of actual physical cores. It is reported that OpenMP version 3.0 and newer added the **task** directive to support deep and/or unbalanced recursion.

## 11.8   Explicit task parallelism

We have been using the OpenMP **for** directive to divide implicitly the iterative workload among threads. We also discussed how the OpenMP **schedule** clause may help us keep the team threads as busy as possible. However, there are some cases in which implicit division of workload is incapable of allowing us to properly divide and synchronize the iterative workload among threads. A simple example is to find the minimum and maximum number in an unsorted array:

```
void apiFindMinMax(std::vector<double> &x,
                   double &dMin, double &dMax)
{
```

```
int        i, num;
num = (int)x.size();
dMin = dMax = x[0];
for (i=1; i<num; i++)
{
    if (dMin > x[i])
        dMin = x[i];
    else if (dMax < x[i])
        dMax = x[i];
}
}
```

If the OpenMP for directive is used to divide the workload of iterative for loop implicitly, we may parallelize the program as follows:

```
void apiFindMinMax(std::vector<double> &x, double &dMin, double &dMax)
{
    int        i, n;

    n = (int)x.size();
    dMin = dMax = x[0];
    #pragma omp parallel
    {
        #pragma omp for nowait
        for (i=1; i<n; i++)
        {
            if (x[i] < dMin)
                dMin = x[i];
            else if (x[i] > dMax)
                dMax = x[i];
        }
    }
}
```

Since both dMin and dMax are shared variables, they are visible to all threads. During the execution time, every thread races to update dMin and dMax concurrently. Accordingly, we may obtain unpredictable results. To avoid the data race condition, we have to divide the workload *explicitly* and synchronize the local results data with the global results. The modified apiFindMinMax is

```
1    void apiFindMinMax(std::vector<double> &x,
2                            double &dMin, double &dMax)
3    {
4        int        num, num_threads = 0;
5
6        dMin = dMax = x[0];
7        num = (int)x.size();
8        #pragma omp parallel
9        {
```

```
10          int     i, i_beg, i_end, id, n;
11          double  loc_min, loc_max;
12
13          num_threads = omp_get_num_threads();
14          n = num / num_threads;
15          id = omp_get_thread_num();
16
17          i_beg = id * n;
18          if (id != num_threads-1)
19              i_end = i_beg + n;
20          else
21              i_end = num;
22
23          loc_min = loc_max = x[i_beg];
24          for (i=i_beg+1; i<i_end; i++ )
25          {
26              if (x[i] > loc_max)
27                  loc_max = x[i];
28              else if (x[i] < loc_min)
29                  loc_min = x[i];
30          }
31
32          #pragma omp critical
33          {
34              if (dMin > loc_min)
35                  dMin = loc_min;
36              if (dMax < loc max)
37                  dMax = loc_max;
38          }
39      } // End of parallel
40  }
```

From line 13 to 15, we check how many threads this computer has and then divide the array into $n$ sub-arrays. The runtime routine omp_get_num_threads has to be called inside the parallel region to determine how many threads are available for parallel computing. If it is called outside the parallel region, the number of thread is always one. From line 17 to 21, we determine the start and end index of the array from which the active thread, denoted by id, will loop through to find the local minimum and maximum. From line 23 to 30, it finds the local minimum and maximum of the sub-array. From line 32 to 38, the global results are compared with and, if necessary, updated by local results. We declare this region as critical to avoid a data race condition. In the critical region, the code block will be executed by only one thread at a time. All other threads have to wait in queue until the current thread completes and exits, which is obviously not fully optimized parallelism. Running the above code in release with a Core i7 processor cuts the CPU time by slightly more than half. An optimized approach is to store local results from each thread in an array and compute the global minimum and maximum from this array after exiting the parallel region. In the following implementation, it is assumed that available threads are less or equal to

16.

```
1   void apiFindMinMax(std::vector<double> &x,
2                      double &dMin, double &dMax)
3   {
4   #define max_num_threads 16
5
6       int     j, num, num_threads = 0;
7       double  min_of_thread[max_num_threads];
8       double  max_of_thread[max_num_threads];
9
10      num = (int)x.size();
11      #pragma omp parallel
12      {
13          int     i, i_beg, i_end, id, n;
14          double  loc_min, loc_max;
15
16          num_threads = omp_get_num_threads();
17          n = num / num_threads;
18          id = omp_get_thread_num();
19
20          i_beg = id * n;
21          if (id != num_threads-1)
22              i_end = i_beg + n;
23          else
24              i_end = num;
25
26          loc_min = loc_max = x[i_beg];
27          for (i=i_beg+1; i<i_end; i++ )
28          {
29              if (x[i] > loc_max)
30                  loc_max = x[i];
31              else if (x[i] < loc_min)
32                  loc_min = x[i];
33          }
34
35          min_of_thread[id] = loc_min;
36          max_of_thread[id] = loc_max;
37      } // End of parallel
38
39      // Find global min and max
40      dMin = min_of_thread[0];
41      for (j=1;  j<num_threads; j++)
42      {
43          if (dMin > min_of_thread[j])
44              dMin = min_of_thread[j];
45      }
46
```

```
47        dMax = max_of_thread[0];
48        for (j=1;  j<num_threads; j++)
49        {
50            if (dMax < max_of_thread[j])
51                dMax = max_of_thread[j];
52        }
53    }
```

The above implementation has eliminated the need for the **critical** region and, hence, kept each thread busy all the time. Consequently, it takes less than one-third of the time needed by the non-parallelized program to find the minimum and maximum number. However, the implementation is noticeably more complex.

It should be pointed out that OpenMP 3.1 and newer versions have expanded the **reduction** clause to support the operation of finding the minimum and/or maximum number. Accordingly, the algorithm may be parallelized as follows:

```
void apiFindMinMax(std::vector<double> &x,
                   double &dMin, double &dMax)
{
    int      i, num;
    num = (int)x.size();
    dMin = dMax = x[0];
    #pragma omp parallel
    {
        #pragma omp for reduction(min : dMin) reduction(max : dMax)
        for (i=1; i<num; i++)
        {
            if (dMin > x[i])
                dMin = x[i];
            else if (dMax < x[i])
                dMax = x[i];
        }
    }
}
```

Private copies of **dMin** and **dMax** are created for each thread, but the values of the local copies will be *reduced* into global **dMin** and **dMax**. Since OpenMP 3.1 and newer versions are not supported by Visual Studio 2010 and 2012, I am unable to test the above implementation.

## 11.9 Parallelize Gaussian elimination

Most examples used in this chapter are not computationally demanding and, hence, may not be parallelized in practice because multi-threaded executables often incur longer startup times. Otherwise, they can actually run much slower than if compiled by a single thread. In studying Gaussian elimination methods in chapter 6, it was noted that Gaussian elimination is $O(n^3)$ in general. When $n$ is large, this method is obviously very expensive. In creating a piecewise polynomial surface (e.g., a B-spline surface) that approximates the point cloud via the least squares approximation method, it is common for us to solve a linear system whose matrix is over $1000 \times 1000$. Accordingly, unoptimized Gaussian elimination becomes a performance bottleneck. In this section, we will show how to improve the performance of Gaussian elimination with partial pivot and Gauss-Jordan elimination with full pivot via parallelism. The approach can analogously be applied to other Gaussian elimination methods.

Gaussian elimination with partial pivoting is performed by selecting the entry with the largest absolute value from the column of the matrix that is currently being considered as the pivot element. It then performs a row exchange so that the row with the pivot element will be used to eliminate all the elements below the pivot in the same column. By parallelizing the `for` loops of the original implementation found in section 6.2, we have:

```
1    void apiGaussPPivot(std::vector<vector<double>> &aug_mat,
2                                           apiError &rc)
3    {
4        int     i, i_p, j, k, n_row, n_col;
5        double  pivot, dMultiplier;
6
7        rc = api_OK;
8        n_row = (int)aug_mat.size();
9        n_col = (int)aug_mat[0].size();
10
11       // Apply Gaussian eliminations to the augmented matrix so that
12       // the matrix becomes the upper triangular matrix
13       for (k=0; k<n_row-1; k++)
14       {
15           // Find the larger pivot element
16           pivot = 0.0;
17           for (i=k; i<n_row; i++)
18           {
19               if (fabs(pivot) < fabs(aug_mat[i][k]))
20               {
21                   pivot = aug_mat[i][k];
22                   i_p = i;
23               }
24           }
25
26           if (fabs(pivot) < zero_tol)
27           {
28               rc = api_DIVIDEBYZERO;
29               goto wrapup;
30           }
31
32           // Check if row exchange is needed
33           if (i_p != k)
```

```
34          {
35              #pragma omp parallel for private(pivot)
36              for (j=0; j<n_col; j++)
37              {
38                  pivot = aug_mat[i_p][j];
39                  aug_mat[i_p][j] = aug_mat[k][j];
40                  aug_mat[k][j] = pivot;
41              }
42          }

44          #pragma omp parallel for private(j, dMultiplier)
45          for (i=k+1; i<n_row; i++)
46          {
47              // Multiply the kth row by the multiplier and add to
48              // the ith row to make a[i][k]=0 (i=k+1, k+2, ...)
49              dMultiplier = - aug_mat[i][k] / aug_mat[k][k];
50              for (j=k; j<n_col; j++)
51                  aug_mat[i][j] += dMultiplier * aug_mat[k][j];
52          }
53      }

55      // Backward substitution
56      for (k=n_row-1; k>=0; k--)
57      {
58          #pragma omp parallel for private(j)
59          for (i=n_row; i<n_col; i++)
60          {
61              for (j=k+1; j<n_row; j++)
62                  aug_mat[k][i] -= aug_mat[k][j] * aug_mat[j][i];
63              aug_mat[k][i] /= aug_mat[k][ k];
64          }
65      }

67  wrapup:

69      return;
70  }
```

It should be noted that we did not parallelize the outermost loop starting from line 13 because there is a dependency in this code block. It depends on the completion of level $k$ elimination to perform level $k + 1$ elimination, then $k + 2$ elimination, and so on. Therefore, $k$ has to be looped in a sequential manner. Furthermore, we did not parallelize the code block that finds the partial pivot because it is not worth the effort for the little performance gain (we will parallelize the pivot-finding code block for the Gauss-Jordan method in a moment). All other inner loops have been parallelized. It should be pointed out that the most significant performance improvement comes from parallelizing the nested loop from line 44 to 52. All others do not contribute much and can be omitted.

To test the performance improvement, the data file `GaussPPivot.d3` has been created. It was extracted from the creation of a piecewise parametric polynomial surface (e.g., a B-spline surface) that approximates digitized points. The augmented matrix is $1225 \times 1228$ – the average size we encounter in modeling B-spline surfaces via an interpolation or least squares approximation method. Without parallelism, it takes about 2.326 seconds to solve the system in release. With multi-threading, it takes 0.385 seconds. The improvement is significant!

It is worth mentioning that `GaussPPivot.d3` contains mostly zeros. These kinds of matrices are known as the *banded* or *sparse* matrices. They are usually solved via specialized numerical methods for performance. If Gaussian elimination method has to be used for solving a sparse matrix, it is often implemented with an auxiliary array of indices to indicate where the non-zero element starts and ends at each row. Consequently, all loop ranges are greatly reduced to improve the performance significantly.

We now parallelize the Gauss-Jordan elimination with full pivot. Since the pivot is searched along the row and column at each elimination level, it is a nested `for` loop and, hence, is worth the effort to parallelize the search method. In addition to find the pivot (the maximum element), we also need to know its corresponding array index for row and column exchanges. Therefore, we cannot directly call `apiFindMinMax`. But we can implement one in a similar way as we did for `apiFindMinMax`. The parallelized Gauss-Jordan method is

```
1    // Find the maximum pivot and corresponding array index (id)
2    // The number of threads is assumed not to be more than 16.
3    inline void pivot_apiGaussJordan(int num, std::vector<double> &x,
4                                     int &id, double &dPivot)
5    {
6    #define max_num_threads 16
7
8        int      j, num_threads = 0;
9        int      pivotID_of_thread[max_num_threads];
10       double   pivot_of_thread[max_num_threads];
11
12       if (num < 50)
13       {
14           // When array size is small, set the number
15           // of thread to 1 to minimize the overhead
16           omp_set_num_threads(1);
17       }
18
19       #pragma omp parallel
20       {
21           int      i, i_beg, i_end, id_thread, id_pivot, n;
22           double   loc_pivot;
23
24           num_threads = omp_get_num_threads();
```

```
25          id_thread = omp_get_thread_num();
26          n = num / num_threads;
27
28          i_beg = id_thread * n;
29          if (id_thread != num_threads-1)
30              i_end = i_beg + n;
31          else
32              i_end = num;
33
34          loc_pivot = x[i_beg];
35          id_pivot = i_beg;
36          for (i=i_beg+1; i<i_end; i++ )
37          {
38              if (fabs(x[i]) > fabs(loc_pivot))
39              {
40                  loc_pivot = x[i];
41                  id_pivot = i;
42              }
43          }
44          pivot_of_thread[id_thread] = loc_pivot;
45          pivotID_of_thread[id_thread] = id_pivot;
46      } // End of parallel
47
48      // Find global max
49      dPivot = pivot_of_thread[0];
50      id = pivotID_of_thread[0];
51      for (j=1;  j<num threads; j++)
52      {
53          if (fabs(dPivot) < fabs(pivot_of_thread[j]))
54          {
55              id = pivotID_of_thread[j];
56              dPivot = pivot_of_thread[j];
57          }
58      }
59  }
60
61  void apiGaussJordan(std::vector<vector<double>> &aug_mat,
62                                          apiError &rc)
63  {
64      int          i, j, jj, k, n_row, n_col, i_p;
65      double       pivot, temp;
66      vector<int> j_p;
67
68      rc = api_OK;
69      n_row = (int)aug_mat.size();
70      n_col = (int)aug_mat[0].size();
71      j_p.resize(n_col);
```

```
72
73      for (k=0; k<n_row; k++)
74      {
75          // Find the pivot for level k elimination:
76          pivot = 0.0;
77          for (i=k; i<n_row; i++)
78          {
79              pivot_apiGaussJordan(n_row, aug_mat[i], j, temp);
80              if (fabs(pivot) < fabs(temp))
81              {
82                  pivot = temp;
83                  i_p = i;
84                  j_p[k] = j;
85              }
86          }
87
88          if (fabs(pivot) < zero_tol)
89          {
90              rc = api_DIVIDEBYZERO;
91              goto wrapup;
92          }
93
94          if (i_p != k)
95          {
96              // Swapping rows. Note column swap is done at next block
97              #pragma omp parallel for private(temp)
98              for (j=0; j<n_col; j++)
99              {
100                 temp = aug_mat[i_p][j];
101                 aug_mat[i_p][j] = aug_mat[k][j];
102                 aug_mat[k][j] = temp;
103             }
104         }
105
106         #pragma omp parallel for
107         for (j=0; j<n_col; j++)
108             aug_mat[k][j] /= pivot;
109
110         // Level k elimination to ensure aug_mat(i,j_p)=0 for i!=k
111         #pragma omp parallel for private(j, temp)
112         for (i=0; i<k; i++)
113         {
114             temp = -aug_mat[i][j_p[k]];
115             for (j=0; j<n_col; j++)
116                 aug_mat[i][j] += temp * aug_mat[k][j];
117         }
118
```

```
119            #pragma omp parallel for private(j, temp)
120            for (i=k+1; i<n_row; i++)
121            {
122                temp = -aug_mat[i][j_p[k]];
123                for (j=0; j<n_col; j++)
124                    aug_mat[i][j] += temp * aug_mat[k][j];
125            }
126        }
127
128        // Adjust the order of results. It could be done by swapping rows
129        // so that the resulting matrix is a unit matrix. For efficiency,
130        // however, we adjust the order of results based on the indices.
131        for (k=0; k<n_row; k++)
132        {
133            for (i=k+1; i<n_row; i++)
134            {
135                if (j_p[k] > j_p[i])
136                {
137                    /// Swapping indices and results
138                    for (j=n_row; j<n_col; j++)
139                    {
140                        temp = aug_mat[k][j];
141                        aug_mat[k][j] = aug_mat[i][j];
142                        aug_mat[i][j] = temp;
143                    }
144                    jj = j_p[k];
145                    j_p[k] = j_p[i];
146                    j_p[i] = jj;
147                }
148            }
149        }
150
151    wrapup:
152
153        return;
154    }
```

Referring to line 12 through 17, we check the array size to determine whether we should call omp_set_num_threads to set a single thread for the parallel region. It is considered unnecessary to use multi-thread if number of data is less than certain specified value due to the overhead in setting up multi-thread computing. Inside the inline function pivot_apiGaussJordan, it is assumed that the number of available threads is not more than 16.

## 11.10   Debug parallel programming

Computers with multiple processors, multi-core processors, or hyper-threading processes
can run multiple threads at the same time. Parallel processing of multiple threads can
greatly improve program performance, but it can also make debugging more difficult
because it introduces the need to keep track of multiple threads.

Debugging OpenMP applications with Visual Studio 2005 and later versions is complicated. In particular, stepping into or out of a parallel region with F10/F11 can be
very confusing. This is because the compiler creates some additional code to call into
the runtime and to invoke the thread teams. The debugger has no special knowledge
about this, so the programmer sees what looks like strange behavior. For example, by
pressing the F11 key we would expect to step into a sub-function. Instead, we are led
to a different place because another thread has kicked in.

My recommendation for debugging an OpenMP application is to turn off multi-thread
programming by either enforcing the parallel region to run on a single thread or disabling
OpenMP (e.g., changing the setting of project as shown in figure 11.2). If a problem
can be reproduced, then the problem is unlikely to be related to parallelism. Otherwise,
we have to debug it in a hard way. Assume that we receive a return error when running
multi-thread. In this case, we set a breakpoint at

```
if (rc!=api_OK)
```

and run the program in debug. When it stops there, we cannot simply step back to a
certain place and execute the program from there, as we usually do for debugging a single
thread application. In this case, we need to enable the **Threads** window by clicking
**Debug->Windows->Threads**. The **Threads** windows will show the various threads that
are running in the thread team as shown below.

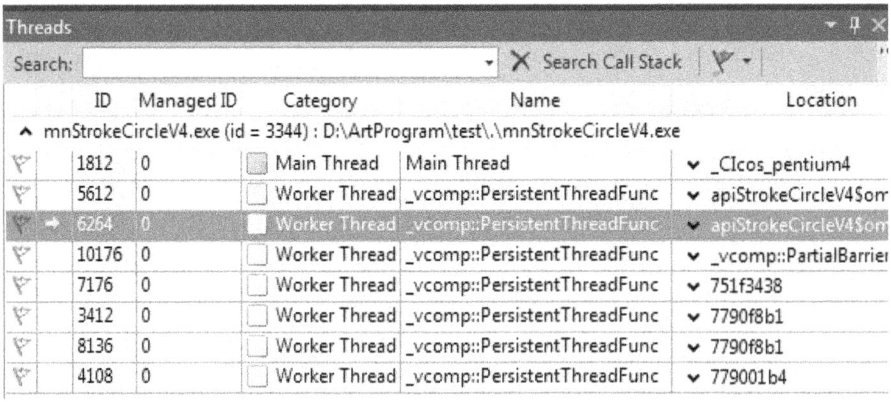

| | ID | Managed ID | Category | Name | Location |
|---|---|---|---|---|---|
| ⌄ mnStrokeCircleV4.exe (id = 3344) : D:\ArtProgram\test\.\mnStrokeCircleV4.exe | | | | | |
| ⚐ | 1812 | 0 | Main Thread | Main Thread | ⌄ _Clcos_pentium4 |
| ⚐ | 5612 | 0 | Worker Thread | _vcomp::PersistentThreadFunc | ⌄ apiStrokeCircleV4$om |
| ⚐ ➡ | 6264 | 0 | Worker Thread | _vcomp::PersistentThreadFunc | ⌄ apiStrokeCircleV4$om |
| ⚐ | 10176 | 0 | Worker Thread | _vcomp::PersistentThreadFunc | ⌄ _vcomp::PartialBarrier |
| ⚐ | 7176 | 0 | Worker Thread | _vcomp::PersistentThreadFunc | ⌄ 751f3438 |
| ⚐ | 3412 | 0 | Worker Thread | _vcomp::PersistentThreadFunc | ⌄ 7790f8b1 |
| ⚐ | 8136 | 0 | Worker Thread | _vcomp::PersistentThreadFunc | ⌄ 7790f8b1 |
| ⚐ | 4108 | 0 | Worker Thread | _vcomp::PersistentThreadFunc | ⌄ 779001b4 |

Figure 11.3: Threads window: active thread is indicated by yellow arrow

The thread IDs will not correlate with the OpenMP thread IDs; however, they will
reflect the Windows thread IDs that OpenMP is built upon. We then highlight all

thread IDs except for the one currently running and click the right mouse button to select `freeze`. This will freeze all highlighted threads. Now, we can step back and execute the program from there to investigate why computation failed.

It should be pointed out that data race, deadlock, threads and synchronization issues may still not be found with the above simple approach. Developers who frequently work on multi-thread programming may have to depend on commercial tools to debug problems. Intel® Inspector is one of such tools. In addition to finding memory leaks, memory corruption, and *dangling pointers* (i.e., pointer is still pointing to a freed memory), it detects deadlock and data race in both heap and stack.

It is reported that Visual Studio 2012 provides an improved Threads window, the new GPU Threads window, the new Parallel Watch window and other user interface improvements to make multi-threaded debugging easier. In addition, Visual Studio 2012 also provides powerful breakpoints and tracepoints, which can be very useful when developers debug multi-threaded applications. It is also said that developers can use breakpoint filters to place breakpoints on individual threads. Readers can visit the MSDN website for detail.

## 11.11 Summary

Parallel computing is the primary way that processor manufacturers are dealing with the physical limits of transistor-based processor technology. Multiple processors (or cores) are joined together on a single integrated circuit to provide increased performance and better energy efficiency than using a single processor. Multi-core technology is now standard in desktop and laptop computers. Mobile computing devices like smart phones and tablets are also incorporating multi-core processors into their designs. The fundamental challenge with multi-core architectures is that application performance does not automatically correlate to the number of processors. The benefits of multi-core processors can only be realized by writing applications that expect and take advantage of parallelism. Therefore, the advent of shared memory multi-core processors is rapidly changing the rules of software development. Developers of technical and scientific applications in industry and in government laboratories find that they need to parallelize huge volumes of code in a portable fashion. But many programmers are not prepared to deal with parallelism, i.e., reasoning about parallel programs requires thinking in a very different way. Dealing correctly with parallelism requires training and practice.

The OpenMP designers have developed a platform-independent set of compiler `pragmas`, directives, `function` calls, and `environment variables` that explicitly instruct the compiler on how and where to insert threads into the application. It is widely regarded as an easy-to-use technique that helps C/C++ developers create multi-threaded applications with minimum and manageable changes in their serial code. However, as was demonstrated in this chapter (especially, in the sections of *Explicit task parallelism* and *Parallelize Gaussian elimination*), programmers are still responsible for both identifying and properly implementing parallelism, which in turn requires sound programming skill and knowledge of parallelism. Examples in this chapter were specifically chosen to provide hands-on experience and to illustrate how parallel programming can speed up or degrade the performance, depending on how it is used.

It should be pointed out that OpenMP version 2.0, packed with Microsoft Visual Studio 2010 and 2012 versions, was released in 2002. It was developed mainly for constructing a parallel region to share the iterative workload with a known bound (e.g., a `for` loop) and finite number of parallel sections. Because of it, parallelism of a `while` loop is not discussed in this chapter. OpenMP version 3.0, released in 2008, added the support to nested loops with the `collapse` clause and `tasks` directive to address common programming structures such as `while` loops, C++ iterators, and unbalanced recursive functions. OpenMP `tasks` are similar to `sections` except that they are more dynamic and greatly improve the performance. Tasks are put into task queue by OpenMP where each task gets eventually executed by some thread from the team. In essence, the new `tasks` directive allows the user to identify units of independent work, leaving the decisions of how and when to execute them to the runtime system. Let's hope that Microsoft Visual Studio 2013 will support OpenMP 3.0 or newer version (OpenMP 4.0 was released in July, 2013).

# Appendix A

# Perl Programming

Languages like C and C++ allow a programmer to write code at a very detailed level which has good execution speed. But in many applications, one would prefer to write a program with a higher level language that makes it easy to crank out code because the programmer is completely freed from mundane tasks like managing memory and checking bounds, and can use extremely simple constructs for string comparison, manipulation, iterators, etc. For example, for text manipulation applications, the basic unit in C/C++ is a character, while for languages like Perl and Python the basic units are lines of text and words within lines. One can work with lines and words in C/C++, but he or she must go to greater effort to accomplish the same thing. C/C++ may usually give better speed, but if speed is not an issue, the convenience of a high level scripting language is very attractive. A *scripting language* is a programming language that supports the writing of scripts – programs written for a special runtime environment that can interpret and automate the execution of tasks which could alternatively be executed one-by-one by a human operator.

Among several scripting languages such as Python, Perl, PHP, Javascript, etc., Perl is an ideal text manipulation language. It was originally developed for text manipulation, but is now also used for a wide range of tasks including system administration, web development, network programming, and GUI development. Perl is a family of high-level, general-purpose, interpreted, dynamic programming languages. The languages in this family include Perl 5 and Perl 6. Perl was originally developed by Larry Wall in 1987 as a general-purpose UNIX scripting language to make report processing easier. Since then, it has undergone many changes and revisions. The latest major stable revision of Perl 5 is 5.16, released in May 2012. Perl 6 is a complete redesign of the language, announced in 2000 and still under active development as of 2013. Perl borrows features from other programming languages including C, shell scripting, and so on.

ActivePerl, developed by a Canadian software company ActiveState®, is the leading commercial-grade distribution of the open source Perl scripting language. Both win32 and win64 are supported. It can be downloaded from ActiveState® web site free of charge under the ActiveState Community License. Installation of ActivePerl is easy, simply accepting all default settings. The installation wizard will usually add `Perl\bin` path to your computer's `PATH` environment automatically. If it failed to do so for some reason, you will have to add the path yourself to ensure Windows operating system can find it.

Perl is a feature-rich language, which clearly cannot be discussed in full detail here. Instead, our goal in this appendix is to help readers quickly become proficient at writing simple Perl programs to manipulate text strings and automate the execution of tasks. Readers can also refer to many excellent online tutorials and published books for detail on Perl programming.

Our first example is assigning a text string to a variable and then performing several string manipulation tasks:

```
1    $myString = "He is a programmer.";
2    print "$myString\n";
3
4    # Replace "He" by "She"
5    $myString = reverse $myString;
6    chop $myString;
7    chop $myString;
8    $myString = reverse $myString;
9    $myString = "She$myString";
10   print "$myString\n";
11
12   # Make the string all lower case
13   $myString =~ tr/A-Z/a-z/;
14   print "$myString\n";
15
16   # Make the string all upper case
17   $myString =~ tr/a-z/A-Z/;
18   print "$myString\n";
```

It is noted that the name of variable begins with $ and a data type of the variable is not declared explicitly in Perl. This is because most scripting languages are intended to be very fast to pick up. This generally implies relatively simple syntax and semantics. At line 1, we simply assign the text string "He is a programmer." to the variable $myString. We then print the text at the command line, the syntax of which is very similar to C language. For printing the output, we could simply write

```
print $myString;
```

In this case, however, there is no end-of-line or newline marker to signify the end of a line of text. Accordingly, the next print statement will print the string at the same line without the word wrap.

From line 4 to 10, "He" is replaced by "She." This is achieved by first reversing the string, then chopping out two ending characters "H" and "e" that stands for "He," reversing the string again, and concatenating the string with "She" for printing out

"She is a programmer." From line 12 to 14, the string is converted to lower case before being printed at the command line. From line 16 to 18, the string is converted to the upper case before being printed.

We now save the above Perl script in D:\ArtProgram\bin as example_1.pl and invoke it in the same directory to display the result at the command line:

```
D:\ArtProgram\bin>Perl example_1.pl
He is a programmer.
She is a programmer.
she is a programmer.
SHE IS A PROGRAMMER.
```

Saving a Perl script in the default suffix has two drawbacks. Firstly, we have to type Perl before the name of a script whenever we invoke it. Secondly, we need to type the full path of the script if it is invoked in a different directory. For example, we have to type

```
D:\ArtProgram\test>Perl D:\ArtProgram\bin\example_1.pl
```

if we are currently not in the D:\ArtProgram\bin directory. As is known, Windows command prompt will search through the Environment Variable PATH for executables, DLLs, and Windows scripts such as .bat and .cmd files. If a Perl script program is saved with either the .cmd or .bat suffix in the folder whose path is listed in the PATH, we can invoke the script anywhere. To save a Perl script as the .cmd file, we have to rewrite the script as

```
1     @rem = '
2     @goto endofperl
3     ';
4
5     $myString = "He is a programmer.";
6     print "$myString\n";
7
8     # Replace "He" by "She"
9     $myString = reverse $myString;
10    chop $myString;
11    chop $myString;
12    $myString = reverse $myString;
13    $myString = "She$myString";
14    print "$myString\n";
15
16    # Make the string all lower case
17    $myString =~ tr/A-Z/a-z/;
18    print "$myString\n";
19
20    # Make the string all upper case
21    $myString =~ tr/a-z/A-Z/;
22    print "$myString\n";
```

```
23
24     __END__
25     :endofperl
26     @perl -S %0.cmd %1 %2 %3 %4 %5
```

Referring to the last line of code, %0, %1, etc. are the potential command-line arguments with %0 being the script name. Therefore, the last statement invokes the same script, denoted by %0.cmd, at the same directory to avoid typing the full path. The @ character placed in front of a statement is to suppress the echoing or printing out the execution of this statement at the command line. We can now invoke this script from the test folder conveniently as illustrated below:

```
D:\ArtProgram\test>example_1
He is a programmer.
She is a programmer.
she is a programmer.
SHE IS A PROGRAMMER.
```

As seen above, it is very easy to write a Perl script to manipulate a text string. On the other hand, it would require considerable effort to achieve the same task via C/C++ programming.

Out second example is writing the Perl script AddCopyright.cmd that opens a named .cpp file to add copyright information to the description. Opening, for example, apiHornerEval.cpp, we shall see the following description

```
/*------------------------------------------------------------------
API Name
    apiHornerEval

Description
    It evaluates polynomial and optionally its first derivative.

Signature
    void apiHornerEval(int ndeg, double *pA,
            double x, double &f, double *q)

    INPUT:
       ndeg      degree of polynomial
       pA        coefficients of polynomial
       x         variable at which polynomial is evaluated
    OUTPUT:
       f         polynomial value
       q         (optional) first derivative of polynomial

History

    Y.M. Li     10/15/2012 : Creation date
-------------------------------------------------------------*/
```

Suppose that we want to add the copyright information before `API Name` and keep the rest of the code to be the same. Then, the Perl script would be

```perl
@rem = '
@goto endofperl
';

if ($ARGV[0] eq "")
{
   die print "\nSyntax: AddCopyright <filename.cpp>\n\n";
}

open(INFILE, "$ARGV[0]") || die "Cannot open $ARGV[0].\n";

$filename = $ARGV[0];
chop $filename;
chop $filename;
chop $filename;
chop $filename;
$filename = "$filename.txt";

open(OUTFILE, ">$filename") || die "Cannot open $filename.\n";

foreach $Line (<INFILE>)
{
  if ($Line =~ /API Name/)
  {
     print OUTFILE "Copyright (C) 2003. All rights reserved.\n\n"
  }
  print OUTFILE "$Line";
}

close(OUTFILE);
close(INFILE);
unlink("$ARGV[0]");
rename("$filename", "$ARGV[0]");

__END__
:endofperl
@perl -S %0.cmd %1 %2 %3 %4 %5
```

Line 5 to line 8 validate the input to make sure the command-line argument is not empty. The statement at line 10 opens the named `.cpp` file as an input file. From line 12 to 17, we replace the suffix `.cpp` by `.txt`. The statement at line 19 opens the named output file whose suffix is `.txt`. From line 21 to 28, we loop through each line of the input file and print the same line to the output file. But if this line contains the string `API Name`, we need to print out the copyright information before printing this line. Statements at line 30 and 31 close the output and input file. The statement at line 32 deletes the original .cpp file, and the statement at line 33 rename the .txt file to .cpp file.

Copy apiHornerEval.cpp to test folder and type the following at the command line:

D:\ArtProgram\test>AddCopyright apiHornerEval.cpp

Opening the newly-updated apiHornerEval.cpp, we should see the copyright information has been added to the description. Everything else in this file is still the same as shown below.

```
/*-------------------------------------------------------------------
Copyright (C) 2003. All rights reserved.

API Name
   apiHornerEval

Description
   It evaluates polynomial and optionally its first derivative.

Signature
   void apiHornerEval(int ndeg, double *pA,
           double x, double &f, double *q)

   INPUT:
      ndeg     degree of polynomial
      pA       coefficients of polynomial
      x        variable at which polynomial is evaluated
   OUTPUT:
      f        polynomial value
      q        (optional) first derivative of polynomial

History

   Y.M. Li     10/15/2012 : Creation date
-------------------------------------------------------------------*/
```

Our last example is writing the Perl script AddCopyrightLib.cmd that adds copyright information to all the .cpp files residing in the current directory. Through this example, we will learn how to loop through every file in a directory and how to call a subroutine. Since this script is similar to AddCopyright.cmd, we make a copy of this script and name it AddCopyrightLib.cmd. Open this script file by any text editor and modify it as follows:

```
1    @rem = '
2    @goto endofperl
3    ';
4
5    opendir(DIR, ".");
```

```perl
 6    @files = readdir(DIR);
 7    foreach $filename (@files)
 8    {
 9      if ($filename =~ /\.cpp/)
10      {
11          addCopyright(@_=($filename));
12      }
13    }
14    close(DIR);
15
16
17    # Subroutine adds copyright information to each named .cpp file.
18
19    sub addCopyright
20    {
21      local($filename) = @_;
22
23      open(INFILE, "$filename") || die "Cannot open $filename.\n";
24
25      $filename_new = $filename;
26      chop $filename_new;
27      chop $filename_new;
28      chop $filename_new;
29      chop $filename_new;
30      $filename_new = "$filename_new.txt";
31
32      open(OUTFILE, ">$filename_new") || die "Cannot open $filename.\n";
33
34      foreach $Line (<INFILE>)
35      {
36        if ($Line =~ /API Name/)
37        {
38            print OUTFILE "Copyright (C) 2003. All rights reserved.\n\n"
39        }
40        print OUTFILE "$Line";
41      }
42
43      close(OUTFILE);
44      close(INFILE);
45      unlink("filename");
46      rename("$filename_new", "$filename");
47    }
48
49    __END__
50    :endofperl
51    @perl -S %0.cmd %1 %2 %3 %4 %5
```

Line 5 opens the current directory, and line 6 reads file names in the opened directory and stores them in the `@files` array. From line 7 to 13, we loop through each filename and, when the filename has the suffix `.cpp`, call the subroutine `addCopyright` to add the copyright information. Note how the filename is passed to the subroutine. The implementation of subroutine is basically the same as `AddCopyright.cmd`. To test this script, copy some source files to the `test` folder and type

```
D:\ArtProgram\test>AddCopyrightLib
```

Upon the completion of execution, we should see that copyright information has been added to every source file in this folder.

These examples were designed to familiarize readers with basic Perl scripting. By walking through these examples, it is adequate for readers to understand the automation scripts used in this book. There are many excellent books and online tutorials on Perl programming, readers can refer to these resources for more information.

# Appendix B

# Interview Questions and Answers

By now readers should be able to answer all pre-interview questions given in the preface. For easy reference and completeness, I will go through the seven pre-interview questions again with my answers and additional comments.

## B.1 Area tolerance

No two components can be manufactured exactly the same. In practice, dimensional or geometric tolerances (e.g., distance and angular tolerances) are introduced in Computer Aided Design systems and manufacturing processes. The smaller the tolerance required, the more expensive the component will be to machine. Therefore, it is often desirable to specify the largest possible tolerance while maintaining proper functionality.

Denoting the distance tolerance by $\varepsilon$, then two circles are considered to be the same if

$$|R_1 - R_2| < \varepsilon,$$

where $R_1$ and $R_2$ are the radii of circles 1 and 2 respectively. Assume that we know the areas of the two circles (denoted by $A_1$ and $A_2$) and the radius of circle 1 (i.e., $R_1$). Please derive the "area tolerance" $\Delta$ in terms of the given distance tolerance $\varepsilon$ such that, when $|A_1 - A_2| < \Delta$, we know two circles are equal with respect to the distance tolerance. One should avoid computing radii via $R_i = \sqrt{A_i/\pi}, i = 2, 3, \cdots, n$, as the square root computation is an expensive arithmetic operation. Although a non-calculus based approach is acceptable, a calculus based approach is preferable since calculus is the study of change.

**Answer:** I have seen in different occasions that developers use $\varepsilon^2$ to check if one lamina (i.e., a closed surface in plane) is equal to the other. Their reasoning is that, since $\varepsilon$ is for one dimensional measurement and area is the two-dimensional analog of the length of a curve (a one-dimensional concept), the area tolerance is simply $\varepsilon^2$ to match the square unit. This is mathematically incorrect and also a much stricter condition than

339

necessary. As will be seen below, the area tolerance of a circle is usually much larger than the distance tolerance since $R$ is, in practice, larger than $\varepsilon$.

- Non-calculus: Assume that $R_2 = R_1 \pm \varepsilon$. Then,

$$\Delta = |A_2 - A_1| = \pi|(R_1 \pm \varepsilon)^2 - R_1^2| = \pi|\pm 2R_1\varepsilon + \varepsilon^2| = \pi|2R_1\varepsilon \pm \varepsilon^2|.$$

Since $\varepsilon^2$ is negligible, we have $\Delta = 2\pi R_1\varepsilon$.

- Calculus: $A = \pi R^2$. By the rule of differential, $dA = 2\pi R \, dR$. Since $dA$ measures the change of the area with respect to the small change of the radius (i.e., $dR$), we have $\Delta = 2\pi R\varepsilon$. Replacing $R$ by the known $R_1$, we obtain $\Delta = 2\pi R_1\varepsilon$.

**Comments**: This question was designed to assess candidates' ability to apply their math skills to solve basic engineering problems. In calculus, the derivative measures how fast the function is changing and the differential represents the *principal part* of the change in a function with respect to the change in a variable. This principal part of function change is what we need to derive the area tolerance. The same technique may be used in other cases. For example, in CAD/CAM systems, parametric polynomial curves and surfaces are used to describe wine glasses, telephone handsets, car bodies, etc. For many geometric operations, it is desirable to compute the parametric tolerance for a given parametric curve. If the change of parameter is less than the parametric tolerance, the change of the curve length is then guaranteed to be within the distance tolerance. Representing a parametric curve in a vector-valued form $r(u)$ and differentiating it with respect to the parameter $u \in [a, b]$ gives

$$\frac{dr(u)}{du} = r'(u) \quad \Longrightarrow \quad \|dr(u)\| = \|r'(u)\| \, du.$$

If we can find the upper bound of the magnitude of the first derivative in $[a, b]$ and denote it by $r'(\xi)$, we can then derive the parametric tolerance as

$$du \leq \frac{\|dr(u)\|}{\|r'(\xi)\|} \leq \frac{\varepsilon}{\|r'(\xi)\|}.$$

As an example, let's see how the parametric tolerance of a circle is derived. Representing a circle in parametric form gives

$$x(\theta) = x_0 + \rho \cos\theta,$$
$$y(\theta) = y_0 + \rho \sin\theta,$$

where $(x_0, y_0)$ is the center of the circle and $\rho$ is the radius. Differentiating $x(\theta)$ and $y(\theta)$ with respect to $\theta$, we have

$$x'(\theta) = -\rho \sin\theta,$$
$$y'(\theta) = \rho \cos\theta.$$

Accordingly,

$$\|r'(\theta)\| = \sqrt{x'(\theta)^2 + y'(\theta)^2} = \rho.$$

Therefore, we have

$$d\theta = \frac{\varepsilon}{\rho},$$

where $d\theta$ is the parametric tolerance. This result can be confirmed by a geometric approach. When the angle changes by $\Delta\theta$, the corresponding arc length change is $\rho \times \Delta\theta$. When $\Delta\theta = 2\pi$, we have $2\pi\rho$ – the circumference of the circle. If we want $\rho \times \Delta\theta < \varepsilon$, we have

$$\Delta\theta = \frac{\varepsilon}{\rho}.$$

This geometric approach leads to the next interview question.

# B.2 Angular tolerance

Again, we denote the distance tolerance by $\varepsilon$ and assume that the model space (the longest model we would create) is $10^4$ meters. Based on $\varepsilon$ and the limit of model space, I would like you to derive the angular tolerance $\Delta$ such that it can be used to determine whether two lines confined in the model space are collinear.

**Hint**: Two lines are considered to be collinear if the maximum deviation between these two lines is less than the distance tolerance $\varepsilon$. From this criterion, you may derive the angular tolerance such that you know two lines are collinear with respect to $\varepsilon$ if the angle between these two lines is less than the angular tolerance $\Delta$. Drawing two lines on a piece of paper may help you analyze the problem.

**Answer**: Assume two longest lines passing through the same point are not exactly collinear and the angle between two lines is $\Delta$. Then, the sweeping arc length between two lines is $\Delta \times 10^4$, which needs to be smaller than the distance tolerance $\varepsilon$. This is to say that $\Delta \times 10^4 < \varepsilon$. Therefore, $\Delta < \varepsilon/10^4$. Alternatively, this can be derived from the right triangle rules: let $10^4$ be the hypotenuse and the cathetus (the opposite leg) be the $h$. Then,

$$\frac{h}{10^4} = \sin\Delta \approx \Delta.$$

Since $h$ needs to be less than $\varepsilon$, we have $\Delta < \varepsilon/10^4$.

**Comments**: The above angular tolerance is much stricter than necessary when the geometry size is much less than the maximum allowed size $10^4$. For example, the angular tolerance for a circle is $\varepsilon/\rho$, where $\rho$ is the radius of the circle. When $\rho$ is shorter than $10^4$ unit, $\varepsilon/\rho$ is much larger than $\Delta = \varepsilon/10^4$. Using the smallest tolerance is a sufficient but not necessary condition.

We may alternatively explain how the angular tolerance and model space limit are derived as follows: For 32-bit computer, a double-precision floating-point format uses 52-bit for the significand, which is equivalent to 15 or 16 significant decimal digits ($\log_{10} 2^{52} \approx 15.654$). We consider five of the least significant digits to represent numeric round-off errors that occur during calculations. Thus, there are roughly 10 digits to represent the dynamic range of numbers (smallest and largest numbers) within an object space. Accordingly, the angular tolerance, which is the smallest of all three tolerances, is set to $10^{-10}$. When the distance and angular tolerances are defined, the longest line we can model would be

$$\frac{10^{-6}}{10^{-10}} = 10,000 \text{ units.}$$

## B.3   Improve performance of circle stroking

Most graphics programming tools provide only a line drawing capability. To display a circle on computer screen, we first need to break the circle into evenly spaced tiny pieces such that each tiny piece can be well-approximated by a line. We then draw these lines on the screen. Because these lines are so small, a circle looks smooth on the screen.

Breaking a circle into many tiny pieces is equivalent to computing many evenly spaced points on the circle, a process known as circle stroking. If we want to stroke $n + 1$ points on circle and start the first point at $\theta_0 = 0$, then the angle increment $\delta$ would be $2\pi/n$ as shown below.

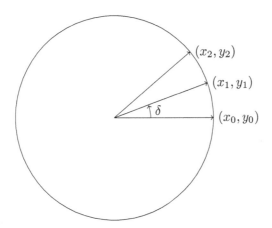

Accordingly, all other points may be computed as follows:

$$x_1 = r\cos(\theta_1) = r\cos(\theta_0 + \delta)$$
$$y_1 = r\sin(\theta_1) = r\sin(\theta_0 + \delta)$$
$$x_2 = r\cos(\theta_2) = r\cos(\theta_1 + \delta)$$
$$y_2 = r\sin(\theta_2) = r\sin(\theta_1 + \delta)$$
$$\cdots$$
$$x_n = r\cos(\theta_n) = r\cos(\theta_{n-1} + \delta)$$
$$y_n = r\sin(\theta_n) = r\sin(\theta_{n-1} + \delta)$$

The above formula indicates that we need to call trigonometric functions (i.e., sin and cos) for $2(n + 1)$ times. Since trigonometric functions are relatively more expensive to compute than multiplication and division, the above approach is not optimized in terms of CPU usage. Please provide a suggestion on how you can speed up the computation.

**Answer:** Form high school math, it is known that

$$\cos(\theta_i + \delta) = \cos(\theta_i)\cos(\delta) - \sin(\theta_i)\sin(\delta)$$

$$\sin(\theta_i + \delta) = \sin(\theta_i)\cos(\delta) + \cos(\theta_i)\sin(\delta)$$

With the above formula, we can compute the $(i+1)$th point as follows:

$$x_{i+1} = r\cos(\theta_i + \delta) = r\cos(\theta_i)\cos(\delta) - r\sin(\theta_i)\sin(\delta) = x_i\cos(\delta) - y_i\sin(\delta)$$

$$y_{i+1} = r\sin(\theta_i + \delta) = r\sin(\theta_i)\cos(\delta) + r\cos(\theta_i)\sin(\delta) = y_i\cos(\delta) + x_i\sin(\delta)$$

Therefore, we compute $\sin(\delta)$ and $\cos(\delta)$ once and use them to derive all stroking points via the recursive relation. The code fragment is given below:

```
sin_delta = sin(delta);
cos_delta = cos(delta);
x[1] = r;
y[1] = 0.0;
for (i=1; i<=n; i++)
{
    x[i+1] = x[i] * cos_delta - y[i] * sin_delta;
    y[i+1] = y[i] * cos_delta + x[i] * sin_delta;
}
```

Alternatively, we may create a rotation transformation with the rotating angle being $\delta$ and then compute $(x_{i+1}, y_{i+1})$ as follows:

$$\begin{pmatrix} x_{i+1} \\ y_{i+1} \end{pmatrix} = \begin{pmatrix} \cos\delta & -\sin\delta \\ \sin\delta & \cos\delta \end{pmatrix} \begin{pmatrix} x_i \\ y_i \end{pmatrix}$$

**Comments:** This question was designed to evaluate candidates' ability to use their basic math knowledge to simplify a problem. However, it should be pointed out that trigonometric functions are widely available across programming languages and platforms. Most CPU architectures have built-in instructions for trigonometric functions. Therefore, it will not be terribly slow if our circle stroking method is implemented as follows:

```
for(i=0; i<nStrkPts; i++)
{
    pStrkPts[i].x = center.x + radius * cos(i * delta);
    pStrkPts[i].y = center.y + radius * sin(i * delta);
}
```

Based on our timing, it is roughly 3 to 4 times slower when repeatedly calling the standard sin and cos math functions. As was seen in chapter 11, the above code fragment can be improved by using multi-thread programming. Even so, it is still outperformed by our first implementation that computes sin and cos once (Timing test was based on a laptop computer with a Core i7 processor that has eight-hyperthread).

## B.4 Approximation by circular arc

A circle in quadratic form is

$$x^2 + y^2 + 2Ax + 2By + C = 0. \tag{B.4.1}$$

Its center and radius are given by $(-A, -B)$ and $\sqrt{A^2 + B^2 - C}$ respectively. Given $n$ points $(x_i, y_i)$ $(i = 1, 2, \cdots, n)$, we want to find a circle that interpolates $(x_1, y_1)$ and $(x_n, y_n)$ and approximates the remaining points in a least squares sense. Substituting $(x_1, y_1)$ and $(x_n, y_n)$ in the above equation gives

$$x_1^2 + y_1^2 + 2x_1 A + 2y_1 B + C = 0 \tag{B.4.2}$$
$$x_n^2 + y_n^2 + 2x_n A + 2y_n B + C = 0 \tag{B.4.3}$$

Subtracting the second equation from the first yields

$$2(x_1 - x_n)A + 2(y_1 - y_n)B + x_1^2 + y_1^2 - x_n^2 - y_n^2 = 0.$$

Assume that $|x_1 - x_n| \neq 0$ so we may express $A$ in terms of $B$, i.e.,

$$A = \frac{y_1 - y_n}{x_n - x_1}B + \frac{x_1^2 + y_1^2 - x_n^2 - y_n^2}{2(x_n - x_1)} = \alpha B + \beta \tag{B.4.4}$$

Replacing $A$ in (B.4.1) gives

$$2(x\alpha + y)B + C + x^2 + y^2 + 2x\beta = 0.$$

If an arbitrary point $p_i = (x_i, y_i)$ is not on the circle, then

$$e_i = \left| 2(x_i\alpha + y_i)B + C + x_i^2 + y_i^2 + 2x_i \right| > 0$$

is the approximation error. The sum of all squared errors is

$$\mathcal{E} = \sum_{i=2}^{n-1} \left( 2(x_i\alpha + y_i)B + C + x_i^2 + y_i^2 + 2x_i\beta \right)^2$$

From calculus, $\mathcal{E}$ is minimized if

$$\frac{\partial \mathcal{E}}{\partial B} = 0 \quad \text{and} \quad \frac{\partial \mathcal{E}}{\partial C} = 0.$$

Optimized $B$ and $C$ are obtained by solving the above two linear equations and $A$ is computed via (B.4.4).

Implementing the above approach will not result in a circle that interpolates $(x_1, y_1)$ and $(x_n, y_n)$. Do you see any reasoning problem in this approach?

**Answer:** A circle is uniquely defined by three non-collinear points. If a circle is required to interpolate two endpoints, two of the three unknowns ($A$, $B$, and $C$) need to be eliminated. The above approach failed to do so. Let's see where it went wrong. Relation

(B.4.4) is not equivalent to relations (B.4.2) and (B.4.3). We need to eliminate two unknowns (e.g., $A$ and $B$) from the two endpoint conditions (or two boundary conditions) and solve the reduced equation for ONE unknown. Relation (B.4.4) destroyed the given conditions. There are several possible ways to solve this least squares approximation problem. A simpler and numerically stabler approach would be: compute the mid-point of the chord that links $(x_1, y_1)$ and $(x_n, y_n)$, and transform all the points to a new coordinate system in which the $x$-axis is parallel to the chord and the origin coincident with the mid-point. In this case, $A = 0$ and equation (B.4.1) involves only two variables:

$$x^2 + y^2 + 2By + C = 0.$$

In the new coordinate system, $(x_1, y_1)$ sits on the $x$-axis. Therefore, $y_1 = 0$ and $C = x_1^2$ (note: we can also use $(x_n, y_n)$ to derive $C = x_n^2$ since it lies on the $x$-axis as well). This further reduces the equation to one unknown

$$x^2 + y^2 + 2By + x_1^2 = 0.$$

Given $n$ points, the sum of the squared errors is

$$\mathcal{E} = \sum_{i=2}^{n-1} \left( x_i^2 + y_i^2 + 2By_i + x_1^2 \right)^2,$$

which can be solved by letting $d\mathcal{E}/dB = 0$.

## B.5    Evaluation of $e^x$

Exponential function $e^x$ and trigonometric functions such as $\sin x$ and $\cos x$ are often evaluated via the Maclaurin series (a special form of Taylor series). Expressing $e^x$ by the Maclaurin series gives

$$e^x = 1 + x + \frac{x^2}{2!} + \frac{x^3}{3!} + \cdots = \sum_{i=0}^{\infty} \frac{x^i}{i!}.$$

This Maclaurin series converges to $e^x$ absolutely and uniformly for $x \in (-\infty, +\infty)$. Please write a program to evaluate $e^x$ via Maclaurin series at $x = 1$ and $\pm 25$ and compare your results with the ones obtained by using either a pocket calculator or the C/C++ internal math function $\texttt{exp(x)}$. An explanation of your implementation and findings is expected.

**Hint:** Let $P_n = \sum_{i=0}^{n} \frac{x^i}{i!}$. Then, $P_n$ is said to be converged to $e^x$ with respect to the given tolerance $\varepsilon$ if $|P_n - P_{n-1}| = \left| \frac{x^n}{n!} \right| < \varepsilon$. Let's assume that $\varepsilon = 10^{-15}$.

**Answer:** One should not directly compute the factorial $i!$ because it is inefficient to do so and can cause an overflow when $i$ is large. By examining the above series, it is noted that the $i$th term is equal to multiplying the $(i-1)$th term by $\frac{x}{i}$. Accordingly, we can evaluate the above polynomial efficiently via the variation of Horner's method:

```
void apiEvalExp(double x, int n, double &f)
{
    int         i;
    double      term, f;

    f = 0.0;
    term = 1.0;
    for (i=1; i<=n; i += 1)
    {
        f += term;
        term = term * x / i;
    }
}
```

The above implementation requires the user to specify $n$, which is not practical. A feasible approach is specifying the convergence tolerance rather than $n$. Denoting

$$P_n(x) = \sum_{i=0}^{n} \frac{x^i}{i!},$$

then $P_n(x)$ is said to be converged to $e^x$ with respect to the given tolerance $\varepsilon$ if

$$|P_n(x) - P_{n-1}(x)| < \varepsilon.$$

It is noted that $|P_n(x) - P_{n-1}(x)|$ gives the last term of $P_n(x)$. Therefore, the convergence criterion is to check whether term is less than the given accuracy. So the complete implementation is:

```
void apiEvalExp(double x, double epsilon, double &f)
{
    int         i;
    double      term;

    f = 0.0;
    term = 1.0;
    i = 1;
    while (true)
    {
        f += term;
        if (fabs(term) < epsilon)
            break;
        term = term * x / i;
        i++;
    }
}
```

Since the Maclaurin series converges to $e^x$ uniformly and absolutely for all $x$, one may assume that the above implementation will always give a correct result for any $x$. This is true only if $x \geq 0$. If $x = -25$ is used to test the above implementation, the result is

$$-7.1297804036720779e - 007.$$

But the correct answer is

$$1.3887943864964021e - 011,$$

which is obtained via the standard C internal function `exp(x)`. Two results are not only significantly different but also have different signs. How could a converging series lead to a diverging result? Many standard computation rules apply only to infinite precision arithmetic. In floating-point computation, it is very important to design an algorithm that minimizes the loss of significant digits. Referring to the above Maclaurin series, the even terms are positive and odd terms are negative, so the numerical instability is caused by subtraction of similar numbers. To avoid such catastrophic problem, we should always treat $x$ as a positive value and compute $f$. If $x < 0$, we have $e^{-x} = 1/e^x$. Accordingly, $1/f$ is the result for $e^{-x}$.

**Comments**: Without thoughtful analysis of numerical stability (the necessary step for a good design), one may implement the evaluation as follows:

```
inline long long Factorial(long long n)
{
    return (n == 1 ? n : n * Factorial(n - 1));
}

void EvaluateExpX(int n, double x, double &f)
{
    int i;

    f = 1.0;
    for (i=1; i<=n; i += 1)
    {
        f += pow(x, i) / Factorial(i);
    }
}
```

It is noted that `Factorial` is declared as an *inline function*. The `inline` specifier instructs the compiler to insert a copy of the function body into each place the function is called. Using inline functions can make our program faster because they eliminate the overhead associated with function calls, but at the cost of larger code size. In computing the factorial $n!$, a `long long` data type is used to avoid overflow. In programming, an overflow occurs when an arithmetic operation attempts to create a numeric value that is too large to be represented within the available storage range. For a 32bit machine, `long long` is equivalent to `_int64` and has the data range of

$$-9,223,372,036,854,775,808 \quad \text{to} \quad 9,223,372,036,854,775,807.$$

This means $n$ should be less than or equal to 20. When $n$ is larger than 20, we will have an integer overflow. Some candidates sent me the following improved code, in which a `double` was used to store the factorial and a call to the `inline` function was eliminated:

```
void EvaluateExpX(int n, double x, double &f)
```

```
{
    int       i;
    double    factorial;

    f = factorial = 1.0;
    for (i=1; i<=n; i += 1)
    {
        factorial *= i;
        f += pow(x, i) / factorial;
    }
}
```

This is a big improvement in terms of eliminating an integer overflow and boosting performance. But the performance can be further improved by eliminating a call to pow(x, i) as demonstrated in my implementation.

## B.6   Implementation of bisection method

Assume a continuous function $f$ is monotonic on the interval $[a, b]$ and $f(a) \times f(b) < 0$. Then, there exists a solution $x$ in $[a, b]$ such that $f(x) = 0$ as illustrated below.

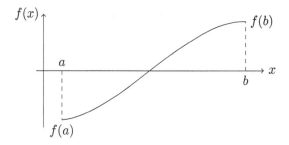

To find the solution numerically, we can use the bisecting method. As the name suggests, we start by selecting $x$ at the mid of the interval $[a, b]$ and compute $f(x)$. If $|f(x)| < \varepsilon$, $x$ is the root of function $f$. Otherwise, we reduce the interval by half using the following criterion:

```
if (f(a) * f(x) < 0.0)
{
    b = x;
}
else
{
    a = x;
}
```

Based on the reduced interval, we compute again $x = 0.5(a + b)$ and check if $|f(x)| < \varepsilon$. Repeating this process should find the root of $f = 0$.

If you are not familiar with object oriented programming, you may simply implement a workable recursive function to compute the root of $f(x) = x^3 + 2x - 2$ in $[0, 1]$. Otherwise, I would like you to demonstrate how you can implement, say, Bisection class to compute the root of the above function. Furthermore, you may want to show me how you can compute the root of another function $f(x) = \sin(x)$ in $[2, 4]$ based on Bisection class with minimum additional implementation.

**Answer:** It is noted that we did not explicitly specify any particular function when discussing how to find the root of $f = 0$ via a recursion method. In other words, this bisecting recursive algorithm is universal to any function. For this reason, we may declare a CBisection class as follows:

```
class CBisection
{
public:

    // pure virtual function to be implemented by derived class
    virtual double EvaluateFunc(double x) = 0;

    double ComputeRoot(double a, double b, double tol)
    {
        double f_a, f_b, f_mid, x_mid;

        // Terminate condition
        x_mid = 0.5 * (a + b);
        f_mid = this->EvaluateFunc(x_mid);
        if (fabs(f_mid) < tol)
            return x_mid;

        // Recuce the complexity via recursion
        f_a = this->EvaluateFunc(a);
        f_b = this->EvaluateFunc(b);
        if (f_a * f_mid < 0.0)
            return ComputeRoot(a, x_mid, tol);
        else
            return ComputeRoot(x_mid, b, tol);
    };
};
```

The method ComputeRoot is a generic implementation of the bisection algorithm. EvaluateFunc is declared as a *pure virtual* function by placing = 0 at the end of its declaration, indicating the derived class must implement it. It is left for the derived classes to do so because the implementation of EvaluateFunc varies with respect to different applications. The pure virtual function is also known as an *abstract* function. It is noted that neither a constructor nor a destructor is implemented since we do not have any specific data needs to be initialized or released.

With the above base class, we can implement a derived class to solve any specific question with minimal coding effort. For example, to find a solution of $\sin x = 0$ in the given interval $[a, b]$, we first define the CSineRoot class whose parent class is the base class CBisection. Since a derived class inherits both data and member functions from a parent class, CSineRoot class has access to the generic bisection method ComputeRoot defined in the parent class. The only thing we need to do inside the derived class is to implement the pure virtual function EvaluateFunc to evaluate $\sin x$:

```
// A class to find x such that sin(x) = 0
class CSineRoot : public CBisection
{
public:
    // Implementation of pure virtual function
    double EvaluateFunc(double x)
    {
        return sin(x);
    }
};
```

Then, the root of $\sin x$ is computed by creating an instance of CSineRoot class and calling the bisection method as follows:

```
CSineRoot   objSin;
x = objSine.ComputeRoot(a, b, tol);
```

Similarly, to find a root of the polynomial function

$$f(x) = \sum_{i=0}^{n} a_i x^i,$$

we derive the CPolynomialRoot class from the base class CBisection.  Inside this derived class, we implement the pure virtual function to evaluate the polynomial:

```
// A class to find x such that a polynoomial function f = 0
class CPolynomialRoot : public CBisection
{
private:
    int       m_ndeg;
    double    *m_pA;

public:
    // Use constructor to initialize polynomial
    CPolynomialRoot(int ndeg, double *pA)
    {
        m_ndeg = ndeg;
        m_pA = new double[ndeg + 1];
        memcpy(m_pA, pA, (ndeg + 1) * sizeof(double));
    };

    // Destructor is responsible to delete memory
```

```
~CPolynomialRoot()
{
    if (m_pA)
        delete [] m_pA;
}

// Implementation of pure virtual function
double EvaluateFunc(double x)
{
    double f;
    apiHornerEval(m_ndeg, m_pA, x, f);
    return f;
}
};
```

Accordingly, the root of $f(x) = x^3 + 2x - 2$ in $[a, b]$ is computed by creating an instance of CPolynomialRoot class and calling the bisection method as follows:

```
double          A[4] = {-2.0, 2.0, 0.0, 1.0};
CPolynomialRoot objCubic(3, A);
x = objCubic.ComputeRoot(a, b, tol);
```

As seen above, there is no need to modify the base class and its implementation to evaluate a different function. Instead, we simply overrides the virtual function with an evaluation method specific to the application. This is known as *inheritance with polymorphism* in object oriented design/programming. If you are C programmers, you can use a callback function to achieve the task of minimizing the code change to find a root of any function.

**Comments**: Object-oriented programming has been around for many decades and taught as a core course in computer science. Many candidates I have interviewed knew the terminologies of *data abstraction, encapsulation, polymorphism*, and *inheritance*. When asked to demonstrate their knowledge and skill to design a bisection method that is capable of finding a root of different functions, very few of them sent back a satisfactory solution.

It appears to me that there is a gap between academic training and real world computing. For example, mammals (or people) are often used in many text books to teach inheritance and polymorphism. Engineering students are taught how mammals form a base class and how dogs and cats are derived from mammals and thus form the derived classes. The need for inheritance and polymorphism sounds very artificial and may fail to draw students' attention to the topic and may even cause their resistance to the idea. Therefore, when asked to use inheritance with polymorphism to design a bisection method that can be used to solve any function, candidates had trouble connecting the dots between what they have learned in the classroom and real engineering applications.

The interview question was designed to evaluate candidates' understanding of object oriented programming. In C++ programming, inheritance allows one data type to acquire properties of other data types. Inheritance from a base class may be declared as *public*, *protected*, or *private*. This access specifier determines whether unrelated and derived classes can access the inherited public and protected members of the base class. Inheritance allows code to be reused between related types. Polymorphism enables one common interface for many implementations, and for objects to act differently under different circumstances. Polymorphism is often achieved by method overriding, which is not the same as method overloading. Method *overloading* refers to methods that have the same method name but different signatures inside the same class. Method *overriding* is where a subclass replaces the implementation of one or more of its parent's methods.

# B.7    Curve/Curve intersection

Simple curves such as lines and arcs are widely used in Computer Aided Design and Manufacturing (CAD/CAM) systems. In addition to a line and arc, a piecewise polynomial curve (either a composite Bézier curve or a B-spline curve) is also used to model complex geometric shapes.

Assume we already have an API to solve a line/line intersection problem. I would like you to derive a method to compute the intersection points of two generic curves as shown below by calling the line/line intersection API.

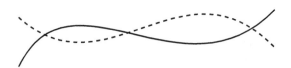

Two curves intersect each other at multiple places

I am not interested in C/C++ code implementation. Instead, I would like to see how you analyze the problem (math) and organize your data (computer science). If you want, you can write the pseudo code to clarify your approach.

**Answer**: If you paid attentions to Question 3 (stroking a circle) and 5 (bisecting algorithm to solve $f(x) = 0$), you should have figured out the solution to this question. In essence, you bisect the solid and dashed curves and save the halved segments (or intervals) in two binary trees (referring to the figure below). It is assumed that the solid curve is defined in the interval $[a, b]$ and dashed curve in $[c, d]$. After the first subdivision, the left- and right-halved solid curves are defined respectively in $[a, b/2]$ and $[b/2, b]$. The intervals are continuously halved when the subdivision process is repeated.

When the segment is almost linear with respect to the given tolerance, you call the line/line intersection routine to obtain an intersection point of two approximating lines. This intersection is then used as a good estimation for the Newton iteration to refine the solution at a much faster convergent speed. To optimize the computation, range boxes (or bounding boxes) are often used to filter out the halved segments whose ranges boxes do not intersect each other. Accordingly, you proceed the operations with preference on the most likely candidates as illustrated below.

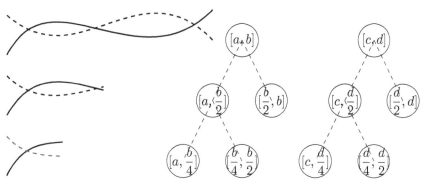

Each node stores the halved candidate curve

Since the two curves may intersect at multiple places, you will need to transverse the two binary trees to make sure you have checked every halved segment in the trees.

A brute force solution to this problem is to stroke each curve with respect to certain tolerance and save the stroking points in two arrays. It then loops through the two arrays to create lines from two adjacent stroking points and to call the line/line intersection routine. Such an approach is an $O(n^2)$ method and should be avoided by all means.

Thank you for purchasing this book. If you wish to obtain the source code, main drivers, and test data used in this book, please send your request together with a copy of your purchase receipt to

request.book.code@gmail.com.

In your email subject line, it is recommended to type "Source code request" for easy grouping.

You may also visit www.infogoaround.org for update and other relevant readings.